GO YE INTO ALL THE WORLD

Sidney B. Sperry

Other volumes in the Sperry Symposium Series
from Deseret Book Company

GO YE INTO ALL THE WORLD

MESSAGES OF THE
NEW TESTAMENT APOSTLES

THE 31ST ANNUAL
SIDNEY B. SPERRY SYMPOSIUM

DESERET BOOK

SALT LAKE CITY, UTAH

Library of Congress Cataloging-in-Publication Data

Sperry Symposium.
　　Go ye into all the world : messages of the New Testament apostles : annual Sidney B. Sperry Symposium / editors, Ray L. Huntington, Thomas A. Wayment, Jerome M. Perkins.
　　　　p.　　cm.
　　Includes bibliographical references and index.
　　ISBN 1-57008-896-9 (hardbound : alk. paper)
　　1. Bible. N.T. Acts—Criticism, interpretation, etc.—Congresses.　2. Bible. N.T. Epistles—Criticism, interpretation, etc.—Congresses.　3. Bible. N.T. Revelation—Criticism, interpretation, etc.—Congresses.　4. Church of Jesus Christ of Latter-day Saints—Doctrines—Congresses.　I. Huntington, Ray L. II. Wayment, Thomas A.　III. Perkins, Jerome M.　IV. Title.

　　BS2617.8 .S64 2002
　　225.6—dc21　　　2002009672

Printed in the United States of America　　　　　　　　　　　　72076-7024
Publishers Printing, Salt Lake City, Utah

10　9　8　7　6　5　4　3　2　1

CONTENTS

PREFACE

*J*UST BEFORE THE SAVIOR ASCENDED into heaven, He commanded His Apostles to be "witnesses unto me both in
Jerusalem, and in all Judaea, and in Samaria, and unto the uttermost
part of the earth" (Acts 1:8). Armed with the power of God's Spirit,
these men boldly proclaimed the gospel, first in Jerusalem and its
surrounding areas and ultimately to the far reaches of the Roman
Empire and perhaps beyond. While we have no scriptural record of
the post-resurrection missionary labors of such Apostles as Andrew,
Bartholomew, or Thomas, the New Testament provides some information about the ministry of Peter, John, and Paul.

According to the book of Acts, the early Christian Church grew
rapidly under the inspired leadership of Peter. For example, within
a few weeks after the Savior's ascension into heaven, three thousand
souls were baptized in Jerusalem on the Day of Pentecost (see Acts
2:41). Many of these Jewish converts were visitors from such places
as Parthia, Cappadocia, Asia, and Rome who would return home
and establish important branches of the Church (see Acts 2:1–11).

As the Church continued to grow in Jerusalem, Judea, and
Samaria, two important events occurred that would have significant

impact. The first was a vision given to Peter in which the Lord authorized the gospel to be taken to the Gentiles (see Acts 10), while the second event was the conversion of Saul (see Acts 9), who would become one of the great missionaries to the Gentile world. Consequently, the Church grew rapidly among the Jewish, Greek, and Roman populations of such places as Antioch, Philippi, Ephesus, Corinth, and Rome. However, the Church's rapid growth also produced some unique challenges. First, there was the need for trained leadership to preside over the growing branches of the Church. Second, as the Church flourished, it attracted the attention of some of the Jewish religious leaders in Jerusalem and the Diaspora, city magistrates and officials in some of the Greco-Roman cities where the Church had been established, and even the attention of several of the Roman emperors. These groups, as well as others, helped orchestrate a rising tide of opposition and persecution against God's Church. Third, the doctrinal purity of the Church was challenged by false doctrines and practices introduced by new converts, apostates, and even local Church leaders intent on establishing their own form of destructive priestcraft. Finally, the immoral practices of the Roman world were an increasing threat to the purity and unity of Church members everywhere.

To deal with these challenges, the Apostles, including Peter, John, and Paul, spent a great deal of time visiting the branches of the Church throughout the Roman Empire. Their personal contact with Church leaders and members was intended to strengthen and train the local leadership, edify the Saints, and purge the Church of false doctrines and immorality. When the Apostles could not visit the churches, they communicated through epistles filled with inspired teachings and counsel. Paul's letters were written to members living in such places as Galatia, Ephesus, Corinth, Rome, and Thessalonica. His letters were doctrinal masterpieces on a variety of subjects, which included faith, marriage, morality, welfare principles, repentance, and the Resurrection. Paul's letters promoted faith in the Savior and a greater understanding of the Atonement, corrected false teachings that were troubling the Saints, and encouraged members to hold "fast the faithful word" (Titus 1:9).

Both Peter and John's epistles were written to members struggling to maintain their spiritual balance during times of severe persecution from the Roman government. Peter counseled the Saints to remain faithful in the face of persecution and to remember that "the eyes of the Lord are over the righteous, and his ears are open unto their prayers" (1 Peter 3:12). Both Peter's and John's epistles contain doctrines relating to the principle of faith, the Atonement, marriage, and the Second Coming, to mention only a few.

In addition to the writings of these men, other inspired Church leaders, such as James and Jude, also wrote epistles to members. All of these epistles, together with the Book of Acts, constitute the second half of the New Testament. The timeless doctrines taught by these individuals are as important and relevant to the modern Church as they were for the New Testament Church. Doctrines of faith in Jesus Christ, the Atonement, morality, marriage, and family taught in the New Testament epistles are applicable for our day as well. The chapters in this volume are based on the writings of these faithful men contained in the books of Acts to Revelation. In many cases, the contributors have sought to add additional insight from the scriptures of the Restoration, such as the Book of Mormon and the Doctrine and Covenants, as well as insights from the Joseph Smith Translation of the Bible. In many instances they have also consulted the Greek New Testament materials for insights. These materials add much to our understanding and appreciation of the doctrines taught in the New Testament epistles. We wish to thank the Religious Studies Center for their assistance in editing, source checking, and preparing the manuscript for printing.

We sincerely hope that your study of this book will strengthen your testimony of the Savior and His Atonement, as well as increase your understanding and appreciation of the important work of the Apostles and the doctrines they taught during the first century A.D.

RAY L. HUNTINGTON   JEROME M. PERKINS
THOMAS A. WAYMENT   PATTY A. SMITH

THE 2002 SIDNEY B. SPERRY SYMPOSIUM COMMITTEE

1

"HE IS RISEN"

L. Aldin Porter

THE PSALMIST SAID, "THY WORD IS A lamp unto my feet, and a light unto my path" (Psalm 119:105). I love the word of the Lord—whether through the scriptures or through His living prophets. My prayer is that the Holy Spirit may attend us that we might have truth and light this evening and throughout this entire symposium.

The golden chain that makes its way through the book of Acts to the book of Revelation and throughout all of the scriptures is that Jesus is the Son of God and has been resurrected. The dominant message of the scriptures in all ages is "He is risen" (Matthew 28:6). As the Prophet Joseph Smith taught, "The fundamental principles of our religion are the testimony of the Apostles and Prophets, concerning Jesus Christ, that He died, was buried, and rose again the third day, and ascended into heaven."[1]

The Apostles Peter, Paul, and others bore personal witness of the Resurrection, and their individual testimonies highlight

---

Elder L. Aldin Porter is an emeritus member of the Seventy of The Church of Jesus Christ of Latter-day Saints.

different aspects of this supernal event. Ultimately the power of their words to bring about conversion in their listeners depended upon the confirming witness of the Holy Ghost, "for when a man speaketh by the power of the Holy Ghost the power of the Holy Ghost carrieth it unto the hearts of the children of men" (2 Nephi 33:1).

There is such power in the witness of the spoken word. The voice has the capability to reach the heart of man in a remarkable manner. When that voice is accompanied by the Holy Spirit, there is light and truth. That light and truth is enjoyed by the speaker as well as the listener (see D&C 50:22).

PETER TESTIFIES OF THE RESURRECTION

On the day of Pentecost, in Peter's first recorded discourse after the Ascension of the Lord, the chief Apostle referred to the prophecies of Jesus Christ and then said:

"This Jesus hath God raised up, whereof we all are witnesses. . . .

"Therefore let all the house of Israel know assuredly, that God hath made that same Jesus, whom ye have crucified, both Lord and Christ.

"Now when they heard this, they were pricked in their heart, and said unto Peter and to the rest of the apostles, Men and brethren, what shall we do?

"Then Peter said unto them, Repent, and be baptized every one of you in the name of Jesus Christ for the remission of sins, and ye shall receive the gift of the Holy Ghost" (Acts 2:32, 36–38).

Later Peter and John at the gates of the temple healed the lame man. As they entered the temple grounds, a large group came running together, greatly wondering. The people in this gathering were obviously very different from the people Peter spoke to on the day of Pentecost. Note the significant change in his instructions:

"But ye denied the Holy One and the Just, and desired a murderer to be granted unto you;

"And killed the Prince of life, whom God hath raised from the dead; whereof we are witnesses. . . .

"Repent ye therefore, and be converted, that your sins may be blotted out, when the times of refreshing shall come from the presence of the Lord;

"And he shall send Jesus Christ, which before was preached unto you:

"Whom the heaven must receive until the times of restitution of all things, which God hath spoken by the mouth of all his holy prophets since the world began" (Acts 3:14–15, 19–21).

This second group of listeners apparently were among those who participated in calling for the Crucifixion of the Son of God, and there would be no baptism until another distant time.

It is interesting that in both cases Peter made a major point of the fact that the Savior had been raised from the dead but gave a call to repentance and to baptism to one group and a call to repent with far-off possibilities to the other.

Each time he boldly gave a witness that God had raised Jesus from the dead. I draw attention to not only the message but the method by which it is transmitted. Peter did not argue, he did not plead, he did not cajole—he simply bore witness of the Master and His Resurrection with a power we can feel as we read the accounts. He knew the fundamental truth, that the convincing power of the Holy Ghost would accompany his words.

Earlier, while Jesus lived in mortality, Simon Peter had an experience that gives background to his testimony:

"When Jesus came into the coasts of Caesarea Philippi, he asked his disciples, saying, Whom do men say that I the Son of man am?

"And they said, Some say that thou art John the Baptist: some, Elias; and others, Jeremias, or one of the prophets.

"He saith unto them, But whom say ye that I am?

"And Simon Peter answered and said, Thou art the Christ, the Son of the living God.

"And Jesus answered and said unto him, Blessed art thou, Simon Bar-jona: for flesh and blood hath not revealed it unto thee, but my Father which is in heaven.

"And I say also unto thee, That thou art Peter, and upon this rock I will build my church; and the gates of hell shall not prevail against it" (Matthew 16:13–18).

The Savior could have said to Peter, "You have seen me feed the five thousand, restore sight to the blind, give hearing to the deaf, and bring life to the dead, and now you know who I am." He did not say those things. What He did say is, "Flesh and blood hath not revealed it unto thee, but my Father which is in heaven."

The Lord's work moves forward on personal revelation and the power of testimony. Today we testify before the world that these things are true. Our parents, teachers, priesthood and auxiliary leaders, missionaries, and apostles and prophets bear witness of the divinity of the Lord's Atonement and Resurrection. We have spiritual progress in this kingdom when our quorums, classes, and pulpits resound with the sure word of testimony.

President Harold B. Lee taught this supernal truth: "More powerful than sight, more powerful than walking and talking with Him, is that witness of the Spirit. . . . When that Spirit has witnessed to our spirit, that's a revelation from Almighty God."[2]

THOMAS FEELS THE SAVIOR'S WOUNDS

From the experience Thomas had with the resurrected Christ, it appears that the Lord required the reality of His physical Resurrection to be understood by those who were to be His special witnesses. Thomas's experience occurred shortly after the Resurrection but before the Ascension, as the scriptures record:

"Thomas, one of the twelve, called Didymus, was not with them when Jesus came.

"The other disciples therefore said unto him, We have seen the Lord. But he said unto them, Except I shall see in his hands the print of the nails, and put my finger into the print of the nails, and thrust my hand into his side, I will not believe.

"And after eight days again his disciples were within, and Thomas with them: then came Jesus, the doors being shut, and stood in the midst, and said, Peace be unto you.

"Then saith he to Thomas, Reach hither thy finger, and behold my hands; and reach hither thy hand, and thrust it into my side: and be not faithless, but believing" (John 20:24–27).

There is little chance that Thomas did not believe that man

survived the grave. How many times had he heard the Master teach the principles of eternity?

Elder Bruce R. McConkie provided this insight: "Thomas apparently did not understand or believe that Jesus had come forth with a literal, tangible body of flesh and bones, one that could be felt and handled, one that bore the nail marks and carried the spear wound, one that ate food and outwardly was almost akin to a mortal body. Obviously he had heard the testimony of Mary Magdalene and the other women, of Peter, and of all the apostles. It is not to be supposed that he doubted the resurrection as such, but rather the literal and corporeal nature of it. Hence his rash assertion about feeling the nail prints and thrusting his hand into the Lord's side."[3]

It was necessary that Thomas believe in the eternal nature of the spirit and also, to fulfill his apostleship, that he know and testify of the physical resurrection of the body. Today the nature of the physical resurrection is often overlooked as we bear testimony. When we do testify of this certainty, the Holy Spirit accompanies our words with power. If we are to enjoy the full benefits of the Holy Spirit we, through revelation, must testify of the certainty of the Lord's life, death, and resurrection.

It is a comfort as well as a warning to understand that the resurrection is physical. Consider the comfort this knowledge brings to those who lay away their children in the grave. Have you not seen the power of this faith in the faces of a bereaved mother and father? The reality of death descends on us in stark tones as we stand at the grave of a loved one. Yet the reality of a literal resurrection comes with the power that only the Comforter can give us. That moment the resurrection ceases to be just a doctrinal subject. Instead a glorious certainty fills the soul with joy.

Does this knowledge not impact us when we realize that we will stand in the flesh before the bar of God? The spiritual confirmation that there is a resurrection brings with it a sureness that we are dealing with life in its most certain eternal forms.

Moroni makes a statement of finality when in his closing words in the last chapter in the Book of Mormon he says, "And I exhort you to remember these things; for the time speedily cometh that ye shall know that I lie not, for ye shall see me at the bar of God; and the Lord God will say unto you: Did I not declare my words unto you, which were written by this man, like as one crying from the dead, yea, even as one speaking out of the dust?" (Moroni 10:27).

One reason the Book of Mormon is given to us in this day is that we may effectively teach and testify of the divinity of the Lord Jesus Christ and of the certainty of His resurrection.

Alma taught, "Yea, every knee shall bow, and every tongue confess before him. Yea, even at the last day, when all men shall stand to be judged of him, then shall they confess that he is God; then shall they confess, who live without God in the world, that the judgment of an everlasting punishment is just upon them; and they shall quake, and tremble, and shrink beneath the glance of his all-searching eye" (Mosiah 27:31).

Ezekiel saw the day when all must accept the Savior's position in the face of evidence which could not be denied:

"Therefore prophesy and say unto them, Thus saith the Lord God; Behold, O my people, I will open your graves, and cause you to come up out of your graves, and bring you into the land of Israel.

"And ye shall know that I am the Lord, when I have opened your graves, O my people, and brought you up out of your graves" (Ezekiel 37:12–13).

It will be a tragedy for those who wait for this final day to accept the Master and His sacrifice. They who "live without God in the world" will have endured so much pain and needless sorrow. For many it will be a dark and fearsome day, but surely it will not be such for those who have received the testimony of Jesus and have overcome by faith. For them it will be a day of most sublime joy.

PAUL TESTIFIES OF THE RISEN LORD

Now we come to the testimony of the Apostle Paul. This great Apostle to the Gentiles was a powerful witness of the Resurrection throughout his life.

"They came to Thessalonica, where was a synagogue of the Jews:

"And Paul, as his manner was, went in unto them, and three sabbath days reasoned with them out of the scriptures,

"Opening and alleging, that Christ must needs have suffered, and risen again from the dead; and that this Jesus, whom I preach unto you, is Christ" (Acts 17:1–3).

Later at Mars' Hill, Paul testified:

"Forasmuch then as we are the offspring of God, we ought not to think that the Godhead is like unto gold, or silver, or stone, graven by art and man's device.

"And the times of this ignorance God winked at; but now commandeth all men every where to repent:

"Because he hath appointed a day, in the which he will judge the world in righteousness by that man whom he hath ordained; whereof he hath given assurance unto all men, in that he hath raised him from the dead" (Acts 17:29–31).

Many months passed, and Paul found himself testifying before King Agrippa:

"Why should it be thought a thing incredible with you, that God should raise the dead? . . .

"Having therefore obtained help of God, I continue unto this day, witnessing both to small and great, saying none other things than those which the prophets and Moses did say should come:

"That Christ should suffer, and that he should be the first that should rise from the dead, and should shew light unto the people, and to the Gentiles" (Acts 26:8, 22–23).

Elder McConkie taught that the Apostle Paul's example is pertinent to all of us who seek to serve the Master:

"Paul testifies that Jesus is the Christ. True, he quotes selected Messianic prophecies to show his witness is in harmony with what other prophets have foretold. But the burden of his message is one of announcement, of bearing record that Jesus was raised from the dead; that he was seen of witnesses who now declare the glad tidings of salvation to others. . . .

"It is the Resurrection of Christ which proves the truth and divinity of the Christian faith. Jesus is shown to be the Son of God because he rose from the dead. The Messianic prophecies are known to apply to him because he broke the bands of death. . . . And so it is with all the Messianic prophecies; their fulfillment is known because Christ gained the victory over death."[4]

THE BOOK OF MORMON TESTIFIES OF CHRIST

The Lord, who knew the end from the beginning, revealed many years ago that we would need the Book of Mormon to carry the work forward in this dispensation:

"The Lord said unto Enoch: As I live, even so will I come in the last days, in the days of wickedness and vengeance, to fulfill the oath which I have made unto you concerning the children of Noah;

"And the day shall come that the earth shall rest, but before that day the heavens shall be darkened, and a veil of darkness shall cover the earth; and the heavens shall shake, and also the earth; and great tribulations shall be among the children of men, but my people will I preserve;

"And righteousness will I send down out of heaven; and truth will I send forth out of the earth, to bear testimony of mine Only Begotten; his resurrection from the dead; yea, and also the resurrection of all men; and righteousness and truth will I cause to sweep the earth as with a flood, to gather out mine elect from the four quarters of the earth" (Moses 7:60–62).

On this passage, Brother Robert Matthews commented: "Five thousand years ago the Lord revealed to the prophet Enoch what the fundamental message of the Book of Mormon would be. Neither history, culture, nor geography were mentioned. The book would testify of the Only Begotten and the resurrection. . . . Almost every prophet in the Book of Mormon makes some reference to the resurrection."[5]

The Book of Mormon's title page explicitly states that it is written "to the convincing of the Jew and Gentile that JESUS is the CHRIST, the ETERNAL GOD, manifesting himself unto all nations." Clearly He who gave us this sacred scripture has made known its divine purposes. These facts were placed in the book to draw our attention to those important doctrines the Lord wants us to understand. Therefore, the Book of Mormon is not merely the history of a people; it is the history of a message, of those who carried that message, and the people's response to it. The testimony of Jesus permeates its pages from the title page to Moroni's final testimony.

REVELATION GUIDES THE CHURCH TODAY

This kingdom moves forward today on the power of the personal revelation that there is a Savior to this world and He is Jesus Christ. A living prophet was the instrument through which the Lord restored the priesthood with all of its power. The overwhelming importance of this revelatory gift is often underestimated by us.

On September 15, 1986, while serving as a mission president, I received a letter from an elder then serving as a missionary in Alabama. He and his companion had been teaching an investigator who had a genuine interest in the Church. Her minister gave her some material which purported to answer the questions of Mormonism. He titles it "The Taproot of Mormonism." I quote:

"Mormons teach that every individual can directly receive divine revelation. In fact, this is the Mormon method for distinguishing truth from error. Mormon missionaries teach non-Mormons that, in order to know whether or not the Mormon teachings are true, people should pray to God to send revelation directly and personally to them—God will send the Holy Spirit to speak directly to their heart.

"The importance of this concept cannot be overemphasized because it is the very means by which Mormons are convinced Mormonism is true. . . . They believe because they are convinced that God himself has personally told them Mormonism is true. This is why few Mormons will reject Mormonism simply if they are shown contradictions between the Bible and Mormonism. They conclude the Bible must be in error (it has been changed through the years, etc.). It cannot be Mormonism is wrong, because they know God has told them it is true! This is the taproot of Mormonism—the source from which all Mormonism flows. It is the foundation of the structure of Mormonism. Destroy it and Mormonism falls."

When I finished reading it, the thought came to me that "the children of this world are in their generation wiser than the children of light" (Luke 16:8). The author had rare insight.

The gentleman then went on to say:

"We seek to show the validity of the following concept of revelation which we affirm is taught in the Bible:

"The Bible is the only revelation from God to man today.

"The time came when God's message was fully revealed and fully recorded in written form in the Bible. There then ceased to be a need, in God's plan, for continued direct revelation to man, so that process ceased." It is a tragedy that so many hold to the position that God no longer speaks through revelation.

MODERN WITNESSES TESTIFY OF CHRIST

Today our prophets, apostles, and other leaders testify of the risen Lord and the power of the Atonement and Resurrection. Years ago, as a new regional representative, I was on assignment to a stake conference with Elder McConkie. In the planning meeting Saturday afternoon with the stake presidency, he asked that he be scheduled for one hour in the evening meeting and one hour in the Sunday meeting. It was Easter weekend. Saturday evening he spoke under the influence of the Holy Spirit on the Atonement. Sunday he spoke with the same power on the Resurrection of the Lord Jesus Christ and of all men. On the way to the airport, I said to him, "Those two discourses were magnificent." Note carefully his response: "Yes, they were. It is amazing how much I learn when I speak under the influence of the Spirit of God."

I have come to know since that day that I receive more revelations while teaching and testifying of the Lord Jesus Christ, of His servant the Prophet Joseph Smith, and of the living prophets of our day than at any other time.

This great and powerful witness that we have so abundantly seen in the scriptures has fallen upon the apostles and prophets and faithful members of the Church in our day. We are blessed with prophets who have a sure and certain knowledge of these basic truths.

President Gordon B. Hinckley testified of the Resurrection, saying:

"Never had this occurred before. There had been only death without hope. Now there was life eternal. Only a God could have done this. The Resurrection of Jesus Christ was the great crowning event of His life and mission. It was the capstone of the Atonement. The sacrifice of His life for all mankind was not complete without His coming forth from the grave, with the certainty of the Resurrection for all who have walked the earth.

"Of all the victories in the chronicles of humanity, none is so great, none so universal in its effects, none so everlasting in its consequences as the victory of the crucified Lord, who came forth from the tomb that first Easter morning.

"Those who were witnesses of that event, all who saw and heard and spoke with the Risen Lord, testified of the reality of this greatest of all miracles. His followers through the centuries lived and died in proclamation of the truth of this supernal act.

"To all of these we add our testimony that He who died on Calvary's cross arose again in wondrous splendor as the Son of God, the Master of life and death."[6]

We here tonight have the honor and the obligation through revelation to bear witness that Jesus literally came forth from the tomb. Our teaching should be permeated with this eternal fact. Ours is the joyful burden of standing as His witnesses in our day and time.

I add my testimony to those of the prophets. God has made known to me in an unmistakable way that He lives and that His Beloved Son, Jesus Christ, is the Savior of the world and was resurrected to lead all men through that incredible transformation. In the name of Jesus Christ, amen.

NOTES

1. *Teachings of the Prophet Joseph Smith,* comp. Joseph Fielding Smith (Salt Lake City: Deseret Book, 1976), 121.

2. Harold B. Lee, *Teachings of Presidents of the Church: Harold B. Lee* (Salt Lake City: The Church of Jesus Christ of Latter-day Saints, 2000), 39.

3. Bruce R. McConkie, *Doctrinal New Testament Commentary* (Salt Lake City: Bookcraft, 1971), 1:860.

4. McConkie, *Doctrinal New Testament Commentary,* 2:126–27.

5. Robert J. Matthews, *Selected Writings of Robert J. Matthews* (Salt Lake City: Deseret Book, 1999), 509.

6. Gordon B. Hinckley, "Special Witnesses of Christ," *Ensign,* April 2001, 15.

2

PAUL THE APOSTLE: CHAMPION OF THE DOCTRINE OF THE RESURRECTION

J. Peter Hansen

"IF CHRIST BE NOT RAISED, YOUR FAITH is vain; ye are yet in your sins," wrote the Apostle Paul to the Saints at Corinth (1 Corinthians 15:17). If Jesus was not resurrected, then what is Christianity? Is it the meager attempt of God-fearing charlatans to rationalize away the greatest of miracles, leaving men nothing but a hopeless empty tomb? Theologian Gerald O'Collins answered: "In a profound sense, Christianity without the Resurrection is not simply Christianity without its final chapter. It is not Christianity at all."[1] The Apostle Paul was not about to let the Resurrection be buried. The doctrine of the Resurrection was a constant theme of his preaching, one which kept him spiritually alive, and one which contributed to his physical death. Paul fought the good fight, even the greatest of fights; he fought for the gospel of Jesus Christ. One of his selected battlegrounds, and one which led to his beheading at the hand of Nero, was the true doctrine of the literal bodily Resurrection of the Savior. It was a doctrine from which Paul

J. Peter Hansen is a Church Educational System coordinator in Pleasant Hill, California.

refused to back down, never equivocating, always testifying—a
champion of the doctrine of the Resurrection. His life of dedication
to Jesus the Christ started on the road to Damascus.

CONVERSION HISTORY

Perhaps as early as A.D. 36,[2] Saul of Tarsus was near to
Damascus. The Light of all lights shone round him and the resurrected Jesus appeared to him, giving him specific instructions. Saul,
now temporarily blind, was led to the house of Judas. Ananias had
been instructed by the Lord to seek out Saul. The Lord further
instructed Ananias to lay his hands upon Saul and restore to him his
sight, baptize him, confer upon him the Holy Ghost, and strengthen
him (see Acts 9:1–19). After Saul tarried with Ananias and the disciples at Damascus for "certain days" (Acts 9:19), he retired to
Arabia[3] for three years. Very little is known of Saul's sojourn to
Arabia. We do know that he did not ask the counsel of any man but
that he sought the Lord to qualify him to preach among the Gentile
nations (see Galatians 1:15–17). After his solitary preparation he
reappeared at Damascus seeking to preach the gospel.

Truly converted and filled with missionary zeal, Saul went
straight to the synagogues. His unrecorded testimony that Jesus was
the "very Christ" was powerful and convincing to some (see Acts
9:22). It confounded others, and after "many days . . . the Jews took
counsel to kill him" (Acts 9:23). Saul heard of the plot and escaped
from Damascus, hurrying off to Jerusalem, where he met Peter, the
senior Apostle.

Saul desired to preach to the disciples in Jerusalem, but they
were understandably wary of him. After all, he was a Pharisee, a
member of the Sanhedrin,[4] and a chief persecutor of the early Saints
(see Acts 26:6–12). He held the coats of the murderers who stoned
Stephen to death (see Acts 7:54–60). Now this man, known as an
enemy to the Christians, claimed to be their fellow, a disciple of the
Lord. He wanted to meet with them and testify of the Lord's divinity. Saul was more than an ordinary disciple.

PAUL'S APOSTLESHIP

John defined the special nature of the calling of an Apostle as he quoted the mortal Messiah: "Ye have not chosen me, but I have chosen you, and ordained you, that ye should go forth" (John 15:16). Luke concurred and enlarged the definition when he wrote that an Apostle is one who is "ordained to be a witness . . . of [Jesus'] resurrection" (Acts 1:22). To "ordain" is to "invest with a ministerial function or sacerdotal power; . . . to set apart for an office; to appoint."[5] Saul met the criteria. He certainly did not choose the Lord of his own volition. The Lord chose him. Saul was handpicked and set apart by the Lord through Ananias as another version of Saul's rudimentary experience accounts. The same hour Saul received his sight under the hands of Ananias, he looked upon the Lord's servant, who told him,

"The God of our fathers hath chosen thee, that thou shouldest know his will, and see that Just One, and shouldest hear the voice of his mouth.

"For thou shalt be his witness unto all men of what thou hast seen and heard.

"And now why tarriest thou? arise, and be baptized, and wash away thy sins, calling on the name of the Lord" (Acts 22:14–16; emphasis added).

Saul was a witness of the literal bodily Resurrection of Jesus Christ. His first vision was on Damascus road.[6] His second recorded vision of the resurrected Lord was at the house of Justus in Corinth. Therein, the Lord visited His newly chosen vessel in a night vision. The resurrected Lord told him to preach boldly and that He would protect him (see Acts 18:7, 9–10). His third visit by the Lord took place in the temple at Jerusalem. His call to serve was reconfirmed. "While I prayed in the temple, I was in a trance; and *saw him* saying unto me, Make haste, and get thee quickly out of Jerusalem: for they will not receive thy testimony concerning me. . . . I will send thee far hence unto the Gentiles" (Acts 22:17–18, 21; emphasis added).

Set apart from the world, the "chosen vessel," was sent out by the Lord to "to bear [his] name before the Gentiles, and kings, and the children of Israel" (Acts 9:15). "Am I not an apostle?" he wrote to the Saints at Corinth. "Have I not seen Jesus Christ our Lord?" (see 1 Corinthians 9:1). Saul, now called Paul (Acts 13:9), was the Lord's anointed Apostle, fully qualified to testify of the divinity and the reality of the Resurrection of the Redeemer.[7]

FIRST RECORDED DISCOURSE ON THE RESURRECTION

With his companions, including Barnabas and others, the Apostle Paul set out on his first of three major missionary journeys. They sailed to the island of Cyprus and then to Attalea in southern Galatia. The company of missionaries traversed mountain valleys and passes dodging robbers and evil countrymen (2 Corinthians 11:26). On a Sabbath morning, Paul and Barnabas found themselves in Pisidian Antioch, a region in modern-day Turkey. They made their way to the synagogue. After the traditional reading of the law, the priest invited anyone to speak, the common practice of the day (see Acts 13:14–15). The new Apostle delivered his first recorded sermon.

"Paul stood up, and beckoning with his hand said, Men of Israel, and ye that fear God, give audience" (Acts 13:16). It is apparent that Paul addressed both Jews and Gentiles. He talked of Moses and the deliverance of Israel, and of King David and his seed, Jesus. He told of the mission of John the Baptist, of Pilate's prosecution, condemnation, and Crucifixion of Christ. He reminded them that Jesus had been laid in a sepulchre. Then came the key doctrine taught best by a special witness:

"God raised him [Jesus] from the dead:

"And he was seen many days of them which came up with him from Galilee to Jerusalem, who are his witnesses unto the people.

"And we declare unto you glad tidings, how that the promise which was made unto the fathers,

"God hath fulfilled the same unto us their children, in that he hath raised up Jesus again; as it is also written in the second psalm, Thou art my Son, this day have I begotten thee.

"And as concerning that he raised him up from the dead, now no more to return to corruption, he said on this wise, I will give you the sure mercies of David.

"Wherefore he saith also in another psalm, Thou shalt not suffer thine Holy One to see corruption [death and decay].

"For David, after he had served his own generation by the will of God, fell on sleep, and was laid unto his fathers, and saw corruption:

"But he, whom God raised again, saw no corruption" (Acts 13:30–37).

Paul taught powerful doctrine: (1) Jesus is the Christ, a fact verified by His Resurrection; (2) there are living witnesses of the Resurrection; (3) messianic prophecies are fulfilled in Christ; (4) though David's dead flesh will be corrupted, that of Christ will never be corrupted, because He is the Resurrection.

Remarkably, the Jews did not stone Paul on the spot. On the contrary, when church was over, "many of the Jews and religious proselytes followed Paul and Barnabas: who, speaking to them, persuaded them to continue in the grace of God. *And the next sabbath day came almost the whole city together to hear the word of God*" (Acts 13:43–44; emphasis added). The bliss was short-lived. The Jews became jealous and challenged Paul and Barnabas. An angry mob persecuted them and ran them out of town. The missionaries moved through other regions, finally arriving at Thessalonica (see Acts 17:1).

TEACHING THE GREEKS ABOUT THE RESURRECTION

Paul went to a synagogue in Thessalonica to preach on the Sabbath. He taught from the scriptures, showing that it was necessary for Christ to suffer and that He rose from the dead. This was the Jesus of whom Paul testified. Some of the Thessalonians believed him. As was often the case, envious Jews forced Paul to flee for his life (see Acts 17:1–9). Paul and his companions passed through Berea, where they had much success, leaving Silas and Timothy (new missionary companions) to do the work. Paul journeyed onward to Athens.

Athens was the cultural and educational center of the world. Many prominent worldly men sent their sons to Athens to be educated. The Greeks were admired as the elite of the world. Their language, architecture, philosophy, art, and customs were modeled throughout the Mediterranean region. Additionally, Athens was a city "wholly given to idolatry" (Acts 17:16). Paul set out to do his work.

He went into the marketplace daily and into the synagogues on the Sabbath to teach his message. He intentionally argued with the locals. He attracted attention. Some called him a babbler. The Athenian philosophers accused Paul of proclaiming false gods and new doctrine "because he preached unto them Jesus, and the resurrection." The Apostle was invited to address the Athenians and found himself in their midst at Mars' Hill (see Acts 17:17–21).

Saul of Tarsus, now Paul the Apostle, stood before the most learned men of his day. He was near an altar dedicated to the so-called unknown God. He desired to speak by the Spirit, to cause a stirring in the hearts of the honest. His proclamation was a marvel. He testified against the gods of the idolater and for the God of heaven. Paul explained to them the resurrected God of Israel, whom they did not know. Paul "intimates that, by the unknown God, God the Creator was in a roundabout way worshipped by the Greeks."[8]

"Ye men of Athens, I perceive that in all things ye are too superstitious.

"For as I passed by, and beheld your devotions, I found an altar with this inscription, TO THE UNKNOWN GOD. Whom therefore ye ignorantly worship, him declare I unto you.

"God that made the world and all things therein, seeing that he is Lord of heaven and earth, dwelleth not in temples made with hands;

"Neither is worshipped with men's hands, as though he needed any thing, seeing he giveth to all life, and breath, and all things;

"And hath made of one blood all nations of men for to dwell on all the face of the earth, and hath determined the times before appointed, and the bounds of their habitation;

"That they should seek the Lord, if haply they might feel after him, and find him, though he be not far from every one of us:

"For in him we live, and move, and have our being; as certain also of your own poets have said, For we are also his offspring.

"Forasmuch then as we are the offspring of God, we ought not to think that the Godhead is like unto gold, or silver, or stone, graven by art and man's device.

"And the times of this ignorance God winked at; but now commandeth all men every where to repent:

"Because he hath appointed a day, in the which he will judge the world in righteousness by that man whom he hath ordained; whereof he hath given assurance unto all men, in that he hath raised him from the dead" (Acts 17:22–31).

When Paul mentioned the Resurrection, some of the Greeks mocked him and he had to stop speaking. Deaf hearts notwithstanding, he taught key doctrine: (1) God is Creator of all things; (2) He is not worshiped with creations of hands—He created all, He needs nothing tangible; (3) all men are one blood—we are brothers; (4) we should earnestly seek Him; (5) we are God's children; (6) because we are His, we should not reckon that He is made of silver or gold; (7) we must live lives of repentance; (8) there shall be a judgment; (9) part of that judgment will be the Resurrection which lives in Christ Jesus. Some mocked Paul, but a few believed his words. He departed from Athens and made his way to Corinth. There, he wrote his first epistle to the Thessalonians.

The Thessalonians, like many Saints, were drifting from the doctrine. Paul wrote and encouraged them to maintain their steadfastness. Toward the end of his letter, Paul encouraged the Saints by promising them a wonderfully bright moment, a moment of the Resurrection of the just. They must have been concerned about the veracity of the Resurrection, but Paul reassured the Thessalonians that "Jesus died and rose again, even so them also which sleep in Jesus will God bring with him" (1 Thessalonians 4:14). In his book *The Savior's Prophecies,* Richard D. Draper wrote: "The day of redemption . . . is the event to which the apostle Paul looked forward, proclaiming that 'the Lord himself shall descend from heaven with a shout, with the voice of the archangel, and with the trump of God: and the dead in Christ shall rise first; then we which are alive and remain shall be caught up together with them in the clouds, to meet the Lord in the air' (1 Thessalonians 4:16–17)."[9] Dr. Draper points out that the phrase "caught up" is translated from the Greek *harpazo*, which connotes being snatched up or carried away with some force involved.[10] From Paul's description of the day of redemption, one can imagine the eagerness with which the Lord will resurrect His sons and daughters and claim them eternally His.

RESURRECTION TAUGHT TO THE CORINTHIANS

Paul journeyed to Ephesus, where he wrote a letter to the Saints at Corinth. Contained therein are some of the greatest thoughts on the Resurrection in all of holy writ. In 1 Corinthians 15, Paul reminds us that there were many who saw, with their own eyes, the gloriously embodied, resurrected Jesus. "He was buried, and . . . rose again the third day. . . . He was seen of Cephas, then of the twelve: After that, he was seen of above five hundred brethren at once [not to mention women and children];. . . . After that he was seen of James; then of all the apostles. . . . And last of all he was seen of me" (1 Corinthians 15:4–8). Over five hundred people witnessed this event at the same time, and Paul points out that most of those witnesses were still alive at his writing. He seems to be saying, "If you don't believe me, go talk to them!"

The Apostle continued as he told the Corinthians that if Christ had not risen from the grave his preaching was for naught. Why bother if there is no afterlife? In fact, if Christ was not resurrected, then faith in Him is futile (see 1 Corinthians 15:13–17). But, "Christ [was] risen from the dead, and [became] the firstfruits of them that slept" (1 Corinthians 15:20). Paul had firsthand knowledge of that fact and made sure that the Corinthians knew of the doctrine. If there are firstfruits of the Resurrection, there must be subsequent fruits.

"In Christ shall all be made alive" (1 Corinthians 15:22). All mortals are rescued from the pangs of death. All will be resurrected. The Prophet Joseph Smith taught that Paul envisioned the resurrection of all men. "Paul ascended into the third heavens, and he could understand the three principal rounds of Jacob's ladder—the telestial, the terrestrial, and the celestial glories or kingdoms."[11] Paul likened glory in each man's individual resurrection to the sun, the moon, or the stars. Live celestially, receive celestial glory; live a lesser standard, receive lesser light. All will be raised incorruptible, empowered, immortal, never again to die (see 1 Corinthians 15:40–43). "Death is swallowed up in victory. O death, where is thy sting? O grave, where is thy victory? . . . But thanks be to God, which giveth us the victory through our Lord Jesus Christ" (1 Corinthians 15:54–55, 57).

A DISPUTE ON THE RESURRECTION

In early June of A.D. 58, Paul made his way back to Jerusalem for the Feast of the Pentecost. By this time Paul was well-known to Jewish antagonists. His reputation proceeded him. While he was in the temple purifying himself, a Jewish mob identified him as a foe, fell upon him, cast him out of the temple, and "went about to kill him" (Acts 21:26–31).

Ironically, when the Roman soldiers arrested him they doubled as his rescuers. Paul asked to speak to the captain of the guard, who was apparently taken by Paul's cultural background. The captain permitted Paul to speak to the mob. Without delay Paul told of his miraculous conversion at Damascus. He testified that he had seen Christ, received his call to be a special witness, and was baptized. Paul then revealed that he went to the temple in Jerusalem, wherein the resurrected Lord visited him again and told him to take the gospel to the Gentiles. At this proclamation, the crowd of Jews went into an uproar, demanding that Paul be killed (see Acts 21:37–22:22). The next day, Paul found himself before the Sanhedrin.[12]

"Men and brethren, I am a Pharisee, the son of a Pharisee: of the hope and resurrection of the dead I am called in question" (Acts 23:6). Immediately upon Paul's mentioning the Resurrection, a dispute ensued. Fearing the worst, the chief captain took Paul into protective custody (see Acts 23:7–10). Paul must have been disconsolate, even into the next night. That was when the Savior, who does not abandon His faithful servants, stood beside Paul and talked with him.[13] "Be of good cheer, Paul: for as thou hast testified of me in Jerusalem, so must thou bear witness also at Rome" (Acts 23:11). Paul had *again* seen the Redeemer, this time standing before him in His resurrected body. Further, Paul received his marching orders. He had to go to Rome to testify before the most powerful man on earth—Nero.

PAUL'S TRIALS AT CAESAREA

Before Paul had his audience with the emperor, he had to be tried at Caesarea before Felix, the Roman governor. "There shall be a resurrection of the dead, both of the just and unjust," Paul witnessed to Felix and his court. "Touching [because of my teaching] the resurrection of the dead I am called in question by you this day" (Acts 24:15, 21). Again Paul did not equivocate. And again, his best efforts landed him in jail. Two years later, Paul was summoned anew to the court of Porcius Festus, the new governor at Caesarea. King Agrippa, great-grandson of Herod the Great, happened to be in Caesarea and was in attendance for another of the Apostle's powerful discourses on the Resurrection.

Paul opened his testimony with a biographical statement of his training as a Pharisee and his own persecution of the Christians. Following his familiar format, Paul told his Damascus story, using it as the basis for his testimony of the Resurrection. Then came the dialogue which confounded the court, leaving the two-man jury hung, and resulting in the Apostle Paul being sent to Rome.

Paul: "[I testify] that Christ should suffer, and that he should be the first that should rise from the dead, and should shew light unto the people, and to the Gentiles."

Festus: "Paul, thou art beside thyself; much learning doth make thee mad."

Paul: "I am not mad, most noble Festus; but speak forth the words of truth and soberness. For the king knoweth of these things, before whom also I speak freely: for I am persuaded that none of these things are hidden from him; for this thing was not done in a corner. King Agrippa, believest thou the prophets? I know that thou believest."[14]

Agrippa: "Almost thou persuadest me to be a Christian."

Paul: "I would to God, that not only thou, but also all that hear me this day, were both almost, and altogether such as I am, except these bonds" (see Acts 26:23–29).

The court could find no reason to sentence Paul to either death or prison. He had asked to be sent to Rome to appeal to Caesar. His wish was granted.

RESURRECTION IN THE PAULINE EPISTLES

While in Rome, sometimes in the Mamertine Prison and other times under house arrest, Paul wrote letters to his friend Timothy, testifying of the Resurrection to the Saints of Colossae, Ephesus, Philippi, Palestine (in Hebrews), and sometime after his Roman imprisonment.

To the Colossians Paul wrote that man is created in the image of God, that He has all power, that He is the head of the Church, that through Christ all will be reconciled to the Father. By Him, "in the body of his flesh," all will be presented before the Father (see Colossians 1:15–23).

Paul reminded the Ephesians that the Father raised Jesus from the dead to rule with Him in the next life (see Ephesians 1:20).

Paul wrote rather graphically to the Philippians. After attributing his own successes to Christ, Paul reported that he had lost all his worldly goods which he had previously valued. Now his treasures were as dung[15] compared to that which he gained in Christ. He knew the Christ and the "power of his resurrection." He further prophesied that he would attain his own resurrection and that each of us "shall change our vile body, that it may be fashioned like unto [Christ's] glorious body" (see Philippians 3:7–8, 10–11, 21).

He recalled to the memory of the Jewish Christians,[16] or the Christians of Jewish ancestry, still in the general area of Palestine, that there are basic principles of perfection in the gospel of Jesus Christ. They include faith in God, repentance, baptism, the laying on of hands, resurrection of the dead, and eternal judgment (see Hebrews 6:1–2).

Still in Rome near the end of his life, Paul wrote two known letters to his beloved Timothy. In the second one, he warned against the errant resurrection philosophies of Hymenaeus and Philetus. They were teaching not that Christ was still in the grave but that the general resurrection was now over.[17] They alleged that the greatest of miracles had ended with Christ. They "have erred," wrote Paul, "saying that the resurrection is past already; and overthrow the faith of some" (2 Timothy 2:18).

PAUL MARTYRED FOR THE CAUSE OF TRUTH

Paul knew that the end of his life was in sight. Some of his final words poignantly testified of the joy of his own pending glory which he knew was certain: "I am now ready to be offered, and the time of my departure is at hand. I have fought a good fight, I have finished my course, I have kept the faith: henceforth there is laid up for me a crown of righteousness, which the Lord, the righteous judge, shall give me at that day" (2 Timothy 4:6–8).

Nero was not in Rome for Paul's first arraignment. Nothing is known of his second hearing, but Nero must have been there. It was he who would have had to sentence the Apostle to death. Tradition holds that Paul was beheaded about two miles southwest of the city on the Ostian Way. Because he was a Roman citizen, he was spared the tortures of crucifixion or the horrors of being coated with pitch and set afire.[18] Early Christian writers agree that Paul was decapitated by Nero's command.

"Examine your records. There you will find that Nero . . . exercised his cruelty against all at Rome. . . . Thus Nero publicly announcing himself as the chief enemy of God, was led on in his fury to slaughter the apostles. Paul is therefore said to have been beheaded at Rome,"[19] wrote Eusebius in his *History of the Church.* Tertullian affirmed: "Paul is beheaded. . . . At Rome Nero was the first who stained with blood the rising faith. . . . Then does Paul obtain a birth suited to Roman citizenship, when in Rome he springs to life again ennobled by martyrdom."[20]

Beheaded? Yes. Crowned by martyrdom? No! Let not death limit the Apostle. Paul's crown is the one of which he testified until it sent him to the executioner's sword. Paul's crown is his resurrection, made possible by the Redeemer whom he knew and loved.

NOTES

1. Gerald O'Collins, *The Easter Jesus* (Valley Forge, Pennsylvania: The Judson Press, 1973), 134.

2. Evangelical New Testament scholar Dr. Craig L. Blomberg of the Denver Seminary proposes that the Crucifixion may have been as early as A.D. 30. That would set Paul's conversion at A.D. 32, and his first meeting with the Apostles in Jerusalem at A.D. 35. See Lee Strobel, *The Case for Christ* (Grand Rapids, Michigan: Zondervan, 1998), 35. Brigham Young University's former dean of religion, Sidney B. Sperry wrote, "From considerations growing out of the author's study of the Book of Mormon, he believes that the Savior was crucified in the year A.D. 33. . . . If this be true, the time of the Apostle's conversion was about A.D. 36." See Sidney B. Sperry, *Paul's Life and Letters* (Salt Lake City: Bookcraft, 1955), 3.

3. Dr. Sperry pointed out that "we cannot determine with any precision the exact place where he [Paul] went." Arabia included a very large area in that day including not only the Sinai Peninsula but also the transjordan region, and possibly even Damascus itself. See *Letters*, 24.

4. Acts 26:10 points to the fact that "many of the saints did [Paul] shut up in prison, having received authority from the chief priests; and when they were put to death, I gave my voice against them." To have voting power in capital cases, one would have been a member of the Sanhedrin.

5. Noah Webster, *An American Dictionary of the English Language* (New York: S. Converse, 1828; reprint, San Fransisco: Foundation for American Christian Education, 1980).

6. Some have contended that the incident on the road to Damascus was limited to Paul's hearing the voice of the Lord and did not include his actually seeing the Resurrected One. A close review of the Apostle's defense before Agrippa settles the argument. He related his Damascus account to the court saying the personage identified Himself as Jesus, who then said, "I have appeared unto thee, . . . to make thee a minister and a witness both of these things which thou hast seen, and of those things in the which I will appear unto thee" (Acts 26:16).

7. The faithful Christian Ignatius wrote in approximately A.D. 105, "I do not, as Peter and Paul, issue commandments. They were Apostles." In *The Ante-Nicene Fathers*, ed. Alexander Roberts and James Donaldson (Grand Rapids, Michigan: Wm. B. Eerdmans, 1989), 1:75.

8. Clementin, *Ante-Nicene Fathers*, 2:321.

9. Richard D. Draper, *The Savior's Prophecies: From the Fall of Jerusalem to the Second Coming* (American Fork, Utah: Covenant Communications, 2001, 44–45.

10. Draper, *Prophecies*, 57, footnote 22.

11. Joseph Smith, *History of the Church of Jesus Christ of Latter-day Saints*, ed. B. H. Roberts (Salt Lake City: The Church of Jesus Christ of Latter-day Saints, 1909), 5:402.

12. It is probable that Paul was, at one time, a member of the Sanhedrin. In Acts 26:10 Luke recorded that Paul admitted to being cruel to the Saints, imprisoning them and "when they were put to death, I gave my voice against them." To cast a vote for death, one must have been a member of the body authorized to sentence in capital cases—the Sanhedrin. Furthermore, Paul seems to have recognized some members of the Sanhedrin when he appeared before them and "perceived that the one part were Sadducees, and the other Pharisees" (Acts 23:6).

13. This marks the fourth recorded visitation of the resurrected Savior to Paul. The others are found in a chain of scriptures: Acts 9:1–9; 18:9–10; 22:17–18.

14. Agrippa, the last of the family of Herod, was a Jew. While Agrippa was probably not a fully practicing Jew, Paul knew that he had been taught, and at minimum knew of, the words of the prophets.

15. "'Dung' is a rendering of the Greek word meaning 'refuse.' Both these words are polite translations." In D. Kelly Ogden and Andrew C. Skinner, *New Testament Apostles Testify of Christ* (Salt Lake City: Deseret Book, 1998), 191.

16. Ogden and Skinner, *New Testament Apostles*, 245.

17. The beginning of the First Resurrection is found in Matthew 27:52–53. Jesus was resurrected, and after Him "the graves were opened" and many who were once dead were now made whole each in his own resurrection. Hymenaeus and Philetus, Paul contends, were incorrect in preaching the resurrection of the dead was complete. If this philosophy were true, only the righteous Saints who died before resurrection morn would qualify to be raised from the dead. The rest of us would be left to molder in the ground.

18. Sperry, *Paul's Life and Letters*, 303.

19. Eusebius, *The Ecclesiastical History* (Grand Rapids, Michigan: Baker Book House, 1955), 80.

20. Tertullian in *Ante-Nicene Fathers*, 3:648. I was directed to this source by Ogden and Skinner in *New Testament Apostles*, 223–24.

3

PAUL AS A WITNESS OF THE WORK OF GOD

Ted L. Gibbons

*T*HE LIFE OF PAUL FOLLOWING HIS conversion allows us to learn significant lessons about what it means to stand as a witness of God "at all times and in all things, and in all places" (Mosiah 18:9). In Paul we find a powerful witness of God. Like Alma[1] and the sons of Mosiah, he threw himself into the work of being a witness in the most hostile of environments.

Following his return to Jerusalem from his third missionary journey, Paul threw much of Jerusalem into an uproar. There Paul was falsely accused of defiling the temple, and the people dragged him out therefrom with the intent to kill him. After his rescue by Lysius and a band of Roman soldiers, Paul asked permission to do what he had been commissioned to do: "I beseech thee, suffer me to speak unto the people" (Acts 21:39). He was then permitted to address the hostile crowd who had assembled.

Standing on the stairs to the castle,[2] speaking to people eager for his death, Paul recounted his conversion and his calling. He told

---

Ted L. Gibbons is an instructor at the Utah State Valley College Institute of Religion.

the people that following three days of blindness and fasting, Ananias had come to him, healed him, and said:

"The God of our fathers hath chosen thee, that thou shouldest know his will, and see that Just One, and shouldest hear the voice of his mouth.

"For thou shalt be his witness unto all men of what thou hast seen and heard" (Acts 22:14–15).

Thus Ananias summarized Paul's life: he would know God's will and see His Son and hear His word, and he would be God's witness "unto all men." Ananias followed his prophetic call with a challenge: "Why tarriest thou?" (Acts 22:16). Paul never *tarried* again. He "received sight forthwith, and arose, and was baptized" (Acts 9:18), spent a few days with the disciples in Damascus, and "straightway he preached Christ in the synagogues, that he is the Son of God" (Acts 9:20). Thus began Paul's ministry, a ministry motivated by his testimony of Christ and by his determination to be a witness of Him "at all times and in all things, and in all places."

A WITNESS OF GOD AT ALL TIMES

During the final months of the Savior's ministry, "there was much murmuring among the people concerning him: for some said, He is a good man: others said, Nay; but he deceiveth the people. Howbeit no man spake openly of him for fear of the Jews" (John 7:12–13).

Jesus Himself warned His followers of the consequences of their unwillingness to be His witnesses in front of His enemies.

"Also I say unto you, Whosoever shall confess me before men, him shall the Son of man also confess before the angels of God.

"But he who denieth me before men, shall be denied before the angels of God.

"Now his disciples knew that he said this, because they had spoken evil against him before the people; for they were afraid to confess him before men" (JST Luke 12:8–10).

In our own day the Lord has added this instruction: "But with some I am not well pleased, for they will not open their mouths, but they hide the talent which I have given unto them, because of the fear of man. Wo unto such, for mine anger is kindled against them" (D&C 60:2).

The Lord warned His disciples that even their longing for personal safety must not cause them to shut their mouths in fear. No such admonition was necessary for Paul. He never sought a safer environment on his own, but at least eight times in the book of Acts when Paul was in danger, the disciples tried to move him out of harm's way.[3] The Lord had commanded him: "Speak, and hold not thy peace" (Acts 18:9). And that is what he did for the final thirty years of his life, regardless of personal danger.

Paul did not believe in sabbaticals. He learned what he was expected and able to do, and he got it done. His continual witness was one of undiluted commitment. He imparted the same sense of duty to Timothy, his own disciple: "Preach the word; be instant in season, out of season; reprove, rebuke, exhort with all longsuffering and doctrine" (2 Timothy 4:2).

The circumstances in which Paul found himself were never a limiting factor, nor were the dangers. If something needed to be said, Paul said it. When personal conversation was impractical or impossible, Paul wrote letters.

But at the time of his conversion, such power and potential were not apparent. When the Lord called Ananias to heal Saul, Ananias debated the issue. "Lord, I have heard by many of this man, how much evil he hath done to thy saints at Jerusalem: and here he hath authority from the chief priests to bind all that call on thy name" (Acts 9:13–14). The concerns of Ananias were justifiable. No reasonable person would encourage a wolf to dwell with the sheep, and Saul had been a wolf. He made "havock of the church" in Jerusalem, "entering into every house, and haling [compelling] men and women committed them to prison" (Acts 8:3). Paul's repeated invasion of Christian homes and his arrest and incarceration of Christian believers is a heartrending image—an image that must have haunted and motivated him through all the years of his discipleship. And Ananias knew Saul had come to Damascus, "breathing out threatenings and slaughter against the disciples of the Lord" (Acts 9:1).

However, Ananias learned, as would so many others, that Saul was a "chosen vessel unto [the Lord]" (Acts 9:15) who would suffer great things for the name of Christ (Acts 9:16). This reality was as invisible to Ananias as it would have been to all of us. Hugh Nibley described the problem of being unable to see the hearts of people:

"The gospel of repentance is a constant reminder that . . . the most wicked are not yet beyond redemption and may still be saved. And that is what God wants: 'Have I any pleasure at all that the wicked should die?' (Ezekiel 18:23). There are poles for all to see, but in this life no one has reached and few have ever approached either pole and no one has any idea at what point between his neighbor stands. Only God knows that."[4]

God knew Paul. He knew what Paul was and what he could become, and even though the potential hidden in this tentmaker's son was at first imperceptible to Ananias, it was nevertheless real. Paul knew that what God had found embodied in him might also be veiled in the hearts of others. Therefore, as Paul demonstrated on the stairs of the Antonia Fortress, he was determined to deliver his witness to everybody at all times. This courageous approach has always typified the greatest missionaries among us: those who have marched into danger armed with the word and their witness, determined to teach the truth. The following events from the missionary journeys of Paul confirm that he was prepared to stand as a witness of God at all times.

• In the synagogue at Antioch in Pisidia, after the reading of the law and the prophets, Paul and his companions were invited to speak, and "Paul stood up, and beckoning with his hand said, Men of Israel, and ye that fear God, give audience" (Acts 13:16). One of Paul's greatest qualities was that he was always ready to "stand up."

• Paul and his companions stayed in Iconium for a long time, "speaking boldly in the Lord" (Acts 14:3).

• While Paul waited for Silas and Timothy in Athens, he could not simply *wait*, because "his spirit was stirred in him, when he saw the city wholly given to idolatry. Therefore disputed he in the synagogue with the Jews, and with the devout persons, and in the market daily with them that met with him" (Acts 17:16–17). His "daily" trips to the market to teach and his testimonies to the devout reveal to us the desires of his heart.

• When Paul came to Corinth, "he reasoned in the synagogue every sabbath, and persuaded the Jews and the Greeks" (Acts 18:4).

• He gave many sermons and, when needed, he gave long sermons. In Troas, "when the disciples came together to break bread, Paul preached unto them, ready to depart on the morrow; and continued his speech until midnight" (Acts 20:7). And he was not done at midnight. After raising Eutychus from death (he had gone to sleep and fallen from a third-story window), Paul "talked a long while, even till break of day" (Acts 20:11).

• To the elders of the church at Ephesus, Paul testified, "by the space of three years I ceased not to warn every one night and day with tears" (Acts 20:31).

• Even as a prisoner in Jerusalem, Caesarea, on Melita (Malta), and in Rome, Paul shared his witness because he was first a prisoner of his love for and testimony of Christ (see Ephesians 3:1; 4:1). He had no desire to please men, but God (see Galatians 1:10; 1 Thessalonians 2:4).

The example of Paul as a witness of God at all times should compel us to renewed efforts. We can never waste an opportunity to be witnesses because we have other things to do or we have done enough or people will not listen. Paul shows us what the Lord expected when He directed His disciples to stand as witnesses "at all times."

A WITNESS OF GOD IN ALL THINGS

Paul delivered his witness through his actions, his example, his obedience, and his message. The verbs used in the King James Bible to describe Paul's ministry paint a stirring portrait of Paul. For example, He "witnessed" (Acts 22:15; 23:11; 26:16), "confounded" (Acts 9:22), "disputed" (Acts 9:29; 15:2), "waxed bold" (Acts 13:46), "returned" (Acts 14:21), "sang" (Acts 16:25), "testified" (Acts 18:5), "strengthened" (Acts 18:23), "taught" (Acts 20:20), "declared" (Acts 20:27), "wrote" (2 Corinthians 2:3–4), "withstood" (Galatians 2:11), "imparted" (1 Thessalonians 2:8), and "exhorted and comforted and charged every one . . . as a father doth his children" (1 Thessalonians 2:11).

Paul's witness of the things he had seen and heard—the things he knew—were varied and powerful.

Paul was a witness of God's goodness to the Gentiles. Luke's arrangement of the conversion and call of Saul in Acts 9 before the invitation to the Gentiles in Acts 10 is probably not a coincidence. Paul was the messenger of God to the Gentiles. As a "chosen vessel" he was to bear the name of the Lord "before the Gentiles, and kings, and the children of Israel" (Acts 9:15). It was in Antioch in Pisidia, when the Jews were "filled with envy, and spake against those things which were spoken by Paul, contradicting and blaspheming," that Paul first said, "Lo, we turn to the Gentiles" (Acts 13:45–46). Decades later, in his defense before Agrippa, Paul explained his ministry:

"I continue unto this day, witnessing both to small and great, saying none other things than those which the prophets and Moses did say should come:

"That Christ should suffer, and that he should be the first that should rise from the dead, and should shew light unto the people, and to the Gentiles" (Acts 26:22–23).

Paul was a witness against the enemies of righteousness. When Elymas the sorcerer attempted to turn one of Paul's converts from the faith, Paul immediately took action:

"O full of all subtilty and all mischief, thou child of the devil, thou enemy of all righteousness, wilt thou not cease to pervert the right ways of the Lord?

"And now, behold, the hand of the Lord is upon thee, and thou shalt be blind, not seeing the sun for a season. And immediately there fell on him a mist and a darkness; and he went about seeking some to lead him by the hand" (Acts 13:10–11).

Paul was a witness of God's power. Paul caused a great commotion when he healed the cripple in Lystra. Residents were convinced that the "gods [were] come down . . . in the likeness of men" (see Acts 14:8–15). In Philippi he healed a young lady who enriched her masters with her "prophetic" gifts. When the irate owners of the slave perceived their financial loss, they had Paul and Silas beaten and committed to prison, from which, like Alma and Amulek (see Alma 14), they were freed by an earthquake (Acts 16:25–26), which gave Paul yet another opportunity to stand as a witness (see Acts 16:28–33).

Paul's miraculous ministry continued in Ephesus.

"And God wrought special miracles by the hands of Paul:

"So that from his body were brought unto the sick hand-kerchiefs or aprons, and the diseases departed from them, and the evil spirits went out of them" (Acts 19:11–12).

In Troas, as mentioned earlier, Paul restored Eutychus to life (Acts 20:9–12). On the island of Melita (traditionally identified as Malta), when he was bitten by a deadly viper, he showed no ill effects from the poison (see Acts 28:3–6).

Paul was a witness of the need for purity in doctrine and ordinances. When Paul found a group of baptized disciples who knew nothing of the gift of the Holy Ghost, he baptized them again and then laid his hands on them to confer that gift. Even though they were called disciples (see Acts 19:2), Paul knew that their instruction in the sequence and importance of the ordinances was incomplete. He performed the ordinances again to ensure that they were done correctly and by proper authority.

Luke related a similar episode, one involving the name of Paul, though not his presence, to show the need for purity in the ordinances. A group of exorcists, referred to as "vagabond Jews," who must have been witnesses of some of the miracles of Paul, undertook to do a similar work in his name and the name of Jesus. They "took upon them to call over them which had evil spirits the name of the Lord Jesus, saying, We adjure you by Jesus whom Paul preacheth.

"And there were seven sons of one Sceva, a Jew, and chief of the priests, which did so. And the evil spirit answered and said, Jesus I know, and Paul I know; but who are ye? And the man in whom the evil spirit was leaped on them, and overcame them, and prevailed against them, so that they fled out of that house naked and wounded" (Acts 19:13–16).

Paul was a witness of what a great missionary should be. In his letter to the Saints at Thessalonica, he spoke of his boldness (1 Thessalonians 2:2), the trust of God in him (1 Thessalonians 2:4), his determination to say what God wanted him to say (1 Thessalonians 2:4), his refusal to flatter to obtain success or advantage (1 Thessalonians 2:5), and his refusal to seek glory for himself or to be burdensome to his converts (1 Thessalonians 2:6). He spoke of his gentleness (1 Thessalonians 2:7), his labor and travail both night and day so that he could stand blameless before God (1 Thessalonians 2:9), his commendable behavior (1 Thessalonians 2:10), and his gratitude to God for the privilege of serving (1 Thessalonians 1:2; 2:13).

In Troas he testified:

"Ye know, from the first day that I came into Asia, after what manner I have been with you at all seasons,

"Serving the Lord with all humility of mind, and with many tears, and temptations, which befell me by the lying in wait of the Jews:

"And how I kept back nothing that was profitable unto you, but have shewed you, and have taught you publickly, and from house to house,

"Testifying both to the Jews, and also to the Greeks, repentance toward God, and faith toward our Lord Jesus Christ" (Acts 20:18–21).

Paul was a witness of the need for patience and long-suffering in the work of God. When God replied to Ananias's concerns over the conversion of Saul, the Lord said, "For I will shew him how great things he must suffer for my name's sake" (Acts 9:16). In this matter of suffering Paul was very much like the sons of Mosiah, to whom the Lord said, "Go forth among the Lamanites, thy brethren, and establish my word; yet ye shall be patient in long-suffering and afflictions, that ye may show forth good examples unto them in me, and I will make an instrument of thee in my hands unto the salvation of many souls" (Alma 17:11).

In 2 Corinthians 11, Paul gives a résumé of his suffering for the cause of Christ. He speaks of labours, prisons, floggings, beatings, stoning, shipwrecks, journeyings, perils, false brethren, weariness, painfulness, hunger, thirst, fastings, cold, nakedness, and "the care of all the churches" (2 Corinthians 11:23–28). In conjunction with the list above, seven recorded instances tell of attempts to take Paul's life (see Acts 9:23; 9:29; 14:5; 14:19; 21:30–31; 23:12; and 25:3).

One of the great images of the New Testament is of the moment when Paul and Silas, stripped and savagely beaten, thrown into a Philippi prison and placed in stocks, "sang praises unto God" (Acts 16:23–25). Patience and long-suffering indeed! He was truly a man willing to be a witness in all things.

But why not sing praises in prison, or anywhere else? Paul's great love was not for his own life, but for Christ (see Acts 20:24; 21:13). That love became his motivation from his encounter with the Lord on the road to Damascus until the day of his martyrdom. It was a love he taught eloquently to others:

"That Christ may dwell in your hearts by faith; that ye, being rooted and grounded in love,

"May be able to comprehend with all saints what is the breadth, and length, and depth, and height;

"And to know the love of Christ, which passeth knowledge, that ye might be filled with all the fulness of God" (Ephesians 3:17–19).

A Witness of God in All Places

The book of Acts and the epistles of Paul indicate some of the places where Paul visited or preached. Some of the locations were Antioch in Pisidia, Antioch in Syria, Athens, Berea, Caesarea, Corinth, Damascus, Derbe, Ephesus, Galatia, Iconium, Jerusalem, Lystra, Melita, Miletus, Mysia, Paphos, Philippi, Phrygia, Ptolemais (Acco), Rome, Salamis, Thessalonica, Troas, Trophimus, and Tyre.

However, Luke shows us something more interesting than the cities where Paul preached. For within those cities, Paul taught in many synagogues (see Acts 13:14; 14:1; 17:1–2, etc.), in "all the coasts of Judea" (Acts 26:20), "by a river side" (Acts 16:13), in a prison (Acts 16:25–32), on Mars' Hill (Acts 17:22), in the market

(Acts 17:17), in a certain man's house (Acts 18:7), over all the country (Acts 18:23), in the school of Tyrannus (Acts 19:9), at a sacrament meeting (Acts 20:7), from house to house (Acts 20:20), on the stairs (Acts 21:40), in the castle (Acts 23:10), in the judgment hall (Acts 23:35), on a ship (Acts 27:21–26), in the quarters of the chief man of Melita (Acts 28:7–8), and in his own house (Acts 28:30–31).

The Lord commanded His disciples to take the witness to "all the world" (Mark 16:15) and "unto the uttermost part of the earth" (Acts 1:8). But in this worldwide ministry, the instruction was to "preach the gospel to every creature" (Mark 16:15). That one-by-one ministry to individuals happens in places smaller than cities and countries. The sons of Mosiah reported that they had preached to the Lamanites in many places: "And we have entered into their houses and taught them, and we have taught them in their streets; yea, and we have taught them upon their hills; and we have also entered into their temples and their synagogues and taught them" (Alma 26:29).

Paul preached in this same spirit, and his determination to be a witness to individuals in every place caused him to emphasize similarities rather than differences.

"For though I be free from all men, yet have I made myself servant unto all, that I might gain the more.

"And unto the Jews I became as a Jew, that I might gain the Jews; to them that are under the law, as under the law, that I might gain them that are under the law;

"To them that are without law, as without law, (being not without law to God, but under the law to Christ,) that I might gain them that are without law.

"To the weak became I as weak, that I might gain the weak: I am made all things to all men, that I might by all means save some.

"And this I do for the gospel's sake, that I might be partaker thereof with you" (1 Corinthians 9:19–23).

The purity of Paul's intent is nowhere better seen than in the passage above. Whatever he needed to do within the framework of agency and his commission from Christ, he would do. President David O. McKay wrote this of Paul:

Before the Royal, he was kingly,
In the prison, noble, true;
In the tempest, mighty captain
Of a terror-stricken crew.

Sunless days nor nights of blackness,
Prison chains—tempestuous wave,
Floundered ship nor deadly viper—
Feared he not the yawning grave.
"God's good angel stood beside me,
His I am and Him I serve,"
This the secret of his power—
Him from Right no power could swerve.[5]

A WITNESS OF GOD EVEN UNTO DEATH

Luke ends his account of the ministry of Paul with the Roman imprisonment, but nonscriptural sources suggest that he died about A.D. 67 or 68 near Rome. Sperry wrote this:

"At the time of Paul's first hearing before the Roman court, it is said that Nero was absent in Greece. What the charge against Paul was we do not know, but it was probably one involving sedition. Nor do we know what happened at the second hearing. Apparently Nero had returned, and his displeasure sealed the Apostle's doom. The Roman Senate had passed an ordinance to the effect that ten days should elapse between the condemnation of a criminal and his execution in order that the Emperor might, if so disposed, grant him a pardon. It was the custom, especially if a demonstration might take place, to take the criminal outside of the city to be executed. The tradition is that Paul was conducted about two miles from Rome on the Ostian Way, southwest of the city, where he was beheaded by the sword. His Roman citizenship saved him from the suffering sustained by many Christians in being crucified or in being smeared with pitch and set on fire. According to the testimony of St. Jerome, Paul met his death in the fourteenth year of Nero's reign, that is, sometime between October 13, A.D. 67 and June 9, A.D. 68."[6]

Such information is useful in understanding what happened to Paul and in understanding Paul himself. Long before the sword fell in Italy, Paul knew at least some of what awaited him. In Miletus, Paul spoke of his future:

"And now, behold, I go bound in the spirit unto Jerusalem, not knowing the things that shall befall me there:

"Save that the Holy Ghost witnesseth in every city, saying that bonds and afflictions abide me.

"But none of these things move me, neither count I my life dear unto myself, so that I might finish my course with joy, and the ministry, which I have received of the Lord Jesus, to testify the gospel of the grace of God" (Acts 20:22–24).

When at Caesarea, Agabus prophesied future afflictions for Paul, and disciples besought him to change his plans, Paul rebuked them, saying, "What mean ye to weep and to break mine heart? for I am ready not to be bound only, but also to die at Jerusalem for the name of the Lord Jesus" (Acts 21:13).

He was ready indeed! His only desire, even at the end of his life, was to glorify Christ through his witness of the Redeemer's merits, mercy, and grace. He was willing to let his life and his death be such a witness.

"For I know that this shall turn to my salvation through your prayer, and the supply of the Spirit of Jesus Christ,

"According to my earnest expectation and my hope, that in nothing I shall be ashamed, but that with all boldness, as always, so now also Christ shall be magnified in my body, whether it be by life, or by death" (Philippians 1:19–20).

Paul was a small man, about five feet tall. But he also had a voice that when elevated resembled the roar of a lion.[7] It is possible to hear the spirit and the resonance of that voice as we read his words. That roar, the thunder of undiluted truth, has changed the Christian world. In fact, as those of us called to a similar ministry read the words of Paul's witness and invitation, it is truly difficult not to hear it:

"We then, as workers together with him, beseech you also that ye receive not the grace of God in vain. . . . Giving no offence in any thing, that the ministry be not blamed:

"But in all things approving ourselves as the ministers of God, in much patience, in afflictions, in necessities, in distresses,

"In stripes, in imprisonments, in tumults, in labours, in watchings, in fastings;

"By pureness, by knowledge, by longsuffering, by kindness, by the Holy Ghost, by love unfeigned,

"By the word of truth, by the power of God, by the armour of righteousness on the right hand and on the left,

"By honour and dishonour, by evil report and good report: as deceivers, and yet true;

"As unknown, and yet well known; as dying, and, behold, we live; as chastened, and not killed;

"As sorrowful, yet alway rejoicing; as poor, yet making many rich; as having nothing, and yet possessing all things" (2 Corinthians 6:1–10).

In his final letter to Timothy, Paul wrote what could have been his own epitaph:

"For I am now ready to be offered, and the time of my departure is at hand.

"I have fought a good fight, I have finished my course, I have kept the faith:

"Henceforth there is laid up for me a crown of righteousness, which the Lord, the righteous judge, shall give me at that day: and not to me only, but unto all them also that love his appearing" (2 Timothy 4:6–8).

Paul's witness of God at all times and in all things and in all places does not end with his death. That witness has echoed down the ages. Perhaps Paul's testimony before Agrippa is an appropriate place to conclude, for it is a reflection of the great longing of Paul's life: "I would to God, that not only thou, but also all that hear me this day, were both almost, and altogether such as I am, except these bonds" (Acts 26:29). This is an appeal that should reach across the years to us. Whether or not we have ever seen the light on the road to Damascus is not the issue; we have all been called to be witnesses of God, at all times and in all things and in all places, until we also have finished our course.

NOTES

1. Elder Bruce R. McConkie refers to Alma the Younger as "the American Paul" (Bruce R. McConkie, *Doctrinal New Testament Commentary* (Salt Lake City: Bookcraft, 1971), 89; and Bruce R. McConkie, *The Promised Messiah* (Salt Lake City: Deseret Book Company, 1978), 268, 333.

2. The *castle* is the Fortress of Antonia. It was built by Herod the Great and was located just north of the temple.

3. See Acts 9:24–25; 9:29–30; 17:5–10; 17:13–14; 19:28–31; 20:22–24; 21:4, 10–13.

4. Hugh Nibley in *Of All Things! Classic Quotations from Hugh Nibley,* comp. and ed. Gary P. Gillum (Salt Lake City, Deseret Book Company, 1993), 6.

5. David O. McKay, *Ancient Apostles* (Salt Lake City: Deseret Book, 1965), 197.

6. Sidney B. Sperry, *Paul's Life and Letters* (Salt Lake City: Bookcraft, 1955), 303.

7. See Andrew F. Ehat and Lyndon Cook, eds. and comps., *The Words of Joseph Smith* (Provo, Utah, Religious Studies Center, Brigham Young University, 1980), 59.

4

THE "I'S" OF CORINTH:
MODERN PROBLEMS
NOT NEW

Mary Jane Woodger

*P*RESIDENT HOWARD W. HUNTER SAID: "The witness of Paul to the saints at Corinth, and the message applies to us in this day, living as we do in a world that can be compared in many ways to Corinth of old. In a society of turmoil, immorality, free-thinking, and questioning of the reality of God, we reach out for the simplicity of the gospel of Jesus Christ."[1]

At times, the society in which we live can infiltrate our congregations. Imagine an Area Authority Seventy receiving a letter from a newly sustained branch president in a secluded area of the world asking for advice on how to handle issues dealing with his branch members. Is it too far-fetched to suppose those problems could include members suing each other in civil court and indiscreetly frequenting social clubs where commodities contrary to Church standards were openly served? Think of that same Area Authority Seventy receiving e-mails that included narratives of intoxicated men participating in the sacrament ordinance and women insisting

---

Mary Jane Woodger is an assistant professor of Church history and doctrine at Brigham Young University.

on conducting meetings, refusing to submit to presiding priesthood leaders. Imagine it being reported that one branch member, rather than bearing testimony, consistently boasted of being baptized by a certain General Authority. Picture a missionary visiting this same branch and finding a Gospel Doctrine teacher who uses the words of a world-renowned philosopher for his curriculum and local Relief Society sisters who are so insecure that they argue about whose spiritual gifts are more important. In addition, imagine an Area Authority Seventy's thoughts upon learning that his warning to excommunicate those involved with fornication had been disregarded—an incestuous relationship was openly being flaunted at meetings by two branch members while local leadership simply looked the other way.

Such a severely troubled branch, in desperate need of a strong local leader or an attentive Area Authority Seventy, was precisely what the Apostle Paul faced. Alarming reports had reached him from several sources concerning Church members in Corinth (see 1 Corinthians 1:11, 5:1–3, 7:1, 16:12–17). If all the problems in the Corinthian branch existed in one congregation today, it would seem overwhelming, but Latter-day Saints can certainly conceive of some of these same situations surfacing in their own wards. This paper will center on the application of gospel principles as taught by Paul to modern-day issues such as intellectualism, inappropriate actions, immorality, indiscretion, insubmissiveness, and insecurity.

INTELLECTUALISM

The Corinth of Paul's day was an important port city of industry and commerce founded by Julius Caesar in 44 B.C. Greek philosophy and Hellenistic culture permeated the cosmopolitan center that lay on a strategic four-mile isthmus.[2] The pool of people from which Paul found converts had been raised as Greeks and were already hellenized.[3] With this hellenization came an inappropriate emphasis on educational opportunities. Greeks boasted of being taught at the feet of self-proclaimed intellectuals and then espoused these mentors' teachings.

The worldly influence of intellectual mentors infiltrated the early Christian Church at Corinth. The pride of the Corinthian Saints in their personal mentors surfaced as they boasted of being baptized by the most reputed priest. They pitted one Apostle against another in a kind of mentor one-upmanship: "Every one of you saith, I am of Paul; and I of Apollos; and I of Cephas; and I of Christ" (1 Corinthians 1:12). Paul denounced their boasting: "I thank God that I baptized none of you" (1 Corinthians 1:14). He explained that it is the message rather than the messenger that takes preeminence in the gospel of Jesus Christ.

Paul proclaimed that the gospel of Jesus Christ would "destroy the wisdom of the wise and . . . bring to nothing the understanding of the prudent" (1 Corinthians 1:19). Paul refused to teach "with [the] wisdom of words" through the intellect alone (1 Corinthians 1:17). Teaching "by the foolishness of preaching," Paul claimed to know nothing except for the gospel of Jesus Christ (1 Corinthians 1:21). Though his pharisaic credentials were impressive, he "determined not to know any thing . . . save Jesus Christ" (1 Corinthians 2:1–2).

In the Church of Christ the wisdom of men is not the deciding factor in becoming a disciple of Christ. God chooses the foolish to confound the wise (1 Corinthians 1:27). Apostles declare adamantly that "true religion is not a matter of intellectuality or of worldly prominence or renown, but of spirituality."[4] Elder Bruce R. McConkie concurred:

"In this life, those who are learned, who have intellectual capacity, who gain scholastic degrees, are held up to dignity and renown; their views are sought; their opinions are valued. But from the Lord's eternal perspective, there is almost no language sufficient to depreciate the importance of intellectuality standing alone and to magnify the eternal worth of spirituality."[5]

In the spirit of their Corinthian counterparts, some modern-day Church members who are also secular scholars suggest that the Church needs to change to fit the culture and intellectual climate in which it exists. In 1993 President Boyd K. Packer discussed having to deal with "the ever-present challenge from the so-called scholars or intellectuals." In Pauline fashion, President Packer explained, "The doctrines of the gospel are revealed through the Spirit to prophets, not through the intellect to scholars."[6]

The intellect has little to do with the preaching of Jesus Christ's gospel. Neither one's measured IQ nor one's academic credentials are a measure of righteousness. Those who preach the gospel of Jesus Christ do not necessarily come "with excellency of speech" (1 Corinthians 2:1–2). Testimony comes through the heart. Nineteen-year-olds would have destroyed the missionary efforts of the Church long ago if mature intellectual experience were required to preach the gospel. The Lord still chooses the "foolish things of the world to confound the wise . . . [and] the weak things of the world to confound the things which are mighty" (1 Corinthians 1:27). Elder Neal A. Maxwell echoes Paul's stance: "Whether . . . a bricklayer or an intellectual we all come to Jesus Christ in the very same way— through the Atonement and the submission of our wills to His."[7]

The Corinthians had to be fed gospel milk because they were not yet able to bear the meaty doctrines (1 Corinthians 3:1–2). The ability to digest the meat of the gospel comes only through a Spirit-born testimony based on the doctrine of Christ, not through intellectual endeavors.

INAPPROPRIATE ACTIONS

Corinthian Church teachers polluted pure doctrine by inappropriately bringing secular philosophies into Church meetings, espousing those ideas rather than the simple gospel. Paul had taught the gospel in its purity in Corinth; however, after he left, others improperly added the wisdom of men to the established doctrinal foundation. Paul responded: "As a wise masterbuilder, I have laid the foundation, and another buildeth thereon. But let every man take heed how he buildeth thereupon" (1 Corinthians 3:10). The master builders are the Apostles, who build upon the foundation of Jesus Christ and His atoning sacrifice. Joseph Smith taught: "The fundamental principles of our religion are the testimony of Apostles and Prophets, concerning Jesus Christ, that He died, was buried, and rose again the third day, and ascended into heaven; and all other things which pertain to our religion are only appendages to it."[8]

In his metaphor of building the Church, Paul used "gold, silver, [and] precious stones" to symbolize doctrines laid upon the foundation of the Savior. Members in Corinth introduced into their preaching secular ideas, symbolized as "wood, hay, and stubble" (1 Corinthians 3:12). No member of the Church of Christ would consider building with such materials, but many symbolically bring less valuable curricula into their teachings. Some ancient and modern Saints argue that doctrines of the gospel are logically or factually unsupported, unsubstantiated, or old-fashioned. Others suggest that man's creative ideas are to be valued more than the simple truths found in apostolic teachings.

For instance, in Gospel Doctrine classes a teacher may try to share the stubble gleaned from some popular book rather than the gold of precious scriptures. Some may feel that if their bishop just understood certain acclaimed, secular business practices, he would make a better administrator. Or when members are asked to speak in sacrament meeting, instead of using a Book of Mormon text they may discuss a contending scientific theory or the latest local newspaper editorial. Others might feel their stake president would be more effective if he just understood certain counseling techniques and relied less on the Spirit. Paul is warning Saints not to replace the godly spirit with secular appearances.

In the same manner, some Corinthians who converted to the primitive Church had a philosophical view of the world to which they were trying to adapt the gospel. Ultimately many Corinthian Saints inappropriately adopted Christianity into the culture that permeated their society. This hellenization resulted with the capstone creeds of false doctrine securely fastened into some sects. President Joseph F. Smith echoed Paul's warnings when he advised modern Saints that the preaching of false educational ideas disguised as truths of the gospel is a dangerous proposition.

IMMORALITY

President Smith also warned of sexual impurity that threatens the Church from within.[9] Immorality among the Saints was also a constant concern for Paul.

As one of the largest cities in the Roman Empire, Corinth enjoyed economic success.

Few documents teach so clearly and powerfully as does Paul's first epistle to the Corinthians that "riches produced luxury and luxury [often brings] a total corruption of morals."[10] Corinth was one of the flesh pots of the ancient world, and Corinthian ports had a reputation of being promiscuous. Following Epicureanism they adopted a "debased way of life."[11] Biblical scholar Russell P. Spittler explains:

"The two harbors of Corinth thus brought to the city numerous travelers, merchants, and sailors, who in turn brought their religion, their wealth, and their morals (or lack of them). . . . Corinth was also famed for its wickedness. Atop the Acro-Corinth . . . was a temple dedicated to the Greek goddess of love, Aphrodite. To this infamous place were attached professional prostitutes (some say 1,000) who had dedicated themselves to the goddess and amassed a fortune to the temple and thus for the city. . . . In fact, the Greek language developed the term *to Corinthianize*, which meant to live a life of drunken immorality."[12]

Amidst this setting there were Corinthians familiar with Aristotle who believed the soul would be eternally "detachable from the body," and looked upon the physical body as "the prisonhouse of the soul."[13] Some followed the father of Greek asceticism, Pythagoras, and imposed food taboos, silence for novices, and sexual restrictions. These philosophical ideas developed into what biblical scholar E. R. Dodds calls the "origin of Puritanism." Dodds tells us that "these beliefs promoted in their adherents a horror of the body and a revulsion against the life of the senses."[14]

The philosophies explained above led many Corinthians to what I refer to as either an ascetic or libertine extreme. Libertines wallowed in fleshy pursuits of permissiveness, while ascetics denied the flesh and espoused celibacy. New Testament historian F. F. Bruce relates that "Paul found it necessary to deal with both tendencies simultaneously, saying 'Liberty, not bondage' to the one group and 'Liberty, not licence' to the other."[15]

Chapter 5 of 1 Corinthians deals with libertines who are

wallowing in the flesh. In Paul's time it was common knowledge that an incestual relationship between a son and his stepmother was taking place, yet local leaders tolerated the situation. Paul declared the seriousness of this situation: "Such fornication as is not so much as named among the Gentiles" (1 Corinthians 5:1). Paul had instructed in a previous epistle long lost to modern readers that individuals involved in fornication "should be handled for their membership." Some may mistakenly think that Paul was counseling Church members to avoid individuals of other faiths who did not share the same values. Rather, his message was that those who made sacred covenants must understand the seriousness of sexual perversion. There are behavioral requirements for membership in the kingdom of God. Corinthians were exposed to the same alternative lifestyles that now face Latter-day Saints, including fornication, adultery, and homosexuality (1 Corinthians 6:9). Paul used clear-cut terminology to inform modern and ancient libertines that you cannot wallow in the flesh, whether in heterosexual or homosexual relations, and remain in full fellowship in the Church.

Paul then approached ascetics who degraded the physical body. Paul instructed that Saints' bodies belong to the Holy Ghost (see 1 Corinthians 6:19). Many in our society negatively compare their physical attributes to those portrayed in the media, thus becoming modern ascetics. The modern diseases of anorexia and bulimia are symptomatic of those who deny the flesh, while others denounce the physical relationship of legal, lawful, marriage.

Latter-day Saints can be grateful that Joseph Smith illuminates a verse that has been misinterpreted by ascetics for centuries. First Corinthians 7 of the King James Version begins with an unrealistic assertion: "It is good for a man not to touch a woman" (1 Corinthians 7:1). This instruction seems particularly out of place as the next few verses highlight intimacy within the marriage bond. Joseph Smith divulged that this statement was part of a question asked in a communiqué: "Now concerning the things whereof ye wrote unto me, saying . . ." (JST 1 Corinthians 7:1). Apparently an ascetic had written Paul and asked if his views were correct. Paul answered that human intimacy is accounted for in the Lord's plan. The solution to the desire for human intimacy is found in the marriage covenant: "To avoid fornication, let every man have his own wife, and let every woman have her own husband" (1 Corinthians 7:2). Using legal terms, Paul instructed that intimacy is an expected and vital part of the marriage contract:

"Let the husband render unto the wife due benevolence: and likewise also the wife unto the husband. The wife hath not power of her own body, but the husband: and likewise also the husband hath not power of his own body, but the wife. Defraud ye not one the other, except it be with consent for a time, that ye may give yourselves to fasting and prayer; and come together again, that Satan tempt you not for your incontinency" (1 Corinthians 7:3–5).

Some mistakenly interpret that Paul spoke only of common courtesy in this verse. In this context he speaks of the contractual agreement between husband and wife, including the role of intimacy. To paraphrase the verse: As a married couple, part of you now belongs to each other. Don't defraud or keep back what you promised to give. Grant your spouse your sexual monopoly and do not deny that access, because if a couple spends too much time apart, Satan will gain leverage.

Readers will also notice that Paul does not mention procreation in these verses. Paul would take issue with those who preach that the only reason for the physical relationship in a marriage is for the begetting of children. No other scriptural writer comes close to being as candid or positive about the role of physical intimacy in marriage.

Latter-day Saint scholars have consistently agreed that Paul was married.[16] His knowledge of an intimate relationship is clearly manifest in his ability to guide others through marital questions and problems. Paul also knew of the relationship of celestial marriage to eternal life. Historically maligning Paul as a celibate, scholars have misinterpreted his statement that the unmarried should "abide even as I" (1 Corinthians 7:8). The Joseph Smith Translation again clears a discrepancy: Joseph Smith learned that Paul counseled young people to go on missions before they married (JST 1 Corinthians 7:29–34). Though wanting his missionary force to grow, Paul counseled prospective missionaries: "If they cannot contain, let them marry: for it is better to marry than to burn" (1 Corinthians 7:9). Modern mission presidents would concur that if a missionary's heart is back home with his girlfriend, he had better change his focus or stay home.

Later in chapter 7, Paul describes the circumstances in which marriage is recommended: "But if any man think that he behaveth himself uncomely toward his virgin, if she pass the flower of her age, and need so require, let him do what he will, he sinneth not: let them marry" (1 Corinthians 7:36). Perhaps in our generation priesthood bearers would instruct a seemingly confirmed bachelor with Lehi's words to "arise from the dust, my sons, and be men" (2 Nephi 1:21). Confronting ascetic and libertine views, Paul's treatise supports the marriages of ancient and modern Christians alike.

INSUBMISSIVENESS

Paul's epistle also defines other eternal truths about the relationship of husbands and wives: "The head of every man is Christ, and the head of the woman is the man; and the head of Christ is God" (1 Corinthians 11:3). Some who read this verse misinterpret Paul's words. In error they feel Paul implies that women are at the bottom of a continuum of value. Paul's focus in this verse is not on gender but on the role of husbands and wives. Paul is not talking about an individual's value; rather, he is describing a flowchart of administration.

In the kingdom of God everyone is in submission to a higher authority. Submissiveness is not gender based, nor does it demean the one who is presided over. It does not lessen Christ to be submissive to Elohim, nor a bishop to be submissive to a stake president. Every Latter-day Saint is voluntarily submissive through common consent with the understanding that those placed above them are to serve as stewards.

Some err in associating the word *submissive* with being inferior. In 1998, while visiting Salt Lake City, members of the Baptist Faith and Message Study Committee counseled, "'Submit' is not a negative word," rather it implies a covenant commitment where "a wife is to submit herself graciously to the servant leadership of her husband."[17] That covenant commitment is made with marital vows. Paul's paradigm for the husband and wife relationship was Jesus Christ and the Church (see 1 Corinthians 11:1–3). Could a woman ask a husband to treat her better than Christ treats His Church? Paul was perfectly comfortable with women teaching, counseling, testifying, praying and exhorting—but not ruling, organizing, or presiding over a branch (see 1 Corinthians 11:13; 14:34; 1 Timothy 5:14).

Paul honored, loved, and showed concern for women (see Philippians 4:3). The degradation of women did not come through Paul or the other original Apostles. John Bristow enlightens us: "It was Socrates who immortalized the Athenian disdain toward women. Often referring to women as 'the weaker sex,' he argued that being born a woman is a divine punishment, since a woman is halfway between a man and an animal."[18] As Greek philosophy pervaded the Christian Church's thinking, it not only accelerated the apostasy but also included an apostate perception of women. A book entitled *Women in Jewish Law and Tradition* advocates such an apostate view of females:

"Augustine wondered how a man could possibly love his wife, knowing what she is and what she represents, and concluded that he should love her as a Christian is commanded to 'love our enemies.' The ascetic Church Fathers identified women with sexuality, which they equated with filth. Their horror of sexual relations became transposed into a horror of women."[19] In contradiction Paul taught, "Neither is the man without the woman, neither the woman without the man, in the Lord" (1 Corinthians 11:11).

INDISCRETION

Along with addressing marital partnerships, Paul also applied the gospel to other social relationships. "Temples and meals in Greco-Roman society functioned in diverse ways. Some meals were knowingly offered to a god while others were not; some meals were held in temples, others were not. The line between the 'secular' and 'sacred' was not always clear."[20] Members sought Paul's clarification regarding the practices of eating idol meat or attending dinner parties held in pagan temples. Reading these verses, one may think that these subjects are irrelevant. For instance, no one would go to a local grocery store and say to the butcher, "I want to buy this T-bone, but I need to know if it has been offered up to Zeus." Such a question would be absurd, but couched in this ancient social problem is great insight that can be applied to modern-day situations.

Paul's response to the question of eating idol meat is found in chapter 8: "As concerning therefore the eating of those things that are offered in sacrifice unto idols, we know that an idol is nothing in the world, and that there is none other God but one" (1 Corinthians 8:4). Though in theory eating idol meat had no religious significance for Christians, Paul adds:

"Take heed lest by any means this liberty of yours become a stumblingblock to them that are weak. For if any man see thee which hast knowledge sit at meat in the idol's temple, shall not the conscience of him which is weak be emboldened to eat those things which are offered to idols; And through thy knowledge shall the weak brother perish, for whom Christ died?" (1 Corinthians 8:9–11)

Paul applied the principle of loving your neighbor as yourself to this social situation. In some contexts, eating meat offered to an idol is correct; in others, inappropriate, depending on how it affects everyone involved. Paul admonished: "Whatsoever is sold in the shambles, that eat, asking no question for conscience sake" (1 Corinthians 10:25). Paul instructs that the Corinthian Saints need not ask where the meat they are going to buy came from unless someone else makes an issue out of it; then the Saints are not to buy it. Church educator Michael Wilcox adds: "Some, he argued, may eat meat because of the examples of other Saints, or through peer pressure, but feel it is wrong. Thus, they would violate or weaken their consciences."[21] The conscience of one's neighbor becomes more important than the principle. The same action may be right or wrong, depending on the context.

Perhaps Paul would say in our day, "If there is something you do, even though it is not a sin, if you put your rights ahead of the spiritual welfare of another, you are in the wrong." In other words, avoid offense. A liberty must not become a stumbling block to a neighbor's testimony, because all people progress in the gospel of Jesus Christ at different paces. "Some members of the Church are being taught elementary courses; others are approaching graduation and can do independent research where the deep and hidden things are concerned. All must learn line upon line and precept upon precept."[22]

Paul asks Christians to be discreet. He is not referring to the commandments but to those issues that have not been defined by the Brethren. Modern-day issues to which we can apply this Pauline principle include discretionary Sabbath activities, dress, dating practices, and a host of other issues. When in gray areas, we must each come to our own conclusions; but at the same time, as covenant Christians, we must be aware of how our interpretation affects others. We may have a hard time exercising such discretion with others' feelings, but as Wilcox promises: "The blessings for decisions of charity above decisions of freedom will be an increase in our own individual sensitivity to the Holy Ghost as well as greater spiritual power."[23]

INSECURITY

Paul also taught the Corinthians about spiritual gifts. Hearing there were divisions among the Saints at Corinth, Paul wrote that he partly believed what he had heard (1 Corinthians 11:18). It had been reported that at sacrament meetings, some were standing and speaking in tongues in the middle of others' talks, and often there was no interpretation of the tongues (1 Corinthians 14:27–28). Those exhibiting the gift of tongues or other spiritual gifts would boast of their talent. Church members who were insecure with their testimonies, personalities, or efforts were trying to compete with one another through spiritual gifts.

Aware that spiritual gifts increase one's feelings of worth, Paul taught that spiritual gifts are not achievements, though they do add to a developed life and sense of worth. He encouraged the Saints to "covet earnestly the best gifts" (1 Corinthians 12:31). When a Saint develops and uses spiritual gifts for the purpose the Lord gave them, a person's sense of worth is developed. Elder McConkie concurred: "Suffice it to say that true greatness, from an eternal standpoint, is measured not in worldly station nor in ecclesiastical office, but in the possession of the gifts of the Spirit and in the enjoyment of the things of God."[24] Gifts are to be used for edification of the Church, exhortation, comfort, and the profit of all including oneself (see 1 Corinthians 12:4, 7; 14:2–3, 12). As Elder Robert D. Hales instructed, it is through the spiritual gifts that "our true destiny will be fulfilled."[25]

Paul related each gift to a member of the body: "There should be no schism in the body; but . . . the members should have the same care one for another" (1 Corinthians 12:25). Paul listed the spiritual gifts in pairs, showing they are to be used in conjunction with the gifts of others ultimately to bless each other's lives (1 Corinthians 12:5–10). He suggests: "When ye come together, every one of you hath a psalm, hath a doctrine, hath a tongue, hath a revelation, hath an interpretation. Let all things be done unto edifying" (1 Corinthians 14:26).

Every converted member of the Church has one or more gifts of the Spirit, and to deny the possession of at least one spiritual gift is demeaning (D&C 46:11). Elder Marvin J. Ashton counseled: "One of the great tragedies of life, it seems to me, is when a person classifies himself as someone who has no talents or gifts. When in disgust or discouragement, we allow ourselves to reach depressive levels of despair because of our demeaning self-appraisal, it is a sad day for us and a sad day in the eyes of God. For us to conclude that we have no gifts when we judge ourselves by stature, intelligence, grade-point average, wealth, power, position, or external appearance is not only unfair, but unreasonable."[26]

Paul makes it clear that the three gifts of faith, hope, and charity are preeminent. One's self-worth is especially dependent on the possession of charity. This truth becomes clear when Paul discloses that if "I . . . have not charity, I am nothing" (1 Corinthians 13:2). Paul was not saying an individual lacking charity is worthless. Even the most wicked and vile of God's sons or daughters is valued and loved by Him. Paul suggests that without charity, we will *feel* like nothing. Jealousy, the antithesis of charity, is personal frustration at another's success, which ultimately diminishes one's own personality and achievement. On the other hand, "charity is the ability to make life more meaningful for others."[27] If we are devoid of charity, we will also be devoid of self-worth and will feel insecure as we pass through mortality.

GUIDANCE FOR THE CHURCH

Paul held at bay the hellenization of the Corinthian Church. His doctrine continues to denounce the problems of intellectualism, inappropriate actions, immorality, indiscretion, insubmissiveness, and insecurity. Though the tactical dimensions of life have changed since Paul wrote his epistle, this storehouse of gospel knowledge still provides guidance as Paul calls the Corinthian Saints to repentance through a letter. Ultimately, however, early Christians did not heed Paul's correction, and apostasy developed. Elder Hartman Rector Jr., emeritus member of the First Quorum of Seventy, explained: "Paul was trying to call people to repentance by writing them letters. Nobody has ever been called to repentance by a letter yet because you have to have a face-to-face confrontation. That's when the Spirit can tell you things about the person that they won't tell. We have lost a kingdom from the earth five times because we couldn't get together to handle the transgressors. If we don't handle transgression, the Church fills up with fornicators and adulterers and the Lord disowns it. He's done it five times, and he will do it again. But it won't happen again, [because] we will handle transgression."[28]

Paul still calls us to repentance through the verses of 1 Corinthians as we struggle with the same problems. However, unlike the dispensation of the Corinthians, ours will not collectively apostatize.

The scenario at the beginning of this paper—the problematic branch in a secluded area of the world—no longer exists. Through the blessings of modern technology, words of the apostles and prophets are as near as a mouse click. Though our dispensation will not end in apostasy, there is no such blanket promise to each individual. By applying Paul's great treatise of doctrine contained in

1 Corinthians to our individual lives, we can avoid the "I's" of Corinth and deter personal apostasy.

―――――――――――

NOTES

1. Howard W. Hunter, in Conference Report, April 1969, 138.

2. David R. Seely, "'Is Christ Divided? Unity of the Saints through Charity,'" in *Studies in Scripture: Volume Six: Acts to Revelation,* ed. Robert L. Millet (Salt Lake City: Deseret Book, 1987), 58.

3. See Martin Hengel, *Judaism and Hellenism: Studies in Their Encounter in Palestine during the Early Hellenistic Period* (Philadelphia: Fortress Press, 1974).

4. Bruce R. McConkie, *Doctrinal New Testament Commentary* (Salt Lake City: Bookcraft, 1971), 2:316.

5. Ibid., 2:327.

6. Boyd K. Packer, "All-Church Coordinating Council Meeting," 18 May 1993.

7. Neal A. Maxwell, Documentary on Neal A. Maxwell by KUTV News, 2 February 1988. Video in Brigham Young University Religious Education Faculty Support Library.

8. Joseph Smith, *Teachings of the Prophet Joseph Smith,* comp. Joseph Fielding Smith (Salt Lake City: Deseret Book, 1976), 121.

9. Joseph F. Smith, *Gospel Doctrine* (Salt Lake City: Deseret Book, 1939), 312–13.

10. Hunter, in Conference Report, April 1969, 135.

11. F. F. Bruce, *New Testament History* (New York: Doubleday, 1969), 42.

12. Russell P. Spittler, *The Corinthian Correspondence* (Springfield, Mo.: Gospel Publishing House, 1976), 9–11.

13. E. R. Dodds, *The Greeks and the Irrational* (Los Angeles: University of California Press, 1951), 135, 143, 149, 152, 154.

14. Ibid., 152.

15. Bruce, *New Testament History,* 325.

16. For a treatise on Paul being married see Richard Lloyd Anderson, *Understanding Paul* (Salt Lake City: Deseret Book, 1983), 24–25, 104–5.

17. Art Toalston, "Southern Baptist Convention Takes Gospel to Salt Lake City," www.bpnews.net (accessed 11 June 1998).

18. John T. Bristow, *What Paul Really Said About Women* (San Francisco: Harper, 1988), 4.

19. Michael Kaufman, *Introduction to the Woman in Jewish Law and Tradition* (New Jersey: Jason Aronson, 1993), xxiv.

20. B. J. Oropeza, *Paul and Apostasy: Eschatology, Perseverance, and Falling Away in the Corinthian Congregation* (Tubingen, Germany: Mohr Siebeck, 2000), 65.

21. S. Michael Wilcox, *Don't Leap with the Sheep* (Salt Lake City: Deseret Book, 2001), 24.

22. McConkie, *Doctrinal New Testament Commentary*, 2:324.

23. Wilcox, *Don't Leap*, 26.

24. Bruce R. McConkie, *The Promised Messiah* (Salt Lake City: Deseret Book, 1978), 574–75.

25. Robert D. Hales, "Gifts of the Spirit," *Ensign*, February 2002, 20.

26. Marvin J. Ashton, "There Are Many Gifts," *Ensign*, May 1987, 20.

27. Hales, " Gifts," 20.

28. Hartman Rector Jr., interviewed by the author, David O. McKay Research Project, Brigham Young University, October 1996.

5

LAW AND LIBERTY IN GALATIANS 5–6

Gaye Strathearn

*M*EMBERS OF THE CHURCH OF JESUS CHRIST of Latter-day Saints believe in agency, or the right to make choices. The scriptures and modern-day prophets have repeatedly taught us the central role of agency in the plan of salvation. The scriptures also teach us that agency was guaranteed by the war in heaven during the premortal life. That war, according to Moses, was initiated when Satan rebelled against God "and sought to destroy the agency of man, which I, the Lord God, had given him" (Moses 4:3). The Doctrine and Covenants teaches us that a third of the hosts of heaven were lost in that war because they exercised their agency unwisely (see D&C 29:36). That agency, which was secured in the premortal life, is central to the plan of salvation and our mortal existence. In fact, President David O. McKay has said, "Next to the bestowal of life itself, the right to direct our lives is God's greatest gift to man."[1]

As important as the doctrine of agency is we would do well to

---

Gaye Strathearn is an instructor of ancient scripture at Brigham Young University.

heed the caution of Elder Dallin H. Oaks. He taught that "few concepts have more potential to mislead us than the idea that choice, or agency, is an ultimate goal. For Latter-day Saints, this potential confusion is partly a product of the fact that moral agency—the right to choose—is a fundamental condition of mortal life. . . . The test in this postwar mortal estate is not to secure choice but to use it—to choose good instead of evil so that we can achieve our eternal goals." He then goes on to remind us that "in mortality, choice is a method, not a goal."[2] Thus Lehi taught his son Jacob that "men are free according to the flesh; and all things are given them which are expedient unto man. And they are free to choose liberty and eternal life, through the great Mediator of all men, or to choose captivity and death, according to the captivity and power of the devil" (2 Nephi 2:27; see also 2 Nephi 10:23). President Gordon B. Hinckley stressed, "This, my brethren and sisters, is our divine right—to choose. This is our divine obligation—to choose the right."[3]In other words, it is not enough that we have choice or liberty; what is really important is that we use that liberty to make the right choices in our lives. One of the difficulties of mortality, however, is learning how to successfully accomplish that obligation in a world of competing calls for allegiance.

These competing calls were certainly an issue for the early Christian Church, in which some members struggled to understand the concept of liberty in a Christian context. In other words, they struggled to understand what liberty they were afforded because of Christ and His Atonement, and also how to use that liberty. Paul deals with this issue throughout his epistles,[4] but in this paper I would like to primarily concentrate our discussion on his teaching in Galatians, particularly chapters 5 and 6. In this epistle, Paul reacts to a group of Christian teachers who came to Galatia and taught, at least in part, that even Christian liberty was grounded in the law of Moses.[5] In the last two chapters, he identifies four important elements that help Saints of all ages to understand the nature of their liberty. These elements include the use of liberty in relation to the law, the Spirit, the principle of love, and the need to understand the relationship between our use of liberty and our need to follow the Brethren.

THE HISTORICAL SETTING FOR GALATIANS

One of the difficulties of understanding Paul's epistles is that they are like hearing only half of a telephone conversation. If we are to understand what Paul is saying then we need to try and re-create the other side of the conversation. In other words, we need to put Galatians 5–6 in its historical context. To do that, we need to appreciate some of the tensions of the early Church and try to re-create what Paul's opponents were teaching in Galatia that upset him and caused him to write this epistle.[6] In Acts, Luke tells us that after Paul and Barnabas returned from their successful first mission, "certain men which came down from Judaea" taught their Gentile converts, "Except ye be circumcised after the manner of Moses, ye cannot be saved." Luke then goes on to record that when Paul and Barnabas found out what was happening there was "no small dissension and disputation with them" (Acts 15:1–2). Paul later claimed that the confrontation was not just about the law of Moses but that it was also centered on the issue of liberty and bondage. He told the Galatian Saints that these men "came in privily to spy out our liberty which we have in Christ Jesus, that they might bring us into bondage" (Galatians 2:4).

This dispute in Antioch eventually led to the convening of the Jerusalem Council, where Peter declared, "Now therefore why tempt ye God, to put a yoke upon the neck of the disciples [i.e., the Gentiles], which neither our fathers nor we were able to bear? But we believe that through the grace of the Lord Jesus Christ we shall be saved, even as they" (Acts 15:10–11; see Acts 15:19–20; 28–29). Paul tells the Galatian Saints that it was also at this conference that the decision was made to have two missions: Paul and Barnabas would be responsible for the Gentile mission, while Peter would have stewardship for the Jewish mission (see Galatians 2:7–10). Yet even the decree of the Jerusalem Council did not put to rest the tensions between the two Christian groups.[7]

We find one of the most significant examples of this tension in

Paul's epistle to the Galatians. When Paul originally arrived in Galatia he taught the people the gospel of Jesus Christ (see Galatians 1:6–11). The letter suggests that he taught the gospel in a context of the fulfillment of the law of Moses.[8] It is difficult to pinpoint exactly who Paul's early converts were in Galatia;[9] most likely they were God-fearing Gentiles; that is, Gentiles who were attracted to the moral teachings of the law of Moses, attended the synagogue, and obeyed their kosher laws without ever fully converting.[10] Acts tells us that this group was an important source of converts for Paul during his early missions (see Acts 13:26; 16:14). Two textual clues suggest that the Galatian Saints were God-fearers. They were Gentiles because they once worshipped pagan gods (see Galatians 4:8–10), and they were not circumcised.[11] If the Galatians were Jews, the debate in chapter 5 over the value of circumcision for them would have been a moot point. But if his audience was Gentiles, why did Paul and his opponents feel the need to argue over the law of Moses and its relationship to the gospel? Surely that discussion would have been more at home with a Jewish audience; that is, unless the Galatian Saints had been God-fearers who were already familiar with, and impressed by, the law and its teachings. The identification of the Galatian Saints as God-fearers helps make sense of two issues. First, it explains why Paul would plead with the Galatians not to be "entangled *again*" (Galatians 5:1; emphasis added) in the law. The word *again* indicates that they had previously been "entangled" in the law. This would not have been the case for most Gentiles. Second, if the Galatians were God-fearers then we can perhaps better understand why the Gentile and Jewish missions intersected in such a volatile way in Galatia even after the pronouncement of the Jerusalem Council.[12] Paul would have identified the Saints as Gentiles and therefore under his stewardship, whereas his opponents would have viewed them as part of the Jewish mission because they had previously committed themselves to the law of Moses. It seems that the best way to reconcile all of this data is if his audience was composed of God-fearing Gentiles.[13]

After Paul had taught the gospel to these Saints and left to continue his missionary journey, another group of Christian missionaries arrived on the scene and began teaching. Paul argues that their teaching is "another gospel" (Galatians 1:6), but then he immediately clarifies this statement by declaring that it is not really "another gospel" because its teachers "pervert the gospel of Christ" (Galatians 1:7). It appears that these teachers were still in Galatia when Paul wrote his letter and that what they were teaching was appealing to the Saints.[14] What we know about this "other gospel" is what we can glean from Paul's epistle because it seems that he is reacting to specific things that the new missionaries were teaching.

We know from the force of Paul's letter that the new missionaries, like the men in Acts 15, were teaching that the gospel must include the law of Moses and circumcision. From their perspective the law was the equivalent of provisions needed for the journey to salvation.[15] One scholar described their teaching in this way: although Christ's Atonement and Resurrection provided the gate for salvation, the law provided the provisions and directions once a person had entered the gate.[16] It also seems, given Paul's response, that they argued that the law is what enabled the Saints to exercise their Christian liberty. The law was not just a system of rules and regulations; it was a system that enabled its followers to be free from sin and tyranny. Historically, there are examples where the people of the covenant sought for political and religious freedom through recommitting themselves to the law. For example, Ezra recommitted his people as they returned from the Babylonian exile so that they would never have to experience bondage again (see Ezra 9–10), Mathathias instituted the Maccabean revolt so that his people would have the freedom that comes from living the law (see 1 Maccabees 1–2), and the people of Qumran fled into the wilderness so that they would also have freedom to live the law as they understood it.[17] So we know that many looked to the law for freedom. Perhaps the new missionaries in Galatia shared similar feelings with groups such as these. They surely argued that liberty can never exist in an absence of law. If there is no law then it is anarchy that prevails, not liberty! It also appears that they, like their counterparts in Rome, interpreted Paul's teachings about the law to actually be "an occasion to the flesh," or a license to sin (Galatians 5:13;

see Romans 3:8; 6:15). Nothing could be further from the intent of Paul's teachings. With this background established we can now turn to Paul's teachings about Christian liberty.

Liberty and Law

It would be inaccurate to think that Paul's view of Christian liberty was independent of law. The force of his teachings in Galatians is specifically directed to those who claim that the law of Moses is *the* means of achieving liberty. Certainly he recognized the important part that the law of Moses had played in its time: it was a "schoolmaster to bring us unto Christ" (Galatians 3:24). Six hundred years before Paul, Nephi taught the same principle: "Behold, my soul delighteth in proving unto my people the truth of the coming of Christ; for, for this end hath the law of Moses been given; and all things which have been given of God from the beginning of the world, unto man, are the typifying of him" (2 Nephi 11:4). But even in its pure form, Abinadi taught that it was only "a law of performances and of ordinances, a law which they were to observe strictly from day to day, to keep them in remembrance of God and their duty towards him" (Mosiah 13:30). By the Christian period the Pharisees had greatly expanded those laws to include a complex system of oral traditions, which acted as "fences around the law" to protect their sanctity (*Aboth* 1.1). Although Peter judged it impossible to live under such a yoke (see Acts 15:10), Paul told the Galatian Saints that he had been "more exceedingly zealous" than his peers in living "the traditions of my fathers" (Galatians 1:14). He knew what it took to try and live that law.

So it seems that the question for some in Galatia was if they weren't to have the law of Moses to guide them in making right choices, how were they to achieve liberty? Paul understood that the whole idea of the law was to bring covenant Israel to a point where they were spiritually prepared to accept the higher law, a law that they had already once rejected at Mount Sinai. That's why he described the law as a schoolmaster.

Jeremiah had plainly taught that the time would come when the Lord would "make a new covenant with the house of Israel, and with the house of Judah," but this new covenant would be written "in their inward parts," and He would "write it in their hearts" (Jeremiah 31:31–33; see 2 Corinthians 3:1–3). Paul recognized this new covenant as the new law—the "law of Christ" (Galatians 6:2; 1 Corinthians 9:21). This was not a law of performances and ordinances or, as one scholar noted, "a detailed code which has a ready-made answer for every circumstance."[18] Instead the law of Christ, a higher law, centers on eternal principles (Matthew 5:21–48).

As Richard Longenecker said: "Paul would have agreed with E. F. Scott's understanding of the ethical teaching of Jesus at this point: 'Instead of framing laws [Christ] stated principles, and made them so few and broad and simple that no one could overlook them. . . . It is true that he enounced a large number of precepts which appear to bear directly on given questions of conduct. . . . But when we look more closely into the precepts we find that they are not so much rules as illustrations. In every instance they involve a principle on which all the stress is laid; but it is applied to a concrete example, so that we may not only grasp it as a principle but judge for ourselves how it works.'"[19]

Latter-day Saints are familiar with this concept from the Prophet Joseph. When asked how he governed such a vast people, he replied, "It is very easy, for I teach the people correct principles and they govern themselves."[20]

The difficulty with this higher law is that while it provides us with a greater liberty to choose, it also comes at a much higher individual cost because it requires that we have a relationship with, and recognize, the promptings of the Spirit.

LIBERTY AND THE SPIRIT

Paul taught the Galatians that "if ye be led of the Spirit, ye are not under the law" (Galatians 5:18). Later, in his epistle to the Romans, Paul expanded this concept:

"There is therefore now no condemnation to them which are in Christ Jesus, who walk not after the flesh, but after the Spirit.

"For the law of the Spirit of life in Christ Jesus hath made me free from the law of sin and death.

"For what the law could not do, in that it was weak through the flesh, God sending his own Son in the likeness of sinful flesh, and for sin, condemned sin in the flesh:

"That the righteousness of the law might be fulfilled in us, *who walk not after the flesh, but after the Spirit*" (Romans 8:1–4; emphasis added).

Paul makes it clear here that he is not just talking about the law of Moses but any law that is imposed because of our fallen nature. Righteousness is not a function of following law per se, but it is a function of following the Spirit. President Ezra Taft Benson taught that "righteousness is the one indispensable ingredient to liberty."[21] With righteousness comes liberty from the demands or consequences of the law. So Paul taught the Corinthian Saints that "where the Spirit of the Lord is, there is liberty" (2 Corinthians 3:17).

Why is the Spirit so critical to our Christian liberty under the law of Christ? The simple answer is that it is the Spirit that guides us in applying the principles Christ taught in our everyday life. But what does that mean for Saints struggling to use their liberty to "choose the right"? Sometimes it seems easier to make choices when there is a specific law to draw upon. The onus then is upon God, parents, or the government to determine how we should act rather than on us. Whereas in the time of Christ the law of Moses had become a complex system of laws to judge actions by, the law of Christ enabled individuals to use their Christian liberty through the promptings of the Spirit. Remember that the Savior promised His disciples that He would not leave them comfortless because He would send them a Comforter who would "teach [them] all things, and bring all things to [their] remembrance, whatsoever I have said unto you" (John 14:18, 26). In other words, Christ could teach principles because the Spirit would help His followers both remember those principles and teach them how to use them in any given situation.

There are two major advantages to a pedagogy that relies on the guidance of the Spirit. First, it recognizes that what is good for a people to do at one time is not necessarily right for them to do under different circumstances.

The law of Moses exemplified that concept for Paul. For centuries it had been "our schoolmaster to bring us unto Christ" (Galatians 3:24), and Paul had once lived that law zealously. As a result, he had progressed in Judaism further than many of his Jewish contemporaries (Galatians 1:14). But now Christ had come, and all of Paul's righteousness in living the law of Moses was no longer applicable. "But now we are delivered from the law, that being dead wherein we were held; that we should serve in newness of spirit, and not in the oldness of the letter" (Romans 7:6).

One of the clearest applications of this principle in the scriptures is Nephi's experience with Laban when he found him "fallen to the earth . . . drunken with wine" (1 Nephi 4:7). All of Nephi's life he had been taught the commandment, "Thou shalt not kill" (Exodus 20:13), but now the Spirit was telling him to do the exact opposite. No wonder he hesitated. But the law could not help Nephi make the right choice in this instance; only the Spirit could do that.

Second, relying on the Spirit enables people at different levels of spiritual progression to journey along the path to salvation. This leads Paul to tell the Galatians that all people, regardless of their background, are children of God. "For as many of you as have been baptized into Christ have put on Christ. There is neither Jew nor Greek, there is neither bond nor free, there is neither male nor female: for ye are all one in Christ Jesus" (Galatians 3:27–28). Paul considered himself to be one of the chiefest of sinners (1 Timothy 1:15) and "the least of the apostles that am not meet to be called an apostle because [he] persecuted the church of God" (1 Corinthians 15:9). Even so, he "press[ed] toward the mark for the prize of the high calling of God in Christ Jesus" (Philippians 3:14). How is it possible to hope for exaltation when a person is just at the beginning of a personal spiritual journey? The Spirit guides them. For new members, keeping the Sabbath day holy may mean refraining from Sunday shopping and attending Church. But as new members progress spiritually they come to realize that keeping the Sabbath holy also means so much more. Recently Elder Oaks gave the following instruction to gospel teachers: "Teachers who are

commanded to teach 'the principles of [the] gospel' and 'the doctrine of the kingdom' (D&C 88:77) should generally forgo teaching
specific rules or applications." He continues, "Once a teacher has
taught the doctrine and the associated principles from the scriptures
and the living prophets, . . . specific applications or rules are generally the responsibility of individuals and families."[22] One of the benefits of such lessons is that members of the class can be uplifted and
motivated regardless of where they are spiritually. Another benefit is
that members, after being reminded of the principle, can then use
their liberty to exercise what President Hinckley defined as their
divine obligation: to "choose the right."

Note also that in Galatians 5:25 Paul makes a distinction
between having access to the Spirit and walking in it. It is not
enough to be confirmed a member of the Church and commanded
to receive the Spirit. The law of Christ can only help us use our
Christian liberty when we have paid the price to recognize the
Spirit's promptings in our lives. Thus President Joseph F. Smith
taught, "The only safe way for us to do, as individuals is to live so
humbly, so righteously and so faithfully before God that we may
possess his Spirit to that extent that we shall be able to judge righteously, and discern between truth and error, between right and
wrong."[23] Likewise, President Woodruff taught that "there is nothing
that we ought to labor more to obtain while in the flesh than the
Spirit of God, the Holy Ghost, the Comforter, which we are entitled
to receive by reason of our having obeyed the requirements of the
Gospel. When you get acquainted with the Spirit, follow its dictates,
no matter where it may lead you; and when you do that, it will
become a principle of revelation in you." Then he bore his testimony and implored the Saints: "I know by experience the value of
it. You . . . should live in such a manner as to be entitled to the operations of the Holy Ghost within you, and, as I have said, it will
become a guide as well as a revelator to you, and never leave or fail
you."[24] Paul says that the fruit of living by the Spirit is "love, joy,
peace, longsuffering, gentleness, goodness, faith, meekness, [and]
temperance" (Galatians 5:22–23). Note that he doesn't say that
these are "the works of the Spirit" that people do when they follow

the Spirit; rather, they are the rewards that come to those who follow the Spirit.[25]

LIBERTY AND LOVE

The third concept that Paul taught the Galatians was that love is an essential element in helping them to use their liberty to make right choices. "For, brethren, ye have been called unto liberty; only use not liberty for an occasion to the flesh, but by love serve one another. For all the law is fulfilled in one word, even in this; Thou shalt love thy neighbour as thyself" (Galatians 5:13–14). Here is the irony. This commandment was a part of the law of Moses that Paul's opponents were advocating (see Leviticus 19:18). But whereas those missionaries had emphasized the law through circumcision, Paul followed Christ's lead when he taught that this was the second great commandment after loving God with all of our heart, soul and mind (see Matthew 22:37–40). I love what President Hinckley had to say on the importance of love: "Love is like the Polar Star. In a changing world, it is a constant. It is of the very essence of the gospel. It is the security of the home. It is the safeguard of community life. It is a beacon of hope in a world of distress."[26] When faced with a decision about how to use our liberty, one of the most important questions we can ask ourselves is "How will my decision affect the lives of others?" If we choose to serve others then we will invariably choose to serve God. Thus King Benjamin taught that "when ye are in the service of your fellow beings ye are only in the service of your God" (Mosiah 2:17).

Perhaps for Paul the greatest evidence of our love for a neighbor was the decision to "restrict [our] personal liberty in matters which are of secondary importance for the sake of the Gospel."[27] This is a concept that Paul introduces in Galatians but develops most fully in 1 Corinthians. There he responds to a dispute over whether Christians should eat meat that was sacrificed at pagan temples. The ruling at the Jerusalem Council was that they should not (see Acts 15:19–20, 28–29). Even so, some of the Saints in Corinth argued that it didn't matter if they ate it because the idols weren't real gods. In one sense Paul agreed with them: there is only one true God. But what really concerned Paul was the fact that in claiming their "right" to eat that meat these Saints had not considered the effect their actions might have on others. So he counsels them to "take heed lest by any means this liberty of yours become a stumblingblock to them that are weak.

"For if any man see thee which hast knowledge sit at meat in the idol's temple, shall not the conscience of him which is weak be emboldened to eat those things which are offered to idols;

"And through thy knowledge shall the weak brother perish, for whom Christ died?

"But when ye sin so against the brethren, and wound their weak conscience, ye sin against Christ.

"Wherefore, if meat make my brother to offend, I will eat no flesh while the world standeth, lest I make my brother to offend" (1 Corinthians 8:9–13).

The issue here for Paul is not that he should become a vegetarian. The issue is that he would rather put aside his liberty to eat meat than risk a new member's salvation. Thus he implores the Corinthian Saints, and all Saints that when we are faced with these types of situations, to "let no man seek his own, but every man another's wealth" (1 Corinthians 10:24). Then he concludes with the following exhortation:

"Conscience, I say, not thine own, but of the other: for why is my liberty judged of another man's conscience?

"For if I by grace be a partaker, why am I evil spoken of for that for which I give thanks?

"Whether therefore ye eat, or drink, or whatsoever ye do, do all to the glory of God.

"Give none offence, neither to the Jews, nor to the Gentiles, nor to the church of God:

"Even as I please all men in all things, not seeking mine own profit, but the profit of many, that they may be saved" (1 Corinthians 10:29–33).

Although Paul's message in 1 Corinthians 8 and 10 deals with the specific issue of eating meat, the real principle that Paul stresses is that we sometimes need to restrict our personal liberty so that another's salvation will not be put in jeopardy. In this way we see, as he told the Galatians, that the liberty Christ provided for us is governed by the commandment to "love our neighbour as ourselves" (see Matthew 22:39).

LIBERTY AND FOLLOWING THE BRETHREN

Our final element in understanding Paul's teachings in these chapters is often overlooked. Granted, he only makes a passing reference to this element in one verse in Galatians, but I believe this verse is significant. The issue is whether a Saint can exercise liberty and still be in subjection to someone who has progressed further spiritually than they have. Is the use of terms such as liberty and subjection in the same sentence an oxymoron? Some have concluded from Paul's teachings on Christian liberty and Christ's principle-centered teaching that "not even an Apostle can tell you what you ought to do."[28] Some modern members have also struggled with this dilemma.[29] However, I believe that this conclusion misrepresents Paul. As an Apostle himself, Paul taught with authority. As one scholar has noted, "He also insisted that he could legitimately reprove, discipline, instruct, and even command."[30] Although he does not use the term Apostle, in Galatians 6:1 Paul teaches that those who are "spiritual," or who are further along in their spiritual progression, should "restore . . . in the spirit of meekness" a "man . . . overtaken in a fault." In Romans, Paul is even more explicit:

"Let every person be subject to the governing authorities.

"For there is no authority except from God, and those that exist have been instituted by God.

"Therefore he who resists the authorities resists what God has appointed, and those who resist will incur judgment.

"For rulers are not a terror to good conduct, but to bad. Would you have no fear of him who is in authority? Then do what is good, and you will receive his approval,

"For he is God's servant for your good" (Revised Standard Version, Romans 13:1–4).

The principle Paul is trying to teach is that Christian liberty is advanced discipleship. The reality is that many of us have not yet progressed spiritually enough where we are sufficiently schooled or confident in discerning the promptings of the Spirit. In such cases, we can turn to those who are further along in their spiritual progression. One of Paul's frequent pleas with the Saints is that they imitate him because he is imitating Christ (see 1 Corinthians 11:1; 2 Thessalonians 3:7).

Is there a lesson here for Latter-day Saints? I think so. President Boyd K. Packer taught that there is no contradiction between liberty and obedience:

"We are all free to choose. . . .

"Choice among my freedoms is my freedom to be obedient. I obey because I want to; I choose to.

"Some people are always suspicious that one is only obedient because he is compelled to be. They indict themselves with the very thought that one is only obedient because he is compelled to be. They feel that one would only obey through compulsion. They speak for themselves. I am free to be obedient, and I decided that— all by myself. I pondered on it; I reasoned it; I even experimented a little. . . .

"Obedience to God [or his servants; D&C 1:38] can be the very highest expression of independence."[31]

FREEDOM IN CHRIST

Paul's teachings on Christian liberty in Galatians came about because some members of the Church sought to undermine that liberty by holding on to the law of Moses. He implored them to "stand fast therefore in the liberty wherewith Christ hath made us free" (Galatians 5:1). Today modern Saints don't have to worry, per se, about the law of Moses, but perhaps we sometimes either consciously or unwittingly bind ourselves to the things of the world. As we do so, we place ourselves in a comparable position to Paul's opponents in Galatia. President Brigham Young taught that "this is the deciding point, the dividing line. They who love and serve God with all their hearts rejoice evermore, pray without ceasing, and in everything give thanks; but they who try to serve God and still cling to the spirit of the world, have got on two yokes—the yoke of Jesus and the yoke of the devil, and they will have plenty to do. They will have a warfare inside and outside, and the labor will be very galling, for they are directly in opposition one to the other. Cast off the yoke of the enemy, and put on the yoke of Christ, and you will say that his yoke is easy and his burden is light. This I know by experience."[32] Christian liberty does not come from an absence of law; it comes from willingly yoking ourselves to Christ. The difficulty comes when we refuse to give up our other yokes, as did Paul's opponents in Galatia. The yoke that they clung to was the law of Moses.

In our day, our yoke, our law of Moses, is anything that prevents or impedes our total commitment to Christ and His gospel. How do we use the liberty that Christ has afforded us? Do we use it as an opportunity to follow the ways of the world or, as Paul said, "an occasion to the flesh" (Galatians 5:13), or do we use it to choose the right and further the work of God in our own lives and in the lives of those around us? If Paul were with us today he would also implore us to "stand fast . . . in the liberty wherewith Christ hath made us free, and be not entangled again with the yoke of bondage" (Galatians 5:1).

NOTES

1. David O. McKay, in Conference Report, October 1965, 8.

2. Dallin H. Oaks, "Weightier Matters," *Ensign,* January 2001, 13–14.

3. Gordon B. Hinckley, "Caesar, Circus, or Christ?" in *BYU Speeches of the Year* (26 October 1965), 8.

4. For a detailed discussion of Paul's teachings on liberty see Richard N. Longenecker, *Paul: Apostle of Liberty* (New York: Harper & Row, 1964).

5. Paul's epistle to the Galatians is clearly a reaction to what his opponents were teaching in Galatia in his absence. It seems to me, therefore, that the best way to understand Paul's pointed remarks on the nature of Christian liberty in this epistle is to understand them as a reaction to what his opponents were teaching.

6. This is the only Pauline epistle where after his introduction he doesn't commend his readers for something. Instead, he immediately chastises them: "I marvel that ye are so soon removed from him that called you into the grace of Christ unto another gospel: which is not another; but there be some that trouble you, and would pervert the gospel of Christ" (Galatians 1:6–7).

7. It should be remembered that the decision of the Jerusalem Council affected Gentile converts only. They made no decision about whether Jews could or should continue living the law of Moses. By the first century A.D. the law had become as much a part of cultural identity as it was a reflection of spiritual commitment. In Acts 21:20, James tells Paul: "Thou seest, brother, how many thousands of Jews there are which believe; and they are all zealous of the law." The Ebionites were a group of Christians who maintained their commitment to the law of Moses. We know that at the end of the first century A.D. there were still such groups because Ignatius denounces them in his letter to the Magnesians (8:1; 10:3).

8. Paul does not specifically mention that he taught the fulfillment of the law of Moses through Christ prior to his Galatian epistle, but the fact that the teachers from Judaea put such a heavy emphasis on it in their teachings suggests that it was in reaction to what Paul had originally taught (see the Savior's teachings in 3 Nephi 15:1–10; Matthew 5:17–48; and Stephen's teachings and the response they elicit in Acts 6:9–15).

9. Scholars have debated this point at great length. There are two main theories for the location of the Galatian church: the North Galatian hypothesis and the South Galatian hypothesis. The South Galatian hypothesis argues that the Churches are located in the southern part of the Roman province. If this was the case then these churches may have been the ones established by Paul during his first missionary journey (see Acts 13–14). We know from that first mission that there were synagogues in many of the cities that he visited and that many of his converts were Gentiles. The North Galatian hypothesis is that the churches were located among the ethnic Galatians in the north around Ankyra and Pessinus. In this area the churches probably consisted of people of Celtic descent, with the possibility of a mixture of "some Greek and a few oriental immigrants" (J. Louis Martyn, *Galatians*, volume 34A of the Anchor Bible [New York: Doubleday, 1997], 15–16), although there was a Jewish element in this area as well (Hans Dieter Betz, *Galatians: A Commentary on Paul's Letter to the Churches in Galatia* [Philadelphia: Fortress Press, 1979], 4–5).

10. Emil Schürer, *The History of the Jewish People in the Age of Jesus Christ* (175 B.C.–A.D. 135), rev. and ed. Geza Vermes, Fergus Millar, and Martin Goodman (Edinburgh: T&T Clark, Ltd., 1986), 3:161–71.

11. The fact that in Galatians chapter 5 Paul insists that circumcision was not an important issue strongly suggests that it was an important issue for his opponents. Richard Lloyd Anderson characterizes "the chief problem of Galatians" as "whether Gentile converts should be circumcised" (*Understanding Paul* [Salt Lake City: Deseret Book, 1983], 151).

12. "Paul can tolerate, and even recognize as God's doing, a *parallel,* Law-observant mission to the Jews, so long as that mission is and remains truly parallel,

that is to say, so long as it does not infect the Gentile mission with the demand for Law-observance. Nothing would have been further from Paul's mind than to indicate that there was a Law-observant mission to Gentiles, considered by at least some members of the church to be authorized by God" (J. Louis Martyn, "A Law-Observant Mission to Gentiles: The Background of Galatians," *Michigan Quarterly Review* 22, no. 1 [1983]: 223).

13. One argument against this reading is if one accepts the North Galatian hypothesis then there were no Jews in that area for the Gentiles to come into contact with. However, archaeological discoveries have uncovered Jewish inscriptions in the north (Betz, *Galatians*, 4–5).

14. Ibid., 8–9.

15. Perhaps these missionaries felt that Paul was acting like some members of the Church in the Americas just after the Savior was born. "And there were no contentions, save it were a few that began to preach, endeavoring to prove by the scriptures that it was no more expedient to observe the law of Moses. Now in this thing they did err, having not understood the scriptures" (3 Nephi 1:24).

16. Martyn, "A Law-Observant Mission to Gentiles," 235.

17. These actions were not just the result of oppressive acts that denied Jews the opportunity to practice their religion, but also reflect the idea that freedom, true freedom is found in the living the law of Moses (Longnecker, *Paul: Apostle of Liberty*, 156–58).

18. Ibid., 191.

19. Ibid., 192.

20. John Taylor, in *Journal of Discourses* (London: Latter-day Saints' Book Depot, 1854–86), 10:57–58.

21. Ezra Taft Benson, *The Teachings of Ezra Taft Benson* (Salt Lake City: Bookcraft, 1988), 346.

22. Dallin H. Oaks, "Gospel Teaching," *Ensign*, November 1999, 79.

23. Joseph F. Smith, *Gospel Doctrine* (Salt Lake City: Deseret Book, 1986), 45.

24. Wilford Woodruff, *Collected Discourses Delivered by President Wilford Woodruff, His Two Counselors, the Twelve Apostles, and Others*, comp. and ed. Brian H. Stuy (Sandy, Utah: B. H. S. Publishing, 1991), 4:327.

25. Betz, *Galatians*, 286.

26. Gordon B. Hinckley, "Let Love Be the Lodestar of Your Life," *Ensign*, May 1989, 66.

27. Longenecker, *Paul: Apostle of Liberty*, 206.

28. Emil Brunner, *Divine Imperative*, trans. Olive Wyon (Philadelphia: Westminster Press, 1947), 118.

29. For one example see, L. Jackson Newell, "Scapegoats and Scarecrows in Our Town: When the Interests of Church and Community Collide," *Sunstone,* December 1993, 22–28.

30. Longenecker, *Paul: Apostle of Liberty,* 197–98.

31. Boyd K. Packer, "Obedience," in *BYU Speeches of the Year* (Provo, Utah: Brigham Young University Press, 1971), 2–3.

32. Brigham Young, in *Journal of Discourses,* 16:123.

6

PAUL'S INSPIRED
TEACHINGS ON MARRIAGE

Kent R. Brooks

*M*ARRIAGE, WHICH IS ESSENTIAL TO GOD'S plan of happiness, was instituted among our first parents, Adam and Eve, even before the Fall.[1] In every dispensation since, prophets bearing the holy priesthood have taught God's eternal plan and have been witnesses to the central nature of marriage and the family in that plan. One of those prophets was Paul. During his ministry in the meridian of times, Paul encountered a Church membership that was changing with the influx of Gentile converts. These converts, many of whom were Greek, had been reared in a morally corrupt society and were often undisciplined and self-conceited. At times, their background created disorder within their branches and prompted numerous questions as they struggled to understand what true discipleship entailed. Questions arose regarding marriage. Paul responded with sensitivity yet directness as he clarified the relevant doctrines. This paper will address some of his inspired teachings on marriage.

Kent R. Brooks is an associate professor of Church history and doctrine at Brigham Young University.

Was the Apostle Paul Ever Married?

Students of the New Testament frequently raise the question as to whether or not Paul was ever married. From the viewpoint of modern Latter-day Saints who understand that marriage and family are central to God's plan of happiness, it seems logical to conclude that one who was called as a special witness of Christ (see Romans 1:1; 1 Corinthians 1:1; 9:1; Galatians 1:1) would have lived in accordance with all of the gospel law and hence would have been married at some point. But from the New Testament record itself is there evidence that would support that conclusion? Yes. Let me suggest four compelling evidences.

First, Paul came from a Judaic background (see Acts 21:39; Romans 11:1) wherein marriage was viewed, traditionally, as a religious duty of utmost importance. According to an early delineation of the 613 precepts contained in the law of Moses, marriage was listed as the first. Customarily, Jewish men and women married between the ages of sixteen and eighteen, although some were as young as fourteen. It is likely that Paul would have wanted to comply with the traditional religious expectation of marriage.[2]

Second, Paul was a Pharisee (see Acts 23:6; Philippians 3:5), one of the strictest bodies of Judaism (see Acts 26:5), and prided himself in being a devout adherent to all of Jewish law. Tutored "at the feet of Gamaliel, and taught according to the perfect manner of the law of the fathers," Paul became, by his own admission, "zealous toward God" (Acts 22:3). In fact, Paul described himself as even "more exceedingly zealous" in fulfilling the requirements of the law than were his peers (Galatians 1:14). It seems plausible that Paul's zealous determination to strictly obey the totality of the law would have extended to marriage. If Paul "lived unmarried as a Jerusalem Pharisee," noted Frederic Farrar, "his case was entirely exceptional."[3]

Third, evidence suggests that Paul was either a member or an official representative of the Sanhedrin, the Jewish senate. As either member or representative of the Sanhedrin, Paul would have been obligated to live in harmony with Jewish customs. The Sanhedrin, comprising chief priests, scribes, and elders, served as the supreme legislative council and court of justice in Judea. Members of the Sanhedrin were required to be married and to be fathers, both considered requirements to the development of wisdom and trustworthiness.[4] As a representative of the Sanhedrin, Paul said, "Many of the saints did I shut up in prison, having received authority from the chief priests; and when they were put to death, I gave my voice against them" (Acts 26:10). Paul's presence as a witness to the stoning of Stephen is further evidence of his association with the Sanhedrin (see Acts 7:58).

Fourth, Paul's teachings on marriage are, themselves, indicative of his conviction to the importance of marriage in God's eternal plan. "Marriage is honourable in all," (Hebrews 13:4) Paul wrote, and "neither is the man without the woman, neither the woman without the man, in the Lord" (1 Corinthians 11:11). Priesthood leaders, Paul counseled, such as bishops, were to be married. In his instructions to Timothy, Paul wrote: "A bishop then must be blameless, the husband of one wife, vigilant, sober, of good behaviour, given to hospitality, apt to teach" (1 Timothy 3:2). Similar counsel was given to Titus (see Titus 1:6). Prophesying of the apostasy of the last days, Paul warned, "In the latter times some shall depart from the faith, . . . forbidding to marry" (1 Timothy 4:1, 3). It would be inconsistent for Paul to characterize those who would forbid or counsel against marriage as having departed from the faith if he were himself antimarriage. So these teachings, as well as others Paul gave during his apostolic ministry, are testaments to the favorable feelings he had toward marriage.

Paul was qualified to speak on marriage. Most likely a married man himself, Paul would have been able to speak from personal experience as he taught Church members about marriage. Since experience and credibility are so closely intertwined in the minds of most people, the Saints of that day would have been more likely to listen to Paul's counsel if they believed he had learned, by his own experience, what a marital relationship was really like. But even more important, Paul was an Apostle, a special witness of Christ. Living and knowing well the doctrine of the Church, he would have been able to teach that doctrine in the authority of his divine calling. Subject to the overall power and authority of Peter, the President of the Church at that time, Paul possessed the right, the power, and the authority to declare the mind and will of God to his people. Paul knew that salvation was not to be found in the tenets of the law, but rather in Christ. His example of discipleship was described by his declaration:

"I have suffered the loss of all things and do count them but dung, that I may win Christ,

"And be found in him, not having mine own righteousness, which is of the law, but that which is through the faith of Christ, the righteousness which is of God by faith" (Philippians 3:8–9).

Convert, disciple, Apostle—Paul was a great advocate and defender of the faith. His teachings, including those on marriage, reflect his discernment of the unique needs and concerns of a disparate, changing Church membership and his inspiration regarding the doctrines that should be taught. Paul's most pivotal teachings on the subject of marriage are found in 1 Corinthians 7, 1 Corinthians 11, and Ephesians 5.

FIRST CORINTHIANS 7

Chastity before Marriage. First Corinthians 7, probably written sometime in the spring of A.D. 57, was a letter Paul wrote in response to questions posed in an earlier correspondence from Corinthian converts. That is made clear in the Joseph Smith Translation (JST) of the first two verses which read: "Now concerning the things whereof ye wrote unto me, *saying,* It is good for a man not to touch a woman.

"Nevertheless, *I say,* to avoid fornication, let every man have his own wife, and let every woman have her own husband" (all Joseph Smith Translation changes in this article are noted in italics).

Unfortunately, we do not have the text of the letter sent from Corinth to Paul and are therefore left to surmise regarding the questions to which Paul was responding. However, President Howard W. Hunter suggested that "the communications revealed that there were factions forming in the branch with different views regarding moral conduct and doctrine. . . . Some were defending loose sexual standards that were rampant in the notorious city."[5] Addressing those inappropriate justifications, Paul teaches the Corinthian Saints in verse 2 that sexual relations between unmarried partners constitute fornication. Sexual desires are to be fulfilled only within the bonds of a legal marriage.

Total Fidelity after Marriage. Having taught the importance of chastity before marriage, Paul counsels members regarding total fidelity after marriage. Recognizing that temptations occur after marriage as well as before, Paul teaches three principles that will help the saints avoid those temptations.

First, in verse 3, Paul suggests that *benevolence* should be the underlying principle in the intimate relationship between husband and wife. "Let the husband," he says, "render unto the wife due benevolence: and likewise also the wife unto the husband." Benevolence is a "disposition to do good" or to "an act of kindness."[6] President David O. McKay said: "Benevolence in its fullest sense is the sum of moral excellence, and comprehends every other virtue. It is the motive that prompts us to do good to others and leads us to live our life for Christ's sake. All acts of kindness . . . of forgiveness, of charity, of love, spring from this divine attribute."[7]

When a marital relationship is characterized by "moral excellence," kindness, forgiveness, charity, and love, then intimacy— including sexual intimacy—seems to naturally follow. In my work as a marriage and family counselor, I have observed that rejection of or withdrawal from intimate relations in marriage generally occurs when those qualities are absent and selfishness sets in. Benevolence and selfishness are opposing forces. Benevolence enlivens a marriage and invites the Spirit. Selfishness weakens a marriage and repels the Spirit.

The second principle Paul teaches to avoid temptation after marriage is *trust*. Trust is an expression of confidence and hope in another. In verse 4, Paul uses an analogy to describe the trust that should exist between a husband and wife. He says, "The wife hath not power of her own body, but the husband: and likewise also the husband hath not power of his own body, but the wife." In other words, marriage and the intimate relationship within it are joint stewardships in which the two separate entities of husband and wife unite in becoming one complementary whole. The couple becomes, as it were, one synchronized body—physically, emotionally, and spiritually. "So ought men to love their wives as their own bodies," Paul wrote to the Ephesians, and "he that loveth his wife loveth himself" (Ephesians 5:28). The husband is as anxious and desirous (if not more so!) for the happiness and well-being of his wife as he is for his own. To make her happy will make him happy. They are one body. The wife does not fear that her "desire . . . be to [her] husband" (Moses 4:22) because she trusts him and feels as safe in his care as she would in her own. Both can be perfectly trusting of the other if both have proven to be perfectly trustworthy, which is possible because the seeds of benevolence have been sown between them. "To be trusted," President David O. McKay taught, "is a greater compliment than to be loved."[8]

Third, to avoid temptation after marriage, there must be *commitment.* In verse 5 of the JST, Paul counsels couples, *"Depart ye not one from the other,* except it be with consent for a time, that ye may give yourselves to fasting and prayer; and come together again, that Satan tempt you not for your incontinency" (emphasis added). President Spencer W. Kimball said: "There are many aspects to love in marriage, and sex is an important one. Just as married partners are not for others, they *are* for each other."[9] Paul's counsel to married couples is that they not depart nor abstain from sexual intimacy except by mutual consent or mutual agreement, and then only for brief periods of time lest they be tempted for their *incontinency.*

"Incontinency," Elder Bruce R. McConkie noted, "is lack of restraint and failure to bridle one's passions (particularly where sex desires are concerned)."[10] What was Paul suggesting, in this context, by the word *incontinency?* Was Paul counseling married couples to restrain or bridle their passions even for each other? Can temptations come to a married couple if they fail to do so? President Boyd K. Packer said: "A married couple may be tempted to introduce things into their relationship which are unworthy. . . . If you do, the tempter will drive a wedge between you. If something unworthy has become part of your relationship, be wise and don't ever do it again!"[11] President Kimball concluded: "Sexual relations in marriage are not unrestrained. Even marriage does not make proper certain extremes in sexual indulgence. . . . If it is unnatural, you just don't do it. That is all. . . . There are some people who have said that behind the bedroom doors anything goes. That is not true and the Lord would not condone it."[12]

But while prophets have counseled married couples to keep their sexual passions and behaviors within appropriate boundaries, the context of 1 Corinthians 7 suggests that Paul is referring to something else. More likely Paul's concern here has to do with a husband or wife who rejects or withholds sexual intimacy from the spouse for long periods of time in an attempt to hurt, manipulate, control, or seek revenge. Abstinence in marriage can cause unnecessary temptations and tensions. Temptations often occur during times of abstinence, particularly vengefully imposed abstinence. The mind of the spouse begins to wander and the heart begins to stray, thereby allowing Satan to gain greater power to tempt and destroy the marriage. Satan can tempt a couple to adopt a recycling pattern of self-justification and other-blaming. Blind to personal sin and thus rejecting any personal responsibility for the dysfunctional pattern, each spouse, in a conscience-salving manner, blames the other and then justifies his or her own continued acts of unrighteousness, which ironically are, in true self-justifying fashion, often perceived to be righteous.

So how do couples break such a cycle? First, they must look *inward.* They must cease their blaming, recognize their own sins, and take personal responsibility for their own thoughts, feelings, and actions. Each could ask "How am *I* contributing to the problem," and "What can *I* to do help my partner?" Second, they must look *forward.* They must be proactive in implementing preventive measures that will keep the cycle from recurring. I would suggest that Paul's counsel to develop benevolence, trust, and commitment is a good place to start. Third, and most important, the couple must look *heavenward.* They must recognize that they cannot break the cycle on their own. They each must come unto Christ through personal repentance and be determined to let the Savior be the center of their lives. Elder Richard G. Scott taught: "Now, the most important principle I can share: Anchor your life in Jesus Christ, your Redeemer. Make your Eternal Father and His Beloved Son the most important priority in your life—more important than life itself, more important than a beloved companion or children or anyone on earth. Make their will your central desire. Then all that you need for happiness will come to you."[13]

"I Would That All Men Were Even as I Myself." Paul begins verse 7 with this statement: "For I would that *all* men were even as myself." What exactly is Paul yearning for here? Some New Testament scholars have used verse 7 as evidence that Paul was never married and thus was advocating a life of celibacy. But, as previously enumerated, there is ample evidence to suggest that Paul was, or at least had been, married and was wholeheartedly in favor of the institution. Other New Testament scholars have suggested that at the time this counsel was given Paul was either widowed or divorced. If so, are we to conclude that Paul wished that all men might experience the trauma of divorce or the loneliness of widowhood or that being divorced or widowed was somehow preferable to being married? In verses 10–11, Paul clearly counseled against divorce. He wrote: "And unto the married I command, yet not I, but the Lord, Let not the wife depart from her husband: But . . . be reconciled to her husband: and let not the husband put away his wife." In reference to young widows, Paul wrote: "I will therefore that the younger women marry, bear children, guide the house, give none occasion to the adversary to speak reproachfully" (1 Timothy 5:14). Thus, it hardly seems likely that Paul's intent in verse 7 was to encourage divorce or extol widowhood.

What, then, did Paul mean by the statement, "I would that *all* men were even as I myself"? Elder Bruce R. McConkie interpreted Paul's statement to mean, "I would that *all* men understood the law of marriage, that *all* had self-mastery over their appetites, and that *all* obeyed the laws of God in these respects."[14] That interpretation would seem to be confirmed by the rest of verse 7: "But every man hath his proper [i.e., his own] gift of God, one after this manner, and another after that." In addition to the spiritual gifts Paul discerned among the Corinthian Saints, he desired that they seek after the gifts of understanding, of self-mastery, and of unqualified obedience to the will of God. Those so endowed would be able to fully consecrate themselves to the work of bringing souls to Christ and make all other interests, including a possible remarriage, secondary.

In verses 8–9 (JST) Paul expanded upon the desire expressed in verse 7 for *all* men by directing specific counsel to a specific audience—the unmarried and widows. He said: "I say therefore to the unmarried [i.e., those currently unmarried rather than those never married] and widows, It is good for them if they abide even as I.

"But if they cannot *abide,* let them marry: for it is better to marry than *that any should commit sin.*" Paul's wish was that they could so completely divest themselves of personal needs, such as the need to be married and to satisfy sexual desires, that they would be able to fully devote themselves to the will and work of the Lord. He counseled, however, that if they could not do that, it would be better for them to marry than to commit sexual sin. Would Paul's counsel in these verses be suitable for all Church members or even for all unmarried and widowed members? Would not many of them be able to serve the Lord better with a marriage companion than without? Could not the satisfying of sexual desires within marriage add to rather than detract from one's ability to serve the Lord? That Paul's counsel, here, may have been intended to have limited applicability is suggested in verse 6 (JST) where Paul makes it clear that his words represented his personal opinion, directed to a particular group of Saints, rather than official doctrine for the general membership of the Church. Paul wrote, *"And now what* I speak *is* by permission, and not by commandment."

Elder McConkie duly noted that "we do not know to whom the instructions here given apply. In any event, they are an exception to the law, and do not apply, even as a personal opinion, to others than those involved."[15] "It may be that he was referring to some particular persons for whom it would have been unwise to contract marriages. Knowing what he did about the doctrine of celestial marriage and exaltation, it is unthinkable that he would have counseled against marriage, except in some peculiar circumstance. There might be cases today in which individuals should not marry, but it is not the general rule, and the principle of not marrying is not the doctrine of the Church now any more than it was in his day. If we knew the situation about which Paul wrote, and had a full transcript of his actual words, there would be no ambiguity as to his meaning and doctrine."[16]

Interfaith Marriage. Another question that Paul apparently dealt with on a frequent basis had to do with the issue of interfaith marriage and whether or not a member so involved should seek a divorce, particularly in cases where the influence of the unbelieving spouse was perceived by the member to be negative or detrimental to gospel living. Paul taught.

"If any brother hath a wife that believeth not, and she be pleased to dwell with him, let him not put her away.

"And the woman which hath an husband that believeth not, and if he be pleased to dwell with her, let her not leave him.

"For the unbelieving husband is sanctified by the wife, and the unbelieving wife is sanctified by the husband: else were your children unclean; but now are they holy. . . .

"For what knowest thou, O wife, whether thou shalt save thy husband? or how knowest thou, O man, whether thou shalt save thy wife?" (1 Corinthians 7:12–14, 16). Paul's counsel, then, was that if married to an unbeliever, one who would permit the spouse's continued activity in the Church rather than divorce; the member should seek to be an influence for good and to have the best marriage possible while maintaining hope that one day the unbelieving spouse would desire to unite with the Church. In our day, prophets and leaders would agree with Paul's counsel.[17] Additionally, to avoid the problems associated with interfaith marriage prophets today would advise the unmarried, as did Paul, to marry within the faith, lest they be "unequally yoked together with unbelievers" (2 Corinthians 6:14; see also D&C 74:5).[18]

What if the children were being negatively influenced by the unbelieving spouse and were being raised outside the Gospel of Jesus Christ? Would divorce be justified then? In Paul's day "there arose a great contention among the people [Christian and non-Christian Jews]" as those who "believed not the gospel of Jesus Christ" [and believed that children were born unholy] held that children "should be circumcised and become subject to the law of Moses" or else remain unholy (D&C 74:2–3). Many of those children, raised in subjection to the law of Moses, gave heed to the "traditions of their [unbelieving] fathers and believed not the gospel of Christ, wherein they *became* unholy" (D&C 74:4; emphasis added). Through modern revelation, the Prophet Joseph Smith learned that children under the age of eight are unaccountable and hence without sin (D&C 29:47; 68:25). They are not unholy but are "redeemed from the foundation of the world" (D&C 29:46) and are "sanctified through the atonement of Jesus Christ" (D&C 74:7). Only when a child *begins* to become accountable at the age of eight (D&C 29:47) and chooses to violate gospel law can he *become* unholy. If he *becomes* unholy, it is only through the Atonement of Jesus Christ that he can once again *become* holy or sanctified. So, if after children reach the age of accountability, they are being drawn away from the Church by an "unbelieving" parent, would the "believing" parent be justified in seeking a divorce? Possibly. In all cases of divorce, the decision should be made only after careful consultation with priesthood leaders, diligent prayer, and confirmation from the Lord through the Holy Ghost.

Missionaries and Marriage. Verses 25–38 of 1 Corinthians 7 address the subject of missionaries and marriage, with the heart of Paul's counsel found in verses 26–33. The inspired changes made in the JST are invaluable to a correct understanding of these verses. Note two key points:

First, in verses 25–26, Paul addresses those who had never been married and who either had been called or expected to be called to serve as full-time missionaries. He counsels that it would be better for them to remain single until they had completed their missionary service so that they could more easily focus on the work, and hence do more good. Paul writes:

"Now concerning virgins [those who had never married] I have no commandment of the Lord; yet I give my judgment, as one that hath obtained mercy of the Lord to be faithful.

"I suppose therefore that this is good for the present distress [a full-time mission], for a man so to *remain that he may do greater good*" (JST). Prophets today have echoed that same counsel.[19]

But, what if a call came, as it sometimes did, to a married man? Should he divorce his wife? Or, what if the call came to a divorced man contemplating remarriage? Should he marry before leaving on a mission? Paul's counsel on both issues is found in verse 27: "Art thou bound unto a wife? seek not to be loosed. Art thou loosed from a wife? seek not a wife." Then, in verse 28 (JST) Paul added: "But . . . if thou [one who is divorced and contemplating a remarriage] marry, thou hast not sinned. . . ." "Nevertheless," Paul warned, "such shall have trouble in the flesh. *For* I spare you *not.*" In other words, married missionaries are not exempt from the temptations of the flesh and may, in fact, feel them more than those who have never married.

The second counsel Paul gave regarding missions and marriage was that all missionaries, single or married, should be fully devoted to the work. He wrote: "But *I speak unto you who are called unto the ministry. For* this I say, brethren, the time that remaineth is but short, *that ye shall be sent forth unto the ministry.* Even they who have wives, *shall* be as though they had none; *for ye are called and chosen to do the Lord's work.* . . . But *I would, brethren, that ye magnify your calling*" (JST 1 Corinthians 7:29, 32). Paul's rationale is further explained in the rest of verse 32 and in verse 33: "I would have you without carefulness [cares or distractions external to the mission]. *For he who is unmarried,* careth for the things that belong to the Lord, how he may please the Lord; *therefore he prevaileth.*

"But he *who* is married, careth for the things that are of the world, how he may please his wife; *therefore there is a difference, for he is hindered.*" Then, in verse 38 (JST) Paul concludes, "So then he that giveth *himself* in marriage doeth well; but he that giveth *himself* not in marriage doeth better."

FIRST CORINTHIANS 11

In one of his greatest teachings on the subject of marriage, Paul declared the eternal doctrine that "neither is the man without the woman, neither the woman without the man, in the Lord" (1 Corinthians 11:11). God Himself declared: "It is not good that the man should be alone" (Genesis 2:18), "so God created man in his own image, in the image of God created he him; male and female created he them.

"And God blessed *them* [not him or her alone] and God said unto *them*, Be fruitful, and multiply, and replenish the earth, and subdue it: and have dominion" (Genesis 1:27–28, emphasis added).

Our Heavenly Father's plan of happiness allows that God's greatest gift, eternal life (D&C 14:7), and the attendant blessing of eternal increase, are extended only to a man and a woman who have been sealed in the temple, by proper authority, and who then subsequently keep their covenants (see D&C 131:1–4). Only in that manner will God grant the blessings of "thrones, kingdoms, principalities, and powers," and of being able to "pass by the angels, and the gods, which are set there, to their exaltation and glory in all things . . . and a continuation of the seeds forever and ever"(D&C 132:19). One cannot obtain those blessings "separately and singly" (D&C 132:17), nor can they be obtained by two men or two women. In Heavenly Father's plan it takes two complementary halves—a man *and* a woman—to make a man *or* a woman and to form a unified, interlocking whole.

Husband, Wife, Christ, and God. The interdependent relationship between a husband, a wife, Christ, and the Father was described by Paul in 1 Corinthians 11:3: "But I would have you know, that the head of every man is Christ; and the head of the woman is the man; and the head of Christ is God." Certainly many people would categorize this counsel as among the most controversial ever given by Paul. The controversy stems largely from an incomplete, if not erroneous, interpretation of Paul's intent. Yet properly understood, this verse entails one of the most powerful and important concepts ever taught on the subject of marriage. It consists of three elements: First, the head of Christ is God the Father. Second, the head of every man is Christ. And third, the head of the woman is the man. Let's consider each element and how it relates to the other two.

The Head of Christ Is God the Father. Jesus declared:

"For I came down from heaven, not to do mine own will, but the will of him that sent me. . . .

"And this is the will of him that sent me, that every one which seeth the Son, and believeth on him, may have everlasting life; and I will raise him up *in the resurrection of the just* at the last day" (JST John 6:38, 40). The will of the Son was "swallowed up in the will of the Father" (Mosiah 15:7), which was to "bring to pass the immortality and eternal life of man" (Moses 1:39). "For God [the Father] so loved the world, that he gave his only begotten Son, that whosoever believeth in him should not perish, but have everlasting life" (John 3:16). And Jesus "so loved the world that he gave his own life, that as many as would believe might become the sons of God" (D&C 34:3). "That they all may be one," Jesus prayed, "as thou, Father, art in me, and I in thee, that they also may be one in us: that the world may believe that thou hast sent me. . . .

"And . . . know that thou . . . hast loved them, as thou hast loved me" (John 17:21, 23).

The Father's love for His Only Begotten Son was unbounded. The Father manifested His great love for each one of us when He "spared not his own Son, but delivered him up for us all," (Romans 8:32) even His "dear" Son, so that we might be "delivered . . . from the power of darkness" (Colossians 1:13). Through His submissive obedience to the Father and His atoning sacrifice for each of us, both voluntary acts (see John 10:17–18), Jesus demonstrated His perfect love for us and for His Father. In fact, it was His love *for* the Father and His obedience *to* the Father that made His love for *us* possible. That is, the more He loved the Father and did His will, the more He could and would be able to love us. That divine pattern is also true in marriage. The more a man and a woman love the Lord, the greater will be their capacity to love each other. Conversely, as Elder Russell M. Nelson noted: "Without a strong commitment to the Lord, an individual is more prone to have a low level of commitment to a spouse."[20]

The Head of Every Man Is Christ. Paul described the second element in the interdependent relationship of God, husband, and wife, teaching that "the head of every man is Christ." When that is true, the love of a husband becomes a mirror-image reflection of the love of Christ (and the Father) for the wife. And as already noted, the greater the degree that a husband loves the Lord and seeks to do the will of the Lord, the greater is his desire and his capacity to love his wife. Why is that so? The more he yields his heart to the Lord, as Paul counseled (see Romans 6:13), the more sanctified he becomes (see Helaman 3:35). Submissiveness is the key to sanctification. Elder Neal A. Maxwell noted that submissiveness is the catalyst that enables us to develop all other godly attributes,[21] including charity, or pure love, which Paul described as "the greatest" of all godly attributes (see 1 Corinthians 13:13). When the will of the husband becomes swallowed up in the will of the Lord, the husband becomes a "man of Christ" (Helaman 3:29), one who emulates the *works* of Christ and acquires the *nature* of Christ.

Regarding the nature of Christ to love, John the Beloved wrote: "We love him, because he first loved us" (1 John 4:19). That statement could be preceded by this one: "Jesus first loved us because the Father first loved him." Can you see a pattern? Could those two statements be followed by "And wives love their husbands because husbands first loved their wives?" Now, certainly we could reverse that and say that husbands love their wives because their wives first loved them. But it seems that part of the role and responsibility of a "head" is to lead out. The Father led out by first loving the Son. The Son led out by first loving us. Perhaps the pattern that would be most pleasing to the Lord, would be for the husband, the head of the wife, to lead out by first loving her. Surely a submissive husband whose Head is Christ would do that. It would be his nature to emulate the works of Christ. Surely in return, a wife would have little difficulty loving a husband who first loved her.

The Head of the Woman Is the Man. The third and concluding element in Paul's counsel is that the "head of the woman is the man." Paul teaches the concept by way of analogy. He says:

"The husband is the head of the wife, even as Christ is the head of the church: and he is the *saviour* of the body. . . .

"Husbands, *love* your wives, even as Christ also loved the church, and *gave himself* for it; . . .

"So ought men to love their wives as their own bodies. He that *loveth* his wife loveth himself.

"For no man ever yet hated his own flesh; but *nourisheth* and *cherisheth* it, even as the Lord the church.

"For we are members of his body, of his flesh, and of his bones.

"For this cause shall a man leave his father and mother, and shall be joined unto his wife, and they two shall be one flesh" (Ephesians 5:23, 25, 28–31; emphasis added).

The Savior's role, in partnership with the Father, is to bring to pass the immortality and eternal life of man, to be the savior of the body of the Church—for those who repent and come unto Christ (see D&C 10:67). The role of a righteous husband, Paul analogizes, is similar. As head of the wife, the husband is to act in partnership with the Lord in being a savior for the marriage body, comprising husband and wife. As the head of that body, the husband bears the responsibility to act as a savior for his wife in helping to sanctify and perfect her. In that endeavor, he is responsible *for* his wife and *to* the Lord. As husbands and wives become sanctified and purified (through Christ), they experience at-one-ment with each other and with the Lord. And if they "are not one, [they] are not mine," the Lord declared (D&C 38:27). A husband accomplishes that Christlike mission, Paul says, by *loving, nourishing,* and *cherishing* his wife and by *giving himself.*

A husband *loves* his wife, President Kimball taught, when there is "faith and confidence and understanding and partnership. There must be common ideals and standards. There must be great devotion and companionship. Love is cleanliness and progress and sacrifice and selflessness. . . . For [true] love to continue, there must be an increase constantly of confidence and understanding, of frequent and sincere expressions of appreciation and affection. There must be a forgetting of self and a constant concern for the other."[22] The Savior instructed His Twelve Apostles that they were to *minister to* and be the *servant of* those they were called to lead (see Matthew 20:25–28). Loving husbands emulate that pattern with their wives.

To *nourish* is to "promote the growth of."[23] President Benson counseled husbands: "Recognize your wife's intelligence and her ability to counsel with you as a real partner regarding family plans, family activities, and family budgeting.

"Give her the opportunity to grow intellectually, emotionally, and socially as well as spiritually."[24] Paul suggested that another way a husband can promote the growth of his wife is by nourishing her through "words of faith and of good doctrine" (1 Timothy 4:6).

To *cherish* is to "hold dear: to feel or show affection for," and cross-referenced with "appreciate."[25] Husbands should offer frequent and sincere expressions of appreciation to their wives, especially for the repetitive tasks they perform day after day that so often go unnoticed and unrecognized. Gratitude, I believe, precedes love. And love precedes progress.

Paul's concluding counsel is that men, like Christ, should *give themselves.* It is interesting to note that Paul didn't say "give *of* himself." The Savior did not just give *of* himself. He *gave himself.* The marriage covenant, President Kimball taught, "presupposes total allegiance and total fidelity. Each spouse takes the partner with the understanding that he or she gives totally to the spouse all the heart, strength, loyalty, honor, and affection, with all dignity."[26] A husband should *give himself* to making his wife happy.

Summarizing Paul's counsel in Ephesians 5, President Benson said: "That is the model we are to follow in our role of *presiding* in the home. We do not find the Savior *leading* the Church with a harsh or unkind hand. We do not find the Savior treating His Church with disrespect or neglect. We do not find the Savior using force or coercion to accomplish His purposes. Nowhere do we find anything but that which *edifies, uplifts, comforts, and exalts* the Church. Brethren, I say to you with all soberness, He is the model we must follow."[27]

EPHESIANS 5

Throughout Paul's writings, the virtue of submissiveness was encouraged in a number of different contexts, each bearing the connotation of supportiveness, cooperation, or subjection to the organizational leadership of another. For example, Paul counseled children to be submissive to their parents (see Ephesians 6:1; Colossians 3:20). All Saints were instructed to submit to their church leaders (Hebrews 13:17) and to "principalities and powers, [and] to obey magistrates" (Titus 3:1). They were to submit to the gospel (2 Corinthians 9:13) and its ordinances of salvation (Colossians 2:20), and were to subject the physical body to the spirit (1 Corinthians 9:27). So, in Ephesians 5, when Paul admonishes wives to "submit yourselves unto your own husbands, as unto the Lord . . . in every thing" (Ephesians 5:22, 24), Paul's oft-repeated theme continued. Paul's admonition, here, was certainly not meant to discriminate against nor to single out wives as the only ones from whom submissiveness was required.

A husband can only function effectively as the head of the wife when the wife is willing to submit to the husband. The idea that a woman should submit to her husband in everything is a controversial notion in our day. For example, to a woman who feels dominated, controlled, or abused by an unrighteous husband who erroneously interprets this teaching as license to exercise unrighteous dominion, Paul's counsel seems frustrating and demeaning. Many wives in that kind of marriage report a correlation between their own submissiveness to such behavior and the increase in severity and frequency in the acts of domination imposed upon them by their husbands. But Paul was neither condoning a husband's unrighteous dominion nor was he lending support for any kind of abuse. Paul's teachings clearly teach otherwise. For example, to the Saints in Rome Paul explained that any man who would use counsel, such as that given in Ephesians 5, to justify unrighteous or domineering acts would be guilty of misusing the truth and therefore changing it into a lie (see Romans 1:18–25). Paul wrote: "For the wrath of God is revealed from heaven against all ungodliness and unrighteousness of men; *who love not the truth, but remain in unrighteousness,* after that which may be known of God is manifest to them" (JST Romans 1:18–19).

Does the Lord require a wife to follow an unrighteous husband or to submit to his unrighteous demands or behavior? Paul's wording in verse 22 of Ephesians 5 would suggest not. He said, "Wives, submit yourselves unto your own husbands, *as unto the Lord*" (emphasis added). It is interesting that Paul teaches the same idea regarding children and parents. He counseled children: "obey your parents *in the Lord:* for this is right" (Ephesians 6:1; emphasis added). So then is Paul suggesting that, as far as the Lord is concerned, wives (or children) are only required to submit to their husbands (or parents) when those husbands (or parents) are righteous or at least striving to be so? It would seem so.

President Joseph F. Smith said, "According to the order that is established in the kingdom of God, it is the duty of the man to follow Christ, and it is the duty of the woman to follow the man in Christ, not out of him."[28] A humorous anecdote is told from the life of Brigham Young. A distraught woman went to the Prophet, lamenting the treatment and language of her husband. "Brother Brigham," she said, "my husband just told me to go to Hell. [What should I do about it?]" The Prophet thoughtfully responded: "Well, sister, don't go."[29] "I have counseled every woman of this Church," Brigham Young taught, "to let her husband be her file leader; he leads her, and those above him in the Priesthood lead him. But I never counseled a woman to follow her husband to hell. . . . I am sanguine and most emphatic on that subject. . . . If a man is determined to expose the lives of his friends, let that man go to the devil and to destruction alone."[30]

President Harold B. Lee added, "Now, you are bound to the law of your husband only so far as he keeps the law of God and no further. . . .

"[But], polish your husband as best you can while you have him with you here and then hope that the Lord will continue the process to aid you even beyond the veil."[31] President Kimball wisely counseled wives: "No woman has ever been asked by the Church authorities to follow her husband into an evil pit. She is to follow him as he follows and obeys the Savior of the world, but in deciding this, she should always be sure she is fair."[32]

Now, what about Paul's counsel that women should submit themselves to their husbands in "every thing." Are women really required to submit to their husbands in *every* thing? Clearly that would not be true if the husband were unrighteous. But if the husband were faithful, then should the wife be willing to submit to her husband in every thing? To answer that question, consider two similar queries: Should a husband be willing to submit to the will of the Lord in every thing? and Was Jesus willing to submit to the will of the Father in every thing? We could answer "yes" to both questions. The Savior's and our submissiveness was (and still is) complete and unconditional. In saying that, we should remember the Lord's counsel to the Saints living in Jackson County, Missouri, in 1831: "For behold, it is not meet that I should command in all things; for he that is compelled in all things, the same is a slothful and not a wise servant; wherefore he receiveth no reward" (D&C 58:26). Thus we could say that it is the will of the Lord that we use our agency and our intelligence to make many, if not most, of the day-to-day decisions—particularly those that are matters of preference rather than principle. In such matters, the Lord's will would likely be "you choose or you decide." That should be true in marriage. When considering matters of personal preference or choices that merely reflect a wife's individuality or uniqueness of personality, a husband should not hesitate to say to his wife, "you choose or you decide." It is important for every husband to allow his wife opportunities to develop and express her own individual talents and to make her own unique contributions to the home, the Church, the community, and the world.

MARRIAGE ORDAINED OF GOD

"Marriage . . . is ordained of God and . . . the family is central to the Creator's plan for the eternal destiny of His children. . . .

"Marriage between man and woman is essential to His eternal plan. . . .

"Happiness in family life is most likely to be achieved when founded upon the teachings of the Lord Jesus Christ. Successful marriages and families are established and maintained on principles of faith, prayer, repentance, forgiveness, respect, love, compassion, work, and wholesome recreational activities."[33]

The Apostle Paul understood and was a witness of those truths. His teachings on the subject of marriage represent significant contribution to our standard works.

"Surely," said President Gordon B. Hinckley, "no one reading the scriptures, both ancient and modern, can doubt the divine concept of marriage. The sweetest feelings of life, the most generous and satisfying impulses of the human heart, find expression in a marriage that stands pure and unsullied above the evil of the world.

"Such a marriage, I believe, is the desire—the hoped-for, the longed-for, the prayed-for desire—of men and women everywhere."[34]

Paul would have understood and concurred with those sentiments.

NOTES

1. Bruce R. McConkie, *Mormon Doctrine,* 2d ed. (Salt Lake City: Bookcraft, 1966), 242; see also McConkie, *Mortal Messiah* (Salt Lake City: Deseret Book, 1980), 3:294–95; Spencer W. Kimball, "The Blessings and Responsibilities of Womanhood," *Ensign,* March 1976, 71; Ezra Taft Benson, *Teachings of Ezra Taft Benson* (Salt Lake City: Bookcraft, 1988), 534.

2. Frederic W. Farrar, *The Life and Work of St. Paul* (London: Cassell & Company, 1885), 46.

3. Ibid., 46.

4. Richard Lloyd Anderson, *Understanding Paul* (Salt Lake City: Deseret Book, 1983), 24.

5. Howard W. Hunter, "The Reality of the Resurrection," *Improvement Era,* June 1969, 106.

6. *Webster's New Collegiate Dictionary,* 10th ed., s.v. "benevolence."

7. David O. McKay, "Christ, the Light of Humanity," *Improvement Era,* June 1968, 4.

8. David O. McKay, *Gospel Ideals: Selections from the Discourses of David O. McKay* (Salt Lake City: Improvement Era, 1953), 187.

9. Spencer W. Kimball, *The Miracle of Forgiveness* (Salt Lake City: Bookcraft, 1969), 73.

10. McConkie, *Mormon Doctrine*, 556.

11. Boyd K. Packer, *Things of the Soul* (Salt Lake City: Bookcraft, 1996), 113.

12. Spencer W. Kimball, *The Teachings of Spencer W. Kimball,* ed. Edward L. Kimball (Salt Lake City: Bookcraft, 1982), 311–12.

13. Richard G. Scott, "The Power of Correct Principles," *Ensign,* May 1993, 34.

14. Bruce R. McConkie, *Doctrinal New Testament Commentary* (Salt Lake City: Bookcraft, 1971), 2:345.

15. Ibid.

16. McConkie, *Mormon Doctrine*, 120.

17. See, for example, Boyd K. Packer, "Begin Where You Are—At Home," *Ensign,* February 1972, 69–74; James M. Paramore, "A Personal Commitment to the Savior," *Ensign,* May 1979, 61; Thomas S. Monson, "Hallmarks of a Happy Home," *Ensign,* November 1988, 72.

18. See, for example, Spencer W. Kimball, *Marriage and Divorce: An Address* (Salt Lake City: Deseret Book, 1976), 7; Ezra Taft Benson, "The Great Commandment—Love the Lord," *Ensign,* May 1988, 5–6.

19. See, for example, Ezra Taft Benson, "To the Young Women of the Church," *Ensign,* November 1986, 82–83; Benson, "To the Single Adult Brethren of the Church," *Ensign,* May 1986, 44.

20. Russell M. Nelson, *Perfection Pending, and Other Favorite Discourses* (Salt Lake City: Deseret Book, 1998), 131.

21. Neal A. Maxwell, "Willing to Submit," *Ensign,* May 1985, 70–71.

22. Spencer W. Kimball, *Faith Precedes the Miracle* (Salt Lake City: Deseret Book, 1972), 159.

23. *Webster's New Collegiate Dictionary,* s.v. "nourish."

24. Ezra Taft Benson, "To the Fathers in Israel," *Ensign,* November 1987, 50.

25. *Webster's New Collegiate Dictionary,* s.v. "cherish."

26. Kimball, *Faith Precedes the Miracle,* 143.

27. Benson, "To the Fathers in Israel," emphasis added.

28. Joseph F. Smith in *Journal of Discourses,* 26 vols. (London: Latter-day Saints' Book Depot, 1854–86), 16:247.

29. Martha Nibley Beck and John C. Beck, *Breaking the Cycle of Compulsive Behavior* (Salt Lake City: Deseret Book, 1990), 225.

30. Brigham Young as quoted in John A. Widtsoe, *Priesthood and Church Government* (Salt Lake City: Deseret Book, 1939), 90.

31. Harold B. Lee, *The Teachings of Harold B. Lee,* ed. by Clyde J. Williams (Salt Lake City: Bookcraft, 1996), 247, 253.

32. Kimball, *The Teachings of Spencer W. Kimball,* 316.

33. "The Family: A Proclamation to the World," *Ensign,* November 1995, 102.

34. Gordon B. Hinckley, "What God Hath Joined Together," *Ensign,* May 1991, 71.

7

"SUBMIT YOURSELVES
. . . AS UNTO THE LORD"

Camille Fronk

*A*s A DIVINELY APPOINTED WITNESS FOR Christ, the Apostle Paul spoke without "flattering words," giving messages that were not always "pleasing [to] men, but [pleasing to] God" (1 Thessalonians 2:4–5). We should not be surprised then if we feel our toes stepped on from time to time when we read Paul's epistles. Such a reaction generally means that he has just uncovered a gospel principle that we have not yet fully understood or faithfully followed. This discomfort is particularly felt in Paul's instruction concerning women. He declared that "the head of the woman is the man" (1 Corinthians 11:3); "wives, submit yourselves unto your own husbands, as unto the Lord" (Ephesians 5:22); and "let your women keep silence in the churches" (1 Corinthians 14:34; see 1 Timothy 2:8–15).

Many of us have reacted to these "hard sayings" by scrambling for the footnotes, hoping for a Joseph Smith Translation insight or another possible translation of the Greek that would exonerate Paul

Camille Fronk is an assistant professor of ancient scripture at Brigham Young University.

from a politically incorrect faux pas. When that fails, we usually respond in one of three ways. First, we may write off Paul's teachings to women as strictly cultural for a first century Judeo-Roman world and therefore not applicable to us today. Second, we may use Paul's words to justify patronizing or belittling women, concluding that women are not equipped to think for themselves, let alone teach doctrines of salvation. This reaction includes biblical humor using Paul's words as fodder to poke fun at women. Finally, we may accuse Paul of chauvinism or even misogyny, concluding that he is blind to women's contributions to the growth of the church and strength of society.

I propose a different response—one that adds nobility and stature to both men and women of Christ while garnering greater reverence for an Apostle who boldly professed God's eternal laws. Upon closer consideration, Paul's statements say as much about men's stewardship in leadership as they do about women's submission, both within the family and in the Church. At a time when strengthening the family and improving communication between the sexes are standard sermons by general Church leaders, Paul's counsel is needed today as much as ever.

CULTURAL BACKGROUND

To begin, consider the cultural milieu for women in Paul's day. Since Paul's epistles were written to address specific concerns within the early Christian Church, identifying cultural characteristics of his audience help to elucidate timeless gospel principles equally applicable to our day. In Jewish society, women's roles and functions were restrictive. Married women were limited in education and inheritance rights while generally being confined to home. During the time of the Savior's ministry among the Jews, Jewish women were typically seen as being without status, voice, or any quality of life without a man's providential care.[1]

By contrast, in Roman cities, educating women was considered very important. Poorer families were at least able to offer their daughters an elementary education; daughters in more affluent homes were taught by personal tutors. In Corinth and Rome, women could initiate divorce proceedings for any reason and were free to manage their own property. In cities like Ephesus in Asia Minor and Thessalonica in Macedonia, women could own private businesses, hold public office, and perform significant roles in various temple rituals.[2] Among Paul's converts were many from this Roman culture such as "chief women" in Thessalonica (Acts 17:4) and "honorable" Greek women in Berea (Acts 17:12). Lydia—a businesswoman from Thyatira in Asia Minor who sold expensive purple dye—was Paul's first convert in Philippi (see Acts 16:14).

The spread of Christianity throughout the Roman Empire in the first century A.D. reflects the potential for misunderstanding of priesthood authority on cultures where tradition either marginalized women or erased role distinction. Two thousand years later, many women (in and outside the home) perceive themselves as patronized and ignored or encouraged to transform themselves into clones of their male colleagues. Priesthood authority may then translate into further seclusion of women or attempts to curtail women's unique voice. Certainly Paul's teachings have as much potential to address men and women's stewardship within our own Christian society as the audience that first encountered them. An understanding of those roles is discovered by knowing Christ and following His example.

SUBMISSIVENESS IN CHRIST

Paul taught that "the head of Christ is God," or that Christ is submissive to God (1 Corinthians 11:3). A search in any dictionary or thesaurus reveals quite an interesting list of synonyms for the characteristic "submissive," such as obedient, pliable, meek, unpretentious, spineless, flexible, long-suffering, sheepish, modest, henpecked, shrinking, apologetic, gentle, humble, subservient, and forbearing. When the list is applied to the Savior, some of the synonyms simply don't fit. Unquestionably, Jesus is humble, meek, gentle, and unpretentious in His perfect obedience to the Father. But henpecked, spineless, and apologetic? Certainly we do not conclude from Paul's statement that Christ is merely a puppet in God's hands or inferior in any way.

We acknowledge both the Father and the Son as equally glorious members of the Godhead with two equally important yet distinct roles to bring about salvation for humankind. In His unique role, Christ leads us back to God because He is submissive to God. Consequently, we have unsurpassed reverence for the Savior, feeling to thank Him continually for His strength of character, supreme wisdom, devotion to covenant, and selfless love for the Father and each of us.

When one uses Christ as the personification of submission, a deeper definition unfolds. True submission requires restraint when one-upmanship is possible; the complete absence of pride when recognition is meted out; strength to stay the Spirit-directed course when letting go may be expected and even rewarded. When Satan tempted Him to display glory, Jesus restrained Himself from showcasing the breadth of His powers (see Matthew 4:1–11). When converted individuals desired baptism, Jesus "himself baptized not so many as his disciples . . . preferring one another" (JST John 4:3–4). On the cross He manifested unparalleled strength and magnificently accomplished the mission His Father sent him to do (see Matthew 27:42–50). Meekness begets meekness; one who is submissive inspires others to have the courage to change, to admit weakness, to "submit to all things which the Lord seeth fit to inflict upon him" (Mosiah 3:19). Whether faced by goodness or evil, the Savior exercised restraint, humility, and commitment to the Father's cause; through His example of submission, His disciples—then and now—have the courage to do likewise.

SUBMISSIVENESS IN WOMEN

Recognizing submission in Jesus Christ provides an appropriate definition when the term is applied to His disciples. The Apostle Paul instructed women to be submissive, but he preceded his counsel with a reminder of his own need for submission. Paul told Saints living in Corinth that he could only expect them to heed his words as he followed Christ: "Be ye followers of me, even as I also am of Christ" (1 Corinthians 11:1). He then admonished: "I would have you know, that the head of every man is Christ; and the head of the woman is the man; and the head of Christ is God" (1 Corinthians 11:3). The general context of 1 Corinthians addresses interactions of Saints in a church setting rather than within the family. Paul's counsel about men being the head of women in this epistle therefore invites us to consider these dynamics within a Church leadership context.

To the Ephesians, however, Paul taught that the same leadership and submission roles exist within the family. He wrote: "Wives, submit yourselves unto your own husbands, as unto the Lord. For the husband is the head of the wife, even as Christ is the head of the church. . . . Therefore as the Church is subject unto Christ so let the wives be to their own husbands in every thing" (Ephesians 5:22–24). Paul perceived a responsibility for women to be meek and unpretentious in both a familial and ecclesiastical setting.

Women who exercise submission with a husband at home and a priesthood leader at Church begin to illuminate the power of a woman's perspective and voice. First Corinthians was written in response to a woman's sensitivity to contentions in the Corinthian branch. Very little is recorded about Chloe and her household in Corinth except that Paul acknowledged their report (1 Corinthians 1:10–11). This lengthy and doctrinally rich sermon identifying the destructive ramifications of disunity is evidence of Paul's respect for a woman's perceptions in spiritual matters.

Remembering that the vast majority of synonyms for the word *submissive* indicate a highly desirable trait, why do we think it means sheepish, spineless, and apologetic when it is used to describe women? Submission is neither giving in to a man's unrighteousness nor giving up on encouraging a man in his potential. In the scriptural context, being submissive does not require women to become doormats for men to walk on. On the contrary, submission requires remarkable strength of character, devotion to covenant, unusual wisdom, and selfless love—reminiscent of the exemplary submissive One.

Furthermore, a broader study of the Bible reveals that Paul did not originate the responsibility for a woman to be submissive. The Lord ordained that role of submission from the beginning. In the

Garden of Eden, God gave woman the assignment of "help meet," because man needed a complement, being unable to accomplish his mission alone (Moses 3:18; Genesis 2:18). The Hebrew word *ezer,* translated *help,* infers strength to succor, support, or rescue. *Meet, or kenegdo,* means "equal to or appropriate for." Eve and her daughters were created by God to be a help to Adam and his sons, who are their equals. God created man and woman to complement each other. He was fully aware that they would need each other to accomplish their missions and reach their full potential.

God's tutelage for Eve did not end at Creation. He empowered her with desires to fulfill her stewardship before she and Adam left the Garden. Not only did man and woman need each other to depart from the Garden and commence mortality, God knew they would need each other to sojourn successfully in a fallen world. So after both Adam and Eve had partaken of the tree of knowledge, God strengthened Eve in her assignment to be a help meet to Adam by giving her a "desire" toward her husband. God gave her an inclination to support, encourage, and remain with her husband as Adam honored his role to "rule" or preside or be "head" of the woman (Moses 4:22; 1 Corinthians 11:3). "We believe that the Church simply will not accomplish what it must without [women's] faith and faithfulness," said Elder M. Russell Ballard, "[without their] innate tendency to put the well-being of others ahead of [their] own, and [their] spiritual strength and tenacity."[3] Again, an inclination to support contributes a spirit of cooperation within the family and the Church. These gifts from God encourage both the partnership God ordained between man and woman as well as their ability to develop their complementary stewardships.

A young returned sister missionary attending BYU taught me that lesson. She described her feelings of discomfort with the assignment to do street contacting and tracting door-to-door at the commencement of her mission. By contrast, she noticed the boldness, courage, and even enthusiasm the elders in her mission displayed when they actively proselytized. She reasoned, why couldn't the sisters be assigned to nurture visitors who attended Church meetings (which she loved to do and the elders seemed to ignore) and let the men go find people to teach (a task they seemed to enjoy so much more)? Then she began to notice elders who had been out for nearly two years. Without losing their courage to boldly bear witness of the restored gospel, whenever or wherever they saw opportunity, they also were sensitive, nurturing, and encouraging to those who had already committed to baptism. About the same time, she recognized what was happening to her as she matured in mission experience. She was losing her fear of tracting. She was becoming more confident in speaking up and bearing witness, while at the same time becoming more effective in encouraging new members by showing greater sensitivity to their needs. Because elders and sisters worked together in a holy cause, they strengthened each other to develop their complementary responsibilities and the work of the Lord progressed.

Most of the confusion, frustration, or anger surrounding the principle of women's submissiveness is grounded in personal experience with men who assume that being "head" of a woman is a license for fathers, husbands, Church leaders, and men in general to abuse, neglect, patronize, dominate, belittle, and disrespect women. When such blatant mistreatment comes at the hands of men ordained to the priesthood, a woman may be cautious or even repulsed by instructions from the Apostle Paul to submit to a man. President Gordon B. Hinckley cautioned:

"Some men who are evidently unable to gain respect by the goodness of their lives use as justification for their actions the statement that Eve was told that Adam should rule over her. How much sadness, how much tragedy, how much heartbreak has been caused through centuries of time by weak men who have used that as a scriptural warrant for atrocious behavior! They do not recognize that the same account indicates that Eve was given as a help meet to Adam. The facts are that they stood side by side in the garden. They were expelled from the garden together, and they worked together side by side in gaining their bread by the sweat of their brows."[4]

In an attempt to protect herself from such offense, a woman may become more aggressive, directive, or even vow to prove that men are not needed in society at all. In short, varying connotations of "head" have confused the lesson Paul was communicating about submission.

The Greek word *kephale,* translated as "head," has been the source of countless word studies and commentaries, producing a variety of suggested meanings such as:

1. "source" or origin, referring to Adam as the source of Eve;
2. "preeminence," as the head has preeminence over the body;[5]
3. "authority over" or "leader";[6]
4. "foremost" as in a military context—not a chief or captain who rules from a safe distance, but "one who went before the troops . . . the first one into battle."[7]

Examining the scriptural context provides the clarifying key to understand the meaning of "head." Before Paul instructed man to be head of woman, he wrote, "the head of every man is Christ." If we appreciate how Christ led, we will understand the meaning for man's leadership role in connection with women.

JESUS, THE PERFECT LEADER

Jesus was the perfect leader as "head" of all God's children. Like the review of synonyms for *submission,* a review of meanings for *head, preside,* and *lead* produces the potential for negative and positive connotations. Consider this list of synonyms: control, supervise, direct, manage, guide, trail-blaze, take precedence, command, regulate, pioneer, boss, dictate, innovate, warlord, show the way, conduct. Which words describe Christ's role as our perfect leader while at the same time reflecting His submission to the Father? Which words do not?

Jesus taught His disciples, "Whosoever will be chief among you, let him be your servant: even as the Son of man came not to be ministered unto, but to minister, and to give his life a ransom for many" (Matthew 20:27–28). Christ served those over whom He presided. He took initiative to act and give direction when challenges arose. He found solutions to problems and involved others in the process. He healed the infirm and was not afraid to praise the faith of those He healed (Luke 8:48). Because of His selfless leadership, men and women desired to "[minister] unto him of their substance" (Luke 8:3). Jesus led by living what he taught. He admonished His disciples to pray always, but it was after hearing Him pray that His disciples *wanted* to pray when they petitioned, "Lord, teach us to pray" (Luke 11:1). He even asked His disciples to pray for Him. Jesus listened without being condescending, spoke candidly and openly without concern over rejection, trusted His disciples to participate in His demanding work, and worked along side them without fearing He would disappoint them. Of his leadership style, President Spencer W. Kimball said, "Jesus was concerned with basics in human nature and in bringing about lasting changes, not simply cosmetic changes."[8]

Christ was fearless in preaching and doing truth while at the same time humble and accepting. He was more concerned with the welfare of souls than the opinions of men. We love and reverence the Savior because He gives clear direction, valiantly blazes a trail we can follow, and never ceases to point us in the direction of the Father.

MEN AS LEADERS

Christ's example of leadership illustrates how men were divinely assigned to be leaders. Paul's declaration that man is the head of woman does not suggest controlling, commanding, demanding, or managing. When God created man and woman, He gave them both dominion over all His other creations (see Moses 2:26–27; Genesis 1:26–27). In other words, the responsibility of dominion was not solely given to man, but to both man and woman together. Being "head" does not then infer that man has dominion over woman, even when the Lord told Eve that her husband was to "rule" over her (see Moses 4:22). President Hinckley's interpretation of that statement was, "The husband shall have a governing responsibility to provide for, to protect, to strengthen and shield the wife."[9] When the man is "head" in the Lord's way, the woman is free to tend to her stewardship.

God emphasized differing roles and responsibilities for His sons and daughters. The challenge is not recognizing that God assigned differing responsibilities to His sons and daughter but in inspiring men and women to work harmoniously and complementarily in their assigned roles. To add complexity to this task, priesthood leadership functions differently in the home than in the Church. President Boyd K. Packer described the difference:

"In the Church our service is by call. In the home our service is by choice. . . . In the Church there is a distinct line of authority. We serve where called by those who preside over us. In the home it is a partnership with husband and wife equally yoked together. . . . While the husband, the father, has responsibility to provide worthy and inspired leadership, his wife is neither behind him nor ahead of him but at his side."[10]

Priesthood leadership follows a vertical pattern in the Church, with every person's Church calling following a line of authority through those men called to preside over them, eventually reaching up to the President of the Church.

This clarification may provide insight for Paul's instruction, "Let your women keep silence in the churches" (1 Corinthians 14:34). Some biblical scholars discount the passage altogether by explaining it as "the work of an interpolator" since it appears to contradict Paul's earlier acknowledgment that women prayed and prophesied in the churches (see 1 Corinthians 11:5).[11] Others suggest that Paul was forbidding women to teach doctrine, not from speaking in general.[12]

The chapter context gives the background for a very different interpretation for women's *silence*. The text describes church meetings in Corinth where people spoke in tongues without an interpreter and where there was general confusion and disruption (JST 1 Corinthians 14:26–34; 1 Timothy 2:11–12). Moreover, the Greek word *hesuchia*, translated *silence*, suggests "a state of rest and contentment" or "a desistance from bustle or language,"[13] as in the manner in which Paul exhorted Thessalonian men to cease being busybodies and idle by working "with quietness" (2 Thessalonians 3:11–12). For these reasons, one scholar concluded that by using the same Greek word in his epistles, Paul intended that the Thessalonian men be "at peace with [their] work" and that the Corinthian women give "peaceful support of their leaders."[14]

This view is further strengthened by the JST insight in the subsequent phase about the women: "For it is not permitted unto them to *rule* . . . in the church" (1 Corinthians 14:34–35). Women are at liberty to speak, bear witness, teach, and offer perspectives but not to provide priesthood leadership in the Church. No matter how much practical leadership training some of these Corinthian women may have received in their businesses and careers—very possibly more than some of the men called as presiding authorities—they were never commissioned by God to be overseers for the Corinthian branch. At Church, the head of the woman is a man in a hierarchical priesthood leadership position.

In the home, the pattern of priesthood leadership is horizontal, as President Packer described. Much of family disharmony over "headship" occurs when the Church application is practiced in the home. In an address during a priesthood session of general conference, President Howard W. Hunter taught:

"A man who holds the priesthood accepts his wife as a partner in the leadership of the home and family with full knowledge of and full participation in all decisions relating thereto. Of necessity there must be in the Church and the home a presiding officer (see D&C 107:21). By divine appointment, the responsibility to preside in the home rests upon the priesthood holder (see Moses 4:22). . . . For a man to operate independently of or without regard to the feelings and counsel of his wife in governing the family is to exercise unrighteous dominion."[15]

A missionary couple, Priscilla and Aquila, exemplify the partnership President Hunter described. Between them, Paul and Luke acknowledged Aquila and Priscilla six times for their contribution to the work. Together Priscilla and Aquila provided their home as the Christian meeting house (1 Corinthians 16:19); "expound[ed]" the gospel to Apollos, an "eloquent man" who was already "mighty in the scriptures," bringing him into the gospel fold (Acts 18:24, 26); and as Paul identified them: "my helpers in Christ Jesus: who have for my life laid down their own necks" (Romans 16:3–4). In his final farewell, Paul identified "Prisca and Aquila" among the stalwarts in the gospel while the greater church was sinking into apostasy

(2 Timothy 4:19). Aquila's inclusion of Priscilla in missionary labors strengthened him in successes and challenges.

Pastor John Piper wrote a remarkable description of "mature masculinity," his term for divinely inspired "headship" based on the Apostle Paul's teachings:

"Mature masculinity expresses itself not in the demand to be served, but in the strength to serve and to sacrifice for the good of the woman. . . .

"Mature masculinity does not have to initiate every action, but feels the responsibility to provide a general pattern of initiative. . . . For example, the leadership pattern would be less than Biblical if the wife in general was having to take the initiative in prayer at mealtime, and get the family out of bed for worship on Sunday morning, and gather the family for devotions, and discuss what moral standards will be required of the children, and confer about financial priorities . . . etc. . . .

"Mature masculinity recognizes that the call to leadership is a call to repentance and humility and risk-taking. . . . In a good marriage decision-making is focused on the husband, but is not unilateral. He seeks input from his wife and often adopts her ideas. . . . His awareness of his sin and imperfection will guard him from thinking that following Christ gives him the ability of Christ to know what's best in every detail. Nevertheless, in a well-ordered Biblical marriage . . .

" . . . The husband will accept the burden of making the final choice."[16]

When a man initiates goodness and respects the knowledge and insight that women provide, he is honoring his stewardship to preside or be "head" of woman. This requires humility that comes from submission, for as Paul cautioned, "the head of every man is Christ." When men lead as God directed, they do not see themselves as their family's savior but do all they can to lead each family member to know God and Jesus Christ, the true Savior.

"Submit Yourselves"—Two Examples

Two illustrations provide examples of how God's pattern works when men and women honor their respective responsibilities.

First, President Boyd K. Packer related a parable to show how men and women need each other to obtain the greatest blessings of God. A man inherited two keys—one to a vault and the other to a safe within the vault. He was told that the treasure inside the safe would produce blessings that are continually replenished for all eternity if he worthily used the contents to benefit others.

"The man went alone to the vault. His first key opened the door. He tried to unlock the treasure with the other key, but he could not, for there were two locks on the safe. His key alone would not open it. No matter how he tried, he could not open it. He was puzzled. He had been given the keys. He knew the treasure was rightfully his. He had obeyed instructions, but he could not open the safe.

"In due time there came a woman into the vault. She too held a key. It was noticeably different from the key he held. Her key fit the other lock. It humbled him to learn that he could not obtain his rightful inheritance without her.

"They made a covenant that together they would open the treasure and, as instructed, he would watch over the vault and protect it; she would watch over the treasure. She was not concerned that, as guardian of the vault, he held two keys, for his full purpose was to see that she was safe as she watched over that which was most precious to them both. Together they opened the safe and partook of their inheritance. They rejoiced, for, as promised, it replenished itself. . . .

"Because some tempted them to misuse their treasure, they were careful to teach their children about keys and covenants.

"There came, in due time, among their posterity some few who were deceived or jealous or selfish because one was given two keys and another only one. 'Why,' the selfish ones reasoned, 'cannot the treasure be mine alone to use as I desire?' . . .

"Those who received the treasure with gratitude and obeyed the laws concerning it knew joy without bounds through time and all eternity."[17]

God's blessings are not diminished with different assignments. On the contrary, combining our complementary responsibilities as men and women magnifies the gifts and opportunities God gives to us. Neither man nor woman can obtain the fullness of God's promises without the other.

Elder Russell M. Nelson provided a second example of men's and women's complementary responsibilities with a recounting of his family's river-rafting vacation. The first time the family approached dangerous rapids and a waterfall, Elder Nelson explained that his fatherly instinct was to "hold them close to me. But as we reached the precipice, the bended raft became a giant sling and shot me into the air. I landed into the roiling rapids of the river. . . . I finally found the side of the raft and rose to the surface. The family pulled my nearly drowned body out of the water." Lucky for him he had a "help meet," one who is his equal with strength to help and rescue!

With all humility and honesty, Elder Nelson then described the most important responsibility a father has in leading his family. When they faced "the most dangerous drop of the journey," Elder Nelson initiated a family council meeting where a plan for survival was outlined. As the one who presides, he directed his family not to hold on to him this time, but to hang on to the only thing that would keep them afloat—the ropes secured to the raft. Lucky for the family they had a father who was submissive to the Lord and knew how to lead them to Him.

Elder Nelson's lesson is clear: "As we go through life, even through very rough waters, a father's instinctive impulse to cling tightly to his wife or to his children may not be the best way to accomplish his objective. Instead, if he will lovingly cling to the Savior and the iron rod of the gospel, his family will want to cling to him and to the Savior."[18] When a man uses his position as "head" to lead those within his priesthood stewardship to Christ and a woman actively sustains that focus, families are strengthened and individuals fortified in their connection to God.

UNITY IN THE LORD

In Paul's day, disunity and contention plagued the early Christian Church in a variety of ways, including confusion and competition over men's and women's differing God-given responsibilities. In our day, Elder M. Russell Ballard observed: "The adversary is having a heyday distorting attitudes about gender and roles and about families and individual worth. He is the author of mass confusion about the value, the role, the contribution, and the unique nature of women."[19]

The Apostle Paul boldly restated God's order to invite unity in Christ by emphasizing the necessity of submission in *every* relationship: "The head of every man is Christ; and the head of the woman is the man; and the head of Christ is God" (1 Corinthians 11:3). No amount of manipulation of these dynamics will make the world a better place. No misinterpretation of *presiding* and *submitting* will finally make right either unrighteous dominion or relinquishing a voice. Only by submitting to God's order are we empowered to lift each other to become what God promised we could be. For what man would not gladly sacrifice, actively serve, and more meekly guide a woman who sincerely trusts, unpretentiously follows, and wholeheartedly supports his Christlike attempts to lead? And what woman would not willingly and joyfully cooperate with a husband, father, or priesthood leader who boldly protects, unflinchingly holds to truth, and gently leads them to Christ and subsequently to an understanding of their potential in the Church, the home, and the world? The Apostle Paul said it best: "Neither is the man without the woman, neither the woman without the man, in the Lord" (1 Corinthians 11:11).

NOTES

1. David Noel Freedman, ed., *The Anchor Bible Dictionary* (New York: Doubleday, 1992), 6:958–60, S.V. "Women (NT)."

2. Ibid.

3. M. Russell Ballard, "Here I Am, Send Me," in *Brigham Young University 2000–2001 Speeches* (Provo, Utah: Brigham Young University, 2001), 199.

4. Gordon B. Hinckley, in Conference Report, October 1991, 72.

5. Wayne Grudem, "The Meaning of Kephale ('Head'): A Response to Recent Studies," in *Recovering Biblical Manhood and Womanhood: A Response to Evangelical Feminism,* ed. John Piper and Wayne Gudem (Wheaton, Illinois: Crossway Books, 1991), 426.

6. Ibid.

7. John Temple Bristow, *What Paul Really Said about Women* (New York: HarperCollins, 1988), 36–37.

8. Spencer W. Kimball, "Jesus: The Perfect Leader," *Ensign,* August 1979, 6.

9. Gordon B. Hinckley, "Daughters of God," *Ensign,* November 1991, 99.

10. Boyd K. Packer, in Conference Report, April 1998, 96.

11. Margaret Y. MacDonald, "Reading Real Women through the Undisputed Letters of Paul," in *Women & Christian Origins,* ed. Ross Shephard Kraemer and Mary Rose D'Angelo (New York: Oxford University Press, 1999), 216.

12. Werner Neuer, *Man and Woman in Christian Perspective* (Wheaton, Illinois: Crossway Books, 1991), 117.

13. James Strong, *The Exhaustive Concordance of the Bible* (McLean, Virginia: MacDonald, N.D.), S.V. "Hesuchia."

14. Richard Lloyd Anderson, *Understanding Paul* (Salt Lake City: Deseret Book, 1983), 352.

15. Howard W. Hunter, in Conference Report, October 1994, 68.

16. John Piper, "A Vision of Biblical Complementarity: Manhood and Womanhood Defined According to the Bible," in *Recovering Biblical Manhood and Womanhood: A Response to Evangelical Feminism,* ed. John Piper and Wayne Gudem (Wheaton, Illinois: Crossway Books, 1991), 38–59.

17. Boyd K. Packer, in Conference Report, October 1993, 31.

18. Russell M. Nelson, "Women Of Righteousness," *Ensign,* November 2001, 69.

19. Ballard, "Here I Am," 199.

8

UNITY AND
ATONEMENT IN EPHESIANS

Amy Blake Hardison

*T*HE ATONEMENT IS "THE ACT OF UNIFYING or bringing together what has been separated or estranged."[1] We usually think of the Atonement in its ultimate manifestation, that of Jesus Christ overcoming sin and death and thereby providing a way for man to be reunited with God. As transcendent as this blessing is, it is only one aspect of the Atonement.

In His intercessory prayer, Christ asked the Father to bless all those who believed in Him "that they all may be one; as thou, Father, art in me, and I in thee, that they also may be one in us" and "that they may be made perfect in one" (John 17:21, 23). In this plea, we see that the Atonement is to operate not only vertically, filling us with the desire to be with and be like God, but also horizontally, moving us to blend in sweet harmony with the people in our lives.

This ideal relationship was first commanded of Adam and Eve in the Garden of Eden. However, fallen, natural human beings tend to be egocentric, proud, and dogmatic—in other words, separate.

Amy Blake Hardison teaches at the Tempe Arizona Institute of Religion.

Becoming at one with spouses, children, neighbors, ward members, and others who regularly irritate, exasperate, and challenge us is graduate work for aspiring Saints. It requires humility, giving up our own agendas and wills, brutal honesty in looking at our own flaws, and most of all repentance. Because of these demands, it is sanctifying. It is exactly what we need to effect the vertical aspect of the Atonement, becoming like God.

It is this very pragmatic side of the Atonement that Paul deals with extensively in Ephesians. In this epistle, Paul not only acknowledges the difficulty of living in unity but also shows how to do so in two very practical and challenging relationships: (1) as members of the Church and (2) as husbands and wives.

The Challenge of Living in Unity

In the premortal existence, we were called and elected to many things: to be members of the house of Israel, to become mothers and fathers in Israel,[2] and to fulfill unique roles in building the kingdom. In Ephesians 1:4, Paul points out one election we often overlook—to live together in love. It is likely we learned how to do this in the premortal world,[3] and we will need to so live in the celestial kingdom (see D&C 105:4). In the interim, living celestial principles in a fallen world with a fallen nature is difficult. Paul acknowledges this when he beseeches the Saints to live with lowliness (humility), meekness (gentleness), long-suffering, and forbearance (see Ephesians 4:1–2), the very characteristics needed to blend gently with mankind.

Ironically, the more separate we are, the easier it is to live in love, or at least it appears to be easier. We are usually quite polite to strangers, but then we don't have to share toothpaste with them or agree on how to raise children or step over their dirty socks. The closer the relationship, the more our lives are intertwined. The more our lives are intertwined, the more another's way of being encroaches on our way of being. That is why Gib Kocherhans has written: "The home is the crucible of Christian commitment. I have done a far better job of living the gospel in public and private than in the mini-society of my family. No other person or group can press upon me, demand of me, or expose me like the members of my family can."[4] These demands are one of the reasons our close relationships are so very important to us; they teach us how to love.

President James E. Faust related a conversation he once had with Elder S. Dilworth Young. Elder Young's wife, Gladys, had had a cruel stroke that left her as an invalid, requiring him to dress her, feed her, and care for her. President Faust remarked that he had never seen a greater example of tender kindness and solicitude than Elder Young's as he tended to Gladys. Elder Young confided to President Faust: "It was the worst thing in the world that could have happened to Gladys and the best thing for me. It made me decent. I learned what love really should be."[5] So it is in our lives. It is only when we surrender the self and care for someone else more than we care for ourselves that we begin to realize true love. That is why parenting is a most intensive course on love. That is why married love can be an "exultant ecstasy."[6] That is why love "is always specific, always costly, [and] always a miraculous event."[7] And that is why it is not easy.

Achieving Unity Within the Church

The Saints of Paul's day faced some especially difficult obstacles as they sought to live in unity and love. No groups were more disparate than Jews and Gentiles. The Jews believed that Gentiles were created to fuel the fires of hell. They were not to eat with Gentiles or sleep in their houses. Contact was to be avoided as much as possible. The Gentiles equally despised the Jews for their exclusiveness. It is not hard to imagine the social crisis brought about when God told Peter that the gospel was to go to all people; former enemies were to become one congregation, one people, one church. To teach the Ephesians about this unity, Paul uses the metaphor of the temple and the balustrade (see Ephesians 2:11–18).

The temple was composed of a series of concentric holy spaces. As one moved farther from the center, the space became less holy and more people had access to it. The innermost space was the Holy of Holies. Only the high priest of Israel was allowed to enter this most sacred space and only once a year on the Day of Atonement. Outside the Holy of Holies was the Holy Place. Together, the Holy of Holies and the Holy Place composed the sanctuary proper, which towered more than 150 feet high. Priests regularly entered the Holy Place to attend to the sacred objects kept therein—to change the shewbread, to keep the golden candlestick burning, and to bring incense from the sacrificial altar to the altar of incense.

A courtyard surrounded the sanctuary. This courtyard was divided into the Court of Priests, wherein only priests and other authorized persons could enter, and the Court of Men. It may have been in this court that the Sanhedrin met and where the sacrifices were offered. Fifteen curved steps led from the Court of Men down to the Court of Women, a large courtyard nearly two hundred square feet in size. All Israel, both men and women, could enter here. These courtyards and the sanctuary constituted the temple proper, which was surrounded by a wall. Outside this wall was the Court of the Gentiles. This court was something like temple square in Salt Lake City in that all people had access to it, up to the balustrade, a four-and-a-half foot railing that surrounded the outer wall of the temple proper. This railing had signs on it in Greek and Latin warning the Gentiles not to pass this railing or they would suffer death. This railing serves as a metaphor for Paul in Ephesians 2.

Paul begins his discourse on unity by pointing out the incredible separation that previously existed between the Gentiles and God. In Ephesians 2:11–12, Paul cites four reasons for this separation. First, the Gentiles needed circumcision, the ordinance by which one entered into the covenant. Second, the Gentiles previously were without Christ. Christ is the Mediator between God and man. Without Christ and His Atonement, man has no access to God. Third, the Gentiles had been "aliens from the commonwealth of Israel." Gentiles didn't belong to the corporate body of Israel. To belong to a group meant to take on the identity of that group—to take on the ideals, standards, and beliefs as one's own. Thus, being a part of the commonwealth of Israel "implies an obligation to observe a godly way of life."[8] Fourth, the Gentiles were "strangers from the covenants of promise." Strangers were resident aliens or legal immigrants. They were protected by law together with the widows and orphans, but they were not brothers or members of the covenant. They were not bound by the law of Moses, except in instances where the observance was national rather than religious, but neither were they blessed by the covenant. Elder Henry B. Eyring has explained that "every covenant with God is an opportunity to draw closer to him."[9] Being without covenants is indeed separation from God. Thus, without covenants and ordinances, without holy behavior, and without Christ, the Gentiles were "without God in the world" (Ephesians 2:12). This separation is symbolized by the balustrade which kept the Gentiles far from the Holy of Holies, or the presence of God.

Paul states that Christ "hath broken down the middle wall of partition" (Ephesians 2:14), and they "who in the past stood far off have been brought near" (Anchor Bible Translation, 2:13).[10] This middle wall of partition has a dual meaning. As mentioned, it is the balustrade. With the balustrade broken down, Gentiles could now pass to the inner courts, even as the Israelites did. The middle wall of partition can also refer to the veil that separated the Holy Place and the Holy of Holies. This veil was rent at the time of Christ's Crucifixion (see Matthew 27:51), symbolizing that all Israel could now approach God. Up to this time, the common Israelite would wait outside the Holy Place, in the Court of Men or the Court of Women, while the priests and the high priest entered the holy sanctuary on his or her behalf.[11] But in Jesus Christ, the law of Moses was fulfilled. Paul declares that those who before stood far off are "made nigh" (Ephesians 2:13). Paul's choice of words is significant for a priest is one who can approach God, one who can draw near to Him.[12] In Jesus Christ, all the spiritual privileges previously reserved for the priests of Israel were extended to the common Israelite and to the Gentile. All who are worthy can approach God.

As incredible as this blessing is, unity with God is not Paul's main emphasis. Paul repeatedly mentions the image of unity between the former Jews and Gentiles. He speaks of "abolish[ing] . . . enmity" (Ephesians 2:15), making "both one" (Ephesians 2:14), making of "twain one new man" (Ephesians 2:15), and "reconcil[ing] both unto God in one body" (Ephesians 2:16). The images of oneness and creation recall the Adam and Eve story. Adam and Eve were commanded to be one flesh. The word for "one" is the Hebrew word *ehad.* It does not reflect cardinal numbers, like one, two, three, and four. Rather, the word *ehad* reflects unity. It is like one cluster of many grapes or the two blades of one pair of scissors. The image here is of two former enemies so united in heart and walk that they enter the temple together as one, *ehad,* to worship God.

The sobering corollary to this is that such unity with our fellowman is not optional. We must be reconciled to our fellowman before we can approach God. This is taught in our temples today as well as in Matthew 5:23–24:

"Therefore if thou bring thy gift to the altar, and there rememberest that thy brother hath ought against thee;

"Leave there thy gift before the altar, and go thy way; first be reconciled to thy brother, and then come and offer thy gift."

For the ancient Israelites, their gifts were their sacrifices. For us, it is a broken heart and contrite spirit. For either gift to be acceptable, it must be accompanied by reconciliation with our fellowman.

The image of making one new person in Ephesians 2:14–16 also recalls the creation of Adam and Eve. In the scriptures, only God has power to create. Becoming one with spouse, child, neighbor, and enemy is a creation achieved only through the power of God. This same idea is expressed when Paul states that Christ "is our peace" (Ephesians 2:14). In the historical context of Ephesians, Christ made peace by fulfilling the law of Moses, the great separator between Jews and Gentiles. Today, when the law of Moses is no longer an issue, Christ is still our peace as we struggle to reconcile with those with whom we are at odds. In other words, overcoming differences, letting go of grievances, pain, and resentment, and filling our hearts with unifying love is not accomplished through sheer willpower but through Christ. This is beautifully illustrated by the touching story of Corrie Ten Boom.

Corrie Ten Boom was a devout Dutch Christian who was interred in a German concentration camp during World War II for helping Jews escape out of Holland. She suffered greatly, but unlike her beloved sister, Betsie, she survived. After the war, she often spoke publicly about her experiences. On one such occasion, a former Nazi guard, one who had actually been a part of Corrie's hideous experience in Ravensbruck, came to her, rejoicing at her message of Christ's forgiveness and love.

"'How grateful I am for your message, Fraulein,' he said. 'To think that, as you say, He has washed my sins away!'

"His hand was thrust out to shake mine. And I, who had preached so often to the people in Bloemendaal the need to forgive, kept my hand at my side.

"Even as the angry, vengeful thoughts boiled through me, I saw the sin of them . . . Lord Jesus, I prayed, forgive me and help me to forgive him.

"I tried to smile, I struggled to raise my hand. I could not. I felt nothing, not the slightest spark of warmth or charity. And so again I breathed a silent prayer. Jesus, I cannot forgive him. Give me Your forgiveness.

"As I took his hand the most incredible thing happened. From my shoulder along my arm and through my hand a current seemed to pass from me to him, while into my heart sprang a love for this stranger that almost overwhelmed me.

"And so I discovered that it is not on our forgiveness any more than on our goodness that the world's healing hinges, but on His. When He tells us to love our enemies, He gives, along with the command, the love itself."[13]

ACHIEVING UNITY IN MARRIAGE

To the modern reader, few passages of Paul's writings cause as much consternation as those in which Paul enjoins wives to submit to their husbands. As we read Paul's epistles, we must remember that we are at best "eavesdroppers on another culture."[14] As western citizens of the twenty-first century, we are living post–French Revolution, post–Civil Rights Movement, and post–Equal Rights

Amendment. All of these have contributed greatly to an egalitarian mindset. We recognize and prize the innate equality of human beings. This was not Paul's world. Paul and his Jewish contemporaries viewed the world as a highly structured cosmos where every person, place, and thing had its proper place. Requiring a wife to submit to her husband upheld Paul's cultural perceptions. But to many people today, his counsel implies that a wife is in some way inferior to her husband. Another complication is the modern connotations of the word *submit*. Today it is almost a dirty word. It evokes images of being lily-livered, a Milquetoast, or a doormat. Such interpretations are incongruent with Paul's writings and the gospel. To understand Paul's statements regarding submission, we must understand not only these vast cultural differences but also the nature, the vocabulary, and the mutuality of submission, and we must view submission and order from a spiritual perspective.

Paul's discussion on submission begins not with Ephesians 5:22, "Wives submit yourselves unto your own husband, as unto the Lord," but with Ephesians 5:21, wherein he requires all—both men and women—to submit. Catherine Thomas explains: "Lines of authority belong to the pattern of the Lord for all his people. The Lord has set each of his children, whether male or female, in a hierarchical chain that requires each to listen carefully to the voice of one set above him or her. Through listening to those the Lord has placed in positions of authority and blessing, one learns how to listen to and obey the Lord."[15] The reason for submission, says Paul, is "because you fear God" (Anchor Bible Translation, 5:21). Fearing God is not apprehensive trembling because an angry God is going to zap us with fire from heaven or consign us to the depths of hell when we err. *Fear* is a covenant word and a covenant requirement. In its covenant context, it means to serve God loyally. It is complete and wholehearted obedience. Thus, because we acknowledge Him as our rightful and beneficent ruler and because we love Him and desire to serve Him faithfully, we submit to His authority, even as it is vested in His earthly representatives. It is not a prospect the natural man relishes. However, it is still a requirement, from the least to the greatest in God's kingdom. Speaking of Christ's appearance in the New World, Elder Jeffrey R. Holland quotes 3 Nephi 11:10–11 and then writes:

"I cannot think it either accident or mere whimsy that the Good Shepherd in his newly exalted state, appearing to a most significant segment of his flock, chooses to speak first of his obedience, his deference, his loyalty, and loving submission to his Father. In an initial and profound moment of spellbinding wonder, when surely he has the attention of every man, woman and child as far as the eye can see, his submission to his Father is the first and most important thing he wishes us to know about himself.

"Frankly, I am a bit haunted by the thought that this is the first and most important thing he may want to know about us when we meet him one day in similar fashion. Did we obey, even if it was painful? Did we submit, even if the cup was bitter indeed? Did we yield to a vision higher and holier than our own, even when we may have seen no vision in it at all?"[16]

Only after discussing submission as a general requirement does Paul then state that wives should submit to their husbands. The word translated "submit" is *hypotasso*. Its meanings include "to place or arrange under, to assign to, to post in the shelter of."[17] On occasion, it is used to express the taking of position in a military unit. There is no thought of inferiority or servility. Rather, the idea is of taking one's place in an established and proper order. This was a desirable action from Paul's cultural viewpoint, for "God expressed holiness by creating a holy/orderly cosmos. God acted to bless this creation precisely by the divine ordering and structuring of all relationships."[18] Taking one's place in this system meant being a part of God's holy order.

As Latter-day Saints, we should not think it strange that God's kingdom is a kingdom of order or that men and women each have an important, but different, place in that order. As "The Family: A Proclamation to the World" states, *"By divine design,* fathers are to preside over their families in love and righteousness. . . . Mothers are primarily responsible for the nurture of their children" (emphasis added).[19] We might compare this to a bishop and a Relief Society president in a ward. Both have important positions of leadership and responsibility. Both have valuable insights and ideas. As individuals, one is not more important than the other. However, for the sake of order, one must stand at the head. Presiding is a priesthood function. The father, as the priesthood holder of the most basic priesthood unit of the Church, the family, is given this position.

In Ephesians 5:23, Paul states that the husband is the head of the wife. The Greek word for head is *kefhale*. It does not mean "chief, boss, ruler, or superior authority" but "source." It is used, for example, for the source or the head of a river. A husband stands at the head of a family, as the source of priesthood power and blessings for that family. In addition, "To say that a man is the head of the wife is to say he is responsible for the wife; he is to care for, he is to give life to, to protect, to guard, to encourage, to guide—he is her source."[20] Again, this is stated in the proclamation on the family when it says that fathers "are responsible to provide the necessities of life and protection for their families."[21]

After speaking of the husband as the head of the family, even as Christ is the head of the Church, Paul then states that "he is the saviour of the body" (Ephesians 5:23). Paul often uses "body" to refer to the body of the Church. As Christ stands in a saving role to the Church, so a husband should stand in a saving role to his family. This saving role is the calling of priesthood holders. They are to labor with all their souls to bring those over whom they preside into the presence of God. We see it in Moses, who "sought diligently to sanctify his people that they might behold the face of God" (D&C 84:23). We see it in King Benjamin, who labored with "all the might of his body and the faculty of his whole soul" (Words of Mormon 1:18) to establish peace in the land, "that essential condition for spiritual progress [which] is evidence of the triumph of spiritual principle and also of the preparation of the people in any size group to receive greater spiritual blessings."[22] Those greater blessings were recorded in King Benjamin's speech and include the promise of being "found at the right hand of God" (Mosiah 5:9). We also see it in Adam, Enoch, Melchizedek, Joseph Smith, and the One upon whom all these prophets modeled their behavior, the Savior Jesus Christ. Therefore, Paul tells priesthood holders to model their lives after the Savior's, loving as He loves, ministering as He ministers, and laboring to purify, sanctify, and present their families without spot, wrinkle, or blemish before Him (see Ephesians 5:26–27). The modern priesthood holder should likewise labor with all his might to bring those he presides over (his family, his quorum, or his ward) to the presence of the Lord, or to the house of the Lord.

Paul next commands husbands to love their wives. So often we think of love as romance and roses. Mature love is far more demanding. It requires the submission of ego and the subjection of self-interest. We must sacrifice the human propensity to insist that we have the right way to live life, to drive a car, to celebrate Christmas, to discipline children, ad infinitum. To truly love, we must honor and cherish the unique and valuable contribution of the one we love. In short, the command to love is a command to submit. Thus, when Paul requires a wife to submit and a husband to love, he is asking them to do the exact same thing.

In addition, Paul demands of men the highest form of love—men are to love their wives "even as Christ also loved the church, and gave himself for it" (Ephesians 5:25). Paul discusses the high demands of Christlike love, or charity, in 1 Corinthians 13. There we read that "charity vaunteth not itself, [and] is not puffed up" (1 Corinthians 13:4). To vaunt is "to boast, a vain display of what one is or has."[23] Charity does not vaunt itself, or in other words, exercise unrighteous dominion or pull rank. "Charity . . . is kind" (1 Corinthians 13:4). "It eases another's pain, soothes anxieties, fears and hostilities and contributes positively to the happiness of others."[24] Thus, charity does not threaten, demand, or intimidate, for such behavior *creates* pain and anxieties, fear and hostilities. Moreover, most modern women would not feel that their husbands had contributed to their happiness unless their husbands had listened to and counseled with them as equal partners. Presiding in love encompasses equality between husband and wife. This is reaffirmed by our modern prophets in the proclamation on the family.

When a husband presides in love and righteousness as outlined in 1 Corinthians, a wife's natural response is to reciprocate with honor and respect. As Paul says, the wife will then "reverence her

husband" (Ephesians 5:33), and his "dominion shall be an everlasting dominion, and without compulsory means it shall flow unto
[him] forever" (D&C 121:46). A wife will only be able to respond
with honor and respect if she is rooted and grounded in Christlike
love. "Charity envieth not" (1 Corinthians 13:4), and "[charity]
seeketh not her own" (1 Corinthians 13:5). Thus, a wife who has
true charity will not envy her husband's position, nor will she subvert it. Moreover, charity "doth not behave itself unseemly"
(1 Corinthians 13:5). The verb translated as "unseemly" can refer to
a kind of disorganization. A wife with charity will honor the God-
ordained patriarchal order. But this order only works upon the
principles of Christlike love. Whenever husband or wife violates the
principles of charity, God's order flounders.

These principles of mutual subjection and love cannot be
understood from a temporal perspective. Paul calls it a great mystery (see Ephesians 5:32). A mystery is something that must be
revealed to be understood. Without the divine revelation of God's
order, an order that honors, exalts, and cherishes the role and contribution of women, Paul's statements are interpreted as sexist and
bigoted. Also, without divine revelation, one thinks of presiding
from a worldly perspective, which equates presiding with exercising
power, ego, and control. From a spiritual perspective, presiding
means serving and loving and giving one's "self" away.

Another great mystery is what it means for men and women to
take different places in God's kingdom. The world tries to tell us
that different places mean unequal places. It insists that when men
preside, women are placed in a secondary role. Nothing could be
further from the truth. In actuality, men and women of God are
called to the same work. This is reflected in a woman's calling to be
a helpmeet. Beverly Campbell, former director of International
Affairs for the Church in Washington, D.C., explains:

"The word that has been translated as 'help meet' is a combination of two root words: *ezer* and *k'enegdo*. The word *ezer* also com-
bines two roots: the first meaning 'to rescue' or 'to save' or 'as a savior,' sometimes coupled with the concept of majesty, and the other

meaning 'strength' or 'to be strong.' The second Hebrew word, *k'enegdo,* is identified as meaning 'equal.'"[25]

Thus, Eve and all women were created to be a majestic, saving power, equal to Adam. It does no dishonor to women that the primary sphere in which she exercises this power is the home and family. If her sphere is not as broad as a man's, who is called to be "a light unto the Gentiles [through missionary work], and through this priesthood, a savior unto my people Israel" (D&C 86:11) through administering saving ordinances, her sphere is more concentrated. Regardless of the differences in scope and administration, the labor is the same.

Perhaps the greatest mystery of all is that the Lord's order fosters interdependence, or unity. A woman must depend on her husband to provide priesthood power and blessings, something she cannot do herself. A man must also depend on his wife. Jewish tradition teaches that a man is not fully a man if he is not married. There is not even a word for "bachelor" in biblical Hebrew, and the modern Hebrew word for bachelor, *ravak,* comes from a root word meaning "empty."[26] Without a wife, a man is empty of the "insight, balance, and unique wisdom"[27] that is given to Eve (and all women) to allow her to perform her divine role as a helpmeet. Without a wife, a man is empty of the enabling power of grace that is given to women to comfort, inspire, ennoble, and give purpose to a husband's protecting and providing. Without a wife and family, a man's opportunities to use his priesthood power to bless are limited. Husbands and wives are given different roles and different strengths so they might bless each other, depend on each other, and ultimately become one.

This mutuality is typified in Abraham and Sarah. When Abraham and Sarah entered Egypt, the Lord revealed to Abraham that when the Egyptians saw Sarah, the Pharaoh would want to take her for his wife and would kill Abraham to do so. The Lord commanded Abraham to ask Sarah to save them both by assuming her role as sister, rather than wife. Human pride and independence would suggest that a husband would prefer to do all in his power to protect his wife and himself. Instead, the Lord required that

Abraham refrain from acting and trust in Him to work through Sarah (and even Pharaoh) to save him and preserve the posterity promises of the Abrahamic Covenant. On the other hand, when Sarah could not bear children, she entreated Abraham to take Hagar to wife so that they might have posterity, according to Hurrian custom and law. When Hagar mocked and taunted Sarah, Abraham protected Sarah's rights, also according to Hurrian custom and law, to the point where he eventually (and painfully) sent Hagar and Ishmael away. Both Abraham and Sarah completely submitted their egos in love and trust. Both protected each other's rights. Both held their mutual best interest above their individual preferences. And both exerted a saving influence for the other. Such is the pattern for the righteous priesthood holder and the virtuous wife.

THE ULTIMATE GOAL

In Ephesians, Paul discusses the Atonement as it pertains to everyday life and everyday relationships. But the work is not ordinary; it is godly. And it requires some of the most difficult things one can do: forgive, let go of hurts and prejudices, conquer the ego, surrender self-interest in favor of caring, support and empower others, live with charity, dedicate one's life to saving others spiritually, and trust in God's perspective of order and importance instead of the world's. When we do these things, we can through the power and gifts of the Spirit achieve unity. We can become truly holy and thus prepare to become one with God and Christ, the ultimate goal of the Atonement.

NOTES

1. Jeffrey R. Holland, *Christ and the New Covenant* (Salt Lake City: Deseret Book, 1997), 197.

2. President Spencer W. Kimball stated: "We made vows, solemn vows, in the heavens before we came to this mortal life. . . . We have made covenants. We made them before we accepted our position here on the earth. . . . We committed ourselves to our Heavenly Father, that if he would send us to the earth and give us bodies and give to us the priceless opportunities that earth life afforded, we would keep our lives clean and would marry in the holy temple and would rear

a family and teach them righteousness. This was a solemn oath, a solemn promise" (quoted in Barbara Winder, "Enjoy Your Journey," *Brigham Young University 1989–90 Devotional and Fireside Speeches* [Provo, Utah: University Publications, 1990], 105).

3. See M. Catherine Thomas, "Zion and the Spirit of At-one-ment," *FARMS Book of Mormon Lecture Series* (Provo, UT: FARMS, 1994), 1. I am indebted to Catherine Thomas for her writings, especially those on at-one-ment, priesthood leaders, and women and the priesthood (see "Alma the Younger," *FARMS Book of Mormon Lecture Series* [Provo, UT: FARMS, 1995] and *Spiritual Lightening* [Salt Lake City: Bookcraft, 1996]).

4. Gib Kocherhans, "The Name 'Melchizedek': Some Thoughts on Its Meaning and the Priesthood It Represents," *Ensign,* September 1980, 18.

5. James E. Faust, "'Brethren, Love Your Wives,'" *Ensign,* July 1981, 37.

6. Spencer W. Kimball, *Teachings of Spencer W. Kimball,* ed. Edward L. Kimball (Salt Lake City: Bookcraft, 1982), 305.

7. Markus Barth, *Ephesians: Introduction, Translation and Commentary on Chapters 4–6,* volume 34A of the Anchor Bible Series (New York: Doubleday, 1960), 428.

8. David H. Stern, *Jewish New Testament Commentary* (Clarksville, Maryland: Jewish New Testament Publications, Inc., 1996), 582.

9. Henry B. Eyring, "Making Covenants with God," *Brigham Young University 1996–97 Speeches* (Provo, Utah: Brigham Young University, 1997), 15.

10. Markus Barth, *Ephesians,* 253.

11. A modern equivalent of this might be if only the prophet and the General Authorities could enter the temple. The average member could only patiently wait outside the temple, praying, singing and worshiping until these privileged leaders came out to the steps of the temple and shared how wonderful their temple experience had been.

12. See Dwight Pryor, "The Covenant and Commitment of Pentecost," *Power of Pentecost* (Dayton, Ohio: Center for Judaic-Christian Studies), audiotape.

13. Corrie Ten Boom, *The Hiding Place* (New York: Bantam Books, 1971), 238.

14. Jerome H. Neyrey, *Paul, In Other Words* (Louisville, Kentucky: Westminster / John Knox Press, 1990), 53.

15. M. Catherine Thomas, *Spiritual Lightening* (Salt Lake City: Bookcraft, 1996), 55.

16. Jeffrey R. and Patricia T. Holland, *On Earth as It Is in Heaven* (Salt Lake City: Deseret Book, 1989), 126.

17. Barth, *Ephesians 4–6,* 709.

18. Neyrey, 26.

19. The First Presidency and Council of the Twelve Apostles, "The Family: A Proclamation to the World," *Ensign,* November 1995, 102.

20. Dwight A. Pryor, "The Ministry of Women in the Church and Synagogue" (Dayton, Ohio: Center for Judaic-Christian Studies), audiotape.

21. The First Presidency and Council of the Twelve Apostles, "The Family," 102.

22. M. Catherine Thomas, "Benjamin and the Mysteries of God," *King Benjamin's Speech,* ed. John W. Welch and Stephen D. Ricks (Provo, Utah: Foundation for Ancient Research and Mormon Studies, 1998), 283.

23. Noah Webster, *An American Dictionary of the English Language,* 1828, electronic edition (Salt Lake City: Deseret Book, 1998).

24. William F. Orr and James Arthur Walther, *I Corinthians: A New Translation,* volume 32 of the Anchor Bible Series (Garden City, New York: Doubleday, 1976), 295.

25. Beverly Campbell, "Mother Eve," *Mentor for Today's Woman: A Heritage of Honor,* http://www.erols.com/jdstone/eve.html (accessed 7 July 1999).

26. Donna B. Nielsen, *Beloved Bridegroom* (USA: Onyx Press, 1999), 3.

27. Sheri Dew, "It Is Not Good for Man or Woman to Be Alone," *Ensign,* November 2001, 13.

9

EPHESIANS: UNFOLDING THE MYSTERIES THROUGH REVELATION

Matthew O. Richardson

IN OUR CURRENT VERNACULAR, A MYSTERY is something that is hidden, inexplicable, or unknown. The term knows no boundaries and can be equally applied to scientific irregularities as to theological principles. Paul, in his letter to the Ephesians, writes of three doctrinal topics that he calls "mysteries." The three mysteries include the dispensation of the fulness of times (see Ephesians 1:9–10), the Gentiles becoming fellow heirs in Christ through the gospel (Ephesians 3:3–6), and marital living and stewardship (Ephesians 5:31–32). For those familiar with the general events of Paul's time, it is clear that these three topics were not only relevant issues but also fiercely debated. Thus, when Paul calls these topics mysteries, one might assume that Paul was stating that the meaning of these topics was hidden, inexplicable, or unknown.

In truth, such conclusions of Paul's treatment of mysteries can only be made from a cursory understanding of Paul's writings and a general lack of understanding of the word *mystery* according to the

Matthew O. Richardson is associate dean of religious education at Brigham Young University.

gospel of Jesus Christ. Therefore, this chapter will consider the gospel meaning of *mystery* and then examine Paul's three gospel mysteries in Ephesians as well as other relevant contributions found in the epistle to the Ephesians.

MYSTERIES

Secular View. While we typically define a mystery as something that is hidden, inexplicable, or unknown, the common perception of mysteries seems to be more than that. For example, it seems that most people accept that a mystery is something that is not only hidden but something hidden from everyone. In other words, if something is determined to be a mystery, no one knows the answer.

Another growing secular perception is that a mystery is not simply something unknown as much as something unknowable. As a result, when something is considered mysterious, it is, at least in a sense, relegated to resolution purgatory. In other words, we can't really hope to discover an answer, for many believe that there is no answer.

Gospel View. While it is true that Paul taught that the wisdom of God is mysterious because it is a "hidden wisdom" (1 Corinthians 2:7), he did not intend to imply that God's wisdom is unknowable. In fact, considering a mystery as unknowable is in sharp contradiction to gospel doctrine, for the scriptures testify that God not only knows the answers but that He is willing to share them with us. The belief that mysteries can and will be unfolded is a rich and vital part of gospel heritage. For example, after Nebuchadnezzar sent for Daniel to interpret his dream, Daniel informed him that "there is a God in heaven that revealeth secrets" (Daniel 2:28). Nephi also testified that "the mysteries of God shall be unfolded" (1 Nephi 10:19). In fact, Nephi not only reminded us that mysteries were revealed in "times of old," but he also testified that they would be made known "in times to come" (1 Nephi 10:19). As prophesied, hundreds of years later, Paul labored to "make known the mystery of the gospel" (Ephesians 6:19), and God has continued to make known His mysteries. In 1832, for example, in a grand vision of the glories of heaven, Joseph Smith learned that the Lord will "reveal all mysteries . . . pertaining to my kingdom" (D&C 76:7).

The word mystery is translated from the Greek *mysterion,* which is also the same word typically translated as secret. Even though both words come from the same Greek origin and should therefore share the same definition, it is interesting that both words do not have the same modern connotation. A mystery, for example, is often perceived as distant, odd, or as unknowable, whereas a secret never implies that the information is unknowable. In fact, the very essence of a secret implies that knowledge is secured but that it is not yet revealed, for the bearer of the secret has decided not to disclose the information yet. This fits nicely with the literal translation of mysterion, which means "to shut the mouth."

Thus, at least textually, we know that a mystery can be known. But Paul's letter to the Ephesians did more than teach that God knows the answers even though He may not be revealing what they are. Paul taught the Ephesians that Christ had "made known unto us the mystery of his will, according to his good pleasure which he hath purposed in himself" (Ephesians 1:9). More than just knowing all things, Paul taught, as Elder Neal A. Maxwell said, that "Heavenly Father and Jesus Christ are actually giving away the secrets of the universe."[1]

Paul later teaches that it was by revelation that the mysteries were made known to him (see Ephesians 3:3; see also D&C 42:61, 65). President Harold B. Lee also connected revelation with mysteries, for he felt that a mystery "cannot be known except by revelation."[2] With this connection in mind, no wonder Jacob warned that we must not "despise . . . the revelations of God," for "no man knoweth of his ways save it be revealed unto him" (Jacob 4:8).

Another important difference between the secular and the gospel orientation of mysteries deals with who can know the secret. The secular concept that if one person does not understand the answers no one else could possibly know the answers is in opposition to the teachings of the gospel of Christ. Alma testified that "it is given unto many to know the mysteries of God" (Alma 12:9). This does not mean, however, that God will reveal all His secrets to all men. Christ, for example, taught: "Unto you it is given to know the mystery of the kingdom of God: but unto them that are without, all these things are done in parables" (Mark 4:11). Obviously then, what is mysterious to some, may not be so mysterious to others. Naturally, this provokes the question: "Why are some able to know the mysteries, while other people are left out?" The answer to this question is not a matter of discrimination but a matter of qualification and disposition.

Both Nephi and Paul testified that mysteries are unfolded by the Holy Ghost (see 1 Corinthians 2:10; 1 Nephi 10:19). This is no surprise to most theologians who believe that it is through the Spirit that all truth is revealed (see John 14:26; D&C 75:10; Moroni 10:5). Just because God unfolds His mysteries to man through the Spirit, however, does not mean that man will receive or understand the mystery. Nephi illustrated this point well when he taught that even though Lehi's dream was revealed to Laman and Lemuel, they found it difficult to understand because of the hardness of their hearts (see 1 Nephi 15:3–11). Paul described this situation well when he wrote, "The things of God knoweth no man, except he has the Spirit of God" (JST 1 Corinthians 2:11). Thus, while God reveals His mysteries through the Spirit, many cannot know that mystery unless they qualify by having the Spirit with them.

PAUL'S TEACHINGS CONCERNING MYSTERIES

"The testimony of the Holy Ghost," President Joseph Fielding Smith taught, "is Spirit speaking to spirit, and is not confined solely to the natural or physical sense."[3] Since God's ways are spiritually transmitted, they can only be "spiritually discerned." This leaves the natural man unable to understand things of a spiritual nature (see 1 Corinthians 2:14), and unless he yields to the "enticings of the Holy Spirit" he will forever remain incompatible—an adversary or enemy—with things of the Spirit (see Mosiah 3:19). In his letter to the Ephesians, Paul emphasized that we must "put off . . . the old man, which is corrupt according to the deceitful lusts . . . and . . . put on the new man, . . . created in righteousness and true holiness" (Ephesians 4:22, 24). Paul then uses much of his letter to the

Ephesians to endorse spiritual behavior which affords revelation and condemns those things that distance man from the Spirit (see Ephesians 4–5).

Unfortunately, it is difficult for natural man to yield to the enticings of the Spirit when he finds spiritual matters unattractive. For those who rely upon their natural or physical senses, it is difficult be interested in the mysteries of God because they "appeal more to the spirit" than to the flesh.[4] Even more limiting than the lack of a spiritual interest or appetite, however, is natural man's inability to comprehend the possible significance of God's ways. The Lord aptly described this clash to Isaiah when He said: "My thoughts are not your thoughts, neither are your ways my ways, saith the Lord. For as the heavens are higher than the earth, so are my ways higher than your ways, and my thoughts than your thoughts" (Isaiah 55:8–9). Since the thoughts of God are foreign to the natural man, God's ways appear to be foolish (see 1 Corinthians 2:14), and as a result man remains in the dark concerning those things of greatest importance. Since the natural man cannot discern a solution to the problem, he confidently declares that there is no solution and that no one else could possibly know what is hidden from him.

With a basic understanding of the gospel perspective dealing with mysteries, we find that Paul's view of mysteries is substantially different from most of our contemporaries, who emphasize the secular perspective. In brief, Paul believed that mysteries could be unfolded (see Colossians 1:26; 1 Corinthians 15:51) and that the Saints should not be ignorant to the mysteries of God (see Romans 11:25). With this in mind, we find Paul's labor dealing with mysteries was meant to reveal and not to obscure. Thus, the three great mysteries in the letter to the Ephesians were actually three secrets made known by revelation to the prophets. Without revelation, prophets, and the Holy Ghost, these three topics would be truly mysterious (unknowable) and would not bring the promised gospel blessings.

Unfolding the Mysteries of Ephesians

Mysteries and the Dispensation of the Fulness of Times. Paul taught that by having the "mystery of his [Christ's] will" made known unto him, "in the dispensation of the fulness of times he [Christ] might gather together in one all things, . . . both which are in heaven, and which are on earth; even in him" (Ephesians 1:9–10). With a cursory reading of these two verses, it appears that the mystery revealed to Paul (Ephesians 1:9) is the dispensation of the fulness of times (Ephesians 1:10). Thus, most students of this segment of Paul's writing focus their attention entirely on the dispensation of the fulness of times and related topics. But a careful textual study of these two verses reveals a different understanding of Paul's first mystery.

Most people in religious circles interpret *dispensation* to mean a "period of time."[5] This interpretation rivets the attention to a specified future event. While this perspective is generally correct for most discussions, it does not fit well with Paul's teachings in Ephesians. In fact, considering a dispensation to mean only a "period of time" can distract from understanding the actual point Paul was trying to make. Paul is the only biblical writer to use the term *dispensation*[6] and his treatment of the term was quite different from contemporary usage. The term *dispensation* is translated from the Greek *oikonomia,* which is the common root for our modern term *economy.* By our standards, economy is generally defined as the "management of affairs" and as such fits nicely with other earlier translations of *oikonomia,* rendered "administration" or "stewardship." By understanding the historical meaning of *dispensation,* we quickly see that Paul's emphasis was not on a period of time per se but on the economy or administration of a time. The relevance of this can only be seen with further textual investigation.

It would be wrong to assume that Paul's mystery unfolded in Ephesians 1:9–10 was merely exposing the outcomes of the fulness of times. Notice that Paul connected the mystery "made known" unto to him (Ephesians 1:9) to the *administration* of the fulness times (Ephesians 1:10) by using the conjunction *that.* The word *that,* at least in this instance, is translated from the Greek *eis,* which means "for" or "by." With this in mind, the literal translation of Ephesians 1:9–10 reads, "making known to us the mystery of the will of Him . . . *for* [the *administration*]of the fullness of the times, to head up all things in Christ, the things both in the heavens and the things on the earth; in Him."[7] Paul creates a mutual dependence between mysteries and the administration of the fulness of times. In other words, we see that mysteries are revealed for (or by) the administration so all things can be gathered in one. Without the revelation of mysteries, it is apparent that the "fulness of times" could not come to pass.

The type of administration that could bring about such unparalleled results is exposed with further review of the term *oikonomia*. The literal translation of *oikonomia* is "house-distributor" or "overseer."[8] Thus, it is by the house-distributor or overseer that the restoration and revelation of all things in the fulness of times will transpire. Throughout the history of man, prophets have been recognized as the Lord's servants and overseers.[9]

Amos taught, "Surely the Lord God will do nothing, until he revealeth the secret unto his servants the prophets" (JST Amos 3:7). As did Amos, Paul testified of the connection between mysteries and prophets. According to Paul, we understand the mystery of Christ when it is revealed unto "his holy apostles and prophets by the Spirit" (Ephesians 3:4–5). Thus, the administration that will bring about the fullness of times is through authorized stewards who manage the affairs of God's house. Through revelation, these stewards, the prophets, administer the kingdom of God on earth.

With this line of reasoning, it is more consequence than coincidence that Paul teaches the importance of prophets in Ephesians 4. The mystery of the administration of the fulness of times was revealed to Paul (Ephesians 1:9), and he understood that it was through prophets that all things would be gathered together in one (Ephesians 1:10). To further expound upon this necessary stewardship and the purpose of their administration, Paul explained: "And he gave some, apostles; and some, prophets; and some, evangelists; and some, pastors and teachers; *for* the perfecting of the saints, *for* the work of the ministry, *for* the edifying of the body of Christ" (Ephesians 4:11–12; emphasis added). By outlining the economy of the times, Paul emphasized that only through authoritative servants can the faith of the Saints be unified so they are brought to a "measure of the stature of the fulness of Christ" (Ephesians 4:13). Paul reminds us that without the administration of prophets, the Saints will be "tossed to and fro, and carried about with every wind of doctrine, by the sleight of men, and cunning craftiness, whereby they lie in wait to deceive" (Ephesians 4:14).

By revealing His secrets (mysteries) to the authorized house-stewards, God declares His word to those willing to listen and obey. Paul taught the Romans that "by the scriptures of the prophets," the mysteries are "made known to all nations for the obedience of faith" (Romans 16:25–26). Our respect and gratitude for prophets is warranted. The Prophet Joseph Smith encouraged us to "search the revelations of God; study the prophecies, and rejoice that God grants unto the world Seers and Prophets. They are they who saw the mysteries of godliness."[10] As the prophets receive revelation regarding the mysteries, it is their responsibility to reveal that which they received as allowed by God (see Alma 12:9–11). Every dispensation (period of time) that has known the fulness of Christ, even in varying degrees, has been due to the administration of the holy prophets.[11]

Surely the Saints of Ephesus looked forward to the day described as the "fulness of times." Today Saints who understand the mysteries look no further than the present day to find the fulness of Christ. In 1841 the Lord told Joseph Smith that He desired to "reveal unto my church things which have been kept hid from before the foundation of the world, things that pertain to the dispensation of the fulness of times" (D&C 124:41). The Lord's yearning to reveal His secrets (mysteries) to the prophets has not waned, for latter-day prophets continue to bring together all things in these marvelous times. Priesthood, ordinances, and doctrines have all been revealed through the prophets from the beginning of the earth and continue to be revealed in present day. Thus, it is by the administration of these times, the fulness of times, that all things have been gathered thus far and will continue to be gathered together.

The importance of Ephesians 1:9–10 is that Paul does more than announce the coming forth of a restoration of all things. He masterfully taught that mysteries are unfolded through prophets and that it is through this process that all things on earth and in heaven will be understood. Thus, through the Lord's authorized servants, mysteries are revealed that make it possible to administer the affairs of God's kingdom.

Salvation of Gentiles. Paul's weaving the mysteries, prophets, and administering the kingdom of God together was necessary to understand other topics considered as mysteries. By being "built upon the foundation of the apostles and prophets" (Ephesians 2:20), Paul taught that we "are no more strangers and foreigners, but fellowcitizens with the saints, and of the household of God" (Ephesians 2:19). This invitation to be fellow citizens included the Gentiles. Thus, Paul reminded the Ephesians that the "Gentiles should be fellowheirs, and of the same body, and partakers of his promise in Christ by the gospel" (Ephesians 3:6). Paul called the relationship of the Gentiles with the Church a "mystery of Christ" (Ephesians 3:3–6) that was "in other ages . . . not made known unto the sons of men" (Ephesians 3:5). Paul testified that this secret of the past was no longer a secret, for it was "now revealed unto his holy apostles and prophets by the Spirit" (Ephesians 3:5). Once again we see not only the connection between unfolding mysteries and revelation but the important relationship of mysteries and the dispensation (administration) of prophets and the kingdom of God.

Cornelius, a devout centurion of the Italian band, received divine direction to seek Peter in Joppa (see Acts 10:1–5). The next day, Peter received a vision where he was directed to eat unclean beasts (Acts 10:10–15), and through a series of directed events Peter, Cornelius, and other Gentiles were gathered together in Caesarea. Peter concluded: "Can any man forbid water, that these should not be baptized, which have received the Holy Ghost as well as we? And he commanded them to be baptized in the name of the Lord" (Acts 10:47–48). This event opened the door to many Gentile converts but it also created a passionate debate among the Jewish members whether the Gentiles should be fellow heirs in the gospel of Christ.

Since the missionary efforts during the mortal ministry of the Savior were restricted primarily to the Jews (see Matthew 10:5–6;

15:24), the membership of the Church was almost exclusively Jewish. After Christ's Resurrection, the scope of missionary labors changed drastically. "Go ye therefore, and teach all nations," Christ commanded His disciples, "baptizing them in the name of the Father, and of the Son, and of the Holy Ghost" (Matthew 28:19). While some of those from the other nations (Gentiles) were converted, they were only baptized after first converting to Judaism (see Acts 2:6–12). This was the accepted procedure of the time and was never really questioned or thought of as problematic until Peter encountered Cornelius, and Gentiles became part of the Church without having to first adhere to Judaic ritual. This became a difficult doctrine to accept for many members and, as a result, they struggled with new Gentile converts for they couldn't understand how a long-standing policy could be changed. Thus, Paul's doctrine concerning the Gentiles was mysterious to many.

Perhaps Paul, the self-ascribed "apostle of the Gentiles" (Romans 11:13; see also 15:16; 1 Timothy 2:7) dealt with this debate more than any other Church leader of the time. It is somewhat ironic that Paul became the champion of the Gentiles; for in his younger days, when he was known as Saul, he zealously fought against the slightest deviation from Judaic worship. Paul's mighty change and conversion was based upon revelation. It was not only his newfound testimony of truth but his testimony of the power of revelation that served Paul well throughout his life. Thus, what seemed to be mysterious to some, even within the Church, was obvious to Paul, for he understood that revelation can literally change the unchangeable. Because of this background, Paul could earnestly teach that allowing Gentiles into the fold of Christ was something that "in other ages was not made known unto the sons of men" but, at the same time, feel comfortable with changes that were "revealed unto his holy apostles and prophets by the Spirit" (Ephesians 3:5).

It was Peter, the President of the Church, who received revelation that unlocked the Gentile mystery. To those who could only see through eyes bound by tradition, pride, and prejudice, the Spirit could not speak. Thus, those who spent a lifetime defending the token of circumcision were strangled by tradition and were unable to understand newly revealed ways of God. They remained in the dark until they were willing to yield to the enticing of the Spirit and see with uncircumcised eyes. Without revelation and prophets, this doctrine regarding the Gentiles would still be mysterious. Only through God's authorized servant, Peter, was the truth revealed.

Although this mystery had particular relevance to the Saints of Paul's time, the principle is still relevant today. For example, in 1978, President Spencer W. Kimball received a revelation that allowed all worthy males to receive the priesthood. Although the priesthood was conferred according to set standards in the past, the pattern was altered according to revelation. In some ways, this event was just as mysterious as allowing Gentiles to be fellow heirs of the Church in Paul's time. At least, it was just as mysterious to some—even in the Church. But those who understood that the administration of the times recognized the prophet as one who held the keys of revelation and the mysteries were able to act in faith and move forward with confidence. Without revelation to make known the secrets of heaven, these principles would still be considered a mystery.

Marital Living and Stewardship. After speaking of the relationship between husband and wife, Paul concludes, "This is a great mystery" (Ephesians 5:32). In consideration of spiraling divorce rates, dysfunctional marriages, and even the trend to avoid marriage and family altogether, many would readily agree that understanding how to make this relationship right is indeed mysterious. When, however, one remembers that Paul's pattern concerning the three mysteries of Ephesians was to illustrate that through revelation and the administration of prophets things are made known, one finds that understanding overcomes confusion, hope endures frustration, and resolve replaces resign.

As we read Paul's treatise on marriage in Ephesians, it becomes clear that Paul was not merely giving practical marital advice for the Saints. In similar manner, President David O. McKay, who often spoke about marital issues, emphasized that happiness in marriage was only attainable through the "form of marriage which God has ordained."[12] Paul taught that divinely ordained marriage begins when a couple submits themselves "one to another in the fear of God" (Ephesians 5:21). This form of submission is more than a couple expressing their love and offering pledges of honor, devotion, and loyalty to each other. The submission Paul speaks of is a submission of a couple to each other *in* fear or reverence[13] of God. President Gordon B. Hinckley describes such an arrangement as "a contract, a compact, a union between a man and a woman under the plan of the Almighty."[14]

The Almighty's plan for marriage emphasized more than a partnership; it required a covenant relationship (see D&C 132). According to God's plan, a couple enters into a relationship that intertwines them with God Himself. This relationship is described in an unparalleled way by an Old Testament teaching: "Two are better than one" (Ecclesiastes 4:9). After extolling the benefits of a partnership (Ecclesiastes 4:9–12), God's form of marriage is succinctly taught in the metaphor of "a threefold cord" (Ecclesiastes 4:12). By weaving a husband, wife, and God together like a traditional hemp cord (rope), a couple receives power that goes beyond their abilities and forms a rope that cannot be "quickly broken" (Ecclesiastes 4:12).

According to God's ways, the marital wrapping of man, woman, and God can only be accomplished by covenants, priesthood power, and sacred ordinances. Only through revelation have the ordinances, priesthood, and covenants been revealed again to the earth. Understanding the power of priesthood covenant in marriages is mysterious to those who lack the spiritual ability to see spiritual things. As a result, many rely only on traditional marital practices. To this, however, Elder Maxwell warns: "Even when secular solutions help, such programmed scratching often goes on after the itching stops. The surf of secularism, therefore, seems so often to carry its sincere seamen against the rude reefs of reality."[15] In contrast, Elder Jeffrey R. Holland taught that those who partake in God's plan "have the most reassuring of all final promises: that power which binds us together in righteousness is greater than any force—any force—which might try to separate us." He then concludes: "That is the power of covenant theology and the power of priesthood ordinances. That is the power of the gospel of Jesus Christ."[16]

Priesthood ordinances and covenants emphasize the protocol of stewardships. Thus, it is of little wonder that Paul outlines a pattern of stewardship for his "marital mystery." He teaches that wives should submit themselves to husbands only as husbands submit themselves to Christ (Ephesians 5:22–24). With Christ as the "head," the power is found in the Savior (Ephesians 5:23) and not in gender or even assumed marital roles. If a steward oversteps the boundaries of the allotted responsibility in vain ambition, to gratify pride or exercise control, dominion, or compulsion in any degree of unrighteousness—power is withdrawn (see D&C 121:36–38). Therefore, Paul admonishes wives to love their husband *as* Christ loved the Church and that husbands should love their wives *even as* the Lord loved the Church (see Ephesians 5:25, 28–29, 33). The outcome of this style of marriage allows the partners to "sanctify and cleanse" their relationship (Ephesians 5:26–28).

It is of little wonder that such teachings are incomprehensible to those who lack spiritual insight. Through prophets, seers, and revelators, priesthood was restored and revealed to make marital covenants possible. Through living prophets, the mysteries of marriage continue to be revealed. In September 1995, for example, President Hinckley stood and proclaimed to the world that "marriage between a man and a woman is ordained of God and that the family is central to the Creator's plan."[17] While prophetic statements may seem to be overly simple to some, in reality, they dispel confusion and offer essential advice that seems to elude the masses. Prophets, seers, and revelators reveal the secrets of marriage and those who understand the connection between revelation and mysteries find wisdom and understanding "what the will of the Lord is" concerning marriage and covenants (Ephesians 5:17).

ENLIGHTENMENT THROUGH THE SPIRIT

A mystery is a truth that is only known by revelation to those authorized to receive the mysteries of the kingdom. Thus, prophets reveal the mysteries as revealed to them. Through revelation, God's ordinances, truths, doctrines, and priesthood have been revealed and continue to be revealed. Without revelation, the fulness of Christ would still be a mystery to mankind. Even though many mysteries have been revealed, some cannot understand the importance of the counsel and are indifferent to the counsel given.

Since the Spirit is required to understand the mysteries revealed through prophets, seers, and revelators, Paul admonishes the Ephesian Saints to "walk not as other Gentiles walk, in the vanity of their mind, having the understanding darkened, being alienated from the life of God through the ignorance that is in them, because of the blindness of their heart" (Ephesians 4:17–18). Because of this relationship, Paul encouraged the Saints to discern spiritual things. As we do that, we find that all truth is revealed according to God's good measure, and we find peace in our existence. Through revelation, God's secrets are unfolded. Paul testified that the Lord "shall make known to you all things . . . that he might comfort your hearts" (Ephesians 6:21–22). In this we find peace.

NOTES

1. Neal A. Maxwell, *The Neal A. Maxwell Quote Book,* ed. Cory Maxwell (Salt Lake City: Bookcraft, 1997), 222.

2. Harold B. Lee, *Ye Are the Light of the World* (Salt Lake City: Deseret Book, 1974), 211.

3. As quoted by Henry D. Moyle in Conference Report, April 1957, 34.

4. Joseph Fielding Smith, *Doctrines of Salvation,* comp. Bruce R. McConkie (Salt Lake City: Bookcraft, 1954), 1:296.

5. This seems to be especially true for Latter-day Saints and is readily apparent in most Latter-day Saint commentaries (see Bruce R. McConkie, *Mormon Doctrine* [Salt Lake City: Bookcraft, 1979], 200–202, s.v. "Dispensations").

6. See 1 Corinthians 9:17; Ephesians 1:10, 3:2; Colossians 1:25.

7. *Interlinear Greek-English New Testament,* 3d ed., Jay P. Green Sr. (Grand Rapids, Mich.: Baker Books, 1996), 590–91.

8. *Oikonomia* is derived from *oikonomos,* which means "house-distributor." A house-distributor was considered an employee with the capacity to manage the affairs of the house. It has also been interpreted to mean "overseer."

9. An excellent example of the Lord's prophet in the role of steward is in the allegory of the olive tree in Jacob 5; see also Doctrine and Covenants 1:38.

10. Joseph Smith, *Teachings of the Prophet Joseph Smith,* comp. Joseph Fielding Smith (Salt Lake City: Deseret Book, 1976), 12.

11. From a Latter-day Saint perspective, the major dispensations are known by the names of the prophetic administrators; namely, Adam, Enoch, Noah, Abraham, Moses, Jesus Christ, and Joseph Smith.

12. David O. McKay, *Gospel Ideals* (Salt Lake City: Deseret News Press, 1953), 465.

13. The Greek *fobos* lends to not merely being afraid of but respecting or reverencing God.

14. Gordon B. Hinckley, *Standing for Something* (New York: Times Books, 2000), 135.

15. Neal A. Maxwell, "Eternalism vs. Secularism," *Ensign,* October 1974, 69.

16. Jeffrey R. Holland, *However Long and Hard the Road* (Salt Lake City: Deseret Book, 1985), 110.

17. Gordon B. Hinckley, "The Family: A Proclamation to the World," *Ensign,* November 1995, 102.

10

THE SETTING AND SACRAMENT OF THE CHRISTIAN COMMUNITY

Mark D. Ellison

*I*N AN UPPER ROOM AT THE LAST SUPPER, our Lord prayed that all His followers might be one, united in love with him, with his Father, and with one another (see John 17:21–26). Then, as now, there were forces which threatened to divide them from each other, to separate brother and sister, parent and child, child of God and Heavenly Father—but Christ taught that those forces could be conquered by the love of God.

We are given a glimpse of that love in action in the New Testament Church at a time when the believers were "of one heart and of one soul" (Acts 4:32). Describing the affairs of these Saints, the book of Acts states: "Breaking bread from house to house, [they] did eat their meat with gladness and singleness of heart" (Acts 2:46). This verse draws our attention to a setting (the house) and a practice (dining together), two seemingly simple elements of the Church's activity. In fact, that setting and practice were of central importance in early Christian worship; they were the backdrop against which the

---

Mark D. Ellison is a Church Educational System coordinator in Tampa, Florida.

Saints of former days either succeeded or failed to "be one." I believe that considering the early Christian house churches and their communal dining worship will help us better understand the New Testament communities, and more fully appreciate the opportunities that are ours in our latter-day worship.

HOUSE CHURCHES

Let us first consider the household setting. In Acts we learn that the Apostles preached of Christ "in the temple, and in every house" (Acts 5:42), and we note that Saul's persecution of the Christians required him to enter "every house" (Acts 8:3). While in Jerusalem, a large company of Saints gathered to pray at the house of Mary, the mother of John Mark (see Acts 12:12). In Philippi Paul and Silas met with Church members in the house of Lydia (see Acts 16:40). The Pauline epistles refer to a "church" in the homes of Nymphas (Colossians 4:15), Philemon (Philemon 1:1–2), Priscilla (1 Corinthians 16:19) and Aquila (Romans 16:3–5).[1] The original concept of "church" (*ekklēsia* in Greek) was not of a *building* but of an *assembly* of people who had been called together.[2]

The *place* of assembly was not as important as its *purpose*. Long before Christians began to build specially constructed church buildings, they assembled to worship in ordinary homes. Noting the significant role those homes played in the apostolic age, one observer wrote: "Even when contact with the Jerusalem Temple and Jewish synagogues was still maintained, it was nevertheless the household which served as the new and vital center for social networks, worship, interprovincial communication, recruitment, baptizing and instruction in the faith, the hosting of traveling missionaries, and the material support essential to the sustenance and growth of the movement across the Roman Empire."[3]

Why did the early Saints use their houses for these activities? It may be simply that since the young Church was poor (see 1 Corinthians 1:26–28), it could not afford a building program; all its resources had to be devoted to caring for its members and accomplishing the apostolic commission to "teach all nations" (Matthew 28:19). Perhaps, too, building permanent edifices was seen as unnecessary in an age when Apostles foresaw apostasy and the Church's eventual retreat into the wilderness (see 2 Thessalonians 2:1–3; Revelation 12:6).[4]

Meeting in houses may also have given the Saints some protection from public persecution. "Christianity in the first century A.D., and for long afterwards, did not have the status of a recognized religion," notes Jerome Murphy-O'Connor, "so there was no question of a public meeting-place, such as the Jewish synagogue. Hence, use had to be made of the only facilities available, namely, the dwellings of families that had become Christian."[5]

Along with all these considerations, there is one more: homes were especially well suited to accommodate the worship service which included the sacrament of the Lord's Supper. For many years, the earliest Saints would partake of the sacrament while sharing a common meal in the homes of fellow Church members.[6]

In time some of the houses which hosted Christian assemblies were renovated and used exclusively for worship. Remains of a few of these "house churches" (*domus ecclesiae*) have been excavated, helping us to visualize the physical worship setting of the early Church.

1. *The House of St. Peter.* Capernaum on the northwest shore of the Sea of Galilee became Jesus' "own city" after he was rejected in Nazareth (Matthew 9:1). Beneath the remains of the fifth-century octagonal church that can be seen there today are the remains of a house built around 100 B.C., which was converted into a church in the latter part of the first century A.D. This first-century house church has been described by archaeologists as "one of the highlights of Christian archaeology in Israel,"[7] and "the oldest Christian sanctuary unearthed anywhere."[8]

At the time of Jesus, before it was converted into a church, the house was a simple structure: two abutting rooms set in a courtyard with walls made of field stones plastered with mud and a roof made of wooden beams, thatch, and mud. In homes like this one, "the simple peasant life of a Galilean family centered around the courtyard, where children played, livestock were kept, and family members worked and ate."[9]

This dwelling may very well have been the "house of Simon and Andrew" mentioned in the Gospels—the place where Jesus healed Peter's mother-in-law, who then appreciatively waited on the Master and His disciples at a meal (see Matthew 8:14–15; Mark 1:29–31; Luke 4:38–39). People sometimes crowded the house of Peter as they brought loved ones who were sick or possessed to Jesus to be healed (see Mark 1:32–34). On one occasion some people even tore through the roof of a house, possibly this house, so they could lower a paralyzed friend down to the Master inside (see Mark 2:1–12). The house of Peter may also have been the private place where, at a quieter time, Jesus instructed His disciples about the meaning of parables and the doctrines of the kingdom (see Mark 4:10–11).

Thus, the house seems to be associated with Jesus' teaching, His power to transform and to heal, and His joyful practice of mealtime fellowship. It is understandable that later Christians would want to remember and venerate the site.

The site's excavator, Virgilio Corbo, states that "after the resurrection, the Jewish-Christian community at Capernaum began using the house as a meeting place."[10] His findings indicate that the house was remodeled later in the first century to be used exclusively for worship. The two rooms were joined, forming a single, nearly square room measuring about seven meters on each side, suggesting that it could have accommodated around twenty people at a time. The rough stone walls of the main room were strengthened, coated with fine plaster, and painted with Jewish-Christian symbols. Thousands of fragments of this plaster were discovered during excavation, including more than a hundred featuring graffiti-like inscriptions in Greek, Aramaic, Syriac, and Latin.

Many of the inscriptions are of a Christian character (references to Jesus as Lord and Christ, and possible references to Peter), indicating that the house church became a pilgrimage destination, receiving visitors from a wide area of the Roman empire. The pilgrim Egeria wrote of her late fourth-century visit there: "Moreover, in Capernaum the house of the *prince of the apostles* has been made into a church, with its original walls still standing."[11] Similar to the way we Latter-day Saints regard the Sacred Grove as "hallowed ground,"[12] this site was greatly revered by Christians from the first century forward, and apparently for the same reason: the Lord had been there.

2. *The House Church at Dura-Europos.* Like the house at Capernaum, a house at Dura-Europos in eastern Syria served as a meeting place for a Christian community.[13] Built in the late second century or early third century, the house featured eight rooms around a central courtyard—much larger and more elegant than the house of Peter. It was converted into a *domus ecclesia* some time before the middle of the third century, apparently to meet the needs of a growing congregation. The courtyard was tiled and benches were installed against the courtyard walls, perhaps indicating that their meetings overflowed into the courtyard.

A small corner room was converted to a canopied baptistery and was decorated with stars and biblical scenes, central among them a depiction of Christ as the Good Shepherd, standing over a flock of sheep and carrying a sheep on His shoulders (see Luke 15:4–7; John 10:1–18). Its prominence in the baptistery suggests that, to the Christians who built it, being baptized signified the creation of a relationship with Christ and being brought into the fold of a caring community.[14] Jesus had never been there personally—Dura was not Capernaum—yet for the sincere who remembered him, the Good Shepherd was there in this sense, and they too felt part of the fold.

How large would that fold have been? A long hall which could have accommodated 65 to 75 people was created when a wall between two of the rooms was removed in the conversion from house to church. A small podium was installed at the east end of this long room, presumably to make an officiator more visible when standing before the congregation. Though the archaeological remains cannot tell us exactly how the Christians here observed the Lord's Supper, Justin Martyr offers an instructive, late second-century description of Sunday sacrament worship. By his day, the congregation did not sit or recline together to eat a meal, but stood to receive only the bread and cup; there were no longer Apostles, but only their "memoirs." There were still efforts to maintain a sense of community:

"All who live in cities or in the country gather together to one place, and the memoirs of the apostles or the writings of the prophets are read, as long as time permits; then, when the reader has ceased, the president verbally instructs, and exhorts to the imitation of these good things. Then we all rise together and pray, and, as we before said, when our prayer is ended, bread and wine and water are brought, and the president in like manner offers prayers and thanksgivings, according to his ability, and the people assent, saying Amen; and there is a distribution to each, and a participation of that over which thanks have been given, and to those who are absent a portion is sent by the deacons."[15]

3. *Other Possible House Churches.* On Mount Zion in Jerusalem, traces of an earlier structure can be seen incorporated into the Crusader Church of St. Mary. Tradition associates the site with the "Upper Room" where the Apostles were gathered when the Spirit was poured out on the day of Pentecost (see Acts 1:9–14; 2:1–8). The various layers of the building's floors indicate that its foundations do date back to Roman times, and so it may be that a well-to-do first-century disciple donated his or her house as a meeting place (see Acts 2:44–45). The evidence available, however, has not been sufficient to create consensus on this.[16] In addition to this site and the others mentioned, there are possible indications of early house churches in Rome and Egypt.[17]

How did meeting in houses like these affect the Church's sense of community? The arrangement had both benefits and detriments.

One of the disadvantages was that a household congregation could accommodate only limited growth; once it surpassed the house's relatively small capacity, another congregation would have to be formed elsewhere. Quite often this would have resulted in there being many small congregations within the same city. While this circumstance would have permitted members in each house church to know each other well, it also carried the potential for a lack of unity between the various congregations.

False teachings and inappropriate practices which sprang up were difficult to manage.[18] This is suggested in 2 John, which warns a Christian community not to receive heretical teachers into their house (2 John 1:10), and possibly also in Titus, with the reference to "vain talkers and deceivers" who "subvert whole houses" (Titus 1:10–11).

The house church setting may also help explain the difficulty mentioned in 3 John: "I wrote unto the church: but Diotrephes, who loveth to have the preeminence among them, receiveth us not . . . neither doth he himself receive the brethren, and forbiddeth them that would, and casteth them out of the church" (3 John 1:9–10). Diotrephes appears to have been the patron of a household congregation who did not want Church leaders to interfere in the meetings and meals he hosted in his own home; he rebelled against the leadership of John, Gaius, and the other brethren of his locality.[19] All these difficulties were among the problems which would ultimately lead to general apostasy (see D&C 64:8).

But for the faithful, assembling in houses had great advantages. The intimate, domestic setting would have contributed to a familial sense within the congregation.[20] Certainly family life was important in the young Church, as is evident from epistles containing instructions for husbands, wives, fathers, children, servants, and masters (see Ephesians 5:19–6:9; Colossians 3:12–4:6; 1 Timothy 3:2–12; Titus 2:2–10). In an early study of house churches, Floyd V. Filson observes:

"It must not be forgotten that both in Jewish and Gentile life religious observance had been largely centered in the home. Moreover, on many occasions entire households, including, no doubt, slaves in some instances, came into the church as a unit (cf. Acts 16:32–33). . . . The need for making the faith work in daily home life must have been greatly intensified by the almost complete concentration of Christian life, fellowship, and worship in the home."[21]

Notice how many New Testament passages employ household language. In several instances the epistles equate the "church of God" with the "house of God" (see 1 Timothy 3:15; Hebrews 3:6; 1 Peter 2:5). The term *house* can indicate either a structure or the people who inhabit it—a household—and the early Church understood itself to be a new kind of "family."[22] Jesus had taught His disciples that they were His brothers and sisters, God's children, and would have a place in His Father's "house" (Mark 3:34–35; Matthew 18:3; John 14:2–3). Paul taught that the Saints were brothers and sisters *(adelphoi)*, "children of God" who had "received the Spirit of adoption"; Jesus' Father was their Father; they were "heirs of God, and joint-heirs with Christ" (Romans 8:14–17; see 2 Corinthians 6:18; Galatians 4:5–7; Philippians 2:15; Hebrews 12:5–9). Among the Christians, an elderly man was to be treated "as a father; . . . the younger men as brethren; the elder women as mothers; the younger as sisters, with all purity" (1 Timothy 5:1–2). Philemon was to accept and forgive a servant who had run away, for as a fellow believer, the servant was now "a brother beloved" (Philemon 1:16).[23] We see that the family *setting* of Christian assembly corresponds to the use of familial *imagery* to illustrate the Saints' relationship with God and with one another.

The idea that the covenant people are a "family" did not originate with the house churches (see Malachi 2:10; Mosiah 5:7; Moses 6:68), but it did seem to find reinforcement in that setting. In a study of the early Christian congregations, Robert Banks conjectures that "the practical necessity for [meeting in houses] blended with a further, theologically based consideration. For, given the family character of the Christian community, the homes of its members provided the most conducive atmosphere in which they could give expression to the bond they had in common."[24] And indeed, one of the most important ways they gave expression to their common bond was through the Lord's Supper—a worship service which, like the worship setting, affirmed their relationship with their Father in Heaven as well as with their brothers and sisters.

THE LORD'S SUPPER

The sacrament was instituted at the Last Supper (see Mark 14:22–25; Matthew 26:26–29, Luke 22:19–20; 1 Corinthians 11:23–25) and for many years continued to be observed in a mealtime setting. These meals were communal dinners shared by the assembled congregation. Acts tells us that the Saints in Jerusalem "had all things common" (Acts 4:32), including their food (Acts

6:1–2).[25] Jude mentions that the saints held "feasts of charity," or *agape* meals, using the Greek word which signified Christian love and came to denote also the common meal in which that love was affirmed (Jude 1:12). An *agape* meal was "a fellowship meal which was a principal occasion for charity to the poorer members of the church."[26] At an *agape* feast which included the sacrament, the bread and wine were usually blessed and distributed at the end of the meal.[27]

One of the most important details in our scriptures about the early Christian sacrament is that the Saints partook "in remembrance" of Jesus (1 Corinthians 11:23–26; JST Matthew 26:22–25; JST Mark 14:20–25; Luke 22:19–20). To appreciate what that "remembrance" would have involved, it is helpful to consider some of the cultural and religious connotations associated with meals in ancient Israel and how they figured in the Lord's mortal ministry:

1. *Fellowship and Reconciliation.* In the culture of the Near East, "meals were much more than occasions for satisfying hunger, for it was understood that persons who ate and drank together were bound to one another by friendship and mutual obligation."[28] James D. G. Dunn explains, "For the oriental, table-fellowship was a guarantee of peace, trust, brotherhood; it meant in a very real sense a sharing of one's life."[29] Since sharing a meal affirmed fellowship, peace, and unity between those who participated, meals could serve to reconcile people who had been estranged from each other (see Genesis 43:32; 45:11; Psalm 23:5; Luke 15:23–24; JST Matthew 7:9).

The Gospels record that during His mortal ministry, the Savior shared many significant meals with His disciples and others.[30] The practice drew criticism from some who did not approve of the company Jesus kept: "This man receiveth sinners, and eateth with them" (Luke 15:2; cf Matthew 11:19; Luke 5:33). The Savior's response, couched in the story of the prodigal whose father celebrated his son's return with a feast, testified that those who were lost could return to God and be welcomed back as beloved children (see Luke 15:11–24; see Mark 2:17; Matthew 9:12–13, Luke 5:31–32).[31] Dining with people was part of the Lord's way of extending an invitation to repent, enter into fellowship with Him, and to be

reconciled to God through Him.[32] A vivid example is the dinner
Jesus shared with Zacchaeus, the chief publican in Jericho (see
Luke 19:2–10). Publicans—Jews who collected taxes for the Roman
government—were looked upon with contempt and excommunicated from the synagogue.[33] For Jesus to dine with this man and tell
him, "This day is salvation come to this house" (Luke 19:9), communicated the dramatic message that in Christ even the despised
and ostracized, along with their loved ones, could be restored to
blessed fellowship with God.

2. *Solemn Covenant.* In the Near East, promises made with the
sharing of food were considered solemn, binding vows (see Genesis
24:54; 26:26–31; 31:46, 54; Joshua 9:3–20; 2 Samuel 3:12–21).[34] The
good news communicated by the Lord's table fellowship is therefore made all the more dramatic. Further, it is amazing to consider
the multitude of profound promises Jesus made to His disciples at
the Last Supper, the occasion when he instituted the sacrament. He
taught them His impending suffering and death would be a ransom
for them (see JST Matthew 26:22–29; Mark 14:22–25; Luke
22:19–20). The Father would send the Spirit of truth, the
Comforter, which would abide with them forever, bring all of Jesus'
teachings to their remembrance, guide them into all truth, and show
them things to come (see John 14:16–17, 26; 15:26; 16:13–14). They
would experience the love of the Father, and the Father and Son
would make their abode with them—a moving image of intimate,
spiritual fellowship (see John 14:23; Revelation 3:20). Jesus' followers would abide, or dwell, in God's love (see John 15:10; 17:26).
They would experience godly peace (see John 14:27). Their prayers
in the name of Christ would be answered (see John 15:7; 16:23–24).
Their sorrow would be turned to a joy that no man could take from
them (see John 16:20, 22). They would become one—united with
each other as the Father and the Son are with each other (see John
17:11, 21–22). Christ would be in them; they would be drawn
towards perfection by the Son of God sharing His spiritual life and
love with them (see John 17:23–26).

3. *Commemoration.* Feasts in ancient Israel often served to help
the children of Israel remember what God had done for them (see

Exodus 12:14, 25–27). The biblical concept of "remembering" (Greek *anamnesis,* Hebrew *zakar*) entails more than might be apparent to a modern Western reader. To the Jews, *remembering* the exodus story at Passover was not merely *recalling* it, but in a sense *re-experiencing* it. As Lee Humphreys explains, the "words accompanied by actions, stories by ritual, bridged the gap between past and present; and the sacred stories were relived as defining life and community in the present."[35]

At Passover families gathered and literally tasted the bitterness of bondage; they ate the pascal lamb and affirmed deliverance from the angel of death by virtue of the blood of the Lamb. It was not just a matter of recalling that the Lord had once delivered their fathers; by participating in the ritual meal, they too were the delivered ones! No matter where they lived or how many years had passed since the exodus, the faithful at Passover were as much God's covenant people as the Israelites who had first camped at Sinai. The English word *remember* is especially fitting because, as Humphreys points out, "in reexperiencing the Moses-Sinai . . . story in this special way Israel was 're-membered' as the individual affirmed her or his membership in that community."[36]

4. *Messianic Anticipation.* Israelite feasts were so joyous and sacred that they came to symbolize the rejoicing, peace, and fellowship that the righteous would share with God when the Messiah would come. Thus the feasts both *looked back,* serving to memorialize and renew the covenant between God and Israel (such as at Passover), and *looked forward* with anticipation to the messianic "feast of fat things" to be enjoyed in the age to come (see Isaiah 25:6–8; 29:8; 55:2; 65:13; Zephaniah 1:7). Jesus drew upon this imagery several times in His teaching. The parables of the ten virgins (Matthew 25:1–13), the marriage of the king's son (Matthew 22:2–10) and the great supper (Luke 14:16–24) are centered around feasts symbolizing the future messianic age. He promised the Apostles that their role in the "feast" to come would be to "eat and drink at my table in my kingdom, and sit on thrones judging the twelve tribes of Israel" (Luke 22:30).

All these meal-related connotations convey great significance to the early Christian observance of the Lord's Supper. The Saints ate as "partakers of the Lord's table" (1 Corinthians 10:21). They, like those to whom the Lord had ministered personally, partook of the promises of the new covenant and experienced the reconciliation, forgiveness, and fellowship with God made possible by the Atonement: "The cup of blessing which we bless, is it not the communion [*koinōnia*, or 'intimate fellowship'] of the blood of Christ? The bread which we break, is it not the communion of the body of Christ?" (1 Corinthians 10:16). They both *looked back* in memory of the Savior: "Christ our passover is sacrificed for us" (1 Corinthians 5:7)—and *looked forward* to His future return: "As often as ye eat this bread, and drink this cup, ye do shew the Lord's death till he come" (1 Corinthians 11:26).

In a touching, personal passage, Paul revealed part of what it meant to "show" (*kataggello*, or "proclaim") the Lord's death—there was, he taught, a sense in which the believer *participated* in the Lord's death and victorious Resurrection: "I am crucified with Christ: nevertheless I live; yet not I, but Christ liveth in me: and the life which I now live in the flesh I live by the faith of the Son of God, who loved me, and gave himself for me" (Galatians 2:20; see Romans 6:3–11).[37] The man he used to be was dead; his new life was in Christ and this reality was part of what was proclaimed by all believers every time they ate the bread and drank of the cup. Like the reenactment of the Passover, partaking "in remembrance" of Jesus in this very personal way applied the Lord's miraculous Atonement—including aspects of His death and His life—to each member's own personal life.

Since the whole community of Saints participated in the Lord's Supper, the ordinance also affirmed a very real bond between all members of the family of believers. This is an important subject in one of Paul's letters to the Corinthian Saints. The Apostle wrote to rebuke the Corinthians for breaking into contentious factions, and to admonish them to be united (see 1 Corinthians 1:10–13). The divisions were especially manifested at their common meals. Paul wrote:

"Now in this that I declare unto you I praise you not, that ye come together not for the better, but for the worse.

"For first of all, when ye come together in the church, I hear that there be divisions among you; and I partly believe it. . . .

"When ye come together therefore into one place, this is not to eat the Lord's supper" (1 Corinthians 11:17–18, 20).

The Joseph Smith Translation changes the final statement into a question: "When ye come together into one place, is it not to eat the Lord's supper?" (JST 1 Corinthians 11:20). Something the Corinthians were doing in their meetings created "divisions"; they were overlooking the real reason for assembling together. The New Revised Standard Version renders Paul's words:

"When you come together, it is not really to eat the Lord's supper.

"For when the time comes to eat, each of you goes ahead with your own supper, and one goes hungry and another becomes drunk" (1 Corinthians 11:20–21).

Apparently, when the members would gather at a host home, bringing with them their food to contribute to the common meal (like a modern-day potluck dinner), they would begin to eat before some of the poorer members could arrive. The latecomers—slaves and others of poorer classes—would arrive in time for the bread and cup, but having missed the main meal they would leave hungry, while others were full (1 Corinthians 11:21).[38]

To Paul, conducting the Lord's Supper in this way was an abuse of the practice, violating the very truths which the sacrament was supposed to affirm. The Christian community, like Israel of old, was to eat the same spiritual food and drink the same spiritual drink (see 1 Corinthians 10:3–4). Partaking of the same bread symbolized that they all were "one body" (1 Corinthians 10:17).[39] Therefore, participating in the sacrament affirmed a "communion" not only with the Lord but also with every other participant in that sacred service (see 1 Corinthians 10:16). They all were "brought together into covenant community."[40]

As they partook they were to be mindful of the Lord's "body," meaning both the *mortal body* of Christ and also *the body of the Church:*

"There should be no schism in the body; but . . . the members should have the same care one for another.

"And whether one member suffer, all the members suffer with it; or one member be honoured, all the members rejoice with it" (1 Corinthians 12:25–26).

The result of the Corinthians' failure to have this kind of care for each other was that their worship was "not for the better, but for the worse"; their common meals were not *really* the Lord's Supper (1 Corinthians 11:17, 20).

Paul's counsel to the Corinthians was to wait for one another when they came together to eat, and (if they thought waiting might be too difficult) to eat something at their own homes before going to the service (see 1 Corinthians 11:33–34). As it was, their abuses of the sacrament were bringing them under condemnation (see 1 Corinthians 11:29–34); it would be preferable, Paul hints, to sever the common meal from the sacrament of the bread and wine, rather than to continue neglecting some members (see 1 Corinthians 11:22).

Corinth was not the only place with problems observing the Lord's Supper. Writing some time after Paul, Jude mentions "spots," or blemishes, which mar the "feasts of charity." Some participants were unruly and looked after themselves only. They were spiritually "dead," like "clouds . . . without water" or "trees . . . without fruit" (Jude 1:12). Greco-Roman religious feasts were somewhat notorious for the raucous, immoral behavior and self-interested contention they sometimes featured; these problems seem to have been brought into the Christian meal setting by some members.[41] It is conceivable that because of abuses like these, partaking of the bread and wine was separated from the *agape* meal in the second century. In the fourth century the common meals were forbidden, as was the observance of the sacrament in houses.[42] Much of the original understanding of the sacrament was lost.

OUR LATTER-DAY WORSHIP

In what we have observed of the early Christian worship service and setting, there is great meaning for us as Latter-day Saints, both individually and collectively. We are reminded that the organization of the restored Church and the first sacrament meeting in the latter-day dispensation took place in a humble farmhouse in Fayette, New York. The Lord began this dispensation where the last had left off.

Since that time, growth and change in the Church—including direction about such matters as where we meet and how we administer the sacrament—have come under the guidance of the Lord, through His living Apostles, as it had in the New Testament Church. In former days, the divine commission was primarily to spread the gospel throughout the world (see Matthew 28:19–20); in the latter days, that same commission was accompanied by callings to gather and build (see D&C 29:7; 37; 88:119; 95; 138:53–54). Though the apostolic age of the early Church was tragically short-lived, today it dramatically goes on. Though our circumstances are different, some things remain the same. We continue to be vitally interested in family life and in making the faith work in our homes. Both at home with our immediate family, as well as at the meetinghouse with those whom we rightly call our "ward family," we strive to make real the ideals of love and community. Of this aspiration Elder Robert D. Hales has taught:

"[We each belong to a] ward family made up of adults, youth, and children—individual brothers and sisters—caring for and strengthening one another. . . .

"We all belong to a community of Saints . . . , we all need each other, and we are all working toward the same goal. Any one of us could isolate ourselves from this ward family on the basis of our differences. But we must not shut ourselves out or isolate ourselves from opportunities because of the differences we perceive in ourselves. Instead, let us share our gifts and talents with others, bringing brightness of hope and joy to them, and in so doing lift our own spirits."[43]

The Church still is not primarily a building; it is all of us—the *ekklēsia*—the assembly of Saints. Wherever we meet, be it farmhouse or stake center, tabernacle or temple, even when only two or three of us gather in Jesus' name, our Lord is there with us in our very midst (see Matthew 18:20; D&C 6:32). As we "break bread" week to week, we have the obligation to partake thoughtfully,

mindful of "the body"—our Lord Himself, and His family of followers. Is there someone in my ward who is in need, who hungers?
In the spirit of love and community, I should seek to wait upon that
brother or sister. In every sacrament meeting around the world, the
body of Christ is "re-membered" as individual Saints reaffirm the
baptismal covenant by which they became members of that body:
"Bear one another's burdens, that they may be light . . . mourn with
those that mourn; yea, and comfort those that stand in need of
comfort, and . . . stand as witnesses of God" (Mosiah 18:8–9). And
because of that, no matter where we live or how many years have
passed since the days of Peter and Paul, the ordinary, faithful
Latter-day Saints at home and at church are as much God's
covenant people as those early disciples who sat with the Savior in
the upper room.

"We no longer include a supper with this ordinance," said Elder
Jeffrey R. Holland, "but it is a feast nevertheless. We can be fortified by it for whatever life requires of us."[44] Elder Holland suggests
that the sacrament can be a deeply personal moment of worship,
akin to how the ancients worshiped "in remembrance":

"This particular ordinance with all its symbolism and imagery
comes to us more readily and more repeatedly than any other in our
life. It comes in what has been called 'the *most sacred*, the *most
holy*, of all the meetings of the Church.' . . . Perhaps we do not
always attach that kind of meaning to our weekly sacramental service. How 'sacred' and how 'holy' is it? Do we see it as *our* passover,
remembrance of *our* safety and deliverance and redemption? With
so very much at stake, this ordinance commemorating our escape
from the angel of darkness should be taken more seriously than it
sometimes is. It should be a powerful, reverent, reflective
moment."[45]

Like a dinner host, the Lord brings us to His house and there
shares with us His sustenance, His nourishment, His life. We sit as
invited guests at His table.[46] In the token meal of the bread and the
cup is His offer of friendship and fellowship, renewal and redemption—just as it was offered to His followers anciently.

If in some way we have become estranged from Him, this

supper, if we are prepared, is an opportunity for reconciliation, a time when we can plea, "Father, open thy house that I may come in and sup with thee," and when He can respond, "Come in, my son; for mine is thine, and thine is mine" (JST Matthew 7:17). When we partake with faith, we may partake of all the blessings of the meal: the fellowship, the acceptance, the reconciliation, the friendship, the peace. We may leave the sacrament meeting with the same blessing the Lord gave His disciples at the Last Supper: "Peace I leave with you, my peace I give unto you: not as the world giveth, give I unto you. Let not your heart be troubled, neither let it be afraid" (John 14:27). Thus reassured, we can go forth from the house, as individuals and as a community, "with gladness and singleness of heart" (Acts 2:46).

NOTES

1. Paul may allude to other house congregations when he mentions "them which are of the house of Chloe" (1 Corinthians 1:11), sends greetings from his host "Gaius . . . and of the whole church" (Romans 16:23), and commends the patron Phebe, who has hosted many people as "a servant of the church which is at Cenchrea" (Romans 16:1–2). See also Richard D. Draper, "New Light on Paul's Teachings," *Ensign*, September 1999, 22–24: "As the Apostle Paul closed his epistle, he sent his salutation to 'them which are of Aristobulus' household' and requested that his reader 'greet them that be of the household of Narcissus, which are in the Lord' [Romans 16:10–11]. The JST changes 'household' in each instance to *church* (JST Romans 16:10–11, footnotes 10*a*, 11*a*). So while the KJV suggests Paul was writing to individual families, the JST shows he is writing to leaders of local church units. As the early Church spread, meetings were held in members' homes. The Apostles assigned leaders to these 'house-churches' to guide and teach the people and to administer to their needs. The JST makes it clear that Paul was addressing these local leaders and their congregations, not just their families."

2. Stephen E. Robinson, "Warring against the Saints of God," *Ensign*, January 1988, 34: "The word *church* (Hebrew *qahal* or *edah;* Greek *ekklesia*) had a slightly broader meaning anciently than it does now. It referred to an assembly, congregation, or association of people who bonded together and shared the same loyalties. Thus, the term was not necessarily restricted to religious associations; in fact, in Athens the Greeks used the term to denote the legislative assembly of government. Originally the term *ekklesia,* formed from two words meaning *call* and *out,* referred to those citizens whom heralds called out or summoned to public

meetings. Thus, it was an ideal word to represent the body of individuals whom God 'calls out' of the world through the Holy Ghost." See also Charles Muldowney, "I Have a Question," *Ensign,* August 1993, 52.

3. John H. Elliot, "Philemon and House Churches," *Bible Today* 22 (May 1984): 147.

4. Significantly, it was not until the fourth century, when Christianity became an official religion under the emperor Constantine, that the tradition of building large, monumental basilicas began. They were buildings of a radically different type from any previous Christian house church. It may be that the new design was intended to facilitate an imperial-style processional of the bishop and clergy (suggested by James Riley Strange, "Christianity: The Fourth Century Basilica," publication pending, in author's possession).

5. Jerome Murphy-O'Connor, "House Churches and the Eucharist," *Bible Today* 22 (January 1984): 33.

6. David Noel Freedman, ed., *The Anchor Bible Dictionary* (New York: Doubleday, 1992), 1:90, s.v. "Agape Meal."

7. Virgilio Corbo, "The Church of the House of St. Peter at Capernaum," in *Ancient Churches Revealed,* ed. Yoram Tsafir (Jerusalem: Israel Exploration Society, 1993): 71.

8. Eric M. Meyers and James F. Strange, *Archaeology, The Rabbis, and Early Christianity* (Nashville, Tenn.: Abingdon, 1981): 130. The house's late first-century renovation suggests that, contrary to Josephus' claims, not all Christians fled to Pella in Transjordan incident to the first Jewish revolt—there were Christians in Galilee, too. "It is reasonable to expect that many [Christians] simply fled northward with their fellow Jews to sink new roots in the historical locus of a major part of Jesus' ministry," ibid., 32.

9. John Dominic Crossan and Jonathan L. Reed, *Excavating Jesus: Beneath the Stones, Behind the Texts* (San Francisco: Harper Collins, 2001), 126.

10. Corbo, *"The Church of the House,"* 71.

11. John Wilkinson, *Egeria's Travels* (London: SPCK, 1971), 194, as cited in Meyers and Strange, *Archaeology, The Rabbis, and Early Christianity,* 185n. In the fourth century, an insula was built around the house-church, the room was enlarged and re-plastered, and the roof was reinforced with an arch. This renovation is the church Egeria would have seen.

12. Gordon B. Hinckley, "Find the Lambs, Feed the Sheep," *Ensign,* May 1999, 110: "The vision that occurred in the Sacred Grove was just as Joseph said it was. We are building a new temple overlooking this hallowed ground to further testify to the reality of this most sacred event."

13. See Carl H. Kraeling, *The Christian Building* (New Haven, Connecticut: Dura-Europos Publications, 1967).

14. Graydon F. Snyder, *Ante Pacem: Archaeological Evidence of Church Life Before Constantine* (Macon, Ga: Mercer University Press, 1985), 23–24. Kraeling, 182: The Good Shepherd was "a symbol which betokened the creation and existence of a personal relation between their Lord and themselves."

15. Justin Martyr, First Apology, 1.67, in Alexander Roberts and James Donaldson, eds., *The Ante-Nicene Fathers: Translation of the Writings of the Fathers Down to A.D. 325* (Grand Rapids, Mich.: 1950–57), 1:186.

16. See Jerome Murphy-O'Connor, *The Holy Land: An Oxford Archaeological Guide from Earliest Times to 1700*, 4th ed., rev. and expanded (New York: Oxford University Press, 1998), 104–106; *contra* Bargil Pixner, "Church of the Apostles Found on Mt. Zion," *Biblical Archaeology Review* 16, no. 3 (May–June 1990): 16–35, 60.

17. In Rome, the original structure at the Church of Saints *Giovanni e Paulo* was a single room, which served as the church edifice until near the end of the third century, when a larger structure was built; in Egypt, street lists indicate that some homes there were used as churches: Snyder, 166. Beneath the church of Saint Clement in Rome are the remains of a house believed by some to date to the first century, perhaps the house of Clement of Rome: Floyd V. Filson, "The Significance of the Early House Churches," *Journal of Biblical Literature* 58 (1939): 107; but see the opposing opinion in Snyder, *Ante Pacem*, 76–77. See also Joan M. Peterson, "House-Churches in Rome," *Vigiliae Christianae* 23 (1969): 264–72.

18. Jerome Murphy-O'Connor, "House Churches and the Eucharist," 36: "While such sub-groups would have tended to foster an intimate family-type atmosphere, they would also have tended to promote divisions within the wider city community. It seems likely that the various groups mentioned by Paul . . . would regularly have met separately. Such relative isolation would have meant that each group had a chance to develop its own theology, and virtually ensured that it took good root before being confronted by other opinions."

19. As suggested by Bart D. Ehrman, *The New Testament: A Historical Introduction to the Early Christian Writings* (New York: Oxford University Press, 1997), 162.

20. Snyder, *Ante Pacem*, 166: Christian art and archaeology before Constantine presents a "picture of the Christians as a democratic, close-knit group. People found in the new faith community a place of deliverance and peace."

21. Filson, *Journal of Biblical Literature*, 109–10. See also Carolyn Osiek and David L. Balch, *Families in the New Testament World: Households and House Churches* (Louisville, Ky.: Westminster John Knox Press, 1997).

22. An example is the well-known verse, "Choose you this day whom ye will serve; . . . but as for me and my house, we will serve the Lord" (Joshua 24:15).

James D. G. Dunn, *Unity and Diversity in the New Testament: An Inquiry into the Character of Earliest Christianity,* 2ⁿᵈ ed. (Valley Forge, Penn.: Trinity Press International, 1990), 104–5: "Jesus thought of his disciples as a family (Mark 3:34f); the disciples were those who had converted and become as little children, members of God's family as well as sharers in his kingdom (Matthew 18:3)."

23. See Elliot, *The Bible Today,* 145–50.

24. Robert Banks, *Paul's Idea of Community,* rev. ed. (Peabody, Massachusetts: Hendrickson, 1994), 57. This is one example of how "Physical space and social structures reflect each other and interact with each other in complicated ways," Osiek and Balch, 36. See also Leslie J. Hoppe, *The Synagogues and Churches of Ancient Palestine,* (Collegeville, Minnesota: The Liturgical Press, 1994), 60: "The early communities did not have the economic resources, the organizational structure, or even the need to develop a distinctive Christian architecture. They met where convenient. But . . . because of the nature of [their distinctive] gatherings, they were held in the homes of believers. The core of the service was a meal and, consequently, the place of meeting needed to be able to accommodate a number of people for 'dinner.'"

25. The Greek *diakonia* "ministration" can refer to serving food (Acts 6:1; compare Mark 1:31). Note also the Apostles' reference to serving tables (see Acts 6:2). See Freedman, *The Anchor Bible Dictionary,* 1:91.

26. Freedman, *The Anchor Bible Dictionary,* 1:90.

27. Freedman, *The Anchor Bible Dictionary,* 4:363. Note, however, that the tradition Paul received was that the Lord had broken the bread before the meal, and offered the wine after it (1 Corinthians 11:24–25). Further, the late first-century *Didache* suggests that "the Eucharist" preceded the meal, and that the wine was blessed before the loaf of bread (*Didache* 9–10). All this suggests, among other things, that the *agape* and the sacrament of the bread and wine were not clearly distinguished from each other at first: the terms "agape" and "eucharist" are used interchangeably into the second century. Pliny the Younger, however, writes at the start of the second century of two daily Christian gatherings for meals, one in the morning and a different, more ordinary one, in the evening. See Freedman, in *The Anchor Bible Dictionary,* 1:90–91.

28. Paul J. Achtemeier, et al., ed., *The Harper Collins Bible Dictionary* (San Francisco: Harper Collins, 1985), 616.

29. Dunn, *Unity and Diversity in the New Testament: An Inquiry into the Character of Earliest Christianity,* 162. Also Louis F. Hartman, trans., *Encyclopedic Dictionary of the Bible* (New York: McGraw-Hill, 1963), 2080–81: "According to the way of thinking of the ancients, those who shared in the same food and drink were regarded as sharing in the same blood and the same principle of life, and thus bound to each other by a sacred bond." See also Ralph Gower,

The New Manners and Customs of the Bible (Chicago: Moody Press, 1987), 241–45; Joachim Jeremias, *The Eucharistic Words of Jesus* (New York: Charles Scribner's Sons, 1966).

30. Matthew 14:14–21; 15:32–38; 26:20–35; Mark 1:30–31; 6:34–44; 8:1–9; 14:17–26; Luke 6:3–4, 7:36–50, 8:1–3; 10:38–42; 11:37–54; 14:1–6; 15:1–2; 19:2–10; 22:14–38; 24:30–31; 41–43; John 4:6–26; 12:1–9; 13–17; 21:9–13.

31. The reunion banquet image is also found in this gem, which the Joseph Smith Translation adds to Matthew 7:9: "What man among you, having a son, and he shall be standing out, and shall say, Father, open thy house that I may come in and sup with thee, will not say, Come in, my son; for mine is thine, and thine is mine?" (JST Matthew 7:17).

32. Dunn, *Unity and Diversity in the New Testament: An Inquiry into the Character of Earliest Christianity,* 167: "Table-fellowship with tax collector and sinner was Jesus' way of proclaiming God's salvation and assurance of forgiveness." Joachim Jeremias, *The Parables of Jesus,* 2nd rev. ed., (New York: Charles Scribner's Sons, 1954), 227: "These feasts for publicans are prophetic signs, more significant than words, silent proclamations that the Messianic Age is here, the Age of forgiveness." Given this cultural understanding, it must have been immensely comforting and reassuring to the disciples when the risen Lord appeared to them and ate with them (Luke 24:13–43; John 21:9–13; Acts 10:41). Though they had fled and faltered the night Jesus was arrested, their fellowship had been renewed. Eating together said to the apostles, as the Lord would later say to another apostle who had faltered: "Thou art still chosen, and art again called to the work" (D&C 3:10).

33. LDS Bible Dictionary, 755, s.v. "Publicans."

34. W. Lee Humphreys, *Crisis and Story: Introduction to the Old Testament,* 2nd ed. (Mountain View, Calif.: Mayfield Publishing Co., 1990), 247: "In the Near East of antiquity, little social or business intercourse was conducted without recourse to the dining table. Contracts were concluded, marriages formed, land exchanged, friendships made and sustained over meals because partaking of another's fare was a sign of respect and trust."

35. Humphreys, *Crisis and Story,* 200.

36. Humphreys, *Crisis and Story,* 200. See also Paul Connerton, *How Societies Remember* (Cambridge University Press, 1989), 46: "In both the Old Testament and the prayer-book 'remembrance' becomes a technical term through which expression is given to the process by which practising Jews recall and recuperate in their present life the major formative events in the history of their community. . . . To remember is to make the past actual, to form a solidarity with the fathers. . . . Seder annually reminds practising Jews of the most formative moment in the life of their community, the moment in which that community was

redeemed from bondage and made into a free people." See also Freedman, *The Anchor Bible Dictionary,* 4:363.

37. For an overview of participationist language in Paul's writings, see Ehrman, *The New Testament,* 304–307.

38. See also Murphy-O'Connor, "House Churches and the Eucharist," 36–38, which argues that the seating arrangement may have contributed to this disparity by segregating the congregation along socioeconomic lines.

39. This symbolism is also seen in the Eucharistic prayer over the bread, preserved in the late first-century *Didache:* "As this piece [of bread] was scattered over the hills and then was brought together and made one, so let your Church be brought together from the ends of the earth into your Kingdom" (*Didache* 9:4, cf. 10:5).

40. Freedman, *The Anchor Bible Dictionary,* 4:363.

41. Freedman, *The Anchor Bible Dictionary,* 1:90.

42. Freedman, 1:90–91. Pliny the Younger also played a role in putting a stop to the agape feasts by enforcing an edict against unauthorized associations. In the first decade of the second century, Ignatius, bishop of Antioch, wrote to other Christian congregations, encouraging them not to participate in Eucharists, baptisms, or "love feasts" which were not under their bishop's direction—implying that some were doing so: *Epistle to the Smyrneans,* 8:1–2; cf. his *Epistle to the Ephesians,* 13:1, and 14:2, where he expresses concern about those who "profess to be Christ's" by "a momentary act of professing," but who are not "persistently motivated by faith." The Council of Laodicea in A.D. 364 produced the following rulings: "Canon 28: It is not permitted to hold love feasts, as they are called, in the Lord's Houses, or Churches, nor to eat and to spread couches in the house of God. . . . Canon 58: Bishops and presbyters may no longer celebrate the offering [the bread and wine] in houses."

43. Quoted in "Elder Hales Counsels Single Adults," *Church News,* 18 November 1995, 4.

44. Jeffrey R. Holland, in Conference Report, October 1995, 91.

45. Holland, in Conference Report, 88–89; italics in the original. Elder Holland's quotation about "the most sacred, the most holy, of all the meetings . . ." is from Joseph Fielding Smith, *Doctrines of Salvation,* comp. Bruce R. McConkie (Salt Lake City: Bookcraft, 1954–56), 2:340.

46. See 1 Corinthians 10:21. Also David O. McKay, *Gospel Ideals* (Salt Lake City: Improvement Era, 1953), 72: "The address, 'O God, the Eternal Father,' is an acknowledgment on the part of the congregation that the Lord is present; at least that his Spirit is in possible communication with the spirit of each one who sincerely seeks him."

11

THE "SAME" ORGANIZATION THAT EXISTED IN THE PRIMITIVE CHURCH

Grant Underwood

*F*OR YEARS NOW, PRIMARY GRADUATES throughout the Church have either memorized, or spent time attempting to memorize, the Articles of Faith. If they are like my children, they "pass them off" with nervous enthusiasm but often without full comprehension of the words they are repeating. Consider the sixth article of faith: "We believe in the same organization that existed in the Primitive Church, namely, apostles, prophets, pastors, teachers, evangelists, and so forth." There are terms here that may be unclear to Latter-day Saints young and old. What, for instance, is a "pastor" or an "evangelist?" Then there is the question of interpretation. How best do we understand the term "same"? In missionary work over the years, much has been claimed, perhaps too much, in the name of this article of faith. A legitimate comparison of any kind is based on an accurate picture of the things being compared. The purpose of this study, therefore, is to explore the nature of Church

---

Grant Underwood is a professor of history and research historian at the Joseph Fielding Smith Institute for Latter-day Saint history at Brigham Young University.

organization in the New Testament and to show how, without distorting history, it can be considered the same as in the Church today.

PRIMITIVE CHURCH

To many people, especially younger Latter-day Saints, the word *primitive* may convey the wrong message. As the word was used in religious discussions in Joseph Smith's day, it did *not* mean "crude, backward, or undeveloped." Rather, it drew directly from its Latin root *primus* to mean "first" and was related to other English words like "prime," "primary," and "primordial." In short, Joseph Smith was talking about the "prime-itive" or "first" church—the one the Savior organized in the first century A.D. As it turns out, in the early 1800s, just at the time the Lord spoke to Joseph Smith, there was considerable interest in America in the primitive Church. Aware of the spiritual barnacles that over the centuries had attached themselves to existing Christian traditions, many religious souls in and out of different denominations sought to reform their churches in the primitive mold. This quest for the primitive Church, not surprisingly, has been labeled by historians of early American religion as "Christian primitivism" or simply "primitivism." Many of those who joined the Church in the early years of this dispensation were primitivists who found in the message of the Restoration precisely what they were looking for.[1]

Awareness of this primitivist impulse in nineteenth century America also helps explain the rest of the wording of the sixth article of faith. Originally, the Articles of Faith were not a stand-alone declaration of beliefs. They constituted the closing sentences (not numbered) of the famous "Wentworth letter" written in 1842 by Joseph Smith for a Chicago editor who requested a "sketch of the rise, progress, persecution and faith of the Latter-day Saints."[2] For our purposes, it is important to observe that these statements were written for a nonmember audience, one familiar with the Bible and exposed to the primitivist sentiment of the day.[3] Such an audience would have recognized the match between the Prophet Joseph Smith's words and the Apostle Paul's characterization of Christ's

Church: "And he gave some, apostles; and some, prophets; and some, evangelists; and some, pastors and teachers" (Ephesians 4:11). The Prophet's use of Paul's words to illustrate what he meant by "primitive church" would have established a common denominator with Bible believers. It would have reassured them that the Prophet's view of the ideal church was scriptural.

Beyond a comforting rhetorical connection to the New Testament, what exactly did Joseph Smith mean by these terms? Was he ticking off an organizational flowchart? Some Latter-day Saints seem to think so. Yet the "and so forth" at the end of the article indicates he was being suggestive rather than exhaustive in his list. As will be seen, the terms used in Ephesians 4:11 and the sixth article of faith are generally best understood in terms of function rather than position. That Joseph was using the words here more allusively than exactingly is apparent from the fact that earlier in the same letter he wrote that the Book of Mormon "tells us" that "they had apostles, prophets, pastors, teachers and evangelists; the same order, the same priesthood, the same ordinances, gifts, powers, and blessing, as was enjoyed on the eastern continent."[4] Technically speaking, of course, this is not true, for in the Book of Mormon, no ancient American servants of the Lord are designated "pastors" or "evangelists."[5] The Prophet seems more concerned with affirming the *nature* of the organization in the primitive Church than with its *nomenclature*.

It is important, therefore, to return to the New Testament and carefully examine what it has to say about such matters. It is also important to keep our eye on the modern side of the comparison. When Joseph wrote, "*We* believe in the same organization that existed in the primitive church," the "we" referred to himself and the Saints in 1842. His point of comparison was LDS Church organization in its earliest years. Thus, we must guard against anachronism on either side of this comparison. For a Latter-day Saint at the dawn of the twenty-first century to assume that the present Church organization and accompanying job descriptions are identical to that of the 1840s, let alone the first century A.D., is problematic. Yet by attending more to function than flowchart, we can discern an

essential "sameness" between the primitive Church and the kingdom of God in latter days.

APOSTLES

Any thorough exploration of New Testament content requires
attention to Greek, the language of the earliest manuscripts. As
Joseph Smith remarked, "in the original language," God "opens our
minds in a marvelous manner, to understand His word."[6] We begin,
therefore, by considering the Greek word group behind *Apostle*.
Based on the verb *apostello* (to send forth), an apostle *(apostolos)* is
literally "one who is sent forth," a messenger, an envoy, a missionary.[7] Of all the terms mentioned in the sixth article of faith, the most
obvious parallels between the ancient and modern churches rests
with *Apostles*. Though *apostoloi* is used less often in the Gospels
than *mathetai* (disciples) or *hoi dodeka* (the twelve), it is clear
enough that these three terms were usually synonymous (e.g.,
Matthew 10:1–2; Luke 6:13; 22:11–14). That the Twelve Apostles
were to be a governing body of set size is illustrated by the account
of the call of Matthias (see Acts 1:15–26). That they were given
weighty responsibility is clear from the Lord's declaration to them:
"Whatsoever ye shall bind on earth shall be bound in heaven: and
whatsoever ye shall loose on earth shall be loosed in heaven"
(Matthew 18:18). Little wonder, then, that Paul wrote, "God hath
set some in the church, first apostles, secondarily prophets, thirdly
teachers" (1 Corinthians 12:28) and that the "household of God"
was "built upon the foundation of the apostles and prophets"
(Ephesians 2:19–20). A final indicator of the Apostles' authoritative
position in the primitive Church was the circulation and preserva-
tion of their letters in the years after their deaths.

That the ancient Twelve, like their modern counterparts, provided the firm foundation on which the Church rested is widely recognized by Latter-day Saints today. Less familiar are the other uses
of *apostolos* in the New Testament. Here it is necessary to keep in
mind the term's broader meaning as "envoy," "messenger," or simply
"one sent forth." It is important to point out to those unfamiliar with
the Greek language that though some Bible translations, like the

King James Version (KJV), occasionally render *apostolos* with other words such as "messenger," the underlying Greek term is neither spelled differently nor set off by any special linguistic markers that would denote a meaning distinct from its use to refer to the Twelve Apostles. In particular, differentiation by capitalization, so important in modern English as a way of according special status, does not exist in Greek.

What, then, are some examples of non-Twelve "apostles"? In 2 Corinthians 8:23 Paul mentions the *apostoloi ekklesion*—literally, the "apostles of the churches"—which the KJV renders as the "messengers of the churches." Paul singles out for commendation one such *apostolos* (KJV, "messenger"), Epaphroditus, whom the Philippians sent as the commissioned representative of their congregation to look after Paul's needs (Philippians 2:25). A missionary connotation to *apostolos* is apparent when Paul calls himself an Apostle "of" or "to" the Gentiles (e.g., Romans 11:13, Galatians 2:8), much as Latter-day Saints in the nineteenth century spoke of Jacob Hamblin, who was never one of the Twelve, as an "apostle to the Lamanites."[8] Other individuals designated *apostolos* that the New Testament does not list with "the twelve" include Jesus (Hebrews 3:1); James, Jesus' brother (Galatians 1:19); Paul (1 Corinthians 9:1; 15:9; often at the beginning of his epistles); Barnabas (Acts 14:4, 14); and, possibly, Andronicus and Junia (Romans 16:7).[9]

It seems clear, then, that in addition to using *apostoloi* to refer to the Twelve apostles, the New Testament also employs the term for a variety of other apostles ranging from missionaries to individuals sent on official Church errands. What unites them all is the notion of proper authorization. This helps explain Paul's use of *pseudapostoloi* (false apostles) to describe those who claimed to be the Lord's legitimate representatives but were not. Similarly, in John's Revelation, the Ephesians are commended for having "tried them which say they are apostles, and are not, and hast found them liars" (Revelations 2:2). The same idea, by the way, is reflected in Doctrine and Covenants 64:39, where the inhabitants of Zion are promised the ability to discern "liars and hypocrites" and thus "they who are not apostles and prophets shall be known." The concern in either dispensation seems to be authorized representation.

The broader New Testament use of *apostle* to designate servants of the Lord other than just the Twelve was perpetuated throughout Christian history. It is not surprising, therefore, that that connotation was part of the vocabulary carried into the Church by the first Latter-day Saints. In the earliest years, men who never became part of the Quorum of Twelve Apostles were sometimes called "apostles." A September 1832 revelation given to Joseph Smith and "six elders" declares, "as I said unto mine apostles, even so I say unto you, for you are mine apostles" (D&C 84:63).[10] The paragraph in "Articles and Covenants" listing the duties of an elder (D&C 20:38–44) begins with the words "an apostle is an elder, and it is his calling to . . ." John Whitmer's elder's "license" dated 9 June 1830 reads, "Given to John Whitmer signifying and proving that he is an Apostle of Jesus Christ an Elder of this Church of Christ."[11] This wider usage is well represented in the 2 December 1830 letter from Joseph Smith and John Whitmer to the Colesville Saints, written the day after Orson Pratt was ordained an elder: "According to our prayers, the Lord hath called, chosen, ordained, sanctified and sent unto you another Servant and apostle separated unto his gospel through Jesus Christ our Redeemer . . . even our beloved brother Orson Pratt, the bearer of these lines."[12] John Taylor reflected this broader meaning of the term available early in this dispensation when in 1837 he wrote to a friend in England: "You ask what is the number of the apostles. There are twelve that are ordained to go to the nations, and there are many others, no definite number."[13] Thus we see that during the 1830s, *apostle* could be applied to more than just the Twelve.

With the passage of time, and especially after the Twelve returned from their successful mission to England in 1840–41, however, the Prophet Joseph was able to teach the Twelve (and, to a degree, the Saints) the deeper significance of the holy apostleship. By 1853, Brigham Young could say, in what has since been viewed as a defining statement, "the keys of the eternal Priesthood, which is after the order of the Son of God, are comprehended by being an

Apostle. All the Priesthood, all the keys, all the gifts, all the endowments, and everything preparatory to entering into the presence of the Father and of the Son, are in, composed of, circumscribed by, or I might say incorporated within the circumference of, the Apostleship."[14] Consistent with this developed understanding, the use of the term *apostle* began to be restricted and eventually came to refer to men who had been ordained to that particular office in the Melchizedek Priesthood and who, as such, were serving in the governing Quorum of the Twelve Apostles.

PROPHETS

Prophetes is a combination of the root *phe(mi)*, which means "to say" or "to speak," and the prefix *pro,* which is usually rendered with neutral terms like "forth," or more loosely, "openly" or "publicly," though it can also mean "fore," as in fore-teller. Thus, *prophetes* is literally one who "speaks forth." Originally, the term was associated with the oracle personnel of ancient Greece. Oracle prophets were understood to "declare something whose content are not derived from themselves but from the god who reveals his will at the particular [oracle] site." Similarly, *prophetes* was sometimes applied to the ancient Greek poet as "the one who declares to men what he has received from the divine Muses."[15] Later, in the Septuagint, *prophetes* was used to translate the Hebrew *nabi,* "a person who serves as a channel of communication between the human and divine worlds."[16] Despite the focus in the popular mind on the predictive work of prophets, the fundamental meaning of the word has always targeted the notion of being an inspired spokesperson for God, regardless of the content of the message.[17]

Consistent with Old Testament usage, in the New Testament, *prophetes* is generally used to describe a "proclaimer of the divine, inspired message."[18] Examples of individuals in the New Testament who are either called prophets or who prophesy include John the Baptist (Luke 7:28), Agabus (Acts 11:27–28 and 21:10–14), Anna (Luke 2:36–38); the four daughters of Philip (Acts 21:9); Barnabas, Simeon, Lucius, Manaen, Saul at Antioch (Acts 13:1); Judas Barsabas, and Silas (Acts 15:32). Indeed, Jesus Christ was regarded by the people (and regarded Himself) as a prophet (see Matthew 21:11; Luke 7:16; Mark 6:2–4).

When Paul writes about *propheteia* (prophecy), he means the divine gift or *charisma* of inspired utterance, of Spirit-guided declarations. This is particularly clear in 1 Corinthians 14. The chapter is not a debate about which dazzling and exotic spiritual gift is superior—speaking in tongues or forecasting the future. Rather it is Paul's impassioned plea for the Saints to seek the blessing of inspired utterance in their services rather than the showy gift of tongues. Understanding of this chapter and other similar New Testament references to the prophecy word group can be greatly enhanced if instead of "predict the future" one mentally inserts "speak under inspiration" every time the verb *propheteuo* (prophesy) appears. For example: "Desire spiritual gifts, but rather that ye may [speak under inspiration]" (1 Corinthians 14:1), "He that [speaks under inspiration] speaketh unto men to edification, and exhortation, and comfort" (1 Corinthians 14:3), or "For ye may all [speak under inspiration] one by one, that all may learn, and all may be comforted" (1 Corinthians 14:31). This is reminiscent of Moses' retort to Joshua: "Would God that all the Lord's people were prophets, and that the Lord would put his spirit upon them" (Numbers 11:29). Similarly, the sense of prophecy as inspiration more than prediction is clearly reflected in the wording of the fifth article of faith: "We believe that a man must be called of God, by prophecy, and by the laying on of hands by those who are in authority."[19]

This understanding also animates a November 1831 revelation to four elders and "all those who [are] ordained unto this priesthood" that they should "speak as they are moved upon by the Holy Ghost. And whatsoever they shall speak when moved upon by the Holy Ghost shall be . . . the voice of the Lord, and the power of God unto salvation" (D&C 68:2–4). In the twenty-first century, it has been common to focus application of this passage on the General Authorities, but originally it was an encouragement for ordinary elders to magnify their calling and be *prophetai*, speaking under inspiration to the edification of others. This seems to be the thrust of the

Prophet Joseph Smith's comments to an eastern correspondent when "he no more professed to be a prophet, than every man must, who professes to be a preacher of righteousness. . . . If a man professes to be a minister of Jesus, and has not the spirit of prophecy, he must be a false witness, for he is not in possession of that gift which qualifies him for his office."[20] Such also was the meaning and intent of the "school of the prophets," a training experience for all "who are called to the ministry in the church, beginning at the high priests, even down to the deacons" (D&C 88:127) to help them be inspired and inspiring preachers of the gospel. "School of the prophets," in the sense of a ministerial school, had in fact been the common designation in colonial America for what we today call theological seminaries or divinity schools. Harvard, Yale, and Princeton all began as "schools of the prophets."[21]

That all priesthood bearers were expected to prophetically speak under inspiration did not, however, mean that those Spirit-inspired utterances *(propheteia)* were to be normative for the Church. Two revelations within the Church's first year clarified that beside Joseph Smith "there is none other appointed unto [the church] to receive commandments and revelations" (D&C 43:3). Oliver Cowdery, and by inference other prophet-elders, was to "be heard by the church in all things whatsoever thou shalt teach them by the Comforter" (D&C 28:1). He was even told that he would "have revelations" but was counseled, "Write them not by way of commandment" (D&C 28:8). Thus, while the elders were to diligently strive to enjoy the gift of prophecy in their teaching ministry, none of their *propheteia* were to be considered binding on the Church.

Semantically, there is a modest divergence between New Testament and Latter-day Saint practice. Our use of the phrase "the prophet" to refer to the senior living Apostle and President of the Church is not known in the New Testament. Still, though "seniority" is not an ecclesiastical concept that figures in the New Testament and though Peter is never called either a prophet or "the" prophet, Peter does appear to have been one of the first Apostles called and later seems to have functioned as the head of the Church after Christ's ascension.[22] With our focus on functional rather than titular similarities, however, the real "sameness" between the primitive and latter-day churches lies in the actual presence of inspired utterance *(propheteia).* That the Latter-day Saints gradually narrowed their application of the term *prophet* is secondary. Authorized governance by Apostles with one acting as leader and Church members who enjoy the gift of inspired utterance in both congregational worship and public ministry, these are the similarities that matter.

PASTORS

The word *pastor,* as a translation of the Greek *poimen,* appears only once in the New Testament, in Ephesians 4:11. In every other instance, the KJV renders *poimen* as "shepherd(s)." Thus, the well-known Christmas verse reads, "There were in the same country *[poimenes]* abiding in the field, keeping watch over their flock by night" (Luke 2:8), and in John 10, Christ declares, "I am the good *[poimen]* . . . and there shall be one fold and one *[poimen]* (John 10:14, 16).[23] That both Paul in Ephesians 4:11 and the Prophet Joseph in the sixth article of faith intended *pastor* in a figurative or functional sense is clear from the fact that no office by that title is attested in either the New Testament or Latter-day Saint churches.[24] Yet pastors and pastoring, in the sense of "shepherding" (feeding, nourishing, caring for) God's flock, have abounded in both dispensations. Responding to one of Peter's replies to His query "Lovest thou me?" the resurrected Lord said *"[poimaino]* my sheep" (John 21:16). Peter later passed on the same advice to the elders of the church: *"[poimaino]* the flock of God which is among you" (1 Peter 5:2).

Three groups in the New Testament seem to have been specially charged with being pastors—*episcopos, presbuteros,* and *diakonos. Episcopos* is a combination of *epi,* "upon" or "over," and *scopos,* "looker" or "watcher." Thus, an *episcopos* is literally one who "looks upon," "watches over," or "oversees."[25] For centuries before Christ, the related Greek verbs *episkopeo* or *episkeptomai* carried the connotation of protective watch-care. They communicated a sense of "the gracious care of the gods for a territory under their protection" or a sea captain's vigilance over his cargo. The words also meant "to inspect," "to investigate," and "to visit," all with the connotation of "looking after."[26] Thus, James declared that "pure religion and undefiled" is to *"[episkeptomai]* the fatherless and widows in their affliction" (James 1:27). Naturally, Church members in any age would benefit from this kind of caring leadership from their "pastors."

Influenced by the ecclesiology of their day, King James translators generally used some form of the word "bishop" to translate the nouns *episcopos* or *episcope.* Hence, the English words *episcopal* and *episcopacy,* which today designate churches that have bishops in their hierarchy. In Acts 20:28, however, the KJV renders *episcopoi* as "overseers," a translation choice that points to the broader meaning of the term. First Peter 2:25 calls Christ "the Shepherd and Bishop of your souls," a verse that, as translated in the KJV, sounds odd to modern Saints. Yet the pairing of *poimen* and *episcopos* in Greek conveys a powerful sense of the pastoral watch-care exercised by the Savior in our lives.

A variant of *episcopos,* the noun *episcope,* accounts for the initial appearance of "bishop" in 1 Timothy 3. Actually, the KJV creates the phrase "the office of a bishop" to translate the one Greek word *episcope.*[27] The same word in Acts 1:20 is rendered "bishoprick." This is significant because Acts 1 is not discussing a three-man bishopric or even the office of bishop. The passage in question—"his bishoprick let another take"—is a rendering of a line from Psalm 69 that Peter uses to introduce the need to call another to the Twelve to take Judas's place. When the underlying word *episcope* is properly understood in its Greek sense, this becomes an entirely appropriate description of the oversight and watch-care over the whole Church rendered by the Twelve.

Another group of pastors with watch-care responsibilities were the *presbuteroi,* or "elders." *Presbuteros,* like "elder" in English, "can be employed both as a designation of age and also as a title of office."[28] "In most civilizations authority has been vested in those who by reason of age or experience have been thought best qualified to rule. It is not surprising therefore that the leaders in many ancient communities have borne a title derived from a root meaning 'old age.'"[29] The "elders of Israel" frequently mentioned in the Old Testament would be a prime example. In the primitive church, unnamed governing "elders" along with the Apostles, presided in Jerusalem (see Acts 11:30; 15:2, 4, 6, 22–23), but mostly the term was applied to congregational leaders. As Paul and Barnabas finished their first missionary tour, revisiting their converts and exhorting them to faithfulness, they "ordained them elders in every church" (Acts 14:23). Paul later wrote to Titus on Crete directing him to "ordain elders in every city" (Titus 1:5).

None of these references are in the context of ordination to the Melchizedek Priesthood; they describe the call of presiding elders for each congregation, pastors whom the Lord put in place to watch over His flock. This helps explain the terminological overlap between elder (*presbuteros*) and bishop (*episcopos*) in the New Testament.[30] In Paul's letter to Titus, after instructing him to ordain elders in every city, he offers the same set of qualifications for their call—blameless, the husband of one wife, etc.—that he gave to Timothy as qualifications for a bishop (compare Titus 1:6 to 1 Timothy 3:2ff). Moreover, in the very next verse (Titus 1:7), Paul refers to an elder as *episcopos*, which the KJV renders "bishop." Understanding *episcopos* in terms of function rather than title, however, makes the passage perfectly intelligible. By the very nature of their call, presiding elders (*presbuteroi*) are "overseers" (*episcopoi*), charged with watching over the flock, and this is precisely what Paul is conveying here to Titus. Even the Latter-day Saint most committed to maintaining titular continuity between the former-day and latter-day churches must realize that functionally no distinction is made in the Church today between a branch president and a ward bishop. The branch president shoulders all the same "episcopal" responsibilities that the bishop does, though he is neither ordained or addressed as such.

Understanding these words more in terms of function than title also helps with other passages in the New Testament. In Paul's famous speech to the Ephesian elders who had gathered at Miletus to bid him farewell (see Acts 20:17), he tells these pastors, "Take heed therefore unto yourselves, and to all the flock, over the which the Holy Ghost hath made you overseers *[episcopoi],* to feed *[poimaino]* the church of God, which he hath purchased with his own blood" (Acts 20:28). Linguistically speaking, there is no difference between this use of *episcopos* and its appearance in 1 Timothy 3, where it is translated "bishop." Acts 20:28 might just as readily have been rendered, indeed, is so rendered in the American Standard Version, "the flock over which the Holy Ghost hath made you bishops." Another example that pulls together all that we have been discussing thus far under the heading of "pastors" is found in 1 Peter 5: "The elders *[presbuteroi]* which are among you I exhort, who am also an elder *[presbuteros]. . . .* Feed *[poimaino]* the flock of God which is among you, taking the oversight *[episkopeo]* thereof, not by constraint, but willingly . . . being ensamples to the flock. And when the chief Shepherd *[archipoimen]* shall appear, ye shall receive a crown of glory that fadeth not away" (1 Peter 5:1–4). In other words, the Apostle Peter here writes as one "church leader" to the others, exhorting them to properly "pastor" the members, "bishoping" them not by constraint but willingly, so that when the "chief Pastor" appears they may receive a fitting reward. This advice and the advice in Timothy and Titus are appropriate for all Church leaders, not just ordained bishops. In recent years, the General Authorities have regularly encouraged local leaders, even home teachers, to love, nurture, and truly "watch over" those they serve. Expressed differently, they have also been trying to teach local leaders to "minister" to the members, not just "administer" Church affairs.

This brings us to yet another pastoral term that is used generously in the New Testament—*diakonos,* sometimes translated "deacon," but mostly "minister" or "servant."[31] The KJV actually uses "deacon" in only two New Testament passages. Immediately after outlining the qualifications for an *episcopos* in 1 Timothy 3, Paul does the same for *diakonos,* using the word group several times (1 Timothy 3:8–13). Here, in addition to choosing the ecclesiastical loan word "deacon" to translate *diakonos,* the KJV also twice renders the verb *diakoneo* not as "minister unto" or "serve," as it typically does, but as "use[d] the office of a deacon." The other New Testament occurrence is when Paul and Timothy greet the Philippian "saints" together with their "bishops and deacons" (Philippian 1:1). In terms of modern Church structure, "bishops and deacons" is an odd pairing, but if translated as "overseers" and "ministers" or "helpers," a couple of rough modern equivalents might be imagined—presidents and counselors, or priesthood and auxiliary leaders. Or perhaps the terms are describing two sides of the same pastoral coin—taking the oversight of, as well as ministering to, the flock of God. To our ears, an even more unexpected usage is when Paul commends to the Romans, "Phoebe our sister, which is a *[diakonos]* of the church which is at Cenchrea" (Romans 16:1). Yet when understood as a servant of the Lord rather than an ordained deacon in the Aaronic priesthood, it is easy to envision Phoebe functioning as something like a modern Relief Society president.

That a variety of Church personnel were involved in "deaconing" *(diakoneo)* is clear in the verse following the Ephesians 4:11 list of the Lord's gifts to the Church, where Paul says that they were given "for the perfecting of the saints, for the work of the *[diakonia]* ministry" (Ephesians 4:12). The *apostolos* Paul asked rhetorically, "Who then is Paul, and who is Apollos, but *[diakonoi]* ministers by whom ye believed, even as the Lord gave to every man?" (1 Corinthians 3:5). Earlier, after selecting two candidates to replace Judas in the Quorum of the Twelve, the Eleven sought divine guidance to discover whom the Lord had chosen "that he may take part of this *[diakonia]* and *[apostole]*" (Acts 1:25). The KJV renders the two terms respectively as "ministry" and "apostleship," but linguistic equivalency would allow the awkward though accurate "deaconship and apostleship." Again, the emphasis on function more than office in the New Testament is apparent. Clearly, the New Testament is not using the *diakonos* word group primarily to refer to the office or actions of twelve-year-old boys in the Aaronic Priesthood.

TEACHERS

"Teachers" is the one word in the Ephesians 4:11 and sixth article of faith list that operates in English like its Greek counterpart *didaskalos* (whence our word "didactic" is derived) does, as either a title or a function. The most frequent use of *didaskalos* in the New Testament is as a way of addressing the Savior. The KJV translators chose to consistently render this term as "Master." Elsewhere in the New Testament, they use the word "teacher."[32] Sadly, with the change in the English language, the sense of addressing Jesus as "Teacher" has been all but lost today. Instead, "Master" connotes hierarchical authority and conjures up synonyms like "ruler" or "supreme one." To be sure, Christ is all of that, but he was also the consummate teacher, and that is what is being highlighted by the use of the term *didaskalos*.

In the remainder of the New Testament, the term *didaskalos* appears only a handful of times. Aside from Ephesians 4:11, which includes "teachers" in its list, there are several other relevant passages. Luke records that there were "at Antioch certain prophets and teachers" (Acts 13:1). Paul tells the Corinthians that "God hath set some in the church, first apostles, secondarily prophets, thirdly teachers" (1 Corinthians 12:28). An active teaching ministry is at the heart of the Teacher's church in any dispensation. By extending our understanding of "teachers" beyond an office in the Aaronic Priesthood and looking at it as a function filled by a variety of Saints, the similarity between the primitive and modern churches is very strong. Latter-day Saints who have long rallied to the divine invitation "teach ye diligently" (D&C 88:78) understand well why Paul would put teachers in the third position behind only apostles and prophets.

EVANGELISTS

Euangelistes, which the KJV renders as "evangelist[s]," appears only three times in the New Testament. Aside from our base text in Ephesians 4:11, Acts 21:8 calls Philip an "evangelist" and Paul encourages Timothy to "do the work of an evangelist" (2 Timothy 4:5). The meaning of this English loan word becomes clear when connected to the rest of its verbal family. *Euangelion* is the word the KJV translates as "gospel" (literally, the "good news"), and *euangelizo* means to "bring or announce good news," or to "declare, show, or bring glad tidings."[33] In other words, an "evangelist" is one who proclaims the good news (gospel) of Christ's atoning sacrifice and is, therefore, a missionary or a preacher. The Church in any dispensation could not grow without such proclaimers of the good news. Today, the energy of sixty thousand Latter-day Saint missionaries acting as evangelists worldwide certainly matches the spirit of determined dissemination of the word of God found in the New Testament.

Yet Latter-day Saints also have applied the term "evangelist" in another, specialized manner. In 1835, shortly after the Quorum of the Twelve was first constituted in this dispensation, a revelation indicated that one of their duties was "in all large branches of the church, to ordain evangelical ministers, as they shall be designated unto them by revelation—The order of this priesthood was confirmed to be handed down from father to son" (D&C 107:39–40). As Joseph Smith later clarified: "An Evangelist is a Patriarch, even the oldest man of the blood of Joseph or of the seed of Abraham. Wherever the Church of Christ is established in the Earth, there should be a Patriarch for the benefit of the posterity of the Saints, as it was with Jacob in giving his Patriarchal blessings unto his sons."[34] Some Latter-day Saints find it fitting to call a patriarch an evangelist since the blessings he dispenses are indeed proclamations of "good news" for the lives of individual Saints. Though nothing is said of the office of patriarch or of patriarchal blessings in the New Testament, this limited, specialized sense of the term does not detract from the well-documented similarity between the primitive and modern churches in their profound commitment to preach the gospel *(euangelizo)* wherever possible.

AN ORGANIZATION TAILORED TO OUR TIMES

The brief symbol "&c" (and so forth) concludes the sixth article of faith. Historically, the temptation for some has been to throw in the rest of the LDS organizational flowchart at this point. Seventies, high priests, and Aaronic priests were not mentioned, so they can be added. Yet as we have seen, to read Paul or Joseph Smith as focusing on formal office titles is misleading and problematic. Better to look at the "and so forth" as extending what the Prophet was really trying to affirm in this article of faith, that the latter-day Church embraces and implements every ministerial impulse and activity that was present in the primitive Church. Exactly who carries them out and what titles they bear is secondary.

A concluding comparison can be drawn from the Primary. Though the Church has changed the names, arrangement, and curricula of its Primary classes a number of times over the years, it is still the "same" Primary organization in the one way that really matters—function, in its abiding commitment to love and teach the children of the Church. Nomenclature, organizational flowchart, and specific practices will always be tailored to contemporary circumstances. Indeed that is the grand design of continuing revelation. Latter-day Saint interest in replicating the primitive Church, unlike some historic forms of Christian primitivism, never has been strait-jacketed into matching the precise configuration of things in the New Testament. A loving Lord is thus free to constantly adjust the Church's outer garment so that it best serves its unchanging inner commitment to "bring to pass the immortality and eternal life of man" (Moses 1:39).

What is crucially the same about the Savior's work in the latter days is its function. He continues to send forth authorized servants of various kinds (as apostles) who act under the inspiration of the Holy Ghost (as prophets) to shepherd His Saints (as pastors), to instruct them in the word of life (as teachers), and to spread the good news of His saving grace to all the world (as evangelists). These functions are the similarities that really count. Indeed, they are the essence of what makes this the "only true and *living* church upon the face of the whole earth" (D&C 1:30).

NOTES

1. See Richard T. Hughes, ed., *The American Quest for the Primitive Church* (Urbana: University of Illinois Press, 1988); Nathan O. Hatch, *The Democratization of American Christianity* (New Haven: Yale University Press, 1989); and Marvin S. Hill, "The Role of Christian Primitivism in the Origin and

Development of the Mormon Kingdom, 1830–44" (Ph.D. diss., University of Chicago, 1968).

2. Joseph Smith, *The Papers of Joseph Smith, Volume 1: Autobiographical and Historical Writings,* ed. Dean C. Jessee (Salt Lake City: Deseret Book, 1989), 429; hereafter, *Papers of Joseph Smith.*

3. That the Prophet wrote this for a nonmember audience is clear from his note that "as Mr. Ba[r]stow has taken the proper steps to obtain correct information, all that I shall ask at his hands, is, that he publish the account entire, ungarnished, and without misrepresentation" (Joseph Smith, *History of the Church of Jesus Christ of Latter-day Saints,* ed. B. H. Roberts, 2d ed., rev. [Salt Lake City: Deseret Book, 1976], 4:535–36; hereafter, *HC*).

4. *Papers of Joseph Smith,* 1:432.

5. The word *pastors* is found once, but it is in an Isaiah quotation recorded by Nephi (see 1 Nephi 21:1). Moreover, in the Book of Mormon, the term *apostles* almost always refers to the Old World Twelve (see 1 Nephi 11:35–36; 13:39–41). The common designation for the twelve called by Christ during his ministry in the New World is "disciples." Where they figure most prominently in the Book of Mormon narrative—3 Nephi—they are always so designated. Later, however, in three passages recorded by Moroni (see Mormon 9:18; Ether 12:41; Moroni 2:2), the term *apostles* is used, but the meaning is ambiguous and could be construed to refer to either group of twelve men.

6. *HC* 2:376. On another occasion, he remarked, "My soul delights in reading the word of the Lord in the original, and I am determined to pursue the study of the languages, until I shall become master of them, if I am permitted to live long enough. At any rate, so long as I do live, I am determined to make this my object; and with the blessing of God, I shall succeed to my satisfaction" (*HC* 2:396).

7. A comprehensive survey of the extensive literature on the meaning of *apostolos* can be found in Francis H. Agnew, "The Origin of the NT Apostle-Concept: A Review of Research," *Journal of Biblical Literature* 105 (March 1986): 75–96. Helpful for the entire *apostello* word group is Gerhard Kittel and Gerhard Friedrich, eds., *Theological Dictionary of the New Testament* (Grand Rapids, Michigan: Eerdmans, 1964–76), 1:398–447; hereafter, *TDNT.* See also Walter Bauer, *A Greek-English Lexicon of the New Testament and Other Early Christian Literature,* 4th ed., rev. (Chicago: University of Chicago Press, 1957), 99.

8. Charles S. Peterson, "Jacob Hamblin, Apostle to the Lamanites, and the Indian Mission," *Journal of Mormon History* 2 (1975): 21–34.

9. The inclusion of Andronicus and Junia hinges on one's interpretation of *en tois apostoloi,* usually rendered "among the apostles." Does this mean they labored alongside the Apostles or were themselves Apostles?

10. Actually, this portion of the revelation was received the next day in the presence of "eleven high Priests save one." *Kirtland Revelation Book,* 24, LDS Church Archives.

11. License for John Whitmer, 9 June 1830, ms., 1 p., Beineke Library, Yale University, New Haven, Connecticut. Years later, someone took a pencil and crossed out "Apostle of Jesus Christ" with sufficient vigor that it made a small tear through the paper. In early January 1831, Sidney Rigdon wrote to his Ohio associates introducing Whitmer as "a brother greatly beloved, and an Apostle of this church" (E. D. Howe, *Mormonism Unveiled* [Painesville: by author, 1834], 110).

12. Joseph Smith and John Whitmer to Dearly Beloved in the Lord, 2 December 1830, in "Newel Knight Autobiography," Allen Manuscript version, 196, in private possession.

13. Cited in *Latter-day Saints' Messenger and Advocate* 3 (June 1837): 514.

14. *Journal of Discourses* (London: Latter-day Saints' Book Depot, 1854–56), 1:134–35.

15. *TDNT,* 6:791, 93; and Bauer, *Greek-English Lexicon,* 730–31.

16. Paul J. Achtemeier, ed., *Harper's Bible Dictionary* (San Francisco: Harper & Row, 1985), 826.

17. Robert R. Wilson, *Prophecy and Society in Ancient Israel* (Philadelphia: Fortress Press, 1980). Sometimes "in the interests of speaking to the present situation," the prophet "undertakes to enlarge upon events yet to come" (J. D. Douglas and N. Hillyer, eds., *New Bible Dictionary,* 2d ed. [Wheaton, Illinois: Tyndale, 1982], 975.)

18. *TDNT,* 6:828. See also David Noel Freedman, ed., *The Anchor Bible Dictionary* (New York: Doubleday, 1992), 5:496, s.v. "Early Christian Prophecy."

19. In fact, Joseph Smith made this point explicit: "And how were apostles, prophets, pastors, teachers, and evangelists chosen? by 'prophesy (revelation) and by laying on of hands:'—by a divine communication, and a divinely appointed ordinance" (*Times and Seasons* 3 [April 1, 1842]: 744). The fifth article of faith reflects Paul's words to Timothy: "Neglect not the gift that is in thee, which was given thee by prophecy, with the laying on of the hands of the presbytery" (1 Timothy 4:14).

20. *Times and Seasons* 4 (15 May 1843): 200. This echoes the famous question-and-answer series published earlier in the *Elders' Journal:* "Question 5th. Do you believe Joseph Smith Jr. to be a prophet? Answer. Yes, and every other man who has the testimony of Jesus. 'For the testimony of Jesus, is the spirit of prophecy.'—Revelation 19:10" (*Elders' Journal* 1 [July 1838]: 43).

21. Richard Warch, *School of the Prophets: Yale College, 1701–1740* (New Haven: Yale University Press, 1973). In 1758 Caleb Smith called Princeton "this school of the prophets" (*A Christian Life: A Biography of Aaron Burr*

(1715/16–1757), President of Princeton College [New York: Hugh Gaine, 1758], 8).

22. Interestingly, Joseph Smith called Paul a "prophet" but not Peter: "Peter and John were apostles, yet the Jewish court scourged them as impostors. Paul was both an Apostle and prophet, yet they stoned him and put him into prison" (*Times and Seasons* 3 [June 15, 1842]: 824).

23. It is of interest that the words translated "flock" or "fold"—*poimne* and *poimnion*—share the same root as the word for "shepherd"—*poimen*. To Greek ears these words sounded like "sheep herd" and "shepherd" do to us, or more literally, like "herd" and "herder" do since the term applied to cattle as well.

24. For a brief period in the mid–nineteenth century, the Church in Britain did have such a position. See William G. Hartley, "LDS Pastors and Pastorates, 1852–55," in *Mormons in Early Victorian Britain,* ed. Richard L. Jensen and Malcolm R. Thorp (Salt Lake City: University of Utah Press, 1989), 194–210.

25. Ralph Earle, *Word Meanings in the New Testament* (Kansas City: Beacon Hill Press, 1974–84), 5:188, 258; Bauer, *Greek-English Lexicon,* 299.

26. *TDNT,* 2:602.

27. *Office* is derived from the Latin *officium,* which grows out of a combination of *opus* (a work) and *facere* (to do).

28. *TDNT,* 6:654.

29. *New Bible Dictionary,* 313.

30. See J. B. Lightfoot's seminal study "The Christian Ministry," written as an appendix to his *Saint Paul's Epistle to the Philippians,* 6th ed. (London: Macmillan, 1881), 181–269.

31. In the KJV, *diakonos* is translated "minister" 20 of 30 times, "servant" 7 of 30 times, and "deacon" 3 of 30 times (J. B. Smith, *Greek-English Concordance to the New Testament* [Scottsdale, Pennsylvania: Herald Press, 1955], 84).

32. Smith, *Greek-English Concordance,* 87.

33. Bauer, *Greek-English Lexicon,* 317–18; Smith, *Greek-English Concordance,* 156.

34. *HC,* 3:381.

12

PETER—THE CHIEF APOSTLE

Andrew C. Skinner

O F ALL THE PERSONAGES IN THE New Testament, none is more important to the Latter-day Saints, save Jesus only, than Peter—Simon bar Jona by name. There is no question that the Church of Jesus Christ is founded upon the "chief corner stone," Jesus Christ Himself (Ephesians 2:20). All that the Church *is* and *was* is rooted in the Master. But Peter was the "seer" and "stone" of the early Church, titles designated by the Savior according to the Joseph Smith Translation of the Bible (JST John 1:42).

Though the Apostle Paul is sometimes regarded by the world as the architect of Christianity,[1] and we ourselves look to him for doctrinal understanding, Peter was the chief Apostle in the meridian dispensation and held the position equivalent to that of the President of the Church of Jesus Christ in our day. Peter was a great prophet, seer, and revelator. He along with James and John, who together constituted "the First Presidency of the Church in their day,"[2] received the keys of the kingdom from the Savior, Moses,

---

Andrew C. Skinner is dean of religious education at Brigham Young University.

Elijah, and others on the Mount of Transfiguration (see Matthew 17:1–13). In June of 1829 Peter, James, and John returned to earth as immortal beings and conferred upon Joseph Smith and Oliver Cowdery the Melchizedek Priesthood and its keys and ordained them to be Apostles of the dispensation of the fulness of times (see D&C 27:12–13). Truly, Peter was a man for all seasons of the Lord's kingdom. Our purpose is to look at his life and actions, and their significance for us today.

PETER'S LIFE AT THE TIME OF HIS CALL

We do not know when Peter was born, only that he was an adult living in Capernaum at the time the scriptures first introduce him to us. John's Gospel says that Bethsaida was "the city of Andrew and Peter" (John 1:44), meaning perhaps that this was the ancestral family home or that these brothers were born there. Peter was married, and we know that his mother-in-law was staying in his house at Capernaum at the time Jesus healed her of a fever (see Mark 1:29–31), though we do not know if she was a permanent occupant of Peter's home.

Peter's house itself has an interesting history of its own that tells something about Peter's open and hospitable personality. Apparently, it was also the home of Peter's brother, Andrew (see Mark 1:29). It seems to have become a kind of headquarters of the Church in Galilee, where lots of people gathered, especially after Jesus was rejected for the first time in His hometown of Nazareth (see Luke 4:23–31), and Capernaum came to be known as His "own city" (Matthew 9:1). One scholar has opined that Jesus "probably chose it because his first converts, the fishermen Peter and Andrew, lived there."[3] Note the way Mark describes one of the many gatherings in Peter's home after Jesus had been rejected in Nazareth:

"And again he entered into Capernaum after some days; and it was noised that he was in the house.

"And straightway many were gathered together, insomuch that there was no room to receive them, no, not so much as about the door: and he preached the word unto them.

"And they came unto him, bringing one sick of the palsy, which was borne of four.

"And when they could not come nigh unto him for the press, they uncovered the roof where he was: and when they had broken it up, they let down the bed wherein the sick of the palsy lay.

"When Jesūs saw their faith, he said unto the sick of the palsy, Son, thy sins be forgiven thee. . . .

"I say unto thee, Arise, and take up thy bed, and go thy way into thine house.

"And immediately he arose, took up the bed, and went forth before them all" (Mark 2:1–5, 11–12).

Archaeology supports this story in an interesting way. The dry-stone basalt walls of the excavated house which is purported to be, and almost certainly is, Peter's domicile could have supported only a light roof and, when viewed on site by anyone familiar with the text, automatically conjures up the episode of the curing of the paralytic. Much evidence shows that this house was singled out and venerated from the mid–first century A.D. One specific room in the house-complex bears plastered walls and a large number of graffiti scratched thereon, some mentioning Jesus as Lord and Christ. In the mid–first century the house underwent a significant change in use, from normal family activity to a general gathering or meeting place, indicating that it became one of the first house-churches in the Holy Land.[4] Additionally, the synoptic Gospels portray Peter's house as being near the Capernaum synagogue, and archaeological excavations reveal that it was indeed situated near both the ancient synagogue of the town, which was situated on a slight rise just north of the house *and* the shores of the Sea of Galilee, immediately south of the house. New Testament passages indicate that Peter was a fisherman with his brother and was an owner of fishing vessels on the Sea of Galilee.

That Peter was married is an important doctrinal statement, for marriage was a vital, even indispensable, institution both in first-century Judaism and among the leaders of the very Church the Lord Himself established while He was on the earth. From a comment in one of Paul's letters to the Corinthian Saints we learn that

Peter carried out his ministry and pursued his apostolic travels with his wife at his side. Speaking for himself and his companion Barnabas, Paul asks rhetorically in his letter, "Have we not power to lead about a sister, a wife, as well as other apostles, and as the brethren of the Lord, and Cephas?" (1 Corinthians 9:5). Though the King James Version is a bit convoluted here, Paul is literally asking, "Don't we have the right to take a believing wife along with us, as do the other apostles and the Lord's brothers and Cephas [the Aramaic form of Peter]?"[5]

It seems significant that Paul gives Peter's name separate mention, apart from the "other apostles" whom he cites in a general way. Perhaps Peter's association with his wife was especially prominent, or perhaps Paul is recognizing Peter's preeminent status and example.

PETER'S CALL

Undoubtedly, Peter was foreordained in the grand council of our premortal life to occupy the singular position he was called to fill by the very Savior who was also foreordained and whom Peter would come to love and value more than life itself. The Prophet Joseph Smith taught, "Every man who has a calling to minister to the inhabitants of the world was ordained to that very purpose in the Grand Council of heaven before this world was."[6] The accounts of the four Gospels indicate that Peter became a disciple of our Lord in the very early days of Jesus' ministry but that the call to service was administered in stages, and the full realization of the significance of that calling was understood in stages. Perhaps curious at first blush, his initial call was bound up with his name. But when fully understood, the episode becomes a powerful illustration of an eternal principle.

Peter's actual given name was probably the Hebrew or Aramaic *Shim'on,* anglicized as Simeon (see Acts 15:14), meaning "one that hears." More often than not he is called Simon or Simon Peter in the New Testament. It has been argued that the frequency of the name *Simon* and the rare use of *Simeon* indicates that *Simon* was an alternate original name, was in common use during Jesus' day, and hints at Peter's contact with Greek culture. Thus, he was not simply an Aramaic-speaking Jew unaffected by Hellenistic forces in Galilee but rather "a bilingual Jew who thereby had some providential preparation for later missionary preaching."[7] Peter's father was Jonah. Hence, when Peter was addressed formally he was called, in Aramaic, Simon Bar Jona, "Simon son of Jonah." This is important information because it helps us to understand the significance of the first recorded encounter between the future Apostle and Jesus.

"Again the next day after, John stood, and two of his disciples,

"And looking upon Jesus as he walked, he said; Behold the Lamb of God!

"And the two disciples heard him speak, and they followed Jesus.

"Then Jesus turned, and saw them following him, and saith unto them, What seek ye? They said unto him, Rabbi, (which is to say, being interpreted, Master;) Where dwellest thou?

"He saith unto them, Come and see. And they came and saw where he dwelt, and abode with him that day: for it was about the tenth hour.

"One of the two who heard John, and followed Jesus, was Andrew, Simon Peter's brother.

"He first findeth his own brother Simon, and saith unto him, We have found the Messias, which is, being interpreted, the Christ.

"And he brought him to Jesus. And when Jesus beheld him, he said, Thou art Simon, the son of Jona, thou shalt be called Cephas, which is, by interpretation, a seer, or a stone. And they were fishermen. And they straightway left all, and followed Jesus" (JST John 1:35–42).

Here we learn several interesting things, not the least of which is the superior reading of the Joseph Smith Translation over the King James Version. However, note in particular that this first call to discipleship includes the promise of a *new* name for *Shim'on bar-Yonah*. This was not simply the offhanded bestowal of a convenient nickname as some have supposed. Rather, it was the application of a sacred and ancient principle, which is still administered in our own day. Whenever a new or higher level of commitment is made to the Lord and administered by the Lord or His servants, those disciples who agree to live on a higher plane or commit to a higher covenant, receive a new name, just as the scriptures of the Restoration teach (see Mosiah 5:9–12; D&C 130:11).

In this case, the new name, Aramaic *Kepha'* (anglicized as Cephas), is the equivalent of the Greek *Petros,* or Peter, meaning "stone." But Joseph Smith presents an expanded interpretation of the Savior's intention by describing the meaning as "a *seer* or a stone," thus implying that the new name is better understood as "seer stone." Simon's new name reflected something of his mature role as "seer stone" or revelatory anchor of God's earthly kingdom. In other words, just as a seer stone is an instrument of revelation, the Savior was outlining the future role of the chief Apostle by saying, in effect, Peter would be the instrument through whom revelation for the Church would come. An example of this may be seen in Peter's vision concerning Cornelius reported in Acts 10.

Also important to note is that Peter and John, the first of the specifically named disciples to be called, had been looking for the Messiah. Their commitment to Jesus of Nazareth as the Christ was not "out of the blue." They had been led to search for the Messiah by a mentor. That mentor, as implied in a few New Testament passages, was none other than John the Baptist, whose testimony occupies a good portion of the prologue or first chapter of the Gospel of John the Revelator. In other words, Peter was a disciple of John the Baptist *before* he became a disciple of the Savior. And probably so had most of those disciples who later became the members of the first Quorum of the Twelve Apostles in the meridian dispensation. This is implied in a statement attributed to Peter himself. During one of the first meetings of the Church held after the Savior's ascension, Peter explained to the congregation—about 120 in number— that another needed to be appointed to fill the vacancy in the Quorum of the Twelve left by Judas' death.

"Wherefore of these men which have companied with us all the time that the Lord Jesus went in and out among us,

"Beginning from the baptism of John, unto that same day that he was taken up from us, must one be ordained to be a witness with us of his resurrection" (Acts 1:21–22).

As indicated above, Peter was called to the ministry in a *series* of episodes, each of which progressively impressed on his mind a fuller understanding of both the nature of the call, as well as the nature of the Being extending it, *and* the need for Peter to live in complete harmony with his new calling, which was to become his vocation. Sometime after Peter's initial call from the Savior, Luke's record indicates that Peter was back fishing in the Sea of Galilee when the Savior again bade Peter to follow Him.

"And [Jesus] saw two ships standing by the lake: but the fishermen were gone out of them, and were washing their nets.

"And he entered into one of the ships, which was Simon's, and prayed him that he would thrust out a little from the land. And he sat down, and taught the people out of the ship.

"Now when he had left speaking, he said unto Simon, Launch out into the deep, and let down your nets for a draught.

"And Simon answering said unto him, Master, we have toiled all the night, and have taken nothing: nevertheless at thy word I will let down the net.

"And when they had this done, they inclosed a great multitude of fishes: and their net brake.

"And they beckoned unto their partners, which were in the other ship, that they should come and help them. And they came, and filled both the ships, so that they began to sink.

"When Simon Peter saw it, he fell down at Jesus' knees, saying, Depart from me; for I am a sinful man, O Lord.

"For he was astonished, and all that were with him, at the draught of the fishes which they had taken:

"And so was also James, and John, the sons of Zebedee, which were partners with Simon. And Jesus said unto Simon, Fear not; from henceforth thou shalt catch men.

"And when they had brought their ships to land, they forsook all, and followed him" (Luke 5:2–11).

Though Peter had had previous encounters with the Savior, this time he was so impressed and overcome by the dramatic miracle

Jesus performed (perhaps precisely in order to get Peter's attention) that Peter not only recognized his own unworthiness in the face of such staggering power and towering righteousness but also forsook his fishing business with wholehearted commitment. Commensurate with Peter's commitment on this occasion, Jesus in turn promised Peter and the sons of Zebedee that thenceforth they would do far more than harvest a few fish to satisfy only temporal desires—they would now "catch men," meaning they would have the ultimate power to perform a greater harvest of souls and bring them within the wide sweep of the gospel net. Hence, the object lesson of the increased catch of fish wrought by the Savior's power moments before would, at that instant, have conveyed a poignantly symbolic message, with the Savior saying, in effect, just as I increased the fish harvest manyfold, the greater miracle is the power I will now give to you to increase the soul harvest.

From this time onward, it appears that Peter and his associates fulfilled their commitment to Jesus and to the kingdom with total devotion. We do not see them returning to their old vocation of fishing until *after* the Savior's Crucifixion and Resurrection. During that period of transition the Apostles knew they were supposed to do something to lead the Church in the absence of their Master but seemed unsure of what exactly they were supposed to do because the Savior was not constantly and directly tutoring them anymore. (It will be remembered that this episode occasioned the Savior's renewed call yet again to Peter to feed His sheep as recorded in John 21.)

Peter's Apostolic Role

Thus, from the day of the Savior's call by the Sea of Galilee to the time Jesus was taken away from him, Peter followed the Savior, first as a full-time disciple, and then as a full-time Apostle, living with his Teacher, learning his Master's message and method of ministry, and performing delegated tasks. The Greek word for "disciple," *mathētēs*, is the equivalent of the Hebrew *talmid* and means "learner," or "pupil/student," hence disciple. The rabbis taught that continual and intimate association with one's teacher was an integral part of the learning process. And so it was with the disciples of Jesus. However, unlike the disciples of the other great rabbis of intertestamental Judaism, who were encouraged to choose for themselves their own master or teacher, Peter and his associates who eventually became members of the Quorum of the Twelve were reminded that they had been chosen by the Master (see John 15:16).

Jesus chose the first members of the Quorum of the Twelve from among all the disciples by the same method by which we may be guided: personal revelation.

"And it came to pass in those days, that he went out into a mountain to pray, and continued all night in prayer to God.

"And when it was day, he called unto him his disciples: and of them he chose twelve, whom also he named apostles;

"Simon, (whom he also named Peter,) and Andrew his brother, James and John, Phillip and Bartholomew,

"Matthew and Thomas, James the son of Alphaeus, and Simon called Zelotes,

"And Judas the brother of James, and Judas Iscariot, which also was the traitor" (Luke 6:12–16).

Noteworthy in this passage, and also typical of others, is the mention of Peter's name first. Whenever the Quorum of the Twelve is discussed in the New Testament, Peter is *always* mentioned and is always the *first one* mentioned or named. In fact, Peter is often singled out even when the rest of the group is noted only in a general way. A few examples will suffice:

• "Simon and they that were with him followed after him" (Mark 1:36);

• "Peter and they that were with him said, Master, the multitude throng thee and press thee, and sayest thou, Who touched me?" (Luke 8:45);

"Peter and they that were with him were heavy with sleep" (Luke 9:32);

• Even the angelic messenger in the sepulchre says to the women, "But go your way, tell his disciples and Peter that he goeth before you into Galilee" (Mark 16:7).

As these passages demonstrate, often Peter's name is given specifically, while "the others that were with him" remain anonymous. But that is not all. In the New Testament, Peter is usually found acting or speaking for the whole group of Apostles and disciples and is inferred to be the authorized spokesman for the group. For example:

• At Caesarea Philippi, after a few comments had been proffered by various members of the Quorum as to what people were saying about Jesus' identity, Peter spoke out boldly, declaring his apostolic witness ultimately for the whole group, and affirmed Jesus' messiahship and divine sonship (see Matthew 16:13–16).

• In Capernaum, after many had ceased from following the Savior owing to their offense at the Bread of Life discourse, Peter spoke for the entire group of Apostles in affirming to Jesus their commitment to remain with Him because they were sure that He was Christ, the Son of the living God (see John 6:66–69).

• In Perea, after their encounter with the rich young ruler who went away sorrowing over his inability to give up his possessions, Peter spoke on behalf of the whole group to remind the Savior that they had forsaken all and followed Him (see Matthew 19:27).

Many other examples of Peter's recognized leadership of the disciples generally, and his preeminent position in the Quorum of the Twelve specifically, could be marshaled. But more important than amassing examples of his preeminence is to understand why Peter was singled out and that such prominence was not based on favoritism but on Peter's role among the Apostles as the senior member of the Quorum. The principle of seniority in the Quorum of the Twelve is critically important in the Lord's Church—not to the men themselves but to the Lord because of the implications such seniority has for determining who the next President of the Church will be.

Peter was the senior Apostle on earth and as such held the keys of the kingdom. President Harold B. Lee taught that "Peter, holding the keys of the kingdom, was as much the president of the High Priesthood in his day as Joseph Smith and his successors, to whom also these 'keys' were given in our day, are the presidents of the

High Priesthood and the earthly heads of the Church and kingdom of God on the earth."[8] From Doctrine and Covenants 132:7 we learn that "there is never but one [man] on the earth at a time on whom this power and the keys of this priesthood are conferred." In other words, the keys of presidency over the whole Church "can be exercised in their fulness on the earth by only one man at a time; and that man in the period just after Jesus ascended into heaven was Peter."[9]

The man who holds the keys in their fulness at any one time on the earth is always the Lord's senior Apostle on earth. That is why seniority is so critical. Elder Russell M. Nelson provided an important insight into an episode from Peter's life which demonstrates the principle of seniority. He said, "Seniority is honored among ordained Apostles—even when entering or leaving a room. President Benson related to us this account:

"'Some [years] ago Elder Haight extended a special courtesy to President Romney while they were in the upper room in the temple. President Romney was lingering behind for some reason, and [Elder Haight] did not want to precede him out the door. When President Romney signaled [for him] to go first, Elder Haight replied, 'No President, you go first.'

"President Romney replied with his humor, 'What's the matter, David? Are you afraid I'm going to steal something?'

"Such deference from a junior to a senior Apostle is recorded in the New Testament. When Simon Peter and John the Beloved ran to investigate the report that the body of their crucified Lord had been taken from the sepulcher, John, being younger and swifter, arrived first, yet he did not enter. He deferred to the senior Apostle, who entered the sepulcher first. (See John 20:2–6.) Seniority in the Apostleship has long been a means by which the Lord selects His presiding high priest."[10]

In this light, it seems significant that after His Resurrection, Jesus appeared to Peter singly and apart from all others (see Luke 24:34). And though Peter always maintained a reverent silence about the nature of the visitation, surely it had something to do with the fact that Peter was the President of the Church and held the keys in their fulness, and as such was the one being on earth commissioned to receive the mind and will of Deity in all matters.[11] In a sense, he was taking the place of Jesus as the head of the Church in mortality.

CAESAREA PHILIPPI AND THE PROMISE OF KEYS

Crucial for our understanding of Peter's role as President of the Church and holder of the keys of the kingdom are two pivotal events occurring only a week apart—both of them associated powerfully with the principle of revelation. In the fall season of the year, some six months before His Crucifixion, the Savior took His disciples to the northern reaches of the Holy Land—a beautiful area at the foot of Mount Hermon called Caesarea Philippi. There Peter, acting as spokesman for the group, testified with certitude that Jesus was both Messiah and Son of the living God. In turn, the Savior then promised the chief Apostle that he would be given the keys of the kingdom of God on earth; that is, the power to direct and administer the use of the priesthood on the earth, the power to seal and unseal all matters relative to eternal life. But the manner in which the Savior instructed Peter and the group surely ranks as one of the great, almost unparalleled, teaching moments in all of scripture. For the Master Teacher used not only a wordplay on the name "Peter," but also employed the surrounding geography (the bedrock base of Mount Hermon) as a grand visual aid to impress upon Peter and the others the fundamental principle underlying all that is done in the Lord's Church. Here are Jesus' words immediately following Peter's declaration of testimony:

"And Simon Peter answered and said, Thou art the Christ, the Son of the living God.

"And Jesus answered and said unto him, Blessed art thou, Simon Bar-jona: for flesh and blood hath not revealed it unto thee, but my Father which is in heaven.

"And I say also unto thee, That thou art Peter, and upon this rock I will build my church; and the gates of hell shall not prevail against it.

"And I will give unto thee the keys of the kingdom of heaven:

and whatsoever thou shalt bind on earth shall be bound in heaven: and whatsoever thou shalt loose on earth shall be loosed in heaven" (Matthew 16:16–19).

Anyone who has stood at the bedrock base of Mount Hermon can almost picture the Savior riveting His gaze upon Peter and saying to the chief Apostle, "You are *Petros*" (meaning "stone" or "small rock" according to the footnote in our LDS edition of the King James Bible). Then, in the same breath, pointing to the bedrock face of the mountainside near where they stood, Jesus declared, "and upon this *petra* [meaning "bedrock"] I will build my church."

Through this very graphic, natural visual aid, the Savior's instruction, and hence His wordplay, becomes clear to us. Though critical to the Lord's true Church, it wasn't the chief Apostle himself who formed the foundation of the Church or the basis that underlies all that the Church does. True enough, Peter was, metaphorically speaking, a seer stone; he was to be the revelator for the Church, the person through whom came the mind and will of the Lord for the members of the Church. But pointing out Peter's role simply serves to underscore the basic principle upon which the Church was founded. The Church, including leaders, members, ordinances, and activities, was built upon the foundation of *revelation,* more specifically the personal revelation that Jesus is the Messiah, the actual Son of God, and the ultimate head of the Church.

Revelation (particularly the revelation that Jesus is the Christ) is the immovable base upon which the Church is built and the foundation upon which every person's testimony must be established, Apostle and layperson alike. Revelation is the foundation upon which Joseph Smith's faith and action were based. It is the principle underlying the First Vision. It is the principle which cannot be replaced by anything else. Possessed of his knowledge of Jesus' divine sonship and the revelatory experience by which that knowledge came, Peter could then serve as the vessel or instrument of revelation for the whole Church, and the possessor and delegator of the keys and authority necessary to make Church ordinances and operations valid.

The Gospels of Matthew and Mark tell us that from this point on in His ministry the Savior began to teach His Apostles of His impending death and Resurrection. But Peter did not receive this idea warmly and attempted to rebuke the Savior, telling him that death could not possibly be his lot (see Matthew 16:21–22). Likely, Peter was still thinking of a Messiah in worldly terms—a political ruler and military conqueror on the order of King David or Solomon, who would restore Israel's grandeur and smash all enemies underfoot. Death at the hands of chief priests and scribes was not very messiahlike, let alone divine. Elder James E. Talmage says, "Peter saw mainly as men see, understanding but imperfectly the deeper purposes of God."[12] Peter still did not understand the nature of the true Messiah and his outburst was an appeal to vanity, an encouragement for Jesus to demonstrate the overwhelming power of the kind Peter thought the true Messiah should possess.

Peter's remonstration evoked from Jesus a stern rebuke of his own. The Savior turned to the chief Apostle and uttered these famous words: "Get thee behind me, Satan: thou art an offence unto me: for thou savourest not the things that be of God, but those that be of men" (Matthew 16:23). Of this Elder Talmage says:

"In addressing Peter as 'Satan,' Jesus was obviously using a forceful figure of speech, and not a literal designation; for Satan is a distinct personage, Lucifer, that fallen, unembodied son of the morning; and certainly Peter was not he. In his remonstrance or 'rebuke' addressed to Jesus, Peter was really counseling what Satan had before attempted to induce Christ to do, or tempting, as Satan himself had tempted. The command, 'Get thee behind me, Satan,' as directed to Peter, is rendered in English by some authorities 'Get thee behind me, tempter.' The essential meaning attached to both Hebrew and Greek originals for our word 'Satan' is that of an adversary, or 'one who places himself in another's way and thus opposes him.' . . . The expression 'Thou art an offense unto me' is admittedly a less literal translation than 'Thou art a stumbling-block unto me.' The man whom Jesus had addressed as Peter—'the rock,' was now likened to a stone in the path, over which the unwary might stumble."[13]

This is not the only instance of Peter being chastened by the Savior. There were others. But this episode provides a significant window of insight into Peter's personality, for it allows us to reflect on one of the truly admirable, even remarkable, qualities of Peter. Whenever he was corrected by his Master, he listened without argument, accepted the chastening, never became embittered, and demonstrated the kind of meekness that the greatest mortals on this earth have shown, including the very men Peter respected most (both Moses and Jesus were described as the meekest of men). Meekness is not weakness; certainly Peter was not weak. Meekness is teachableness in the face of correction or even provocation.

Speaking to a group of young people years ago, Elder Neal A. Maxwell provided a much needed reminder about this virtue of meekness possessed by the chief Apostle. He said:

"Meekness, however, is more than self-restraint; it is the presentation of self in a posture of kindness and gentleness, reflecting certitude, strength, serenity, and a healthy self-esteem and self-control. . . . President Brigham Young, who was tested in many ways and on many occasions, was once tried in a way that required him to 'take it'—even from one he so much adored and admired. Brigham 'took it' because he was meek."[14] This not only describes Brigham Young but Simon Peter as well. He was chastened and he "took it" because it was administered by the perfect judge, and it was proper. However, a lesser man may not have reacted so well. In fact, was this Judas Iscariot's problem?

THE MOUNT OF TRANSFIGURATION

Almost one week after Peter's historic declaration of testimony, the Savior's promise of forthcoming keys was fulfilled when Peter, James, and John accompanied their Master to a high mountain where they were transfigured in order to endure the presence of heavenly beings (Moses, Elijah, John the Baptist,[15] and probably others[16]). They heard the voice of God the Father bear witness of His Son in words reminiscent of Joseph Smith's First Vision, and they were shaken by it.

"Then answered Peter, and said unto Jesus, Lord, it is good for us to be here: if thou wilt, let us make here three tabernacles; one for thee, and one for Moses, and one for Elias.

"While he yet spake, behold, a bright cloud overshadowed them: and behold a voice out of the cloud, which said, This is my beloved Son, in whom I am well pleased; hear ye him.

"And when the disciples heard it, they fell on their face, and were sore afraid" (Matthew 17:4–6).

We note again Peter's role as spokesman for the three Apostles and his offer to build tabernacles, indicating that the Feast of Succoth or Tabernacles was at hand. Several happenings marked this experience of the Apostles, and it is clear from Peter's mature reflection about the event, recorded sometime afterward, that it affected him deeply. Elder Bruce R. McConkie indicates that Peter and the other two Apostles apparently received their own endowments while on the mountain[17] and that Peter himself said something even more significant about his experience on the mount. From Peter's second epistle we read:

"Wherefore the rather, brethren, give diligence to make your calling and election sure: for if ye do these things, ye shall never fall: . . .

"For we have not followed cunningly devised fables, when we made known unto you the power and coming of our Lord Jesus Christ, but were eyewitnesses of his majesty.

"For he received from God the Father honour and glory, when there came such a voice to him from the excellent glory, This is my beloved Son, in whom I am well pleased.

"And this voice which came from heaven we heard, when we were with him in the holy mount.

"We have also a more sure word of prophecy; whereunto ye do well that ye take heed, as unto a light that shineth in a dark place, until the day dawn, and the day star arise in your hearts" (2 Peter 1:10, 16–19).

Elder McConkie seems to interpret Peter's language in light of Doctrine and Covenants 131:5, for he concludes that while Peter was on the Mount of Transfiguration he and his associates were sealed up to eternal life and this was made known to them by revelation. Doctrine and Covenants 131:5 states that "The more sure word of prophecy means a man's knowing that he is sealed up unto eternal life, by revelation and the spirit of prophecy, through the power of the Holy Priesthood." Thus, Elder McConkie wrote:

"Those members of the Church who devote themselves wholly to righteousness, living by every word that proceedeth forth from the mouth of God, make their *calling and election sure*. That is, they receive the more sure word of prophecy, which means that the Lord seals their exaltation upon them while they are yet in this life. Peter summarized the course of righteousness which the saints must pursue to make their calling and election sure and then (referring to his experience on the Mount of Transfiguration with James and John) said that those three had received this more sure word of prophecy."[18]

The context of 2 Peter 1 lends some support to Elder McConkie's statement. Here Peter seems to be devoting an entire chapter to encouraging the Saints to make their "calling and election sure" (2 Peter 1:10) by discussing principles associated with this doctrine. This further leads Peter to discuss his own personal eyewitness experience of Christ's glory on the Mount of Transfiguration, which discussion he concludes by stating that he and the others with him received the more sure word of prophecy.

The Joseph Smith Translation of 2 Peter 1:19 provides another insight into Peter's thinking when it states, "We have therefore a more sure knowledge of the word of prophecy, to which word of prophecy ye do well that ye take heed . . ." In other words, the heavenly voice gave the Apostles a more sure knowledge of the word of prophecy. They knew that the Old Testament prophecies were fulfilled regarding the Messiah; they had a surer sense of the accuracy of prophecies because they saw them actually fulfilled.[19]

However one chooses to view Peter's experience on the Mount of Transfiguration as described in his second epistle, it seems absolutely clear that by the time 2 Peter 1 was written the chief Apostle knew a great deal about the doctrine of being sealed up to eternal life, undoubtedly through personal experience.

Peter also witnessed several other happenings of import on the

Mount of Transfiguration, including a vision of the transfiguration of the earth. That is, he and his fellow Apostles saw the earth renewed and receive again its paradisiacal condition at the Second Coming and beginning of Christ's millennial reign. The Prophet Joseph Smith wrote:

"Nevertheless, he that endureth in faith and doeth my will, the same shall overcome, and shall receive an inheritance upon the earth when the day of transfiguration shall come;

"When the earth shall be transfigured, even according to the pattern which was shown unto mine apostles upon the mount; of which account the fulness ye have not yet received" (D&C 63:20–21).

Peter's experience on the Mount of Transfiguration was monumental by any standard and may well have been the most significant event for the Church between the start of Christ's mortal ministry and His atoning sacrifice. It secured the keys of the kingdom to man on earth and taught the Lord's prophet about the reality of visions, heavenly beings, and the true relationship between Jesus and His Father, who is the true and living God.

WITNESS TO MIRACLES

It was Peter's special privilege to witness powerful miracles performed by Jesus, often in the company of few others. He was singled out, for instance, with James and John to see the Savior raise the daughter of Jairus from death back to life (Mark 5:37–43). He was present on one occasion with the other disciples when the Savior fed five thousand with just a few morsels of food (see John 6:5–13, 68). He was in the boat when Jesus stilled the storm-tossed waves of the Sea of Galilee and then saw evil spirits cast out of someone of the Decapolis region (see Luke 8:22–33). He witnessed the Savior heal the blind, deaf, and crippled and perform several other healings which demonstrated the Lord's compassion and power (see Luke 8:1; Mark 1:30–34). By the time the Lord's mortal ministry came to an end, the chief Apostle was no stranger to supernatural occurrences, for he was an eyewitness to marvelous manifestations of the powers of faith and priesthood.

On one occasion, immediately following the feeding of the five thousand, Jesus sent the Apostles on ahead in a boat across the Sea of Galilee, while he went to "a mountain apart to pray" (Matthew 14:23) because the people wanted to "take him by force, to make him a king" (John 6:15). When night had fallen, and the wind on the sea became "boisterous," Jesus began walking on the water to go to the Apostles in their boat, sometime between 3:00 and 6:00 A.M., the time when fishermen on the Sea of Galilee are concluding their nightly fishing expeditions. The Apostles were naturally afraid, believing they were seeing a ghost. But Jesus identified himself and encouraged His disciples to "be of good cheer" (Matthew 14:27). Certainly the Savior's power to perform mighty miracles was confirmed to Peter, and perhaps emboldened by a demonstration of that incomparable power, Peter requested of the Savior to bid him to come to Him. But once upon the water, and seeing the tumultuous wind and waves all around, Peter began to sink.

We glean from Peter's experience a significant lesson—one doubtlessly recounted many times in our New Testament classes: when Peter's focus was taken off the Savior and attracted to the surrounding conditions and great turbulence, he floundered. How like life for us! We must ever stay focused on the Savior. But if we flounder, as did Peter, we too may be lifted up by the Savior's outstretched hand of help (see Matthew 14:28–31).

But also we learn from this experience, as did Peter, another lesson: that faith and fear are incompatible (see Matthew 14:31). How many times do we take counsel from our fears and ultimately forfeit a glorious reward we might have received if we had pressed forward in faith? Perhaps this is why Oliver Cowdery was not allowed to continue his initial efforts at translating the Book of Mormon—distractions and fears overcame his capacity to receive revelation (see D&C 9:5).

I believe Peter learned much about himself as well as the Savior on this occasion. But I also wonder if this episode didn't come back into sharp remembrance for Peter on a future occasion when he came across another person years later at the entrance to the

Jerusalem Temple who was struggling—only with a physical infirmity. Luke describes the episode with poignancy.

"Now Peter and John went up together into the temple at the hour of prayer, being the ninth hour.

"And a certain man lame from his mother's womb was carried, whom they laid daily at the gate of the temple which is called Beautiful, to ask alms of them that entered into the temple;

"Who seeing Peter and John about to go into the temple asked an alms.

"And Peter, fastening his eyes upon him with John, said, Look on us.

"And he gave heed unto them, expecting to receive something of them.

"Then Peter said, Silver and gold have I none; but such as I have give I thee: In the name of Jesus Christ of Nazareth rise up and walk.

"And he took him by the right hand, and lifted him up: and immediately his feet and ankle bones received strength" (Acts 3:1–7).

The parallel can hardly be missed. The chief Apostle took the floundering man at the Temple by the hand and lifted him out of his distress just as Jesus had lifted Peter out of his distress years earlier on the Sea of Galilee. This shows us just how much Peter was destined to become like his Master when he became the earthly head of the Church.

THE LAST SUPPER

Peter's prominent role among the Twelve during the planning of and participation in the Last Supper is reported by the four Gospels. Mark and Matthew indicate that as Passover approached, the disciples asked about preparing for the feast (see Mark 14:12; Matthew 26:17). Knowing how Peter usually acted as the spokesman for the group, one wonders if he wasn't the one asking the question for the disciples. Luke says Jesus sent Peter and John to prepare the Passover, giving them specific instructions on where to make ready the feast and giving them a prophetic sign on how they would find the preappointed place.

"And he said unto them, Behold, when ye are entered into the city, there shall a man meet you, bearing a pitcher of water; follow him into the house where he entereth in.

"And ye shall say unto the goodman of the house, The Master saith unto thee, Where is the guestchamber, where I shall eat the passover with my disciples?

"And he shall shew you a large upper room furnished: there make ready" (Luke 22:10–12).

This instruction is interesting for at least two reasons. A man bearing a pitcher of water was an unmistakable sign since it was such an unusual sight. Also, it is obvious that the man whose house was to be used for the Passover or Seder meal that evening was himself a disciple of the Savior. Jesus tells Peter and John that the owner would know they were making the request on behalf of the Savior when they invoked the phrase, "The Master saith unto thee . . ." The owner of the house would not understand who "The Master" was unless he was a disciple.

As the actual Passover supper unfolded in the Upper Room, several significant events occurred that directly involved Peter. Jesus revealed His knowledge of a betrayer, and Peter was the one who prompted John to ask of Jesus the identity of the betrayer (see John 13:24). During the course of the evening, two great ordinances were instituted that have had lasting impact. One was the transformation of the Passover meal into the Sacrament of the Lord's Supper, and the other was the washing of the feet. As Jesus prepared to wash His disciples' feet, Peter objected—perhaps believing that such a menial task was beneath the dignity of his Master. However, the Savior both reproved and instructed the chief Apostle, teaching him that he would someday come to a knowledge of the true significance of the ordinance and thus appreciate why it was performed the way it was (see John 13:6–11).

Of tremendous significance during the Upper Room experience was the Savior's instruction to His Apostles about their ultimate reaction to the evening's proceedings—"All ye shall be offended because of me this night"—and Peter's response, even protest, that "Though all men shall be offended because of thee, yet will I never be offended" (Matthew 26:31–33). Jesus' pointed and specific rejoinder to Peter teaches profound lessons, especially the confidence Jesus had in Peter's faithfulness and the potential He knew Peter possessed.

"And the Lord said, Simon, Simon, behold, Satan hath desired to have you, that he may sift you as wheat:

"But I have prayed for thee, that thy faith fail not: and when thou art converted, strengthen thy brethren" (Luke 22:31–32).

The thought that any prayer offered by the Savior would not come to pass, nor any prediction of His not be fulfilled, is unthinkable. Peter's faith would not fail even though he had a deeper conversion yet to experience. The texts of all four Gospels indicate that even up to that point Peter still did not fully comprehend the earthshaking events soon to overtake the Savior and the early Church. But again the Savior patiently tried to teach Peter of things that must come to pass.

"Simon Peter said unto him, Lord, whither goest thou? Jesus answered him, Whither I go, thou canst not follow me now; but thou shalt follow me afterwards.

"Peter said unto him, Lord, why cannot I follow thee now? I will lay down my life for thy sake.

"Jesus answered him, Wilt thou lay down thy life for my sake? Verily, verily, I say unto thee, The cock shall not crow, till thou hast denied me thrice" (John 13:36–38).

Peter was never one to shrink from danger, and we cannot doubt that at that moment and all the moments before and after that point Peter would have forfeited his life for his Master's.

PETER'S DENIAL

Of all the episodes associated with the life of Peter, perhaps the most famous and oft-repeated is his denial of the Lord when the latter was being arraigned before the high priest. The sequence leading up to this scene is important for helping us understand the nature of the denial. After the Last Supper concluded, events moved quickly as the Apostles followed Jesus to the Garden of Gethsemane. Again, Peter's prominent status was manifested as he and the sons of Zebedee, James and John, were given a special vantage point from which to witness the Savior's suffering—though fatigue and doubt ultimately prevented them from both receiving the blessings that could have been theirs and from providing the kind of support to their Master that He so desperately needed at that hour in the Garden (see Joseph Smith Translation, Mark 14:36–38). Three times the Savior came to reprove their murmurings and their weariness. However, in all fairness to the Apostles, we need to remember that they had been awake for a long time and had just gone through a long and emotionally draining Passover experience with the Savior.

When the Savior finished praying the same prayer for the third time in Gethsemane, the Jerusalem temple police force appeared on the scene ready to arrest Jesus. What happened next is stunning, to be sure, but completely in harmony with everything we know about the boldness, fearlessness, and death-defying willingness of Peter to defend his Master. John's Gospel tells the story best.

"Then asked he them again, Whom seek ye? And they said, Jesus of Nazareth.

"Jesus answered, I have told you that I am he: if therefore ye seek me, let these go their way:

"That the saying might be fulfilled, which he spake, Of them which thou gavest me have I lost none.

"Then Simon Peter having a sword drew it, and smote the high priest's servant, and cut off his right ear. The servant's name was Malchus.

"Then said Jesus unto Peter, Put up thy sword into the sheath: the cup which my Father hath given me, shall I not drink it?

"Then the band and the captain and officers of the Jews took Jesus, and bound him" (John 18:7–12).

It must be remembered that Peter's selfless act of protection was done in the face of an armed mob who could have easily overwhelmed the chief Apostle. And it should be noted that Jesus rebuked Peter for trying to stop the arrest. It should also be noted that with the retelling of this episode John highlights a theme woven throughout the evening's happenings. Jesus was extremely protective of His Apostles.

Jesus was taken to the palace of the high priest, where He first appeared before the former high priest, Annas (father-in-law of the current high priest), then arraigned before Caiaphas and others. All the Gospels report Peter's denial, suggesting to us that this was truly a pivotal event. The details need not detain us here, how Peter stood outside of the high priests' house on that cool night and denied knowing Jesus after interrogation by two women and a man (see Matthew 26:69–75; Mark 14:66–72; Luke 22:56–62; John 18:17–27). What gives us great pause, however, is consideration of Peter's motivation. Why did he deny knowing his Master? The reasons usually given range from fear of personal harm, to weakness, to embarrassment, to pride, to indecision or some other reason centering on a flaw or weakness in Peter's character.

However, this seems to contradict everything else we know and have read about Peter in the New Testament, including his confession of the Savior's sonship at Caesarea Philippi and his single-minded resolve to not allow anyone to harm the Savior, especially evil men. In every instance where the impending arrest or death of Jesus had come to Peter's attention, he had been both quick and forceful to say that he would not let such a thing happen (see Matthew 16:21–23) and he would protect Jesus at all costs, even at the peril of his own life, which is what we saw happen in Gethsemane when the armed forces of the chief priests could not intimidate a chief Apostle who was ready to battle them all (see John 18:7–12). Now we are to believe that in the face of a challenge initially put forward by a slave girl, the most unimportant person imaginable in Jewish society, Peter denied even knowing Jesus for fear of being exposed as a follower? (The word *damsel* used in the KJV does not convey the true, lowly position of Peter's first interrogator.)

Years ago, President Spencer W. Kimball invited us to reevaluate our understanding of Peter's actions in a magnificent article entitled "Peter My Brother." Here another chief Apostle, writing about his model and mentor, asks crucial and penetrating questions: Do we really know Peter's mind and heart? Are we sure? Do we understand the circumstances of Peter's denial as well as we think we do? President Kimball discusses the tremendous strength, power, faithfulness, and apostolic attributes of Peter, including his boldness, and then says:

"Much of the criticism of Simon Peter is centered in his denial of his acquaintance with the Master. This has been labeled 'cowardice.' Are we sure of his motive in that recorded denial? He had already given up his occupation and placed all worldly goods on the altar for the cause. . . .

"Is it conceivable that the omniscient Lord would give all these powers and keys to one who was a failure or unworthy? . . .

"If Peter was frightened in the court when he denied his association with the Lord, how brave he was hours earlier when he drew his sword against an overpowering enemy, the night mob. Later defying the people and state and church officials, he boldly charged, 'Him [the Christ] . . . ye have taken, and by wicked hands have crucified and slain.' (Acts 2:23.) To the astounded populace at the healing of the cripple at the Gate Beautiful, he exclaimed, 'Ye men of Israel . . . the God of our fathers, hath glorified his Son Jesus; whom ye delivered up, and denied him in the presence of Pilate. . . . ye denied the Holy One. . . . And killed the Prince of life, whom God hath raised from the dead; whereof we are witnesses.' (Acts 3:12–15.)

"Does this portray cowardice? Quite a bold assertion for a timid one. Remember that Peter never denied the divinity of Christ. He only denied his association or acquaintance with the Christ, which is quite a different matter. . . .

"Is it possible that there might have been some other reason for Peter's triple denial? Could he have felt that circumstances justified expediency? When he bore a strong testimony in Caesarea Philippi, he had been told that 'they should tell no man that he was Jesus the Christ' (Matthew 16:20)".[20]

To what then might we attribute Peter's denial? Simply, to Jesus Himself—to the Savior's request that Peter deny knowing the

Savior, not deny the Savior's divinity but deny knowing the Savior. Why? To ensure Peter's safety as chief Apostle and to ensure the continuity and safety of the Quorum of the Twelve.

By the time of His arrest, Jesus had become very protective of His Apostles, and the safety of the Quorum had become a major concern for the Savior. In His great highly priestly prayer the Savior prayed for the safety of the Apostles. "I have given them thy word; and the world hath hated them, because they are not of the world, even as I am not of the world. I pray not that thou shouldest take them out of the world, but that thou shouldest keep them from the evil" (John 17:14–15). When He was arrested in the Garden, He said to the mob, "I have told you that I am he: if therefore ye seek me, let these go their way" (John 18:8). Jesus did not want and could not let anything happen to those who were ordained to take over the earthly leadership of the Church. Jesus had told Peter at the Last Supper that He had prayed that Peter's faith would not fail—and it did not. As President Kimball stated: "Peter was under fire; all the hosts of hell were against him. The die had been cast for the Savior's crucifixion. If Satan could destroy Simon now, what a victory he would score. Here was the greatest of all living men. Lucifer wanted to confuse him, frustrate him, limit his prestige, and totally destroy him. However, this was not to be, for he was chosen and ordained to a high purpose in heaven, as was Abraham."[21]

In sum, it is apparent that Jesus knew of Peter's fearlessness in defending Him. He had seen several manifestations of Peter's unswerving, almost reckless, commitment to prevent any physical harm from coming to the Savior. And this was something Jesus knew could get Peter into trouble if not tempered. It would put the chief Apostle in grave physical danger. Therefore, I believe that when Jesus told Peter he would deny Him thrice before the cock crowed twice, it was not a prediction; it was a command. This is, in fact, a possible reading of the synoptic texts, according to the grammatical rules of Koine Greek found in the New Testament. Matthew 26:34, 75; Mark 14:30, 72; and Luke 22:61 all use the same verb and verb form, *aparnēsē*, which can be read as an indicative future tense or as an imperative (command) tense.[22] We are grateful to a prophet of the stature of President Kimball, for helping us to look at events in the New Testament differently.

Some might ask, "Why then did Peter weep bitterly after his denial?" I believe these were tears of frustration and sorrow in the realization that he was powerless to change the Lord's fate. He had done what needed to be done, but every impulse inside him was to act differently—to prevent the suffering of the Savior. This was a bitter pill for Peter to swallow. These were tears of frustration precisely because he was obedient but now also fully cognizant of the fact that he was going to lose his Messiah to the inevitability of death. In my view, Peter's denial adds to his stature—not detracts from it!

JUST BEFORE THE ASCENSION

No doubt Peter endured some awful moments during and just after the Savior's horrible Crucifixion, but the joy of seeing for himself his risen Lord again and knowing that all the messianic promises were truly fulfilled in the Being he had followed the previous three years surely must have made up for the anguish. After His Resurrection, the Savior appeared to Peter at the Sea of Galilee (called Tiberias in John 21:1) to reinforce the most important lessons of Peter's life. John tells us that this was the Savior's third post-resurrection appearance to His disciples (see John 21:14). Peter and his associates may have been frustrated, struggling to find their niche during this challenging period of transition. For when Peter announced that he was going fishing, the others said they were going too (see John 21:3). What else was there to do besides return to their old profession now that things had changed so radically after the Resurrection and they were not sure exactly how to proceed with the work of the Lord?

After the group had fished all night and caught nothing, Jesus appeared on the shore, told them where to cast their nets, and watched them gather a miraculous harvest. When Peter realized it was Jesus, he became so eager to be reunited with his Master that he jumped into the water to hurry to shore. There he found that the Savior had fixed a fire and cooked breakfast for him and his associates. What a scene it must have been, and what emotions must have swelled within the disciples. They were cold and tired and hungry. They needed help, and once again there was the Savior to minister to their needs. We must be clear about this. The Savior of the universe had already performed an eternity's worth of service to them and all humankind through the infinite Atonement. He was God! And yet it was not beneath His dignity to care for their personal needs, to demonstrate His personal concern for their economic circumstances, to warm them and make them comfortable, and even to cook for them. In this atmosphere of total service and against the backdrop of His personal example of selfless concern for others, Jesus was able to teach Peter what he must do for the rest of his life—feed the Savior's sheep as the Savior had fed him that morning (see John 21:9–17). The rest of the New Testament from this point on shows us that the lesson was not lost on the chief Apostle.

A MIGHTY CHURCH PRESIDENT

After the Savior's ascension, it is clear that Peter assumed the reigns of Church leadership with the same boldness he executed his role as chief Apostle when Jesus was on the earth. He guided the selection of Judas Iscariot's replacement in the Quorum of the Twelve by teaching powerfully from the scriptures (see Acts 1:15–26). In fact, he taught from the scriptures on many occasions. He received a reconfirming witness from the Holy Ghost on the day of Pentecost regarding the divinity of the work and issued his clarion call to the pentecostal converts to be baptized and receive the gift of the Holy Ghost (see Acts 2). He was arrested, imprisoned, and threatened by the Sanhedrin for powerfully declaring his eyewitness testimony of the Savior's Resurrection without equivocation, as well as charging the Jewish leaders with the death of his Master without flinching (see Acts 3:12–26; 4:8–20).

When the Lord was ready to expand His Church, He revealed to Peter His plan to allow Gentiles to be admitted to the ranks of Church membership. And it was simultaneously to Cornelius that the Lord revealed His will that Cornelius send messengers to bring Simon Peter to Caesarea (see Acts 10). This helps us to remember that as the President of the Church and the holder of the keys of the kingdom, such monumental changes in the Church were mandated by the Lord to come through Peter and through no one else.

Peter continued to have marvelous manifestations after the Lord's ascension, as when the angel of the Lord came at night to release Peter from prison and protect him from the fate that James, the brother of John, had suffered at the hands of Herod Agrippa I (see Acts 12). In fact, the first twelve chapters of Acts center on the actions of Peter, while chapters 13–28 highlight the ministry of Paul—the great Apostle to the Gentiles. But other books make it clear that Peter continued an active ministry to and was the revered leader of the Jewish segment of the Church while Paul was working with the Gentiles (see Galatians 2:8). During this time Paul had an open dispute with Peter over the Gentiles in the Church. Apparently, at one point after submitting to the influence of James, Peter withdrew from eating with the Gentiles, for which Paul "withstood him to the face" (Galatians 2:11). Yet, as Elder McConkie pointed out, even though Paul may have had a legitimate issue to raise, Peter was still the President of the Church and Paul was still his junior.[23]

CLOSE OF HIS MINISTRY

Toward the end of his life, Peter ended up in Rome. In one of his personal letters addressed to the Saints in the five major provinces of Asia Minor, he sends greetings from "Babylon," which is probably none other than the great capital city of the Roman Empire (see 1 Peter 5:13). The early Church historian Eusebius tells us that 1 Peter was written in Rome.[24] Even more interesting is the statement telling us of those who were with Peter at that time in his life, particularly Marcus (see 1 Peter 5:13)—likely the same who was the author of the Gospel of Mark and scribe for the chief Apostle. One can imagine the younger John Mark recording the teachings and reminiscences of Peter, copying down the eyewitness testimony of all the Lord said and did including the foundational doctrines learned. Surely it was from these experiences with Peter that Mark gleaned the necessary information for his Gospel record as well as the content for the two surviving letters sent by the chief Apostle.

Within Peter's two epistles is to be found an important and helpful survey of some of the major doctrines of the early Church of Jesus Christ, including the sinlessness of Jesus; the redemptive power of His atoning blood (see 1 Peter 1:18–20; 2:24–25; 3:18); the postmortal, spirit-prison ministry of Christ (1 Peter 3:19–20; 4:6); baptism (1 Peter 3:21); priesthood (1 Peter 2:9); and others. Some of the greatest contributions towards helping the Saints (ancient and modern) understand, appreciate, and withstand life's trials and tribulations come from Peter's two epistles. These include such encouraging exhortations as:

• The Saints must remember that they are the elect according to the foreknowledge of God and are kept by the power of God (see 1 Peter 1:2–5).

• The Saints should remember that adversity has eternal value (see 1 Peter 4:12–14).

• The Saints must endure in righteousness and bear afflictions patiently (see 1 Peter 2:19–20).

• The Saints will receive great blessings if they do not render evil for evil or railing for railing (see 1 Peter 3:9).

• The Saints should love and strengthen one another (see 1 Peter 1:22; 3:8).

• The Saints should remember that mortality is temporary, but God's promises are eternal (see 1 Peter 1:24–25).

• Husbands and wives should strive to strengthen marriage and family bonds (see 1 Peter 3:1–7).

• The Saints should remember the reward of false prophets, false teachers, and false disciples (see 2 Peter 2:1–4, 9, 12–14, 20–21).

• The Saints can make their calling and election sure through faith and effort (see 2 Peter 1:4–12, 18–19).

In a very touching and uplifting section of his first letter, Peter teaches us about the Savior's basic nature. Though "he was reviled, [he] reviled not again; when he suffered, he threatened not" (1 Peter 2:23). Because of the Savior's meekness and patience in bearing His sufferings and "stripes" without revenge, by His stripes are we healed (see 1 Peter 2:24). One has little doubt that Peter saw in his Master the desirable pattern and much-to-be-sought-after ideal for his own life. Thus, as Paul did in his second letter to Timothy, Peter stated in his own second letter that he shortly "must put off this . . . tabernacle, even as our Lord Jesus Christ hath shewed me" (2 Peter 1:14). This is undoubtedly a reference to the resurrected Lord's prophecy of Peter's own crucifixion as recorded in John 21:18–19:

"Verily, verily, I say unto thee, When thou wast young, thou girdest thyself, and walkedst whither thou wouldest: but when thou shalt be old, thou shalt stretch forth thy hands, and another shall gird thee, and carry thee whither thou wouldest not.

"This spake he, signifying by what death he should glorify God. And when he had spoken this, he saith unto him, Follow me."

CONCLUSION

According to reputable tradition, recorded in the statements of various early authorities of the Christian Church, Peter's death fulfilled the prophesy of the Savior. The chief Apostle died in Rome—martyred in the last years of the reign of Emperor Nero (A.D. 67–68). In 1 Clement 5:4 it is said of Peter that he suffered not one or two but many trials, and having given his testimony, he went to the place which was his due. Ignatius, bishop of Antioch, refers to the deaths of Peter and Paul in Rome, as does Eusebius of Caesarea. Tertullian refers to three martyrdoms at Rome: Peter, Paul, and John. And, finally, Origen reported that Peter "at the end . . . came to Rome and was crucified head downwards."[25]

To the very end, Peter followed his Lord and Master in both word and deed. He acted like him, taught like him, was rejected like him, and in the end, suffered in the same kind of ignominious death like him. Thus, "Peter holds up the goal of becoming godlike in every sense of the term."[26]

Few men in history had the experiences that Peter had. Fewer still refined their understanding of the things of God and honed their spiritual sensitivity as did Peter. Even fewer served the Savior and the kingdom from start to finish with such unflagging courage and selfless dedication as did Peter. Only a handful of prophets have ever been commissioned to teach the gospel in more than one dispensation and restore their keys in this, the dispensation of the fulness of times (see D&C 7:7; 27:12; 128:20). Peter continues to be our model missionary. In giving instruction to elders of the Church in this dispensation, the Lord commanded them to do exactly as Peter of old: preach faith, repentance, baptism, and the gift of the Holy Ghost (see D&C 49:11–14). But Peter also made it clear that Christlike love is the ultimate measure of spiritual progression (see 1 Peter 1:22; 4:8; 2 Peter 1:7).

NOTES

1. This is the judgment of many historians. See, for example, John P. McKay, et. al., *A History of World Societies,* Second Edition (Boston: Houghton Mifflin Company, 1988), 199.

2. Bruce R. McConkie, *Mormon Doctrine* (Salt Lake City: Bookcraft,1966), 571.

3. Jerome Murphy-O'Connor, *The Holy Land: An Archaeological Guide from Earliest Times to 1700,* Third Edition (New York: Oxford University Press, 1992), 223.

4. Murphy-O'Connor, *The Holy Land,* 225.

5. This is the actual NIV wording of this passage, which is closer to the modern colloquial meaning intended by the Greek text than the KJV demonstrates.

6. Joseph Smith, *Teachings of the Prophet Joseph Smith,* comp. Joseph Fielding Smith (Salt Lake City: Deseret Book, 1970), 365.

7. Floyd V. Filson, *The Interpreter's Dictionary of the Bible* (Nashville: Abingdon, 1962), 3:749, s.v. "Peter."

8. Harold B. Lee, in Conference Report, October 1953, 25.

9. *The Life and Teachings of Jesus and His Apostles* (Salt Lake City: Church Educational System, 1979), 200.

10. Russell M. Nelson, in Conference Report, April 1993, 52.

11. Bruce R. McConkie, *Doctrinal New Testament Commentary,* 2:143.

12. James E. Talmage, *Jesus the Christ* (Salt Lake City: Deseret Book, 1962), 364.

13. Ibid., 368.

14. Neal A. Maxwell, "Meekness—A Dimension of True Discipleship," *Ensign,* March 1983, 71.

15. Joseph Smith Translation, Mark 9:3.

16. McConkie, *Doctrinal New Testament Commentary,* 1:400.

17. Ibid.

18. McConkie, *Mormon Doctrine* (Salt Lake City: Bookcraft, 1966), 109.

19. I am indebted to Richard D. Draper for articulating so well the concept being taught by JST 2 Peter 1:19.

20. Spencer W. Kimball, "Peter, My Brother," in *Life and Teachings of Jesus and His Apostles,* 488–89.

21. Ibid., 489.

22. Luke 22:34 also uses *aparnēsē* (identical to all the other synoptic texts); however, the context seems to force a different sense. Yet when Luke repeats the verb form in verse 61 of the same chapter, he falls back to the same construction and sense that Matthew and Mark use. Personal communication with Richard D. Draper.

23. McConkie, *Doctrinal New Testament Commentary,* 2:463–64.

24. Eusebius, *Ecclesiastical History,* 2.15.2.

25. Eusebius, *Ecclesiastical History,* 3.1.2. For an excellent summary of these sources see Floyd V. Filson, "Peter," in *Interpreter's Dictionary of the Bible,* 3:755, s.v. "Peter."

26. Richard L. Anderson, "Peter's Letters: Progression for the Living and the Dead," *Ensign,* October 1991, 7.

13

PETER'S PRINCIPLES: AN APPROACH TO THE FIRST EPISTLE OF PETER

Terry B. Ball

ETER'S FIRST EPISTLE IS A CHALLENGING TEXT for students and scholars of the New Testament. Even the very purpose of this short letter, written to elect strangers residing in Asia Minor (see 1 Peter 1:1–2),[1] is an issue of debate and differing opinions. Some have viewed it as a baptismal sermon or liturgy, others as a collection of hymnic material and commentary, and still others as a simple ethical treatise.[2]

Yet another widely held and helpful approach is to view the letter as being written to warn, prepare, and bolster the Saints for difficult times ahead—times when their lives would be threatened and their faith challenged. In this context the epistle can be understood to be serving the same purpose as the 58th section of the Doctrine and Covenants, which is a revelation given on 1 August 1831 through Joseph Smith to the Saints then eagerly gathering to Jackson County, Missouri.

The Saints hoped to build Zion in the land and usher in the

Terry B. Ball is associate dean of religious education at Brigham Young University.

millennial reign of the Savior. It was a time of great excitement, enthusiasm, and optimism for them. Amid that idealism, the message of the revelation may have seemed confusing, for therein the Prophet issued this warning: "Ye cannot behold with your natural eyes, for the present time, the design of your God concerning those things which shall come hereafter, and the glory which shall follow after much tribulation. For after much tribulation come the blessings" (D&C 58:3–4). The Lord reminded those Saints, "Blessed is he that keepeth my commandments, whether in life or in death; and he that is faithful in tribulation, the reward of the same is greater in the kingdom of heaven" (D&C 58:2). He pled with them to "remember this, which I tell you before, that you may lay it to heart, and receive that which is to follow" (D&C 58:5).

Today we know that the Lord and His prophet were trying to prepare the Saints for the Jackson County persecutions. In the same way, the First Epistle of Peter seems to be trying to prepare the early Saints for the terrible persecutions that they would soon face. For example, in July of A.D. 64, Nero set fire to Rome and then to absolve himself blamed the Christians for the act. The historian Tacitus described the ruthless persecution that followed.

"But all human efforts, all the largesses of the emperor, all the propitiations of the gods, failed to dispel the sinister belief that the conflagration had been ordered. Consequently, to scotch the rumor, Nero fastened the guilt and inflicted the most exquisite tortures upon a group hated for their abominations, whom the populace called Christians. Christus, from whom the name had its origin, had been condemned to death in the reign of Tiberius by the procurator Pontius Pilate, and the pernicious superstition, thus suppressed for the moment, was breaking out again not only in Judea, the original source of this evil, but even in Rome, where all things horrible or shameful from all parts of the world collect and become popular. First, then, those who confessed membership were arrested; then, on their information, great numbers were convicted, not so much of guilt for the conflagration as of hatred of the human race. And mockery was added to their deaths: they were covered with the skins of wild beasts and torn to death by dogs, or they were nailed to crosses and, when daylight failed, were set on fire and burned to provide light at night. Nero had offered his gardens for the spectacle, and was providing circus games, mingling with the populace in the dress of a charioteer or driving a chariot. Hence, though they were deserving of the most extreme punishment, a feeling of pity arose as people felt that they were being sacrificed not for the public good but because of the savagery of one man."[3]

In addition to the Neronian persecutions, we know early Christians also had to endure brutalities during the reign of the emperor Domitian (ca. A.D. 95) and later Trajan (ca. A.D. 112–13). Perhaps Peter,[4] knowing that these times of pain and persecution lay just over the horizon, sent out his first epistle to bolster and prepare the Saints before the turmoil began.

Studying the letter in this context reveals many powerful principles of how one can endure and respond to persecution while maintaining faith. The counsel given and the principles taught can apply today as well. A father might use this epistle to help a child experiencing negative social pressure and rejection because of his or her righteous standards. A bishop or quorum leader could use the principles taught in the text to counsel someone having difficulty at work due to adherence to gospel values, or who may be sacrificing the opportunity for some reward or advancement because of his or her faith. Those of any age questioning the value of maintaining faith in adversity will find comfort and strength in Peter's words. His inspired and inspiring counsel is timeless.

REMEMBER WHO YOU ARE

Most of us can recall instances when a parent or leader, concerned that we might be about to face some serious temptation or challenge, gave us the admonition, "Remember who you are!" Certainly our choices and actions are better when we follow this admonition in the exercise of our agency. It is difficult to sin or fall away while concentrating on the truth that we are children of God striving to become like Him.

Peter apparently realized that keeping a perspective of our divine heritage and eternal goals is especially important in the face of adversity and persecution. He reminded the Saints that because of their "obedience and sprinkling of the blood of Jesus Christ," they are the "elect" of God, and have enjoyed "sanctification" through the Spirit (1 Peter 1:2).

Because of God's mercy and the Resurrection of Christ, Peter assures them that they have a "lively hope" of receiving an "inheritance incorruptible, and undefiled, and that fadeth not away, reserved in heaven" for them (1 Peter 1:3–4). He wanted them to remember that they had been redeemed by "the precious blood of Christ" (1 Peter 1:19–20), and that they are "a chosen generation, a royal priesthood, an holy nation, a peculiar people" (1 Peter 2:9), even "lively" or living stones from which God would build "a spiritual house" (1 Peter 2:5). Such a conviction can be a great source of strength for a covenant people in the face of persecution, anciently and today.

REMEMBER THE VALUE OF ADVERSITY

Shakespeare wrote:
"Sweet are the uses of adversity,
"Which like the toad, ugly and venomous,
"Wears yet a precious jewel in his head."[5]

Peter likewise understood that blessings can be found in trials and adversity. He testified to the Saints that "though now for a season, if need be, ye are in heaviness through manifold temptations [trials and afflictions]: That the trial of your faith, being much more precious than of gold that perisheth, though it be tried with fire," for "the end" of such tried faith will be salvation for their souls (1 Peter 1:6–9).[6] His use of the "tried with fire" imagery perhaps foreshadowed what the Saints would face under the Neronian persecutions. Peter further encouraged the Saints to "rejoice, inasmuch as ye are partakers of Christ's sufferings" and observed that "if ye be reproached for the name of Christ, happy are ye; for the spirit of glory and of God resteth upon you" (1 Peter 4:13–14). Ultimately, "after that ye have suffered a while," Peter assured those Saints, God will "make you perfect, stablish, strengthen, [and] settle you," as you "resist steadfast in the faith" (1 Peter 5:9–10).

ENDURE IN RIGHTEOUSNESS

In the sixth lecture on faith, Joseph Smith taught that "an actual knowledge to any person, that the course of life which he pursues is according to the will of God, is essentially necessary to enable him to have that confidence in God without which no person can obtain eternal life. It was this that enabled the ancient saints to endure all their afflictions and persecutions, and to take joyfully the spoiling of their goods, knowing (not believing merely) that they had a more enduring substance."[7]

Peter also understood that we must have confidence that we are trying to live a righteous life in order to maintain faith in adversity. Accordingly, he counseled the Saints, "Gird up the loins of your mind, be sober, and hope to the end . . . as obedient children, not fashioning yourselves according to the former lusts," but rather "be ye holy" (1 Peter 1:13–14, 16).

He warned that though in times past they may have "walked in lasciviousness, lusts, excess of wine, revellings, banquetings, and abominable idolatries," those doing so now would have to "give account to him that is ready to judge" (1 Peter 4:3, 5).

He further admonished them to lay "aside all malice, and all guile, and hypocrisies, and envies, and all evil speakings" and to "abstain from fleshy lusts . . . having your conversation honest" (1 Peter 2:1, 11–12).

Peter testified that "he that will love life, and see good days, let him refrain his tongue from evil, and his lips that they speak no guile: let him eschew evil, and do good. . . . For the eyes of the Lord are over the righteous" (1 Peter 3:10–12).

LOVE AND STRENGTHEN ONE ANOTHER

When persecution rages, the community of Saints has historically found faith-encouraging love and support within itself. Peter seemed to know that such would be required to endure the trials that lay ahead of the faithful in Asia Minor. He besought them to "love one another with a pure heart fervently" (1 Peter 1:22), to have "compassion one of another, love as brethren," being tenderhearted and courteous to one another (1 Peter 3:8).[8] He especially encouraged the elders among them to do as he himself was exhorted by the Savior—to willingly "feed the flock of God" by example, neither with constraint nor for reward, with the promise that "when the chief Shepherd shall appear, [they] shall receive a crown of glory that fadeth not away" (1 Peter 5:1–2, 4; cf. John 21:15–17). He exhorted the younger to respect and follow the elders and for all to humbly care one for another (1 Peter 5:5).

Peter seems to have been especially concerned that families be strong. Certainly the family should be the primary source of love, support, and comfort in difficult times. Accordingly, he gave counsel to husbands and wives to see that their relationships were loving. He encouraged wives to support and "be in subjection" to their husbands, even as "holy women," such as Sarah, who trusted God and followed their husbands. He suggested that even those husbands who are not converted to the gospel might be "won" by the obedient and righteous example of their wives (1 Peter 3:1, 5–6).

Peter likewise admonished husbands to "dwell" with their wives "according to knowledge," meaning they should be thoughtful and considerate of their spouses. He further urged them to honor their wives, reminding them that they were "heirs together" of the "grace of life" (1 Peter 3:7). The wording suggests Peter understood that the gift of eternal life is received as couples (see D&C 131:1–3; 132:19–20).

REMEMBER MORTAL SUFFERING IS ONLY TEMPORARY

While strengthening and supporting one another during times of persecution, Peter wanted the Saints to remember that suffering during mortality is always temporary, but God's promises are eternal. Keeping that perspective would certainly help them faithfully endure adversity. Likening mortal existence to the grasses and flowers that so quickly complete their life cycles in the Holy Land, Peter testified: "All flesh is as grass, and all the glory of man as the flower of grass. The grass withereth, and the flower thereof falleth away: But the word of the Lord endureth for ever" (1 Peter 1:24–25).

Later in the text he assured the Saints that "the end of all things is at hand: be ye therefore sober, and watch unto prayer" (1 Peter 4:7). He promised that ultimately they would receive an "inheritance incorruptible, and undefiled, and that fadeth not away, reserved in heaven for you" (1 Peter 1:4).

GIVE NO JUSTIFICATION TO PERSECUTORS

Peter was anxious for the Saints to understand that they should live above reproach and thereby give no justification to those looking for excuse to persecute them. He urged the Saints to be honest, law abiding, and obedient to governing entities (see 1 Peter 2:12–14; 4:15). He exhorts them to "honour all men," as well as those of the faith, and to not only fear God but also "honour the King" (1 Peter 2:17). He commands servants to be subject to their masters whether those masters be good or evil (see 1 Peter 2:18). He promises them that with such "well doing ye may put to silence the ignorance of foolish men" and that God is pleased if they are willing to "endure grief, suffering wrongfully" for their faith (see 1 Peter 2:15, 19). He reasons that there is no glory in suffering patiently for their faults, but if they patiently suffer for well doing "this is acceptable with God" (1 Peter 2:20). He repeated the admonition later in the text:

"But and if ye suffer for righteousness' sake, happy are ye: and be not afraid of their terror, neither be troubled;

"But sanctify the Lord God in your hearts: and be ready always to give an answer to every man that asketh you a reason of the hope that is in you with meekness and fear:

"Having a good conscience; that, whereas they speak evil of you, as of evildoers, they may be ashamed that falsely accuse your good conversation in Christ.

"For it is better, if the will of God be so, that ye suffer for well doing, than for evil doing" (1 Peter 3:14–17).

Moreover, when the Saints were being persecuted, Peter wanted them to know that they should not strike back, "not rendering evil for evil, or railing for railing: but contrariwise blessing"

(1 Peter 3:9). Certainly striking back at persecutors would only give those persecutors more justification to continue their attacks.

REMEMBER THE SAVIOR'S EXAMPLE

Perhaps more than anything else, Peter wanted the Saints to look to the Savior as an example of how to faithfully endure suffering. He testified:

"Christ also suffered for us, leaving us an example, that ye should follow his steps:

"Who did no sin, neither was guile found in his mouth:

"Who, when he was reviled, reviled not again; when he suffered, he threatened not; but committed himself to him that judgeth righteously" (1 Peter 2:21–23; see 3:18).

Peter's counsel suggests that Christ asks us to do as He had done—to cleave to our faith and do the will of the Father, even if it requires us to suffer pain and grief. "For Christ also hath once suffered for sins, the just for the unjust, that he might bring us to God, being put to death in the flesh, but quickened by the Spirit" (1 Peter 3:18).

CONCLUSION

Peter had firsthand experience at applying these principles, for he had faithfully faced great persecution and grief. He had been arrested, threatened, and beaten by the Sanhedrin yet boldly bore testimony of Christ to them and his countrymen (see Acts 4:1–23; 5:17–42). He mourned the martyrdoms of Stephen and James and was himself imprisoned in chains under heavy guard, likely to face the same fate. Upon being miraculously delivered, he continued in the ministry knowing that doing so put his own life in jeopardy (see Acts 7:54–60; 12:1–19). He knew as he bore witness in his second epistle that he, like Christ, would soon be called upon to surrender his life for the gospel's sake, yet he did not abandon his faith (see 2 Peter 1:14). Thus, not only did Peter teach but he also modeled the principles by which the faithful should endure trial and adversity. Saints in any dispensation can find strength in Peter's example, and will be able to follow that example in the face of persecution if they will apply the principles he taught:

Remember Who You Are.

Remember the Value of Adversity.

Endure in Righteousness.

Love and Strengthen One Another.

Remember Mortal Suffering is Temporary, but God's Promises are Eternal.

Give No Justification to Persecutors.

Remember the Savior's Example.

NOTES

1. The Greek word translated as "strangers" in this context means resident aliens, while "elect" seems to refer to faithful followers of Christ. Thus the epistle is written to members of the Church who are, in a very real sense, strangers, or resident aliens, living in a wicked world. In particular this epistle was initially addressed to such "strangers" living in several provinces of Asia Minor; i.e. Pontus, Galatia, Cappadocia, Asia, and Bithynia.

2. For a discussion of various views on the purpose of the epistle, see A. R. C. Leany, *The Cambridge Bible Commentary on the New English Bible: The Letters of Peter and Jude* (Cambridge: Cambridge University Press, 1967), 8–9; John H. Elliott, *The Anchor Bible Dictionary* (New York: Doubleday, 1992), 5:270, s.v. "Peter, First Epistle of"; J. Ramsey Michaels, *Word Biblical Commentary: 1 Peter* (Waco, Texas: Word Books, 1988), 49:xliii; Bo Reicke, *The Anchor Bible: The Epistles of James, Peter, and Jude* (Garden City, New York: Doubleday, 1964), 37:74; W. C. van Unnik *The Interpreter's Dictionary of the Bible* (New York: Abingdon Press, 1962), 3:760, s.v., "Peter, First Epistle of."

3. Naphtali Lewis and Meyer Reinhold, eds., *Roman Civilization* (New York: Columbia University Press, 1955), 2:226–27.

4. While the opening verse of this letter clearly states that Peter was the author, some modern researchers, especially those trained in the discipline of textual criticism, question his authorship for a variety of reasons. For a review of the issue see: Leany, 7–12; Elliott, 276–8; Michaels, lv–lxvii; Reicke, 69–73; van Unnik, 762–64. It should be noted however that early Church leaders and historians, centuries closer to the issue than modern scholars, accepted this epistle as genuine, written by Peter. The list of those so accepting Peter's authorship includes Eusebius, Irenaeus, Tertullian, and Clement of Alexandria. (For a good discussion and a list of primary sources for early church acceptance of Peter's authorship of

1 Peter, see "Peter, First Letter of," 761.) I likewise accept the epistle as being written by Peter, likely from Rome around A.D. 62–65 just before the Neronian persecutions. It is perhaps worth noting that regardless of the authorship, the principles taught in this beautiful epistle are true and inspiring.

5. William Shakespeare, *As You Like It,* act 2, scene 1, lines 12–14.

6. The Greek word translated as "temptations" in 1 Peter 1:6 is perhaps more properly translated as "trials" or "afflictions."

7. Joseph Smith, *Lectures on Faith,* comp. N. B. Lundwall (Salt Lake City, Utah: Bookcraft, 1985), 5:7.

8. The Greek word translated as "pitiful" in 1 Peter 3:8 literally means "healthy bowels" or "good insides" and in this context is best understood to mean "tenderhearted."

14

"THINK IT NOT STRANGE CONCERNING THE FIERY TRIAL"

Sherrie Mills Johnson

ART OF LIFE FOR ANYONE TRAVELING the path of righteousness includes what can be called a wilderness trial—an experience similar to what the Savior endured after his forty days in the wilderness. This type of trial is peculiar in that it consists of a period of adversity caused by a contrast between our current earthly reality and the promises the Lord has given us. Enduring the test forces us to confront ourselves and decide not only who we are but who we choose to follow. In this paper, we will examine Peter's first epistle to the Christians who lived in the provinces of what is now Asia Minor to see how he encouraged the Saints who were suffering a wilderness trial and how he advised them from the vantage point of his own experience with such trials.

But before we look at the epistle, let us examine the Savior's ordeal that is recounted in Matthew and Luke to identify what is meant by a wilderness trial. In the Joseph Smith Translation (JST) we are told that Jesus was taken into the wilderness by the Spirit and

---

Sherrie Mills Johnson is an instructor of ancient scripture at Brigham Young University.

after forty days of fasting, prayer, and communion with God, Satan came to tempt him (see JST Matthew 4:1–2; Luke 4:1–2). Two of the three temptations recorded begin with Satan challenging the Savior by saying, "If thou be the Son of God" (Matthew 4:3, 6). These words are loaded with insinuation that is calculated to cause doubts and misgivings. "If you *really* are the Son of God, you shouldn't be hungry. You shouldn't be suffering like this. You're King! You should have power to make food out of this stone. That is, *if* you really are the Son of God." But the Savior was not influenced by Satan's insinuations. He calmly answered, "It is written, That man shall not live by bread alone, but by every word of God" (Luke 4:4).

Satan persisted, however. Appealing to appetite hadn't worked, so Satan appealed to vanity and pride, using the same tactic of insinuation: "If you are the Son of God, you should have power. Prove it. Cast yourself down from this pinnacle and let the angels protect you as is promised in scripture. That will show everyone! That is, *if* you really are who you say you are." Despite the repeated temptations, Jesus never faltered. Instead He commanded, "It is *written,* Thou shalt not tempt the Lord thy God" (JST Luke 4:11).

At last Satan gave up on insinuations and resorted to out-and-out deceit by offering the Savior powers and kingdoms that were not his to give (see Matthew 4:8–9). At this point the Savior dismissed Satan with the words, "Get thee hence, Satan" (Matthew 4:10).

Afterward Jesus returned to Galilee and proclaimed to the people that He was the one sent "to heal the brokenhearted, to preach deliverance to the captives, and recovering of sight to the blind, to set at liberty them that are bruised, to preach the acceptable year of the Lord" (Luke 4:18–19). As in all things, He set the pattern for us. If we will valiantly endure the trials, we will be strengthened and learn more about the duties of our missions here upon the earth.

WILDERNESS TRIALS OF OUR FOREFATHERS

Life in general can be thought of as a wilderness experience in that we leave our spirit home with our Father in Heaven to live for a time in the wilderness known as the lone and dreary world. However, what is meant here by "wilderness" trials are the period of time in our lives when we are tempted, as the Savior in the wilderness, by thoughts that cause us to question our basic beliefs and values and that can be phrased in a format such as "If you are . . ." or "If the Church is . . ." These trials accentuate the fact that we are wandering in a "wilderness" and are calculated to make us feel so far from our heavenly home that we doubt its reality.

Throughout the scriptures we find many examples of trials that fit the wilderness definition. For many years Abraham had to wrestle with the dilemma: "If you are to have seed without number and be the father of many nations, why are you childless?" Later the question became even more poignant: "If Isaac is to provide your posterity, why is he to be slain?" Joseph's wilderness test included, "If you are to be ruler over your brethren, why were they able to sell you into slavery?" For Moses, part of the test was, "If you are to free your people from slavery in Egypt, why are you in exile?" Lehi's wilderness test included, "If you are to inherit a promised land, why are you wandering in the desert for eight years?"

At one point Joseph Smith had to face many of these questions. For example, "If God has a work for you to do, why are you spending so many months in a cold and filthy prison?" And among the questions our forefathers in these latter days had to deal with was, "If you are to establish Zion, why are you being driven from state to state?"

These apparent discrepancies between the promises of the Lord and the reality we are experiencing can last moments, months, or years, and, as with Abraham, they often recur in various forms at different times in our lives. Moses spent forty years in exile before returning to Egypt to free the Hebrews, Joseph spent thirteen years in servitude before he was made a ruler in Egypt, and Abraham was one hundred years old when Isaac was born. The length of time varies, but time is not the important issue. What is important is that these people endured and were better, stronger people because of what they learned from their suffering.

PETER'S WILDERNESS EXPERIENCES

As with other great prophets, Peter was no stranger to wilderness trials. According to John, Peter, who was at that time known by the name of Simon or Simeon, was introduced to Jesus by his brother Andrew. Jesus' first words to Simon were, "Thou art Simon the son of Jona: thou shalt be called Cephas" (John 1:42). *Cephas* is Aramaic and *Peter* Greek for the word "stone" or "rock," and the JST for this verse adds that the Lord also called him a "seer." What a lasting impression this must have had on Simon. He and Andrew had obviously been awaiting the promised Messiah. Finally they met, and the Master's first words to Simon were to proclaim him a seer and a rock. Think about it. A rock is solid, firm, unyielding. A seer is all of this plus wise and knowing. How his heart must have burned at the words and the confidence the Savior was expressing in him.

The first encounter Mark and Matthew recorded between Simon and the Savior differs but is just as dramatic. It took place on the shores of the Sea of Galilee. In these accounts, Jesus approached Simon and Andrew while they were casting a net into the sea and said, "Follow me, and I will make you fishers of men" (Matthew 4:19; see also Mark 1:17).

Luke's account is similar to Matthew's and Mark's, but he added some details the others do not. Luke tells us that the Savior asked Peter to take Him out in his boat so He could teach the multitude. Peter did as he was asked, and after Jesus taught the people He said to Simon, "Launch out into the deep, and let down your nets for a draught" (Luke 5:4). Surprised by the request, Simon protested that he had toiled all night and caught nothing. Despite this he added, "Nevertheless at thy word I will let down the net" (Luke 5:5). No sooner did he obey than the net was filled with so many fish it broke. Calling another boat to help, Simon filled both boats until they began to sink. Seeing the incredible catch, Simon fell at Jesus' knees and said, "Depart from me; for I am a sinful man, O Lord" (Luke 5:8).

Jesus replied, "Fear not; from henceforth thou shalt catch men" (Luke 5:10).

Simon knew the prophecies. He had heard the marvelous teachings of John the Baptist. He had been anxiously awaiting the coming of the Messiah who would heal, recover, and deliver mankind. He recognized that Jesus was indeed that Messiah. Now he was being told by the Messiah that he was to be part of the Savior's work. He was to "catch" men. When the ships landed, Simon and his brother forsook all and followed Jesus.

How these promises and words must have resounded through Peter's mind the next three years as he labored with the Savior. The Messiah promised him that he would be a fisher of men! He proclaimed him a rock and a seer. He was the first called to be an Apostle and was ordained to preach and to heal and to cast out devils (see Mark 3:14–15). Those were the promises, but what were the actual experiences?

During those years Peter witnessed some of the most sacred and marvelous occurrences of all time. He saw storms calmed, people raised from the dead, invalids healed, devils cast out of people, and thousands fed from a few fish and loaves of bread. If that weren't enough, he spent his days listening to Jesus teach his message of peace and love with great authority. Yet despite all the teachings and the things he had seen the Savior do, when the Savior asked who in the multitude had pressed upon Him and touched His clothing, instead of confidently replying something like, "Certainly thou knowest," Peter was bewildered and responded, "Master, the multitude throng thee and press thee, and sayest thou, Who touched me?" (Luke 8:45).

Later, in a great storm, Peter saw the Savior walking on water and called out, "Lord, if it be thou, bid me come unto thee on the water" (Matthew 14:28).

The Lord did bid him come, so Peter stepped out of the ship onto the water and began to walk toward the Savior. But as he walked, the boisterous wind roared in his ears, the waves lapped violently around him and his focus changed from faith to fear. Sinking into the water, Peter cried, "Lord, save me" (Matthew 14:30).

Accordingly, Jesus stretched forth his hand, caught Peter, and tenderly chided, "O thou of little faith, wherefore didst thou doubt?" (Matthew 14:31).

But despite these moments of human frailty, Peter was given glimpses of the rock and seer he was to become and the promises continued. For example, one day while on the coasts of Caesarea Philippi, Jesus asked His disciples, "Whom do men say that I the Son of man am?" His disciples answered, "Some say that thou art John the Baptist: some, Elias; and others, Jeremias, or one of the prophets."

The Savior continued, "But whom say ye that I am?"

Peter responded, "Thou art the Christ, the Son of the living God" (see Matthew 16:13–16).

"Blessed art thou, Simon Bar-Jona," the Savior replied, "for flesh and blood hath not revealed this unto thee, but my Father who is in heaven.

"And I say also unto thee, That thou art Peter; and upon this rock I will build my church, and the gates of hell shall not prevail against it.

"And I will give unto thee the keys of the kingdom of heaven; and whatsoever thou shalt bind on earth, shall be bound in heaven; and whatsoever thou shalt loose on earth, shall be loosed in heaven" (JST Matthew 16:18–20).

The Church would be built upon the rock of revelation, and Peter would hold the keys of the kingdom of heaven. This was another incredible promise for Peter.

However, immediately after this account we are told that the Savior began to explain what was going to happen to Him—that He would be called upon to suffer many things and eventually be killed by those who hated Him. At these words Peter responded, "Be it far from thee, Lord; this shall not be *done* unto thee" (JST Matthew 16:23).

"Get thee behind me, Satan," Jesus rebuked, "thou art an offence unto me: for thou savourest not the things that be of God, but those that be of men" (Matthew 16:23). This stinging rebuke stands in sharp contrast to the promise Peter has just received.

Shortly after this experience, Peter, along with James and John, was present on the Mount of Transfiguration. He heard the voice of God introduce Jesus as His "beloved Son" (Matthew 17:5). But at the sound of the heavenly voice the "rock" fell to his face in fear.

But the climax occurred the night of the Last Supper. On that occasion, Jesus said to Peter, "Behold Satan hath desired you, that he may sift the children of the kingdom as wheat. But I have prayed for you, that your faith fail not; and when you are converted strengthen your brethren" (JST Luke 22:31–32).

At that time Jesus also told His Apostles that "all ye shall be offended because of me this night." In response, Peter vehemently cried out, "Though all men shall be offended because of thee, yet will I never be offended" (Matthew 26:31, 33). And yet before the cock crowed the next morning, Peter—the rock, the seer—had denied the Savior three times. "And the Lord turned, and looked upon Peter. And Peter remembered the word of the Lord, how he had said unto him, Before the cock crow, thou shalt deny me thrice" (Luke 22:61–62). And Peter "went out, and fell upon his face, and wept bitterly" (JST Mark 14:82).

For three years Peter had listened to and pondered the promises. Surely the thought crossed his mind, "If you are the rock, the seer, why do you keep faltering?" But despite the discrepancy between the promises of the Savior and what he was experiencing, Peter did not stop following Jesus. He did not give up or turn away. On the morning of the Resurrection, Peter was among the first at the tomb. Along with the other Apostles, he received the Holy Ghost (see Acts 2:1–4), and the Savior, during his forty-day ministry, appeared to Peter and fed him physically and spiritually on the shores of Galilee after a night of fishing. At the close of this later experience, Jesus turned to Peter and asked, "Lovest thou me more than these?"

"Yea, Lord; thou knowest that I love thee," Peter answered.

"Feed my lambs," Jesus instructed and then asked again, "Lovest thou me?" Peter answered again in the affirmative, and the Savior told Him, "Feed my sheep."

Then once more Jesus asked if Peter loved Him. "Peter was

grieved because he said unto him the third time, Lovest thou me? And he said unto him, Lord, thou knowest all things; thou knowest that I love thee." And Jesus replied once more, "Feed my sheep" (John 21:15–17).

This experience surely reminded Peter of the original promises Christ made to him. He was to catch men—to feed the Lord's sheep! Some may interpret this experience to be one of chastisement, but it seems more to be intended as encouragement. The Savior knew the wilderness experiences that Peter had endured and knew that even though Peter occasionally faltered, his heart was good, his intent was sincere. He had passed the test. But more than that, the Savior knew that the wilderness experiences had not only tried Peter but prepared him. He was now ready to feed the Lord's sheep. This was a turning point for Peter. We next see him on the day of Pentecost boldly teaching the Lord's flock and proclaiming, "Repent, and be baptized every one of you in the name of Jesus Christ for the remission of sins, and ye shall receive the gift of the Holy Ghost. For the promise is unto you, and to your children, and to all that are afar off, even as many as the Lord our God shall call" (Acts 2:38–39). And that day there were about three thousand souls baptized (see Acts 2:41).

We next learn of Peter on his way to the temple with John. A man lame from birth cried out to them, begging for alms. Peter stopped and instructed, "Look on us." Obediently, the beggar lifted his face to them, expecting to receive alms, but instead Peter confidently said, "Silver and gold have I none; but such as I have give I thee: In the name of Jesus Christ of Nazareth rise up and walk" (Acts 3:4, 6).

There was no more doubt. Peter was solid as the rock he was named for. He was a seer. Peter now went forth in power healing the sick, teaching the people, and leading the Church or in other words, feeding the Lord's sheep and catching men in safety nets.

THE FIRST EPISTLE OF PETER

When reading the first epistle of Peter, we learn much more when we keep in mind the author and his background. Peter is writing to people who are suffering a wilderness trial. Bart D. Ehrman, a New Testament scholar, explained: "The word for 'suffering' occurs more often in this short letter than in any other book of the New Testament, even more than in the much longer works of Luke and Acts combined. Even where the author is not talking directly about how to handle suffering, he appears to be speaking about it indirectly."[1] These people are converts to Christianity; some are Jews and some are Greeks. They have been taught the promises. For many those promises were a basis for their conversion. But their reality was not matching the promises. They had been taught they were the elect of God (see 1 Peter 1:2), yet they were being persecuted and tormented by their former friends and neighbors and by the Romans.

For many years the Roman government tolerated all religions, including the new Christian Church. However, as the Apostles taught the gospel, the message that the King of the Jews who had been crucified by Roman soldiers was resurrected, it began to cause a disturbance in the Roman Empire. The Romans did not like the missionaries proclaiming that a coming judgment would destroy the wicked and usher in the Savior's reign of righteousness, so they began efforts to stamp out the new religious movement. Peter's epistles were written just before this persecution erupted into frenzy during the reign of Nero. Hatred and persecution against the Christians throughout the empire were increasing.

If this were not enough, on the local level the Christians were experiencing additional problems. The converts were no longer interested in the "same excess of riot" (1 Peter 4:4), or in other words they were not interested in participating in the same entertainments and past times as they were before they were converted. Because of this, their former friends and neighbors and sometimes even family members may have turned against them and were making life miserable for them. Unable to endure the persecution, some were leaving the Church. Understanding what they were experiencing, Peter wrote the epistles to encourage the members to endure their trials; and being a man who had been tried and tested and prevailed, Peter knew how to do that. The general theme of the epistle is that the Saints are the elect of God and as such they are entitled to the promised blessings, but they should not be surprised when reality contradicts the promises because that is part of the test of life. However, if they will be faithful and turn more fully to Christ, they will be able to endure the contradictions and persecutions.

Peter begins the epistle by addressing them as "strangers" (1 Peter 1:1) and reminds them later that they are sojourners on earth (1 Peter 1:17). In other words, this wilderness is not really their home. Heaven is their home, and it is to be expected that their spirits will feel this discrepancy. However, they are "the people of God" (1 Peter 2:10) and are chosen by God to succeed or to endure the trial. He then reminds them that Jesus Christ "according to his abundant mercy hath begotten us again unto a lively hope by the resurrection" (1 Peter 1:3). Therefore, this condition of being strangers in this foreign place can and will be rectified because of Jesus Christ. It is temporary.

Peter explains that if they can endure the vicissitudes of this "strange" place they will eventually rejoice because they are promised "an inheritance incorruptible, and undefiled, and that fadeth not away, reserved in heaven for you" (1 Peter 1:4). However, before they can get to this promised blessing "for a season" they are going to suffer grief in all kinds of trials so that their faith may be proved genuine (1 Peter 1:6–7). The heading to chapter 1 in our Latter-day Saint edition of scriptures underscores this point. It says, "The trial of our faith precedes salvation."

"Wherefore gird up the loins of your mind," Peter admonishes. "Be sober, and hope to the end for the grace that is to be brought unto you at the revelation of Jesus Christ" (1 Peter 1:13). Grace is enabling power, and Peter of all people knows that it is only because of grace that they can endure the trials of life. They can't do it alone. Peter urges the people to be obedient and not to follow after their former way of life but to strive after holiness in all they do and speak. "Because it is written, Be ye holy; for I am holy" (1 Peter 1:16). Notice that he does not say, "Be ye holy *as* I am holy." Peter has learned that in and of ourselves we cannot be holy. No matter

how much willpower or self-discipline or sincere desire we have, we
cannot be holy without Christ. But *because* Christ is holy—because
He has atoned for us, because He will share His grace with us—we
can be holy with Christ. Peter then reminds them of who Jesus is
and what He has done for us.

In chapter 2 Peter explains more of the promises: "Ye also, as
lively stones, are built up a spiritual house, an holy priesthood, to
offer up spiritual sacrifices, acceptable to God by Jesus Christ"
(1 Peter 2:5). They were to be temples and temples are places of
healing. Also "ye are a chosen generation, a royal priesthood, an
holy nation, a peculiar people; that ye should shew forth the praises
of him who hath called you out of darkness into his marvelous
light" (1 Peter 2:9). But after explaining these promises Peter again
acknowledges the reality by saying, "I beseech you as strangers and
pilgrims, abstain from fleshly lusts, which war against the soul"
(1 Peter 2:11). Then Peter encourages them to be honest and
diligent that all who see their good works even in the face of persecution will be taught about God. After all, Peter explains, it is
commendable if a person endures the suffering he or she deserves,
but how much more commendable when a person endures suffering that is not deserved. That is what Christ did. What's more He
endured the unearned suffering for us (see 1 Peter 3:13–18).

Chapter 4 continues this theme beginning with the words,
"Forasmuch then as Christ hath suffered for us in the flesh, arm
yourselves likewise with the same mind" (1 Peter 4:1). And what is
that mind? A mind centered on righteousness, of course, but also a
mind that understands that just because you are following righteousness and striving to do what is right does not mean you will be
free from suffering. The rains, storms, and tempests beat upon the
house built upon the rock the same as on the house built upon the
sand. The promise has never been that there will be fewer storms if
we follow Christ. The promise is that if we build upon the rock we
will be sustained despite the storms (see Helaman 5:12).

Repeatedly Peter reminds them that Christ, the only pure and
perfect person, suffered more than any of us. Suffering and trial are
a basic part of our mortal experience. Peter pleads with the people

not to turn away from the gospel and Jesus Christ just because they are suffering temptations, persecutions, and trials. Instead he urges them to be sober and to pray (see 1 Peter 4:7) and to help one another through the trials (1 Peter 4:8–11). But most of all, he says, "Think it not strange concerning the fiery trial which is to try you, as though some strange thing happened unto you" (1 Peter 4:12). The New International Version (NIV) renders this verse beautifully: "Dear friends, do not be surprised at the painful trial you are suffering, as though something strange were happening to you. But rejoice that you participate in the sufferings of Christ" (1 Peter 4:12–13). And through all of it, remember that after you have suffered a little while, Christ "will himself restore you and make you strong, and firm and steadfast" (NIV 1 Peter 5:10). He knows that "whom the Lord loveth he chasteneth" (Hebrews 12:6). He knows trials are normal. The persecution they are experiencing is simply part of the trial and test of mortality.

In chapter 5 Peter admonishes the leaders to "feed the flock of God" (1 Peter 5:2) and reiterates the promise that if they will do so "when the chief Shepherd shall appear, ye shall receive a crown of glory that fadeth not away" (1 Peter 5:4). Therefore, they should humble themselves (1 Peter 5:6) and cast their cares upon the Savior (1 Peter 5:7) because the Savior loves them.

Peter concludes his epistle by telling them that after they have suffered a while the Lord will make them perfect. He will strengthen them and establish them (1 Peter 5:10). "And the God of all grace, who called you to his eternal glory in Christ, after you have suffered a little while, will himself restore you and make you strong, firm and steadfast" (NIV 1 Peter 5:10). Peter knows.

OUR OWN WILDERNESS TRIALS

It is tempting to skip over these small letters of Peter when studying the New Testament. However, Joseph Smith said that "Peter penned the most sublime language of any of the apostles."[2] By this did the Prophet Joseph mean that it was the most poetic? Or is it the message that makes it sublime? Perhaps it is the message and the language together. Peter's words encourage, uplift, and advise us. By studying these epistles carefully and returning to them when we need encouragement, we can gain strength and courage to endure when our own wilderness trials cause us to doubt.

As he did to Peter and the early Saints, Satan tempts us to have a negative mindset or attitude instead of being of the "same mind" (1 Peter 4:1) as Christ. Wilderness challenges are as real for you and me as they were for Peter. We may be tempted, "If you are a son of God, and are paying your tithing and doing what the Lord says you should be doing, why are you experiencing financial difficulties?" Or "If you are a member of the only true Church and have lived the Word of Wisdom, why are you having health problems?" Or "If you are a daughter of God, and are to help multiply and replenish the earth why are you not yet married?" Or "If this is the true Church that you have joined, why do so many members have so many faults?" But we, like the people in the provinces of Asia Minor, should not think this strange. Suffering and temptation are normal.

Elder Dallin H. Oaks explains: "Adversity will be a constant or occasional companion for each of us throughout our lives. We cannot avoid it. The only question is how we will react to it. Will our adversities be stumbling blocks or stepping stones?"[3] The only way to endure, the only way to make adversity into stepping-stones, is by turning to Christ.

This is how Peter grew through his adversity. Despite repeated personal trials, he refused to let doubt or discouragement change his course or defeat him. We do not know how many of the Saints in Asia Minor took Peter's advice and were sustained, but we know that he knew the way and that if we follow that way we will be sustained.

Peter's counsel points to one important thing. Whatever happens, the Saints should follow after the good, for all good comes from Jesus Christ (see 2:15; 3:10–13). Peter knew from experience that by choosing the good we put ourselves in a position to be strengthened by the Lord. When we choose the negative and evil, we deny ourselves the blessings.

And how do we consistently choose the good in this world of evil? We trust in Jesus Christ. Peter learned that when the question

"Who touched me?" was asked it wasn't because the Savior needed an answer. Jesus knew who had drawn upon His healing power. Instead the question was asked because Peter needed an answer. Peter learned that we can trust in Jesus because He knows all and will teach us. Peter also knew that when we focus on Christ despite the winds and waves of persecution and suffering that attempt to distract us, we can do miraculous things—things we never dreamed we could do. He knew that even if we falter the Lord still loves us. But most of all Peter knew that we can't do it alone. He knew that when we cry out, "Lord, save me!" the Lord will reach out to us. Peter knew as did President Spencer W. Kimball that "no pain suffered by man or woman upon the earth will be without its compensating effects if it be suffered in resignation and if it be met with patience."[4]

As we read the first epistle of Peter, we can be assured that the man advising us to "have fervent charity among yourselves; for charity preventeth a multitude of sins" (JST 1 Peter 4:8) knows what he is talking about. When we are discouraged, we can turn to his words for comfort and for direction. If we follow his advice and trust in the promises of Jesus Christ despite the reality we are experiencing, we can and will overcome any wilderness trial we are called upon to endure, for it is written, "Jesus Christ, your advocate . . . knoweth the weakness of man and how to succor them who are tempted" (D&C 62:1).

NOTES

1. Bart D. Ehrman, *The New Testament: A Historical Introduction to the Early Christian Writings* (Oxford: Oxford University Press, 2000), 399.

2. Joseph Smith, *Teachings of the Prophet Joseph Smith* (Salt Lake City: Deseret Book, 1976), 301.

3. Dallin H. Oaks, "Adversity," in *Brigham Young University 1994–95 Devotional and Fireside Speeches* (Provo, Utah: Brigham Young University, 1995), 83.

4. Spencer W. Kimball, *The Teachings of Spencer W. Kimball* (Salt Lake City: Bookcraft, 1982), 168.

15

"IF ANY OF YOU LACK WISDOM": JAMES'S IMPERATIVE TO ISRAEL

Craig K. Manscill

*T*HE APOSTLE JAMES STATES, "LET PATIENCE have her perfect work, that ye may be perfect" (James 1:4). *Perfect* is a favored word with James. Besides its repeated use in this verse, it occurs also at James 1:17, 25; 2:22; and 3:2. Here James urges that his readers set before them the goal of becoming perfect and complete, lacking in nothing.

There is no avoiding the awkward, even frightening challenge of this word *perfect* in the New Testament. It is by no means only in James that we hear it. Indeed the reason we meet it here is likely because James had heard the doctrine taught by his half-brother Jesus Christ when He said: "Ye are therefore commanded to be perfect, even as your Father who is in heaven is perfect" (JST Matthew 5:50). The achievement of perfection in its full, positive sense may seem infinitely remote. Nevertheless, the obligation to make it our persistent and urgent aim in life is made unmistakably clear in the New Testament and in the book of James.

Craig K. Manscill is an associate professor of Church history and doctrine at Brigham Young University.

James's counsel to be perfect is followed up with this imperative:[1] "If any of you lack wisdom, let him ask of God, that giveth to all men liberally, and upbraideth not; and it shall be given him" (James 1:5). Wisdom is an attribute of God, and if we are to become perfect even as our Heavenly Father is perfect then it is important to apply to God for wisdom. One of God's foremost gifts for His children who are striving for perfection is the endowment of His wisdom (see Moroni 10:8–9, 18). James expresses that "every good gift and every perfect gift is from . . . the Father of lights, with whom is no variableness" (James 1:17). Therefore, "how much better is it to get wisdom than gold! and to get understanding rather to be chosen than silver!" (Proverbs 16:16). Wisdom, then, is in the deepest sense a divine gift (see 1 Corinthians 12:8).

To James, wisdom is the principal object. As with Paul and faith, John and love, Peter and hope, so it is with James and wisdom. James speaks of many problems that exist among the members of the Church: sinful speech, disobedience, unconcern about others, worldliness, quarreling, arrogance, and evil inclinations toward the rich. James advises those who struggle with temptation to apply to God in prayer for wisdom (James 1:5–6). With wisdom from God, we are able to judge soundly and wisely in the practical matters of life and conduct. James also claims that wisdom "from above is first pure, then peaceable, gentle, and easy to be intreated, full of mercy and good fruits, without partiality, and without hypocrisy" (James 3:17). These are the fruits of wisdom and are to motivate behavior that leads to perfection. This paper focuses on wisdom and its attributes that lift the follower of Christ above the "divers temptations" (James 1:2) of the world which beset the Saints at the time of James.

BACKGROUND TO THE BOOK OF JAMES

It is important to briefly review the background of the epistle of James in order to better understand why James is exhorting his listeners to obtain and apply wisdom in troubling times. His epistle is not addressed to any particular person or branch of the Church but is a general letter to all who care to read it: an open letter to followers of Christ everywhere. The letter is addressed "to the twelve tribes which are scattered abroad" (James 1:1) throughout the Roman Empire; that is, to Jewish Christians of the dispersion. Earlier the Jewish people had proved themselves unworthy of their position and responsibility by their rejection of Jesus, God's Messiah; in their place God had adopted the Christian community as His own people and nation. Hence, the twelve tribes, of which the northern tribes had disappeared entirely from known history, can be considered the whole company of Christian people throughout the known world, in this case the Roman Empire.[2]

Most scholars agree that the letter is authored by James the Just, the brother of Jesus Christ (see Galatians 1:19), for which the dispatch is titled.[3] James occupied a prominent, if not chief, place in the Church in Jerusalem (Galatians 2:9), conducted the first council (Acts 15:13), and with the elders, received Paul upon his return from his third missionary tour (Acts 15:12–13) in A.D. 57.

The epistle of James is presumed to be one of the earliest letters written to the Church. This notion is supported by the early martyrdom of James, which may have taken place in the year A.D. 61. The situation depicted in the letter best fits a period before A.D. 66, when the Jewish war with Rome took place. Over a century before this time, the Roman general Pompey had reduced Judean territory and made many Jewish peasants landless. This, coupled with the exorbitant taxes of Herod the Great, must have driven many small farmers from their employment. Consequently, many peasants worked as tenants on larger, feudal estates; others became landless day laborers in the marketplaces, finding work only sporadically. In Jerusalem the aristocracy became an object of hatred to Zealots, who felt that God alone should rule the land. Various outbreaks of violence eventually culminated in a Zealot revolt in A.D. 66, followed by a massacre of priests and the Roman garrison on the temple mount. This eventually led to the downfall of Jerusalem at which time, A.D. 70–73, its temple was destroyed.[4] Caught up in these social tensions, the Jewish Christians eventually went to war. Once understood in the context of the situation, James's call for wisdom is essential to his argument; that is, with wisdom from God humankind may better cope with trials.

WISDOM

Wisdom plays an important part in this epistle. Some Bible scholars even claim that it may be regarded as the most characteristic word of James.[5] Wisdom for James is intimately related to divine knowledge from God, manifesting itself in the selection of proper ends with the proper means for their accomplishment.[6] Wisdom, from above, is the means. The end is perfection, and the reward is to receive the crown of life which the Lord has promised to those who love Him (see James 1:12).

In biblical times the word *wisdom* (Hebrew *hokma*) had a very narrow meaning as well as a general meaning. The confined definition of wisdom was associated with the demonstration of a person's dexterity in a skill or in art (see Exodus 28:3; 36:1–2). The more general meaning of the word was identified with intelligence, sensibility, judiciousness, with reason, and skillful to judge (see Proverbs 10:1; Deuteronomy 4:6; 34:9). Combining the narrow with the more general meaning of the word, the connotation is one who is skillful in reason and careful judgment (see 1 Kings 2:9). Solomon, the exemplar of wisdom in the Old Testament, revealed his wisdom by being able to devise a test by which it could be determined which two women claiming to be the mother of a child was in fact the real mother (see 1 Kings 3:26). Solomon's wisdom is what we call "moral discernment," or that endowment of heart and mind which is needed for the right conduct of life. It is what Paul prayed that his readers might gain, the power to discern "what is that good, and acceptable, and perfect, will of God" (Romans 12:2).[7] Thus, wisdom means the capacity of judging soundly and dealing broadly with facts, especially in their practical relations to life and conduct. It is this type of wisdom that James extols to his readers.

James uses an intriguing metaphor, "engrafted," to describe the process of how wisdom comes from God to man (James 1:21). To engraft, or to graft, is to insert one part into another so that a permanent union is effected. The purpose of grafting is to create growth resulting in a hybrid. James is advocating the planting of God's wisdom into souls of the children of men that they may judge soundly and wisely in the practical matters of life and conduct. Engrafted wisdom from God, James teaches further, is able to save our souls.

James derives his concept of wisdom from the Old Testament and Jewish thought rather than from Greek writers.[8] For the Greeks, wisdom came to be associated with "cleverness" and subtlety of thought and rare erudition, implying the ability to make fine verbal distinctions and follow abstruse arguments. For the devout Jew, however, wisdom was an endowment of practical usefulness. It was the power to discern right from wrong and good from evil. A wise decision in an emergency was one which led to the greatest possible good in the circumstances.

Another kind of wisdom, which Paul calls "the wisdom of the wise," is intellectual speculation about life and the universe—often divorced from a recognition of moral responsibility. It is this that Paul denounces in 1 Corinthians 1:18–31.[9] This "wisdom" could only mock the truths of God and seek to convince men of what is truth and wisdom through the philosophies and sophistries of men. James refers to this type of wisdom as earthly wisdom (James 3:13–15). Says James, "This wisdom descendeth not from above, but is earthly, sensual, and devilish" (James 3:15). Advancing this type of wisdom, results in envying and strife that perpetuates "confusion and every evil work" (James 3:16).[10]

Elder Gene R. Cook of the Seventy said the student should look for the Lord's definition of wisdom, not the world's. He asked what the world would say to the question, "How do you learn wisdom?" The world's answers might include: go to the university, study, research, and learn from experiences. "Interestingly, none of those are the answer the Lord gives to this question," said Elder Cook. "In fact, they have little to do with His answer. The Lord says one is to learn wisdom by: (a) ' . . . humbling himself,' (b) 'and calling upon the Lord his God, that his eyes may be opened that he may see, and his ears opened that he may hear; for my Spirit is sent forth into the world to enlighten the humble and contrite'" (D&C 136:32–33).[11]

Wisdom starts with an acknowledgment of God and a willingness to understand His will for man. Wisdom is the gift specially needed by one to whom people go for counsel in their spiritual, moral, and domestic dilemmas. This is seen in the role of a ward bishop.

Wisdom is the gift of being able to sense the course that will most likely lead to the good of all concerned—the gift of being able to guide people to an understanding of God's will for them in their individual situations. This gift may be found in those of high intellectual equipment, but it is also found in those who have had few educational advantages and who are of little academic ability. It is God's gift to those who ask in faith, not an achievement of human skill or endeavor. Wisdom then is also the ability to understand God's will and to help others, in their perplexities and lack of understanding, to understand His will as it relates to them.

THE FEAR OF THE LORD IS THE BEGINNING OF WISDOM

Wisdom is also a product of our knowledge. Knowledge is an acquaintance with, or clear perception of, facts. Wisdom is the capacity of judging soundly and dealing broadly with facts, especially in their practical application to life and conduct. This being the case, it follows that wisdom, although more than, is nevertheless a product of, and dependent upon, knowledge.

The Book of Mormon specifically relates God's wisdom to His knowledge. Speaking of the Lord's plan for our salvation, Lehi says, "All things have been done in the wisdom of him who knoweth all things" (2 Nephi 2:24). James asks, "Who is a wise man and endued with knowledge among you?" (James 3:13). Thus, as God's perfect wisdom is a product of His knowledge of all things, man's wisdom is dependent upon his knowledge. But since individuals do not know all things, it is possible for them to be knowledgeable about many things, and still be short on wisdom—that is to say, be without the capacity of judging soundly and dealing wisely with the known facts in their practical relations to life and conduct. Hence, humankind, including James's audience, in its present state of development is lacking in wisdom on two counts. First, individuals do not have all the facts; and second, they do not have the capacity to make maximum beneficial use in their lives and conduct of the facts they do have.

Is there then no hope for James's audience or for the people of the world to improve their situation? Yes, there is a way, but only one way whereby humankind may obtain the benefit of the wisdom which will save them from their situation. That way is for individuals to come to a knowledge of the true and living God by approaching God in prayer. Psalms explains further that "the fear of the Lord is the beginning of wisdom" (Psalm 111:10). The meaning of the word fear as used here was not intended to mean dread, fright, terror, or dismay but rather "profound reverence."[12] A more descriptive, clear version of the statement in Psalms would follow: "Profound reverence" for the Lord is the beginning of wisdom. Let us consider now for a moment the significance of profound reverence. One definition of *profound* is "arising from the depth of one's nature."

Reverence is the soul of true religion. Its seedbed is sincerity. Its quality is determined by the esteem in which one holds the object of reverence as evidenced by his or her behavior toward that object. When that object is God, the profoundly reverent person has an adoration coupled with a respectful behavior toward Him and all that pertains to Him. One who has a profound reverence for God loves Him, trusts in Him, prays to Him, relies upon Him, and is inspired by Him. Wisdom from God has always been and now is available to all men who have a profound reverence for Him. Conversely a lack of wisdom is a lack of profound reverence for God. What better way to overcome a lack of wisdom and obtain a profound reverence for God than to follow James's advice and turn to Him in prayer and ask for wisdom.

Sound judgment, a function of wisdom, is a form of inspiration that can and often does compensate for unknown facts, that is, for lack of knowledge. For example, if a stranger at the crossroads, not knowing which way to turn, can receive inspiration from the Lord, his or her decision will be as wise as if he or she had known all the facts. Why? Because the Lord does all things "in the wisdom of him who knoweth all things" (2 Nephi 2:24). Inspiration from Him is an expression of total wisdom.

The fourteen-year-old Joseph Smith was at that very crossroads. Joseph Smith, who had been effaced by the wisdom of the world, lacked true wisdom. With profound reverence for God and the knowledge he had, Joseph did as James directed and prayed. The promise of James was fulfilled in a heavenly manifestation (Joseph Smith—History 1:7–20). Joseph's faith turned to knowledge and his knowledge turned to wisdom that led him through a turbulent life that ended in martyrdom. If members of the Church are to overcome the divers temptations that have beset them and demonstrate sound judgment they, like Joseph Smith, must turn to God for inspiration.

DIVERS TEMPTATIONS AND AFFLICTIONS: THE NEED FOR WISDOM

During the times of James the need for wisdom is apparently due to "divers temptations" which had befallen the Jewish Christians (James 1:2–4). The Joseph Smith Translation of James 1:2 indicates that the "divers temptations" refer to many types of afflictions. These afflictions may be due to outward trouble of different kinds such as: high taxes resulting in the loss of land and poverty, oppression from the aristocracy and the rich, and subjugation of government officials and pagan neighbors.

James speaks in his letter about many problems that exist among the members of the Church: sinful speech, disobedience, unconcern about others, worldliness, quarreling, arrogance and evil inclinations toward the rich. James addresses the pride of the rich (see James 1:9–11; 2:1–9; 4:13–17), persecution by the rich (James 2:6–7; 5:5–6), and pay withheld by the rich (James 5:4). He also addresses those tempted to retaliate with violent acts (James 2:11; 4:2) or words (James 1:19–20, 26; 3:1–12; 4:11–12; 5:9). Furthermore, James condemns those who have been drawn away from the fold by lusts, enticements (James 1:14–15), filthiness, and "superfluity of naughtiness" (James 1:21). Finally James questions the discipleship of those who profess faith yet do not match their faith with works (James 2:14–17). These undesirable attributes are not consistent with a person who is striving for perfection and is in possession of wisdom.

James responds to these situations with a call for wisdom rather than violence, sin, hypocrisy, and cursings (James 1:5). To the rich who are withholding pay and persecuting the poor, James expresses, "But the rich, . . . as the flower of the grass he shall pass away" (James 1:10). To those who are tempted to be drawn away with lusts and enticements the motivation is given, "Blessed is the man that endureth temptation: for . . . he shall receive the crown of life" (James 1:12). Advice is given to those who offend in word, stating:

"For in many things we offend all. If any man offend not in word, the same is a perfect man, and able also to bridle the whole body.

"Behold we put bits in the horses' mouths, that they may obey us; and we turn about their whole body.

"Behold also the ships, which though they be so great, and are driven of fierce winds, yet are they turned about with a very small helm, whithersoever the governor listeth.

"Even so the tongue is a little member, and boasteth great things. Behold how great a matter a little fire kindleth!" (James 3:2–5).

To those who speak cursings, envying, and strife comes the caution, "But the tongue no man can tame; it is an unruly evil, full of deadly poison" (James 3:8). To adulterers and adulteresses James warns, "Know ye not that the friendship of the world is enmity with God? whosoever therefore will be a friend of the world is the enemy of God" (James 4:4). James alerts those who hold grudges against others, stating, "Behold, the judge standeth before the door" (James 5:9).

Father Lehi promised his son Jacob that God would "consecrate [his] afflictions for [his] gain" (2 Nephi 2:2). Most of us, like the Saints during the time of James, experience some measure of what the scriptures call "the furnace of affliction" (Isaiah 48:10) in our lives. If the means to the end is divers temptations and affliction and the end result is a net gain in wisdom, then let the furnace of affliction do its work.

The Effects of Wisdom

Wisdom from above is not in any individual's power to achieve by his or her own endeavors and devices. The wisdom of this world may be acquired by wit and perseverance, but God's wisdom comes only as God's gift, to be received humbly and gratefully. Its only source is in God, a truth emphasized also in Proverbs 2:6, "The Lord giveth wisdom."

James enumerates the effects that divine wisdom from above should produce. "But the wisdom that is from above is first pure, then peaceable, gentle, and easy to be intreated, full of mercy and good fruits, without partiality, and without hypocrisy" (James 3:17). These fruits of wisdom are to motivate certain kinds of behavior that lead to perfection and also help to cope with the problems, afflictions, and temptations previously mentioned.

The overarching attribute of wisdom is purity. God's wisdom as bestowed on people reveals itself in conduct that is pure. One author writes of the purity of wisdom, "Wisdom which is free from any stain or blemish would be incapable of producing anything evil."[13] This inner quality governs everything else related to it. Christ Himself is pure; the wisdom from above reflects its source. James explains that a religion that is "pure . . . and undefiled before God and the Father is this, To visit the fatherless and widows in their affliction, and to keep himself unspotted from the world" (James 1:27). To be pure is to be free from self-interest and selfish ambition, to have an eye single to the purposes of God. It is not "double minded," to use James's own term (James 1:8).

From the basic quality of purity come seven outward attributes of wisdom. The first, "peaceable," describes heavenly wisdom as peacemaking rather than perpetuating strife. James criticizes those who falsely claim to be wise for their contentiousness (James 3:14; 4:1–2). Peaceable wisdom conciliates, unites, and promotes peace. It is proactive in seeking to remove all causes of ill will and bringing about circumstances that favor harmonious cooperation.

The second attribute is "gentle," or considerate of others, making allowances for their feelings, weaknesses, and needs. Gentleness is the unwillingness to mercilessly demand the strict claims of justice. Those who are gentle are also considerate, reasonable, forbearing, and forgiving.

"Easy to be intreated" is the third attribute. It explains heavenly wisdom as obedient or compliant and also connotes that one is easy to persuade. It describes a character which is the opposite of stubborn, self-opinionated, impervious to persuasion or appeal.

The fourth attribute of wisdom is "full of mercy." James provides his own definition of mercy: the neighborly love that presents itself through action (James 2:8–13). Mercy abounds in good works and in being sensitive to the unfortunate. This contrasts with the resulting evil works of earthly wisdom (James 3:15). To be full of mercy means to be compassionate to those in trouble, even if their trouble is of their own foolish making. Mercy is a quality of God Himself. According to Jesus, it is also what God looks most of all for in men (see Matthew 9:13; 12:7).

The fifth effect of wisdom is "full of good fruits," and it is by their fruits that we determine the real quality of both trees and people (Matthew 7:17–20). Good fruits here mean deeds of practical usefulness to others in need, deeds prompted by mercy and compassion.

The sixth attribute of wisdom is impartiality. The term describes someone who is not discriminatory, neither toward others nor inwardly doubting or being uncertain. Such a person has clear discernment of God's will and thus can be confident regarding the wisdom of his or her actions. James illustrates the partiality exhibited from the rich to the poor man,

"For if there come unto your assembly a man with a gold ring, in goodly apparel, and there come in also a poor man in vile raiment;

"And ye have respect to him that weareth the gay clothing, and say unto him, Sit thou here in a good place; and say to the poor, Stand thou there, or sit here under my footstool:

"Are ye not then partial in yourselves, and are become judges of evil thoughts?" (James 2:2–4).

Mormon, in his epistle to Moroni, says, "For I know that God is not a partial God" (Moroni 8:18).

The seventh attribute of wisdom from above is sincerity. It is open and forthright, without lying, hypocrisy, deceit, or pretense. No schemes or subterfuges will form a part of this wisdom. James again alludes to this undesirable behavior,

"Doth a fountain send forth at the same place sweet water and bitter?

"Can the fig tree, my brethren, bear olive berries? either a vine, figs? so can no fountain both yield salt water and fresh" (James 3:11–12).

These qualities of wisdom are the qualities of Christ Himself, who embodies the Wisdom of God (see 1 Corinthians 1:24). The attributes assist us to gain "the measure of the stature of the fulness of Christ" (Ephesians 4:13); that is, to become like Him. These attributes of wisdom should be part of our thoughts and acts in progressing to what we hope to become.

OUR NEED FOR WISDOM

The Lord, knowing all things, foresaw our present state of confusion and lack of wisdom: Long ago, speaking through His prophets, Isaiah and Nephi, the Lord declared, "The wisdom of their wise men shall perish, and the understanding of their prudent men shall be hid" (Isaiah 29:14; cf. 2 Nephi 27:26).

Confirming that fact, He has said in our day that the wisdom of men has perished and their understanding has come to naught. And He has specified that the reason for their loss of wisdom is the forsaking of Him. His words are:

"They have strayed from mine ordinances, and have broken mine everlasting covenant;

"They seek not the Lord to establish his righteousness, but every man walketh in his own way, and after the image of his own god, whose image is in the likeness of the world" (D&C 1:15–16).

These could have been the very words of James describing his people who had fallen into "divers temptations" and therefore were in a state where they lacked wisdom.

Wisdom, as it was in James's time, is of short supply because men and women do not turn to God for wisdom nor do they profoundly reverence God. Until we apply to God in prayer, in good faith and with persistent works, we will be forever learning and never able to come to a knowledge of the truth. Until we come to a knowledge of God we will continue in distractions, regardless of how much other knowledge we acquire.

Though James has spoken in his letter about many problems, we owe a great deal to him for his teachings about wisdom and the fruits of wisdom. In learning wisdom and reaping its fruits we can rise above the temptations, problems, and afflictions that present themselves in our everyday lives, and thereby "patience [will] have her perfect work, that ye may be perfect" (James 1:4).

NOTES

1. Of the 108 verses in the book of James, about 60 have imperatives of one notion or another.

2. Douglas J. Moo, *The Letter of James: An Introduction and Commentary* (Grand Rapids, Mich.: William B. Eerdmans, 1986), 32–33.

3. Sophie Laws, *A Commentary on the Epistle of James* (San Francisco: Harper & Row, 1980), 38–39.

4. Leslie Mitton, *The Epistle of James* (London: Marshall, Morgan, and Scott, 1966), 233.

5. J. B. Mayor, *The Epistle of James* (London: Macmillan, 1892), 36.

6. Cf. Merrill F. Unger, *The New Unger's Bible Dictionary* (Chicago: Moody Press, 1988), s.v. "wisdom."

7. Ibid.

8. Moo, *The Letter of James*, 52–53.

9. Kent A. Homer Jr., *Faith That Works: Studies in the Epistle of James* (Grand Rapids, Mich.: Baker Book House, 1986), 139.

10. Moo, *The Letter of James*, 134–35.

11. "Preparing for Spirit Is a Role of Students," *Church News*, 24 March 1990, 10.

12. *Webster's Third New International Dictionary of the English Language*, unabridged, s.v. "fear."

13. Moo, *The Letter of James*, 135.

16

DISCIPLESHIP AND THE EPISTLE OF JAMES

David M. Whitchurch

I FIRST BECAME INTERESTED in the Epistle of James years ago as a religion instructor. I discovered that whenever I taught the New Testament the writings of James received little attention. By the time I reached the Epistle of James, I was far enough behind in my teaching schedule that I made a conscious decision to hurry through his writings so that I could get to those of John. In my mind, no student should miss the Revelation of St. John the Divine! Somehow it made sense. Yet each semester I felt that I was doing the scriptures (and my teaching) a disservice. One year I determined to study the Epistle of James in greater depth. What I learned enthralled me.

Historically, the Epistle of James has been shrouded in controversy. One New Testament scholar wrote, "There is no writing in the New Testament, on which critical opinion has varied so widely."[1] Indeed, the impact of such a statement became very real for me. I recently turned in an article on the topic of James for review. The

David M. Whitchurch is an associate professor of ancient scripture at Brigham Young University.

responses from the reviewers were varied and passionate. After reexamining my earlier research, I realized that many of the points made by my reviewers represented areas of scholarly debate. Although the historical intrigue and questions surrounding James are worthy of detailed study, for this paper I have determined to provide a limited overview of its background and focus my attention on the epistle's teachings and application. I will begin with a brief historical overview, followed by a discussion of James's teachings regarding discipleship.

AUTHENTICITY AND AUTHORSHIP

Two areas often debated regarding the Epistle of James include its authenticity and authorship.[2] The earliest extant manuscript fragments of James date to the third century, and the earliest available complete manuscripts from the fourth century.[3] However, the first Christian writer to mention the epistle of James dates to Origen (A.D. 185–253), an Alexandrian scholar, who makes a distinct reference to the epistle as being authored by "James the Just" and "being scripture."[4] It may well be that Origen came into contact with the writings of James after moving from Alexandria to Palestine, where historically the early "church of Jerusalem took pride in preserving links with James, its traditional founder."[5] This makes sense in light of the epistle's Jewish audience. One scholar wrote regarding the Epistle of James: "There is nothing in the thought and teaching of James that does not find resonance in the world of Judaism. In fact, the theological stance of James is consistent with the basic theological perspectives of Judaism."[6] It may well be that some of the problems associated with the epistle's inclusion into canon stem from the fact that the Gentile Christian church was not aware of it because of its isolated use in Jerusalem; or, more likely, they saw less relevancy of its teachings to their personal needs because of the epistle's Jewish audience.

The views regarding the authorship of the Epistle of James vary dramatically. A recent New Testament writer graphically depicted that of fifty-six twentieth century scholars, 13 percent argue that the Epistle of James was written by a non-Christian of Jewish origin,

9 percent attribute partial credit to James, 37 percent consider it to be written pseudonymously, and 41 percent conclude that it was written by James the brother of the Lord.[7] As to the traditional Catholic view, it seems to have its beginnings with Jerome, the 4th century Christian scholar, who struggled with the notion of a familial relationship between James and Jesus. He resolved his conflict by concluding that the book's authorship must be James the son of Alphaeus (see Matthew 10:3). This view largely continues within the Catholic tradition today.[8]

The Protestant position frequently attributes the authorship of James with James the brother of the Lord (see Galatians 1:19; Matthew 13:55). The reasoning comes in part from the writings of Josephus, a first century Jewish historian, who identified James as "the brother of Jesus, who was called Christ"[9]; and Eusebius, a fourth century Christian historian who indicated that following Paul's "appeal unto Caesar" (Acts 25:11), the Jews of Jerusalem turned their attention toward "James the Lord's brother, who had been elected by the apostles to the episcopal throne at Jerusalem."[10] These statements, together with scriptures that depict James as sympathetic toward the Gentile gathering and, at the same time, supportive of some elements of Mosaic law (see Acts 15:13–20; 21:18–20; Galatians 2:9, 12), guide many to conclude that the Epistle of James was written by James the brother of Jesus.

When examining the statements and writings of prophets and leaders of The Church of Jesus Christ of Latter-day Saints on James, Presidents Heber J. Grant[11] and Joseph Fielding Smith[12] both make reference to James as an "Apostle," while Elder Bruce R. McConkie states, "The author of this General Epistle is not known for certain. It is generally believed by Biblical scholars that he is that James who is identified as being the Lord's brother."[13]

DATING THE EPISTLE OF JAMES

There is much evidence to suggest the Epistle of James can be dated prior to the destruction of the Second Temple (A.D. 70). The justification for such a dating partially comes from the text itself. One scholar stated, "There are no signs of heresy or schism, . . . no marks of incipient gnosticism, whether speculative or even, as we might expect in this Epistle, moral . . . such as is characteristic of Jewish Christianity in the latter half of the New Testament."[14] External evidence also suggests an early dating. Josephus records that upon the death of Herod Agrippa I the political stability of the Holy Land dramatically deteriorated along with the hope of economic security due to prevailing famine in the region.[15] Although dates are speculative, these economic and social conditions during this period are reflective of the type of message the Epistle of James delivers.[16]

MARTIN LUTHER AND THE EPISTLE OF JAMES

One last historical controversy worth noting about the Epistle of James deals with the disparaging reviews made about it by Martin Luther. For Luther, the writings of James argued directly against his view that man was justified by faith alone and not by works (compare Romans 3:28; Galatians 2:16; James 2:14–18). Luther, unable to resolve such a conflict, relegated James to the end of his translated volume of the New Testament and did not assign it any number in the table of contents.[17] Luther viewed these books as profitable for edification but believed they should not be given full canonical authority.[18] Luther's statements make his feelings clear regarding the writings of James. For example, in Luther's 1522 "Prefaces to New Testament," he characterizes James as an "epistle of straw" in comparison to those of Paul, Peter, and the Gospel of John, which "show you Christ."[19] On another occasion he said of James, "He throws things together so chaotically that it seems to me he must have been some good, pious man, who took a few sayings from the disciples of the Apostles and thus tossed them off on paper."[20] To help justify his position regarding faith and salvation, Luther dismissed the Epistle of James by saying it was not written by an Apostle.[21] Certainly such caustic discourse influenced many a religious leader as they preached and wrote to their respective audiences.

THE MEANING OF TRUE DISCIPLESHIP

Before examining the content of James's writings, it may be helpful to discuss the concept of discipleship. The word *disciple* as used in the New Testament derives from the Greek *mathetes* and indicates those who direct their minds to something. The substantive meaning denotes "pupil" and implies relationship to a teacher.[22] In regards to Jesus, discipleship requires a willingness to leave everything (see Matthew 10:37–39) and obediently follow the teachings and commandments of Christ (see Matthew 9:9). Elder Neal A. Maxwell said: "This journey of deepening discipleship, therefore, is not one step but many. It is the work of this lifetime, and more. Indeed, as already shown, our journey actually began long, long ago."[23]

Discipleship looms large in the mind of anyone committed to the gospel of Jesus Christ. It mandates fidelity and consistency. The test of true discipleship may find its greatest expression during episodes of trial and tribulation. Certainly, discipleship requires commitment of heart and mind. Elder Maxwell stated, "True discipleship is for volunteers only."[24] Furthermore, he indicated that "much more burdening than that avoidable fatigue, however, is the burden of personal frailties. Almost all of us as members fail to lighten our load for the long and arduous journey of discipleship. We fail to put off the childish things—not the tinker toys, but the temper tantrums; not training pants, but pride. We remain unnecessarily burdened by things which clearly should and can be jettisoned. No wonder some are weary and faint in their minds (see Hebrews 12:3)."[25]

We enter into this pathway of discipleship when we take upon us the name of Christ (see Mosiah 5:5–7). The word or name of *Christ* when examined from a scriptural perspective is not simply used as a label of identification; instead, it becomes "an expression of the essential nature of its bearer. A man's name reveals his character. . . . In Hebrew as in Babylonian thought, name is inextricably bound up with existence. Nothing exists unless it has a name. . . . To cut off a name, therefore, is to end the existence of its bearer."[26] Thus, *life* is indispensably connected to taking upon us the name of

Christ. This is accomplished through covenant (see Mosiah 5:5). King Benjamin stated it simply and succinctly: "And now, because of the covenant which ye have made ye shall be called the children of Christ, his sons, and his daughters; for behold, this day he hath spiritually begotten you; for ye say that your hearts are changed through faith on *his name*" (Mosiah 5:7; emphasis added). When we take upon us the name of Christ, the very personality and innermost self "exercises a constraint upon its bearer. . . . Hence a change of name accompanies a change in character."[27] Therefore, discipleship, in effect, changes the very essence of one's character and transforms us into new creatures (2 Corinthians 5:17).

DISCIPLESHIP

To understand the Epistle of James and its implication toward discipleship, we begin by looking at James's audience and his own commitment (discipleship) to Jesus Christ. James commences his epistle, "James, a servant of God and of the Lord Jesus Christ, to the twelve tribes which are scattered abroad, greeting" (James 1:1). Shortly after the martyrdom of Stephen, Luke explained, "And at that time there was a great persecution against the church which was at Jerusalem" (Acts 8:1). This persecution resulted in the scattering of Christian Jews to cities such as Damascus (see Acts 9:2,10,19) and likely far beyond (see Acts 8:4). It should be no surprise then, that James addresses his letter "to the twelve tribes, which are scattered abroad" (James 1:1). The identification of the Jews as the "twelve tribes" is consistent with scripture from the time of the Babylonian captivity. For example, in speaking to Ananias of Damascus the Lord commanded him to "Go thy way: for [Saul] is a chosen vessel unto me, to bear my name before the Gentiles, and kings, and *the children of Israel*" (Acts 9:15; emphasis added). As indicated earlier, James's epistle resonates to the world of Judaism. Even his name brings to mind the Jewish nature of his letter. The name *James* is the King James Version substitute for the Greek *Iakobos* or *Jacob*—a name found throughout the Old Testament in reference to the father of the twelve tribes of Israel. Such symbolism should not be lost in the King James translation.

Immediately following his introduction, James demonstrates his commitment to the Savior by indicating he is a "servant of God and of the Lord Jesus Christ." That single phrase evokes depth of commitment and determination to serve. The Greek word for *servant* is *doulos,* which means "bondman or slave." Metaphorically, it is "one who gives himself up to another's will; those whose service is used by Christ in extending and advancing his cause among men."[28] Thus, from the very beginning of his letter, James outwardly declares to his audience that he is duty-bound to do all that God and His Son, Jesus Christ, demand of him. In a way, he presents himself as the epitome of one who follows his own counsel.

No greater introduction could be given for any disciple of Jesus. President Hugh B. Brown, a member of the First Presidency, tells the story of being called as an Assistant to the Twelve Apostles in 1953. While working as an attorney for an oil company in Edmonton, Alberta, he described how it looked like he would soon become a multimillionaire. However, prior to achieving such worldly success he experienced feelings of tremendous depression and uneasiness. The prayers that followed led him to an assurance that all would be well. President Brown stated: "That night at 10:00 o'clock, October 1953—the telephone rang. Sister Brown answered. She called me and said, 'Salt Lake's calling.' . . . I took the phone and said, 'Hello.' 'This is David O. McKay calling. The Lord wants you to give the balance of your life to Him and His Church.'" President Brown responded to that call and left all that he had to serve the Lord. He concludes his story by stating, "The men with whom I was associated have made millions," and yet he was willing to leave all that he had to serve God.[29] Such is the message of *doulos.* Unlike the rich young ruler described by Matthew, true disciples give their all to follow Jesus Christ when called upon to do so (see Matthew 19:16–22).

PERFECTION VERSUS DOUBLE-MINDEDNESS

Rather than the chaotic text described by Luther, the message of James presents itself as both unified and harmonious. James's message is the message of Christ:[30]

"My brethren, count it all joy when ye fall into divers temptations; knowing this, that the trying of your faith worketh patience.

"But let patience have her perfect work, *that ye may be perfect and entire,* wanting nothing" (1:2–3; emphasis added).

James wants his hearers to strive for perfection. Such is the message of Jesus: "Ye are therefore commanded to be perfect, even as your Father who is in heaven is perfect" (JST Matthew 5:50). The word *perfect* translates from the Greek *teleos* and signifies "fulfillment," "fully," or "to the end."[31] In God's plan the true test of Christianity means overcoming tribulation. For James, we should "count it all joy" (James 1:2) when we are tried, for only through testing can ultimate perfection be realized (James 1:4).

James proceeds to outline the particular challenges disciples face and how best to overcome them. Perfection can only be achieved when we avoid duplicity, or, as James calls it, "double-mindedness" (James 1:8, 4:8). True discipleship means uniting inner belief with outward behavior in a manner consistent with God's expectations. What we do on the Sabbath day may be far more telling than anything we say about keeping it holy.

Actions reveal our true belief of Christ. The theme is ageless. In the Book of Mormon, Nephi teaches that upon entry into the waters of baptism and reception of the Holy Ghost that we "must press forward with a steadfastness in Christ . . . feasting upon the word of Christ, and endure to the end" (2 Nephi 31:20). In the Old Testament, those that serve God are commanded to "love the Lord their God with *all* [their] heart, and *all* [their] soul, and *all* [their] might" (Deuteronomy 6:5; emphasis added). Jehovah constantly condemned the ancient Saints for forsaking Him in favor of other gods (see Isaiah 46:1–11; Jeremiah 2:13). Elijah demanded to know from his apostate constituency, "How long halt ye between two opinions?" (1 Kings 18:21).

James systematically provides examples of what it means to resist double-mindedness:

"Be ye doers of the word, and not hearers only, deceiving your own selves.

"For if any be a hearer of the word, and not a doer, he is like unto a man beholding his natural face in a glass [mirror]: for he beholdeth himself, and goeth his way, and straightway forgetteth what manner of man he was" (James 1:22–24).

Then, as if to make certain his audience understands, James says, "If any man among you seem to be religious, and bridleth not his tongue, but deceiveth his own heart, this man's religion is vain" (James 1:26). Greek translations for *vain* include "devoid of force," "useless," or "of no purpose."[32] True religion, therefore inner belief, *lacks* force, *is* useless, and *has* no purpose unless one's behavior manifests inner belief. James continues:

"If there come unto your assembly a man with a gold ring, in goodly apparel, and there come in also a poor man in vile [dirty] raiment;

"And ye have respect to him that weareth the gay [goodly] clothing . . . are ye not then partial [or double-minded] in yourselves, and are become judges of evil thoughts?" (James 2:2–4).

James again teaches the principle of unified action and belief when he says:

"If a brother or sister be naked, and destitute of daily food,

"And one of you say unto them, Depart in peace, be ye warmed and filled; notwithstanding ye give them not those things which are needful to the body; what doth it profit?" (James 2:15–16).

There is no escape—double-mindedness in its various manifestations excludes us from discipleship and therefore from perfection.

A case for the damning nature of duplicity can be seen in the story of John E. Page. During a general conference of the Church held on 6 April 1840, Elder Orson Hyde addressed the conference at length regarding a mission to Jerusalem. Following his remarks a motion carried that Elder Hyde proceed on his mission. Elder Page then "spoke with much force on the subject of Elder Hyde's mission."[33] Two days later Joseph Smith Jr. "stated that since Elder Hyde had been appointed to visit the Jews, he had felt an impression that it would be well for Elder John E. Page to accompany him on his mission."[34] What followed demonstrates the dangers of faltering commitment. Although Elder Page left for the mission, by the time he reached Philadelphia Elder George A. Smith met him and advised him to sail to England and catch up to Elder Hyde. Elder Page rejected the proposition, even though he had sufficient money to do so.[35] In time John E. Page was excommunicated from the Church. Faith without works is dead (see James 2:17).

James provides additional insights into nonconformity and its counterproductive influence on discipleship and how double-mindedness derails perfection. He addresses how even the spoken word betrays our fidelity to Christ. Not only must faith be manifest through deed, it must also be evidenced through speech. Ancient literature demonstrates that in "Hellenistic moral teaching that speech was dangerous and, in order to avoid error, either silence or brevity was best . . . a bias that was shared as well by Jewish wisdom."[36] James provides several examples of how such a small bodily appendage as the tongue effects the behavior of the whole body (see James 3:3–8). He declares:

"Therewith [the tongue] bless we God . . . and therewith curse we men. . . .

"My brethren, these things ought not so to be" (James 3:9–10; emphasis added).

In our day we are no less vulnerable to double-mindedness. President Brigham Young stated it most plainly when he said, "If I attain to the knowledge of all true principles that have ever existed, and do not govern myself by them, they will damn me deeper in hell than if I had never known anything about them."[37] President Gordon B. Hinckley warned: "And as we move forward into a wonderful future, there are what some may regard as the lesser commandments but which are also of such tremendous importance. I mention the Sabbath day. The Sabbath of the Lord is becoming the play day of the people. It is a day of golf and football on television, of buying and selling in our stores and markets." Then to make the point, President Hinckley asks, "Are we moving to mainstream America as some observers believe? In this," he says, "I fear we are."[38]

James identifies yet another trial that the Saints in his day must overcome—economic disparity (James 2:1–10). Duplicitous behavior and economic class distinction go hand in hand. Ancient Israel was certainly challenged and condemned for these wrongs. In Amos, the Lord rebukes His covenant people "because they sold the righteous for silver, and the poor for a pair of shoes" (James 2:6). The sins of "pride," "fullness of bread," and refusal to "strengthen the hand of the poor and needy" were sins of Sodom (Ezekiel 16:49).

The basis of the prophetic insistence that the wealthy help the poor is embodied in Israelite law (see Leviticus 19:9–10). James describes the problem by saying, "Let the brother of low degree rejoice in that he is exalted: but the rich, in that he is made low" (James 1:9–10). In an attempt to provide perspective, James tells his brethren that if they can just be patient, there will come a time when the heavy-handedness of the wealthy will fade (James 1:10). James pursues his theme of poverty as he condemns Church members for giving undue benevolence to the wealthy at the expense of the poor (James 2:1–4). Instead of members being sympathetic to the poor, the Saints had become their own enemies and were reminded:

"Hath not God chosen the poor of this world rich in faith, and heirs of the kingdom which he hath promised to them that love him?

"But ye have despised the poor. . . . Do not they [the rich] blaspheme that worthy name by the which ye are called?" (James 2:5–7).

Boethius, a fifth-century Christian philosopher, said of riches: "When riches are shared among many it is inevitable that they impoverish those from whom they pass. How poor and barren riches really are, then, is clear from the way that it is impossible for many to share them undiminished, or for one man to possess them without reducing all the others to poverty."[39] To achieve perfection we must relinquish our dependency upon temporal wants and set our hearts upon the affairs of God. To do so means to treat all people with equality, regardless of social class or status. Jesus also warned against this form of double-mindedness by reminding His disciples that it is impossible to "serve God and mammon," *mammon* being an Aramaic word meaning "earthly goods"[40] (Matthew 6:24).

James continues his theme of the wealthy and their inequitable treatment of the poor. This time he leaves out the endearing term "my brethren" (James 5:1) and states:

"Go to now, ye rich men, weep and howl for your miseries that shall come upon you.

"Your riches are corrupted, and your garments are motheaten.

"Your gold and silver is cankered [rusted or tarnished]; and the rust [venom or poison] of them shall be a witness against you, and shall eat your flesh as it were fire" (James 5:1–3).

James concludes his comments to the wealthy by condemning their hiring practices along with their luxurious lifestyle (see James 5:4–6).

It is no surprise that the trials derived from the economic disparity manifest themselves in both directions. President Ezra Taft Benson said: "Pride is a sin that can readily be seen in others but is rarely admitted in ourselves. Most of us consider pride to be a sin of those on the top, such as the rich and the learned, looking down at the rest of us (see 2 Nephi 9:42). There is, however, a far more common ailment among us—and that is pride from the bottom looking up. It is manifest in so many ways, such as faultfinding, gossiping, backbiting, murmuring, living beyond our means, envying, coveting, withholding gratitude and praise that might lift another, and being unforgiving and jealous."[41]

In addition, King Benjamin warns the poor that they must remain guiltless by not condemning others because they "have not" (Mosiah 4:24). As stated earlier, true disciples must eliminate every type of disparity since God's people must be "of one heart and one mind, and [dwell] in righteousness; and [have] no poor among them" (Moses 7:18).

James has made it clear that the trial and test of this life is both *living* and *being* what we profess. From the outset, he declares that we should rejoice in this test because it brings us ever closer to completion or, as he calls it, *perfection* (James 1:4). James provides a clear unwavering answer how we can avoid double-mindedness and achieve perfection: "If any of you lack wisdom, let him ask of God, that giveth to all men liberally, and upbraideth not; and it shall be given him" (James 1:5). James's solution is wisdom! Even at this point, James warns of the consequences of double-mindedness: One must either "ask in faith, *nothing* wavering" or be tossed and driven like a wave before the wind (James 1:6; emphasis added).

In our day, President Benson has said, "The Lord will increase our knowledge, wisdom, and capacity to obey when we obey His fundamental laws. This is what the Prophet Joseph Smith meant when he said we could have 'sudden strokes of ideas' which come into our minds as 'pure intelligence.' . . . *This is revelation.* We must learn to rely on the Holy Ghost so we can use it to guide our lives and the lives of those for whom we have responsibility."[42] Wisdom, therefore, is the key to receiving knowledge that unifies our will with His.

For James, wisdom is the "good gift" and "perfect gift" from above (James 1:17). This is the gift that descends "from the Father . . . with whom is no variableness, neither shadow of turning" (James 1:17). President Brigham Young stated that, "There is no doubt, if a person lives according to the revelations given to God's people, he may have the Spirit of the Lord to signify to him his will, and to guide and to direct him in the discharge of his duties, in his temporal as well as his spiritual exercises. I am satisfied, however, that in this respect, we live far beneath our privileges."[43]

The wisdom of God eliminates double-mindedness. James warns that not all wisdom is from God. He specifically cautions against earthly wisdom that manifests itself through "bitter envying," "strife," "confusion," and "every evil work." This type of wisdom is "sensual" and "devilish" (James 3:14–16). The characteristics of earthly wisdom are the antithesis of godly wisdom, which is "pure, then peaceable, gentle, and easy to be entreated, full of mercy and good fruits, without partiality, and without hypocrisy" (James 3:17). Each of these qualities lucidly describe what it means to be a disciple or pupil of Christ. For when divine wisdom is sought after and received, that is when behavior and belief intertwine to become one. The catalyst for receiving "every good gift," including wisdom, is prayer, born of a sincere heart (James 1:4–5, 17). James warns his brethren, not to be lured away after the things of the world because of lust, which causes them to pray for that which they ought not (James 1:14–15; 4:1–3). The end result of such behavior "bringeth forth death" (James 1:15).

Regardless of the controversy surrounding the Epistle of James's historical background, its message is of preeminent importance. Its powerful homiletic style directs us ever closer to greater discipleship. Throughout his text he addresses members of the Church[44] who are faced with the challenges of "snobbery, oppression, strife, self-righteousness, hypocrisy, greed, [and] worldliness."[45] When combined with economic disparity, and self-justification, the Epistle of James becomes a prophetic voice to guide us toward discipleship in a modern age that parallels those to whom he wrote. James concludes his letter by reminding us to "be patient . . . unto the coming of the Lord" (see James 5:7). With patience we must find humility—a willingness to draw nigh unto God and submission of our will to His (see James 4:8). It requires us to resist the devil (James 4:7), free ourselves from resentment (James 4:11; 5:9), mourn for our sins (James 4:9), and purify our hearts (James 4:8). Only then can we escape double-mindedness (James 4:8). The Epistle of James truly becomes a prophetic voice which will guide us toward ever greater discipleship. When we take upon us Christ's name through covenant, our thoughts, speech, and behavior become inextricably bound with His. His Divine will manifests itself to us directing us ever closer to the Christ—where peace, harmony, happiness, and the "crown of life" abound (James 1:12).

NOTES

1. Ernest Findlay Scott, *The Literature of the New Testament* (New York: Columbia, 1936), 210.

2. James B. Adamson, *James: The Man and His Message* (Grand Rapids, Mich.: Eerdmans, 1989), 3.

3. Luke Timothy Johnson, *The Letters of James* (New York: Doubleday, 1995), 4.

4. Peter H. Davids, *The Epistle of James: A Commentary on the Greek Text* (Grand Rapids: Mich.: Eerdmans, 1982), 7. The Epistle of James is not included in the Muratorian Canon, ca. A.D. 200 or the Cheltenham List, ca. 359 (see David

Noel Freedman, et al., eds., *The Anchor Bible Dictionary* [New York: Doubleday, 1992], 3:621, s.v. "James Epistle of").

5. Freedman, *Anchor Bible Dictionary,* 3:621. Other early Christian writers such as Tertullian (A.D. 160–215), Eusebius (A.D. 260–340), Jerome (A.D. 346–420), and Augustine (A.D. 354–430) provide differing views on its authenticity (see Adamson, *James: The Man and His Message,* 150; Johnson, *The Letter of James,* 135).

6. Patrick J. Hartin, *A Spirituality of Perfection: Faith in Action in the Letter of James* (Collegeville, Minn.: Liturgical Press, 1999), 7.

7. Davids, *The Epistle of James,* 4.

8. Freedman, *Anchor Bible Dictionary,* 3:622; and David Hutchinson Edgar, *Has God Not Chosen the Poor? The Social Setting of the Epistle of James* (Sheffield, England: Sheffield Academic Press, 2001), 19.

9. William Whiston, trans., *Josephus: Complete Works* (Grand Rapids, Mich.: Kregel, 1960), *Antiquities* XX:IX.1.

10. Eusebius of Caesarea, *The History of the Church from Christ to Constantine,* trans. G. A. Williamson (New York: Dorset Press, 1965), 99.

11. Francis M. Gibbons, *Heber J. Grant: Man of Steel, Prophet of God* (Salt Lake City: Deseret Book, 1979), 88.

12. Joseph Fielding Smith, *Answers to Gospel Questions* (Salt Lake City: Deseret Book, 1966), 5:188.

13. Bruce R. McConkie, *Doctrinal New Testament Commentary* (Salt Lake City: Bookcraft, 1980), 3:245. See also the Bible Dictionary, 709, s.v. "James, Epistle of."

14. Quoted in Adamson, *James: The Man and His Message,* 26.

15. Paul L. Maier, trans., *Josephus Antiquities* (Grand Rapids, Mich.: Kregel, 1994), 280–81. For an excellent overview of historical context and economic circumstances of the day, see Peter H. Davids, *New International Greek Testament Commentary: The Epistle of James* (Grand Rapids, Mich.: Eerdmans, 1982), 33.

16. Even though James's epistle mentions trials, it never states the type of challenges the Saints are facing (James 1:2–3). His allusion to fighting and warring among the members is vague (James 4:1–2). It could be symbolic representation demonstrating the spiritual consequences of their greed. There seems to be little debate that the Jewish people as a whole, including Christian members, had to contend with persecution directed at them from Rome. Part of this longstanding persecution resulted from the Jews themselves who were of the "opinion that it was unlawful for them to pay taxes to an idolatrous master . . ." Edward Gibbon in his book, *Decline and Fall of the Roman Empire,* wrote, "It might therefore be expected that [Rome] would unite with indignation against any sect or people which should separate itself from the communion of mankind, and, claiming the

exclusive possession of divine knowledge, should disdain every form of worship except its own as impious and idolatrous." It may well be that very few of the tribulations James refers to were attributable to Rome. A careful reading of James suggests that many of the trials resulted from selfishness, greed, and economic disparity existing among themselves. Even though Rome may have contributed in many ways to the social climate, The *Pax Romana,* in all likelihood, provided a certain degree of protection for the Saints. The more open and forceful persecution and intolerance seen in other writings of the New Testament seems to come much later. It wasn't until Nero and his placement of responsibility for the burning of Rome upon the Christians (A.D. 64) that we see intense, open persecution (see Edward Gibbon, *Decline and Fall of the Roman Empire,* 111; see also Adamson, *James: The Man and His Message,* 29).

17. Along with Jude, Hebrews, and Revelation. James Hardy Ropes, *A Critical and Exegetical Commentary on the Epistle of St. James* (New York: Charles Scribner's Sons, 1961), 106–7.

18. Ibid. Other statements by Luther refer to James as a "really dangerous and bad book" and on one occasion he even threatened to burn the writings of James when he said, "For you will judge that none of it must be set forth contrary to manifest Holy Scripture. Accordingly, if they will not admit my interpretations, then I shall make rubble also of it. I almost feel like throwing Jimmy into the stove, as the priest in Kalenberg did." Quoted in Adamson, *James: The Man and His Message,* ix. The preacher of Kalenberg burned wooden statues of the Apostles when visited by a duchess (see Lewis W. Spitz, ed., *Luther's Works: Career of the Reformer IV* [Philadelphia: Muhlenberg, 1960], 34:317).

In fairness to Luther, it should also be stated that these terse views do not negate the importance of his accomplishments and the work he achieved regarding the Reformation. Several statements by leaders of The Church of Jesus Christ of Latter-day Saints give powerful testimony regarding the importance of Martin Luther. He played an important part in bringing about the conditions necessary for a latter-day restoration of the gospel of Jesus Christ. President Ezra Taft Benson stated, "The great religious leaders of the world such as Mohammed, Confucius, and the Reformers, as well as the philosophers—Socrates and others—received a portion of God's light . . . to enlighten whole nations and to bring a higher level of understanding to individuals" (*The Teachings of Ezra Taft Benson* [Salt Lake City: Bookcraft, 1988], 271–72). President Gordon B. Hinckley said of the Reformation, "Would there ever have been a Reformation without the certitude that drove with boldness such giants as Luther, Huss, Zwingli, and others of their kind?" ("Faith: The Essence of True Religion," November 1981, 6). Lastly, Elder McConkie says of Martin Luther, "In its very nature Romans is an epistle capable of differing interpretations. Those without prior and full knowledge of the doctrines involved find it exceedingly difficult to place Paul's comments about these doctrines into their true perspective. For instance, it is on a misunderstanding of the Apostle's statement about justification by faith alone that the whole sectarian world is led to believe that men are not required to work out their own salvation; and it was this very passage that enabled Martin Luther to justify in his own mind his break with Catholicism, *an eventuality of vital importance to the furtherance of the Lord's work on earth" (Doctrinal New Testament Commentary* [Salt Lake City: Bookcraft, 1970], 2:212–13; emphasis added).

19. E. Theodore Bachman, ed., *Luther's Works: Word and Sacrament I* (Philadelphia, Penn.: Muhlenberg, 1960), 35:362.

20. Ibid, 397.

21. Ibid, 396.

22. Gerhard Kittel and Gerhard Friedrich, eds., *Theological Dictionary of the New Testament,* trans. Geoffrey W. Bromily (Grand Rapids, Mich.: Eerdmans, 1985), 555–56.

23. Neal A. Maxwell, *But for a Small Moment* (Salt Lake City: Bookcraft, 1986), 110.

24. Maxwell, *Not My Will, But Thine* (Salt Lake City: Bookcraft, 1988), 89.

25. Maxwell, *Men and Women of Christ* (Salt Lake City: Bookcraft, 1988), 3–4.

26. George A. Buttrick, ed., *The Interpreter's Dictionary of the Bible* (New York: Abingdon Press, 1962), 3:500–501.

27. Ibid., 501–2.

28. *LDS Collectors Library '97*, Lexicon of New Testament Greek, s.v. "doulos."

29. Hugh B. Brown, "Eternal Progression," address to the student body, Church College of Hawaii, 16 October 1964, 8–10.

30. At least 36 parallels exist from the writings of James to those of Jesus in the Synoptic Gospels. Davids, *The Epistle of James,* 47–48.

31. Kittel, *Theological Dictionary of the New Testament,* 1161.

32. *LDS Collectors Library '97*, s.v. "mataios."

33. B. H. Roberts, ed., *History of The Church of Jesus Christ of Latter-day Saints* (Salt Lake City: Deseret Book, 1976), 4:106.

34. Ibid, 4:109.

35. Ibid, 4:372.

36. Johnson, *The Letters of James,* 256.

37. John A. Widtsoe, comp., *Discourses of Brigham Young* (Salt Lake City: Deseret Book, 1978), 429.

38. Gordon B. Hinckley, "Look to the Future," *Ensign,* November 1997, 64.

39. V. E. Watts, trans., *Boethius: The Consolation of Philosophy* (New York: Penguin, 1969), 65.

40. The word *mammon* "most probably derives from the root *'mn* ('that in which one trusts')." In the New Testament it denotes "earthly goods" and stresses their materialistic character (see Kittel, *Theological Dictionary of the New Testament*, 552, s.v. "Mamonas").

41. Ezra Taft Benson, "Beware of Pride," *Ensign*, May 1989, 5.

42. Ezra Taft Benson, "Principle with a Promise," *Ensign*, 1983, 54.

43. Widtsoe, *Discourses of Brigham Young*, 33.

44. James uses the phrase "brethren" or "my brethren" fifteen times throughout his letter.

45. Adamson, *James*, 26.

17

"AS THE BODY WITHOUT THE SPIRIT": JAMES'S EPISTLE ON FAITH AND WORKS

Brian M. Hauglid

*W*HEN LATTER-DAY SAINTS EMPHASIZE the importance of exhibiting faith in Christ by works, we commonly refer to the second chapter of the Epistle of James. Surely this epistle is one of the most pragmatic of the twenty-seven books of the New Testament. James considers works to be the lifeblood principle of faith: "For as the body without the spirit is dead, so faith without works is dead also" (James 2:26). James consistently focuses on the *actions* of individuals—for example, the use of the tongue and the treatment of widows.

After I briefly address the historical authenticity and authorship of the Epistle of James, I will analyze the Greek words for *faith* and *works* and discuss Elder James E. Talmage's teachings on these terms. I will then demonstrate that all the chapters in James's epistle, even while not specifically referring to the terms *faith* and *works*,[1] support James's primary injunction to be "doers of the word, and not hearers only" (James 1:22).

Brian M. Hauglid is an assistant professor of ancient scripture at Brigham Young University.

HISTORICAL AUTHENTICITY AND AUTHORSHIP

Surprisingly, the Epistle of James was not readily accepted as part of the New Testament canon. Even though it was considered one of the Catholic Epistles (i.e., written to a general rather than a specific audience),[2] the Epistle of James was not included in early Christian canons such as those by Marcion (d. A.D. 144),[3] Irenaeus (d. 202), Muratorian (d. ca. second century), and Eusebius (d. 340). It is not known for certain why this epistle was disputed; it may have been a question of authorship. Jerome (d. 420), speaking of James as the brother of the Lord, said: "He wrote only one Epistle, which is reckoned among the seven Catholic Epistles, and even this is claimed by some to have been published by some one else under his name, and gradually, as time went on, to have gained in authority."[4] However, from as early as the third century, both Origen (d. 254) and Eusebius refer to James as the author of the epistle.[5]

Although specific reasoning and evidence concerning the question of authorship no longer exist, these divergent views do indicate that concerns arose over this issue. In any case, in A.D. 367, Athanasius included the Epistle of James in his authorized collection of the twenty-seven books of the New Testament, which became the officially accepted canon in 382. Inclusion of the Epistle of James was not questioned again until 1522 when Martin Luther, in his Preface to the New Testament, called it "an epistle of straw."[6] "Because of what he saw to be James's rejection of the Pauline doctrine of justification by faith, Luther denied that the epistle had apostolic authority; and in his translation of the NT he relegated it from its canonical position to the end, together with his equally disliked Hebrews, Jude, and Revelation."[7] Despite the previous questions of authorship and Luther's concern with James's emphasis on works, James's teachings are generally highly valued by Christians.

FAITH (PISTIS) AND WORKS (ERGON)

Among the most quoted verses in the Epistle of James is the declaration that "faith without works is dead" (James 2:26). Throughout his epistle James uses the Greek terms *pistis* for "faith" and *ergon* for "works." Identifying these Greek words and defining them helps us see that James's use of *pistis* and *ergon* varies from the generally accepted view in Christianity.

Faith is seen in two distinct ways in the modern Christian context: (1) "It is applied objectively to the body of truth ('the Christian faith') to be found in the Creeds, . . . Councils, . . . teachings of doctors and saints, and, above all, in the revelation contained in the Bible." (2) Subjectively, "it is the human response to Divine truth, inculcated in the Gospels as the childlike and trusting acceptance of the kingdom and its demands."[8] Christians view the subjective part of faith as a supernatural event wherein the "Christian can make an act of faith only in virtue of God's action in his soul," and this is possible "only in the context of the Christian revelation."[9] Latter-day Saints also recognize faith as a spiritual gift (see Moroni 10:11). However, an important difference emerges regarding the emphasis on obedient activity, which grows out of faith.

Christian faith in its subjective sense as a "childlike and trusting acceptance"[10] likely emerges from the Greek word *pistis*, which has both the sense of "trusting" and "worthy of trust."[11] However, "inasmuch as trust may be a duty, *[pistis]* can come to have the nuance 'obedient.'"[12] In fact, the Septuagint renders a common form of *pistis* from the Hebrew *amin*, which when referring to "God's requirement, order, or command . . . implies acknowledgment of the requirement and man's obedience."[13]

Even in later Judaism, "faithfulness is also obedience. Hence the Law and commandments are among the objects of faith. In the [Rabbinic] writings to believe in God and to obey God are equivalent in meaning."[14] Faith as obedience is an idea found in the New Testament, particularly in Hebrews 11, which cites examples of many Old Testament prophets who exhibited their faith through obedience.[15] Although most modern Christians now interpret *pistis* as the "saving faith which recognizes and appropriates God's saving work in Christ," with obedience being implied,[16] I believe James says it differently—for one to exercise faith in Christ, one *must* exhibit obedience to God through good works.

The Greek term *ergon* is translated as "works." Its fundamental meaning is to "denote action or active zeal in contrast to idleness."[17] In the Septuagint "many words which denote conduct in general are brought under the concept of work."[18] According to rabbinic Judaism, "he who has learned Torah and yet acts contrary to it blasphemes God. Christianity, however, demands a preaching of action, . . . and contradiction between word and act is a denial of Christ."[19] Many Pauline scholars view *ergon* in a "completely negative sense whenever it is a matter of human achievement."[20] James, on the other hand, emphasizes works within the context of faith in Christ, not as a negative but as a natural, positive outgrowth of faith: "Yea, a man may say, Thou hast faith [in Christ], and I have works: shew me thy faith [in Christ] without thy works, and I will shew thee my faith [in Christ] by my works" (James 2:18). James's epistle follows the meaning of *pistis* and *ergon* as defined by the Septuagint and rabbinic Judaism, connecting them to faith in Christ.

The epistle of James clearly teaches that faith and works complement each other and belong together. In fact, it is impossible to separate them. In a way, faith is like water. We think of water most often in its liquid form, but when the temperature is substantially increased or decreased, the water eventually changes to steam or ice. In comparison to each other, ice and steam may look different, but they are still essentially the same compound of chemicals. In the form of steam, water can serve to power engines. When it converts to ice, it can be used as a cooling agent or to provide a solid layer over bodies of water on which heavy vehicles may drive. So it is with faith. Our service in the Church, our enduring of trials and tests, our obedience to commandments—these works are all expressions of our faith. Faith and works are of the same compound. They are inseparable. You cannot have one without the other. In other words, good works are to faith as steam and ice are to water. This is the essence of the epistle of James.

TALMAGE ON FAITH AND WORKS

A review of Elder Talmage's understanding of faith and works helps Latter-day Saints better appreciate James's teachings. In 1899, Elder Talmage published the first edition of *A Study of the Articles of Faith*. This highly valued and well-known study represented the first formal analysis of each of the Articles of Faith by a Latter-day Saint scholar. Talmage's eloquent examination of faith, like James's, clearly distinguishes between faith and belief. He writes, "belief, in one of its accepted senses, may consist in a merely intellectual assent, while faith implies such confidence as will impel to action."[21] Talmage defines belief, faith, and works (very much in harmony with the Hebrew and Greek definitions stated above) and emphasizes how both faith and works should be centered in Christ. "Belief is in a sense passive, an agreement or acceptance only; faith is active and positive, embracing such reliance and confidence as will lead to works. Faith in Christ comprises belief in Him, combined with trust in Him. One cannot have faith without belief; yet he may believe and still lack faith. Faith is vivified, vitalized, living belief."[22]

In a 1914 article titled "Prove Thy Faith by Thy Works,"[23] Elder Talmage demonstrates his concern that modern translations of the Bible view the terms *faith* and *belief* as synonyms:

"Belief is the mechanism, like a locomotive standing with tank empty and fire-box cold upon the track; faith is the fire and the resulting steam that gives it power and makes it work such miracles as had never been dreamed of in days of yore. Faith is vitalized, energized, dynamic belief. . . . Strange, is it not, that there are yet those who hold that the use of the term belief in the Holy Scriptures means empty, intellectual, negative belief, and that alone? Because of the fact, already cited, that in early English the term belief was used as a synonym of faith, we find it occurring and recurring in our translation of the Scriptures given to us as the Holy Bible, when by the context it is absolutely plain, and, by derivation beyond all question, that living belief, or actual faith, was intended, and that the term meaning this did occur in the original."[24]

Elder Talmage further notes, "James, an Apostle of the Lord Jesus Christ, found it necessary to warn the people against belief as a saving principle if left to stand alone."[25] Elder Talmage demonstrates that the entire Epistle of James was written with the fundamental assumption that true faith in Christ will lead to good works.

Textual Study of the Epistle of James

In his epistle James emphasizes the need to exercise faith and identifies appropriate works that grow out of true faith, such as prayer, visiting the sick and afflicted, controlling the tongue, and using the priesthood. He also shows that lack of faith is demonstrated through inappropriate works such as double-mindedness, deception, pride and riches, and sin in general. James wrote this epistle "to prevent the danger of separation *(diastasis)* between faith and works. . . . It is this coherence of faith and deeds that gives the unifying theme to the entire document and makes it a genuinely Christian writing."[26] James identifies various activities that the follower of Christ should pursue. Faith is the element that holds these disparate subjects together. James illustrates the active faith of believers with his instruction to follow the path to perfection, seek wisdom, and avoid the sins of pride. His use of the imperative tense throughout the text further evidences James's concern that we put our discipleship into action.

Perfection

According to James, afflictions try faith, which then strengthens patience. "But let patience have her perfect work, that ye may be perfect and entire, wanting nothing" (James 1:4).[27] The word for perfection in the Greek *(telos)* refers to "fulfillment" or "completion" and "denotes that which has reached maturity or fulfilled the *end* contemplated."[28] Perfection, then, in the Epistle of James is more akin to spiritual maturity rather than absolute sinlessness.

James clearly teaches that to gain perfection one must perfect faith through good works:

"Thou believest that there is one God; thou doest well: the devils also believe, and tremble.

"But wilt thou know, O vain man, that faith without works is dead?

"Was not Abraham our father justified by works, when he had offered Isaac his son upon the altar?

"Seest thou how faith wrought with his works, and by works was faith made perfect?" (James 2:19–22). The phrase "the devils also believe, and tremble," indicates that passive belief is not enough: faith must impel the disciple to acts of righteousness. Joseph F. Smith explains Satan and his followers' fatal flaw as a lack of pure intelligence:

"There is a difference between knowledge and pure intelligence. Satan possesses knowledge, far more than we have, but he has not intelligence or he would render obedience to the principles of truth and right. I know men who have knowledge, who understand the principles of the Gospel, perhaps as well as you do, who are brilliant, but who lack the essential qualification of pure intelligence. They will not accept and render obedience thereto. Pure intelligence comprises not only knowledge, but also the power to properly apply that knowledge."[29]

President Smith would agree with James that faith (pure intelligence) and obedience (works) are inseparably connected.

Interestingly, a number of parallel verses can be identified between James's path of faith to perfection and the Savior's teachings in the Sermon on the Mount in Matthew. A comparison of the two shows that James's epistle reiterates the Savior's command that His disciples "let [their] light so shine before men, that they may see

Matthew	*James*
Rejoice in trials (5:12).	"Count it all joy when ye fall into many afflictions" (JST 1:2).
"Ask, and it shall be given you" (7:7).	"Ask of God, that giveth . . . liberally" (1:5).
"Be ye therefore perfect" (5:48).	"Be perfect and entire, wanting nothing" (1:4).
"Judge not unrighteously, that ye be not judged" (JST 7:1).	"For he shall have judgment without mercy, that hath shewed no mercy" (2:13)
"Let your communication be, Yea, yea; Nay, nay" (5:37).	"Let your yea be yea; and your nay, nay" (5:12).

"Blessed are the meek" (5:5).	"Shew . . . meekness of wisdom" (3:13).
"Lay not up for yourselves treasures upon earth" (6:19).	"Your riches are corrupted" (5:2).
"Whosoever is angry with his brother shall be in danger of his judgment" (JST 5:24).	"The wrath of man worketh not the righteousness of God" (1:20).
"Not every one that saith unto me, Lord, Lord, . . . but he that doeth" (7:21).	"What doth it profit . . . though a man say he hath faith, and have not works?" (2:14).[30]

[their] good works and glorify [their] Father which is in heaven" (Matthew 5:16).

As Jesus does in the Sermon on the Mount, of which James likely was aware, James gives counsel on what the faithful should do to reach perfection or spiritual maturity. One powerful example James uses to illustrate the connection between spiritual maturity and faith is in the controlling of the tongue: "For in many things we offend all. If any man offend not in word, the same is a perfect man, and able also to bridle the whole body" (James 3:2). James characterizes the tongue as "a little member, and boasteth great things" (James 3:5), "a fire, a world of iniquity: . . . and setteth on fire the course of nature; and it is set on fire of hell" (James 3:6), "but the tongue can no man tame; it is an unruly evil, full of deadly poison" (James 3:8). President N. Eldon Tanner was as blunt as James. He said:

"The tongue is the most dangerous, destructive, and deadly weapon available to man. A vicious tongue can ruin the reputation and even the future of the one attacked. Insidious attacks against one's reputation, loathsome innuendoes, half-lies about an individual are as deadly as those insect parasites that kill the heart and life of a mighty oak. They are so stealthy and cowardly that one cannot guard against them. As someone has said, 'It is easier to dodge an elephant than a microbe.'"[31]

Learning to control the tongue, according to one commentator, is "overcoming the tendency of the mouth 'to stay open when it were more profitably closed.'"[32]

To attain perfection, or completeness, according to the Epistle of James, the believer is expected to exhibit a living, vitalized faith. This faith is manifest by good works such as patience and control of the tongue.

WISDOM

James discusses two kinds of wisdom: the wisdom of the world and the wisdom of God:

"Who is a wise man and endued with knowledge among you? let him shew out of a good conversation his works with meekness of wisdom.

"But if ye have bitter envying and strife in your hearts, glory not, and lie not against the truth.

"This wisdom descendeth not from above, but is earthy, sensual, devilish. . . .

"But the wisdom that is from above is first pure, then peaceable, gentle, and easy to be intreated, full of mercy and good fruits" (James 3:13–15, 17).

James inextricably ties wisdom to good works. Like true faith that leads to righteous works, true knowledge, correctly applied, is wisdom that will lead to appropriate action. Nowhere is this more poignantly portrayed than in the account of the First Vision. After reading James 1:5, "If any of you lack wisdom, let him ask of God, that giveth to all men liberally, and upbraideth not; and it shall be given him," Joseph Smith recorded,

"Never did any passage of scripture come with more power to the heart of man than this did at this time to mine. It seemed to enter with great force into every feeling of my heart. I reflected on it again and again, knowing that if any person needed wisdom from God, I did; *for how to act I did not know,* and unless I could get more *wisdom* than I then had, I would never know; for the teachers of religion of the different sects understood the same passages of scripture so differently as to destroy all confidence in settling the question by an appeal to the Bible. At length I came to the conclusion that I must either remain in darkness and confusion, *or else I must do as James directs, that is, ask of God.*" (JS—History 1:12–13; emphasis added).

Joseph Smith's willingness to act on his faith, "as James directs," produced consequences beyond what even the Prophet himself could understand at that time. The effects of Joseph's decision to apply James's directive continues to unfold in both collective and individual ways and will likely do so until the work is done. Joseph may have read many other verses that taught about faith, but it was this verse in James that most profoundly compelled him to go into the grove of trees and offer his prayer of faith. Elder Bruce R. McConkie expressed it well: "This single verse of scripture has had a greater and a more far reaching effect upon mankind than any other single sentence ever recorded by any prophet in any age. It might well be said that the crowning act of the ministry of James was not his martyrdom for the testimony of Jesus, but his recitation, as guided by the Holy Ghost, of these simple words which led to the opening of the heavens in modern times."[33]

WORKS OF PRIDE

James exposes some common manifestations of pride that the spiritually alert should avoid. These sins of pride are opposite of the fruits or works that grow out of true faith. James identifies some of these vices as coveting and killing (James 4:2), adultery (James 4:3), and greed (James 5:1–5). James clearly ties these acts to pride with the question, "Know ye not that the friendship of the world is enmity with God?" (James 4:4). President Ezra Taft Benson observed that the meaning of pride is enmity or hostility toward God or our neighbor.[34] Well aware that pride is the source of evil, James counsels, "God resisteth the proud, but giveth grace unto the humble. . . . Humble yourselves in the sight of the Lord, and he shall lift you up" (James 4:6, 10).

Whether encouraging one to attain perfection, to seek wisdom, or to abhor the sins of pride, the Epistle of James bases its approach on the application of faith. Its pragmatic themes build on the notion that "faith without works is dead."

James's Use of the Imperative Tense

The imperative command found throughout the letter displays James's desire for our dynamic discipleship. The following are some examples of his imperatives:

Chapter 1
> "Be perfect and entire" (1:4).
> "Ask of God" (1:5).
> "Ask in faith" (1:6).
> "Rejoice in that he is exalted" (1:9).
> "Be swift to hear, slow to speak, slow to wrath" (1:19).
> "Lay apart all filthiness," etc. (1:21).
> "Receive with meekness," etc. (1:21).
> "Be ye doers of the word" (1:22).
> "Visit the fatherless" (1:27).

Chapter 2
> "Hearken, my beloved brethren" (2:5).
> "Love thy neighbor" (2:8).
> "Keep the whole law" (2:10).
> "So speak ye" (2:12).
> "Shew me thy faith" (2:18).

Chapter 3
> "Shew out of a good conversation," etc. (3:13).
> "Lie not against the truth" (3:14).

Chapter 4
> "Submit yourselves . . . to God" (4:7).
> "Resist the devil" (4:7).
> "Draw nigh to God" (4:8).
> "Cleanse your hands" (4:8).
> "Purify your hearts" (4:8).
> "Be afflicted, and mourn, and weep" (4:9).
> "Humble yourselves" (4:10).
> "Speak not evil" (4:11).

Chapter 5

"Go to now" (5:1).

"Be patient" (5:7).

"Stablish your hearts" (5:8).

"Grudge not" (5:9).

"Swear not" (5:12).

"Confess your faults" (5:16).

"Pray one for another" (5:16).

THINGS OF LASTING VALUE

James counseled:

"Go to now, ye that say, To day or to morrow we will go into such a city, and continue there a year, and buy and sell, and get gain:

"Whereas ye know not what shall be on the morrow. For what is your life? It is even a vapour, that appeareth for a little time, and then vanisheth away.

"For that ye ought to say, If the Lord will, we shall live, and do this, or that" (James 4:13–15).

These verses point out that the time we are given in this life will eventually pass like a vapor and that we should focus our attention on the things that are most worthy—things that bring us closer to God. In the same vein, the Nephite prophet Amulek said: "For behold, this life is the time for men to prepare to meet God; yea, behold the day of this life is the day for men to perform their labors" (Alma 34:32).

Although James's epistle may have raised questions in the minds of some earlier Christians, it is a blessing that his inspired message on faith and works was providentially preserved for later generations. The words *faith (pistis)* and *works (ergon)* were defined to demonstrate their strong connection to obedience and faith as a living belief. Elder Talmage's thoughts on faith and works helped to illuminate James's views. The concepts of faith and works throughout the epistle were examined according to three of James's general themes: perfection, wisdom, and pride. Finally, James's use of the imperative tense was shown to demonstrate his desire to reinforce an active faith.

Like the instructions of James to couple our faith with good works, the Lord has given similar counsel today: "Wherefore, if ye believe me, ye will labor while it is called today" (D&C 64:25). The Epistle of James is an articulate expression of the interrelationship between faith and works for Christians of his day and ours: "For as the body without the spirit is dead, so faith without works is dead also" (James 2:26).

NOTES

1. The term *faith* is used sixteen times in the Epistle of James, thirteen in chapter 2. *Works* occurs thirteen times, twelve times in chapter 2.

2. Traditionally there are seven Catholic Epistles: James; 1 and 2 Peter; 1, 2, and 3 John; and Jude.

3. Marcion rejected the entire Old Testament and accepted only the Gospel of Luke and ten epistles of Paul.

4. As found in Bruce M. Metzger, *The Canon of the New Testament* (Oxford: Clarendon Press, 1997), 235.

5. Eusebius assumes James is the brother of Jesus (see David Noel Freedman, ed., *The Anchor Bible Dictionary* [New York: Doubleday, 1992], 3:622–23).

6. Freedman, *The Anchor Bible Dictionary,* 3:622.

7. Ibid. "It is sometimes suggested that James's argument is prior to Paul's and that Paul wrote in part to answer it, but while Paul's argument on justification does not require James's to explain it, the strongly polemical tone of James's language indicates that he knows a position which he is concerned to refute: 'and not by faith alone'" (ibid., 625). See section 2 on James and Paul in the entry "James, Epistle of" for further study.

8. F. L. Cross, ed., *The Oxford Dictionary of the Christian Church* (Oxford: Oxford University Press, 1985), 499.

9. Ibid.

10. Ibid.

11. Gerhard Friedrich, ed., *Theological Dictionary of the New Testament* (Grand Rapids, Mich.: Eerdmans, 1968), 6:175.

12. Ibid.

13. Ibid., 6:187. See also Deuteronomy 9:23; Psalm 119:66.

14. Ibid., 6:199.

15. Ibid., 6:205; see also Ether 12:7–22.

16. Ibid., 6:208.

17. Ibid., 2:635.

18. Ibid., 2:637.

19. Ibid., 2:651.

20. Ibid.

21. James E. Talmage, *A Study of the Articles of Faith* (Salt Lake City: Deseret Book, 1983), 87.

22. Ibid., 88; see also James E. Talmage, *The Vitality of Mormonism* (Boston: Gorham Press, 1919), 79.

23. *Improvement Era*, 17 (1914): 940–47.

24. Ibid., 941.

25. Ibid., 942. Concerning the writings of Paul, Talmage writes, "The spirit of all of Paul's writings is to the effect that when he thus spoke of a saving faith he meant faith; he did not mean mere belief, but belief plus the works which that belief comprises and postulates, and such combination is faith" (ibid., 943).

26. Ralph Martin, ed., *World Biblical Commentary* (Waco, Texas: Word Books, 1988), lxxix.

27. "Note James' characteristic corroborations of a positive statement by a negative clause: *entire, lacking in nothing; God that giveth and upbraideth not; in faith, nothing doubting*" (Martin R. Vincent, Word Studies in the New Testament [Grand Rapids, Mich.: Eerdmans, 1975], 1:725).

28. Ibid., 1:724.

29. Joseph F. Smith, *Gospel Doctrine* (Salt Lake City: Deseret Book, 1977), 58.

30. Adapted from the World Biblical Commentary, lxxv–lxxvi. Note other parallels this commentary cites.

31. N. Eldon Tanner, in Conference Report, April 1972, 57.

32. Martin, *World Biblical Commentary*, 109.

33. Bruce R. McConkie, *Doctrinal New Testament Commentary* (Salt Lake City: Bookcraft, 1973), 3:246–47.

34. Ezra Taft Benson, in Conference Report, April 1989, 3.

18

AGENCY AND SELF-DECEPTION IN THE WRITINGS OF JAMES AND 1 JOHN

Terrance D. Olson

HEREFORE, TO HIM THAT KNOWETH to do good, and doeth it not . . ." (*James 4:17*).

Think of the last time you felt it was right to do something and you refused to do it. Perhaps it was a little thing like reading a bedtime story to your five-year-old or visiting your brother in the hospital. It could have been an act that required more time, such as driving to your niece's wedding in a neighboring state or giving a Saturday of service cleaning up after girls' camp. No matter what the example, each consists of something you sense is right to do. But you are a moral agent—capable of living true or false to your sense of what is right. If you act favorably and willingly on your feeling regarding what is right, you proceed to read the book, make the visit, drive to the wedding, or help with girls' camp. You do these things without a second thought, and probably without moral fanfare. As examples or stories of moral or ethical conduct, there is little to tell about these incidents except to recall the memories.

Terrance D. Olson is a professor of marriage, family, and human development at Brigham Young University.

However, if we do not do these good things or we do them resentfully, there is a story to tell. Suddenly, an otherwise straight-forward and perhaps even mundane event becomes significant. Now the story is a moral tale, for the heart of the story is in our refusal to do as we believe. Had we been true to our sense of what was right, it would not occur to us to have to explain ourselves. But when we are false to our beliefs, there is much to explain.

When my response to my five-year-old is to go against what I believe is right, I might say to myself, *I am really tired tonight,* or *He wasn't very well-behaved at dinner,* or *I have a big report due tomorrow.* When these kinds of comments are delivered by some-one who knoweth to do good but doeth it not, they become ration-alizations of wrongdoing. They become attempts to make the wrong we are doing appear to be right, or at least not wrong.[1] They are symptoms of a problem being experienced by someone who is no longer living the truth in relationships with others. These symptoms are evidence of more than mere ignorance and more than being blinded by the demands or pressures of life. They are signs of self-deception.

In everyday life and in our attempts to explain ourselves to each other, it seems we have neglected the idea and implications of being self-deceived. Yet the scriptures indicate that when responsible agents engage in self-deception, they engage in sinful activity. Evidently, self-deception is more than an abstract term that describes someone who does not see the truth. It is a concept that accounts for how it is possible to be blind to the truth. By definition, to be self-deceived is to participate in an act that produces a false view of one's circumstances. To be self-deceived is to be blind to the truth of a situation. This blindness includes at least two features: (1) seeing the truth falsely—as untruth, and (2) being blind to the fact that one's own act has produced the false view.

Given this kind of blindness, it seems that if I am self-deceived I cannot access the knowledge that would set me free, so I cannot escape. Also, since I do not know I am deceived and do not know I have produced the deception, I will even reject the attempts of observers to enlighten me. I will see such efforts as evidence that they are meddlers, prejudiced, or irrational. Clearly, to take the idea of self-deception seriously might seem impossible to the self-deceived.

The epistles of James and John address the problem of self-deception more fully than any other place in the scriptures, and both of them ground the problem as a symptom of wrongdoing.

JAMES ON DOUBLE-MINDEDNESS

James understood the link between knowing the truth and living the truth, and described the instability in life that comes when we are "double minded" (James 1:8) and willfully refuse to live that which we know:

"Be ye doers of the word, and not hearers only, deceiving your own selves.

"For if any be a hearer of the word, and not a doer, he is like unto a man beholding his natural face in a glass:

"For he beholdeth himself, and goeth his way, and straightway forgetteth what manner of man he was" (James 1:22–24).

The complete rendition of James 4:17 is "Therefore to him that knoweth to do good, and doeth it not, to him it is sin." Thus, sin and self-deception are inextricably linked.

Sin is not a popular explanation of what our culture has come to see as mere imperfection or inescapable human failings. To deny sin as a source of some mortal troubles can itself be a symptom of being self-deceived. After all, if I can attribute my sins to things I can't help—imperfections—I have nothing to repent of, and the best I can do, even with those failings, is cope. Besides, if James is going to lay blame at my feet for something that is just human nature, then it creates guilt. I certainly do not need guilt as an additional stumbling block! But perhaps there is a better answer. Perhaps we can actually be free of certain recurring attitudes and feelings that seem inescapable. Perhaps James takes seriously an idea our culture too readily dismisses. Perhaps dismissing James's testimony is already an act of self-deception, and that dismissal leaves us blind and trapped in a self-deceived world.

JOHN ON SELF-DECEPTION

John sustains James's witness regarding wrongdoing and blindness. The book of 1 John is a testimony of Jesus Christ and a call to obedience. In almost every chapter, the author contrasts the condition of the obedient with that of the disobedient. In testifying of the fellowship the Saints can experience with the Father and the Son, John unequivocally declares:

"This then is the message which we have heard of him, and declare unto you, that God is light, and in him is no darkness at all.

"If we say that we have fellowship with him, and walk in darkness, we lie, and do not the truth:

"But if we walk in the light, as he is in the light, we have fellowship one with another, and the blood of Jesus Christ his Son cleanseth us from all sin.

"If we say that we have no sin, we deceive ourselves, and the truth is not in us" (1 John 1:5–8).

So a contrast is established immediately between walking in light and walking in darkness. Walking in darkness is characterized by our *doing not the truth;* by the truth not being *in us.* This is significant commentary, because it suggests that those who are self-deceived no longer see, experience, or understand the truth. This blindness to the truth is not due to ignorance but to a refusal to walk in the light. But that refusal is something we are *doing* ("and do not the truth"), and that kind of doing makes the truth inaccessible to us ("the truth is not in us").

In 1 John 2, the author continues the theme:

"He that saith, I know him, and keepeth not his commandments, is a liar, and the truth is not in him. . . .

"He that loveth his brother abideth in the light, and there is none occasion of stumbling in him.

"But he that hateth his brother is in darkness, and walketh in darkness, and knoweth not whither he goeth, because that darkness hath blinded his eyes" (1 John 2:4, 10–11).

And in a final example from chapter 4:

"There is no fear in love; but perfect love casteth out fear:

because fear hath torment. He that feareth is not made perfect in love. . . .

"If a man say, I love God, and hateth his brother, he is a liar: for he that loveth not his brother whom he hath seen, how can he love God whom he hath not seen?" (1 John 4:18–20).

Perhaps the reason obedience is the first law of heaven is that without obedience, we do not see clearly the possibility or reality of heaven. We do not see that the Savior is the light of the world. We are in darkness, we stumble, we "forget" what manner of person we are. But we can not attribute these problems to sources outside ourselves. We are blind because of our own refusal to see. As Jacob, the son of Lehi, noted, "Wo unto the blind that *will not see;* for they shall perish" (2 Nephi 9:32; emphasis added). It is likely that the first casualty of refusing to see is a loss of an understanding of the truth, because "that darkness hath blinded his eyes" (1 John 2:11).

It is evident, then, that it is in our *response* to the gospel—how we act upon it, and not how it acts upon us—that reveals who and what we see; who and what we are, in any given moment. Our disobedience changes our world—what we see and what we understand, and how we relate to others. Being blind to the truth is the condition of those who refuse to live by the truth they have been offered.

Since our blindness is produced by walking in darkness, and since we are "free" to walk in darkness, our blindness to the truth is self-inflicted. Or, regarding the stumbling metaphor used by James, we do not stumble at all spiritually when the hallmark of our life is love for our brother. It is our refusal to love that creates our spiritual problems, and those problems cause us to stumble.

THE BLINDNESS OF SELF-DECEPTION

Thus far we know that self-deception is produced by disobedience, which is, by definition, sin. So what? Either this is a conclusion so obvious that it need not take up too much of our time or we have failed to see its significance in our everyday lives—especially for those who generally seek to take the gospel seriously. Seemingly, the counsel to those self-deceived is to repent—end of story. But since to be self-deceived is to be blind to the truth, including the truths that others might tell us about our being in sin, how does a person who is self-deceived respond to the truth telling of others? If self-deception is produced by a refusal to walk in the light, self-deceived persons will resist light offered them about their sin.

This act of refusal is evidence of humans as moral agents, for if the act of refusal were not voluntary—freely chosen—the individual could not be held accountable for the act. As affirmed by Samuel the Lamanite in the Book of Mormon:

"And now remember, remember, my brethren, that whosoever perisheth, perisheth unto himself; and whosoever doeth iniquity, doeth it unto himself; for behold, ye are free; ye are permitted to act for yourselves; for behold, God hath given unto you a knowledge and he hath made you free.

"He hath given unto you that ye might know good from evil, and he hath given unto you that ye might choose life or death; and ye can do good and be restored unto that which is good, or have that which is good restored unto you; or ye can do evil, and have that which is evil restored unto you" (Helaman 14:30–31).

When we have a sense of what is right to do and we do not do it, we create a false way of seeing—and a false way of being—to which we are blind. We are as blind to the solutions to these types of problems as we are to our role in creating them in the first place. My own experience affirms this possibility.

When I was irritated about how one of the neighbor's children had stomped through my newly planted garden, I confess that there was no room in my heart, during my irritation, for forgiveness. Nor, if you had asked me at the time why I was troubled, would I have thought I had any need for repentance. Yet, at that moment, I was neither forgiving nor repentant. Rather, I was consumed with how my gardening efforts had been ruined by a thoughtless child. And make no mistake, in my irritation, that child had become my enemy. No other way of seeing the situation made sense to me.

On another occasion, I found myself delayed at an intersection where I was waiting with my signal flashing to turn left. I had to wait because of one—only one—oncoming and amazingly slow-moving car. It seemed that I had been waiting for an eternity for this creeping mass of metal to get by me. Then as the car entered the intersection, it turned left without warning. Had I known earlier of the driver's intention, my path would have been clear. Because the driver hadn't exercised the same courtesy I had—using the left turn signal as automakers and the state driving manual had intended—I had waited unnecessarily. That wait must have cost me at least 20 seconds—all because some other driver was so frivolous and discourteous as to not use a simple turn signal. My car's tires squealed as I made my long awaited left turn. I'm sure I muttered something about what kind of people they let drive these days. I don't recall the phrase "Do unto others," or "Love thy neighbor" coming into my mind as I drove the final few blocks to my house. Such ideas would have seemed so unrealistic in that situation anyway.

I also remember once speaking in a public meeting where I was being critical of the practices of one of my child's teachers. I didn't name the teacher, but my wife was pulling on my sleeve. I successfully ignored her until I realized the teacher about whom I was complaining was in the audience. It was not enough that the audience didn't know who I was speaking of. The teacher knew. I knew. I felt, fleetingly, that it was a shame someone's incompetence had to be publicly displayed like that. Unfortunately, the idea of conducting myself with meekness and lowliness of heart was foreign to me in that meeting.

These are everyday incidents, I know. Some would even claim that they are merely mundane evidences that we are imperfect or that we lose control, or that all of us are trying to learn to cope better with the challenges of life. Those who see the garden or turn-signal incident as trivial might even say that there are so many much-greater things to worry about in life, that we should bite our collective tongues over the little things and worry about coping with the big things.

I believe that these so-called everyday incidents—these so-called "little things"—have much to do with the quality of our lives, and are the foundation of the quality of our marriage, family, business, and Church relationships, not only in the present moment, but in the kingdoms we look forward to inheriting after this life. In each of these incidents, the person telling the stories—me—is self-deceived. That means in the moment I am living these stories, I am more than merely ignorant. It means I am doing more than denying the truth of the situation. The truth of the situation is that I don't even see the truth. If, during my irritation with the child, or during my impatience with the driver, or during my public criticism of the teacher, someone had told me I was hard-hearted, unforgiving, or unrepentant, I would have met the charge with what I would have considered to be justified disbelief. I would have been blind to the need for my compassion for the child (I would have seen such a notion as mere indulgence), for the driver of the other car (who didn't deserve to be rewarded for being inconsiderate), or for the teacher. In fact, instead of considering *my* attitude, *my* actions, as being a problem in these situations, I would have considered myself as being victimized by the other people. *They* are causing the problem. *They* are responsible for disrupting my world. *They* are the source of my difficulties. Preach to *them*, I might say to anyone challenging my responses. Moreover, I would have seen even those challenging my responses as stumbling blocks.

These responses are more than human failings that we can't help doing, or merely denials of the truth. They are expressions of having refused to see and live by the truth. Such refusals are symptoms of disobedience, of a refusal to walk in the light, if you will. As James and John testify, such disobedience means we begin to deceive ourselves about the truth. I know this because these are my stories. I know now what I didn't know during those incidents: that while I was being uncompassionate, hard-hearted and so on, I was absolutely blind to the truth. Only when I later quit refusing to live the truth, did I see the truth I had been refusing to live. I began living obediently to all that I knew about how I am to treat my neighbors (and let's see—who is my neighbor?). The truth was now a blessing to me, whereas in my refusal, I found the truth unrealistic and a burden. It may be that only moral agents can become self-deceived.

Once I gave up my sin, John's testimony made perfect sense to me, and his phrases began echoing in my soul. I was saying I had no sin. I was deceiving myself. The truth was not in me (see 1 John 1:8). John's description of the reality of self-deception and of the cause—my refusal to admit to sin when I was, in fact, sinful—was either lost on me or an irritant. But once I repented and returned to the light, the idea of self-deception made perfect sense and became a relatively important feature of my understanding the human condition. After all, if through disobedience, I become blind to the truth—the truth is not in me—how am I to understand the truth of myself and my condition at all? In such a condition, all my explanations of my actions will also be self-deceived.

It is not the truth that the reason I did not read the book to my child was because he or I were tired or that he had misbehaved or that I had a report looming. Those explanations only occurred to me *after* I had become self-deceived. I became self-deceived when I became disobedient. In my disobedience, my "explanations" became justifications or rationalizations for wrongdoing, rather than straightforward descriptions of an honest, moral choice. Similarly, I was walking in darkness in my attitude toward the oncoming car, and my irritation over their lack of use of a turn signal was just self-righteousness. My complaints against the teacher in a public meeting were not "honest criticism" but dishonest resentment. All those meanings eventually changed for me, not because any of those people changed, but because I did. I have wondered how my change came about.

OTHER SYMPTOMS OF SELF-DECEPTION

James and John identify additional symptoms of how we are when self-deceived. They see the consequences fully. James links many specific acts of disobedience to rationalizations born of blindness. One example is, "Let no man say when he is tempted, I am tempted of God; . . . neither tempteth [God] any man" (James 1:13). Do we see ourselves as victims of God when in temptation? This is a deceived view compared to the truth: "But every man is tempted, when he is drawn away of his own lust, and enticed" (James 1:14). This is an example of being a hearer of the word and not a doer, and thus "deceiving your own selves" (James 1:22). Also, "If any man among you seem to be religious, and bridleth not his tongue, but deceiveth his own heart, this man's religion is vain" (James 1:26). To *seem* to be religious stands in contrast to being religious, and is an expression of being self-deceived. Think for a moment. The last time your tongue was unbridled, did you feel justified? What was your rationalization?

Similarly, John notes that to be self-deceived is to be a liar. Yet, in sin, we not only lie about the truth, but believe the lie that we tell. Terry Warner calls this more than telling a lie—it is living a lie.[2] A simple example is that one who uses tobacco while ignorant of the spiritual law against it may suffer health problems but does not perish spiritually over it unless he refuses to obey the law once it is received by him. In other words, the prices we pay for our ignorance do not include the cost to us of knowing to do good and doing it not. Self-deception is resistance to light and truth, while ignorance is lack of knowledge of light and truth.[3] As described by John, "the truth is not in him" (1 John 2:4); or, "If a man say, I love God, and hateth his brother, he is a liar: for he that loveth not his brother whom he hath seen, how can he love God whom he hath not seen?" (1 John 4:20). The idea of simultaneously loving God and hating a brother is conceptually and practically impossible. But those immersed in hate, those who are self-deceived by their own sin of a refusal to love, are blind to the truth of that statement.

The common threads of how self-deceived persons see themselves and their circumstances include, not surprisingly, a sense of being helpless in the face of what others are doing to them, and a defensiveness that looks absolutely necessary to them. This view swallows up any sense of personal responsibility for creating or perpetuating the problem and obliterates the possibility that they are participating in any way in a willful refusal to walk in the light. Nor would it occur to the self-deceived that they are engaging in a freely chosen walk in darkness. But these are the fruits of self-deception consistent with how self-deception is described in James and 1 John. When we're in that darkness, born of our refusal to do the good that we know, we do not see our way out. After all, we now don't see how we played any role in getting ourselves in (to self-deception). Moreover, no sense of being personally responsible for the help-lessness is experienced either. If so, the individual would not be deceived about their role in producing the problem. This illustrates the reality of "the truth is not in us" (1 John 1:8).

At a more general level, being self-deceived is to find the gospel to be a burden. This is not because the Lord's commandments are burdensome, but because, when we fail to respond to them in humility and meekness, we deceive ourselves about their meaning. Seeing the commandments as a burden is a perfect way to rational-ize and justify our refusal to respond to them in humility. When we "do not the truth," we are "doing" a lie. That lie includes the self-deceived view that our refusal to give our best and call upon the atonement is someone else's fault—perhaps even God's fault. The self-deceived see their own imperfections, the gospel, and often life itself, as a burden instead of a blessing.

THE AVENUE OF ESCAPE

Escaping self-deception begins with a willingness to admit that we are, after all, moral agents. The crucial point about being moral agents is not in the mere matter of choice, but in our free, unre-stricted opportunity and obligation to choose the right. Lehi's wit-ness about moral agency matches the position of Samuel the Lamanite, cited earlier. Lehi affirms that when we do not choose the right, we choose consequences that we can not escape: "men are free according to the flesh. . . . Free to choose liberty and eternal life, through the great Mediator of all men, or to choose captivity and death" (2 Nephi 2:27).

Remember, John, in his discourse on living the truth, identified the problem of self-deception and also declared the avenue of escape: "if we walk in the light, as he is in the light, we have fellow-ship one with another, and the blood of Jesus Christ his Son cleanseth us from all sin" (1 John 1:7).

Giving up a self-deceived view of others reveals that we have not only become free of our resentments toward them, but often, that they had never sinned against us in the first place. When we *do* not the truth, the truth of the motives, attitudes, and actions of others is unavailable to us, and our fellowship with one another can range from being shallow to hypocritical.

In a way, the difference between doing the truth and doing self-deception is the difference described by King Benjamin of the mighty change of heart: "because of the Spirit of the Lord Omnipotent, which has wrought a mighty change in us, or in our hearts, that we have no more disposition to do evil, but to do good continually" (Mosiah 5:2). Essentially, we have awakened from the evil, resistant, alternative way of living described elsewhere as being in a deep sleep as to the things of God (see Alma 5:7).

The attitudes and even emotions of the two worlds (doing self-deception versus doing the truth) are incompatible. A disposition to do evil, or walking in darkness, cannot simultaneously be an expression of having lost that disposition, and be walking in the light. So the world of sin and self-deception are absolutely distinguishable from the alternative world of obedience. Once a person is living (or doing) qualities associated with obedience, the alternative disobedient qualities are not "in us." Examples of these incompatibilities from James and John include:

1. Be swift to hear rather than slow (James 1:19).

2. Be slow to wrath rather than quick-tempered (James 1:19).

3. Be doers of the word, not hearers only (James 1:22).

4. Bridleth his tongue, versus unbridled—and thus "deceiveth his own heart" (James 1:26).

5. Visit the fatherless and widows, versus neglecting them (James 1:27).

6. Faith without works, versus faith "by my works" (JST James 2:15).

7. Knoweth to do good, versus doeth it not (James 4:17).

None of the categories of being obedient can coexist with the categories of a refusal to be obedient. And in that refusal comes our self-deceived understanding of what we have done.

Consider this—if self-deception is produced by a free act, then escaping it must be a free act also. If being self-deceived is a refusal to live the truth, then giving up that refusal is the heart of being restored to an understanding—even a vision—of the truth. Thus, the problem is not a matter of ignorance or lack of skill or even lack of practice in some behavior. Being free of self-deception begins in willingness, not ability. If being free of self-deception requires a change of heart, then only a moral agent willing to be true to the light can experience the fellowship with Christ promised those who walk in the light. The change necessary to be free of self-deception is a matter of obedience. Yet all of us have sinned and fallen short of the glory of God (see Romans 3:23) so all of us are imperfect; thus all of us have participated in self-deception.

A harsh term for our condition is hypocrisy, and many Christians whose failings are all too visible have been subjected to such an accusation. Also, other hearers of the word who fail to be doers sometimes report they feel guilty—so guilty that they are burdened by the commandments, ever fearful that since they can never be perfect, they are doomed to guilty despair. This presents a curious situation. The gospel is a gospel of hope, not despair, and James and John are issuing a call to obedience meant to nourish the idea that "If we confess our sins, he is faithful and just to forgive us our sins, and to cleanse us from all unrighteousness" (1 John 1:9).

An honest rendition of gospel principles reveals there is no need for would-be Saints to experience burdensome, paralyzing guilt when they read passages such as James 4:17: "Therefore to him that knoweth to do good, and doeth it not, to him it is sin." Rather, they are free to see it as merely "guilt unto repentance" and an invitation to give up their burdened world of experience. At the least, we can propose that those whose response to the call of the gospel is to despair, are somehow deceived about the spirit and meaning of the call in the first place. And, according to James and John, seeing the truth falsely is evidence of *self*-deception. The truth is "not in" those who are offended by the truth or burdened by the light, precisely because they are "do[ing] not the truth" (1 John 1:6).

Specifically, we can offer hope for people like me who, although disobedient (hard-hearted) in past moments, can, in the present moment, give it all up and be left with compassion for neighbor children, fellow drivers, and imperfect teachers. I neither need to indulge others when they are engaged in wrongdoing by excusing them or by pretending they have not sinned, nor will I feel to harshly condemn others as a way of justifying my own hostility. I will tell the truth in love and sorrow. If I must testify to an officer regarding how a car weaving in traffic startled a girl whose car then rolled three times, I will do so in sorrow, not in arrogance or in a self-promoting way. In brief, I will love others, pray for them in humility, sorrow when they sin, and nourish them in their concern for others. Only by walking in the light myself, and repenting of the times I do not, will I likely be able to invite others to live a life of love and sacrifice and commitment and humility. Others will either take offense (Terry Warner's term for becoming hard-hearted or in sin) at my self-deceptive way of being—or even at my humility; or they will see me honestly. If, in their honesty, they see I am being hard-hearted, they will sorrow. If they see a person of compassion and humility, we will resonate. Their response to me reveals whether they have joined me in my world of self-deception or have remained true to the faith, being an example to me to repent. Either way, it is always possible for us to continue to offer responses in the light, even if others begin or continue to walk in darkness.

The world others live in may include rejecting our honest offerings, but we need not join them in darkness. To consider ourselves above or below them are examples of dark responses. We must continue in love and humility and boldness as our concern for them and the Spirit prompts us. To give up self-deception is to be realistic, honest, full of hope and to experience all the "symptoms" of walking in the light.

Self-deception, then, is an inescapable consequence of wrongdoing. Giving up self-deception is only possible in the act of obedience, that act that comes from within. It is that act moral agents are capable of. It is an affirmation of our love of God to love our brother. The Savior's call to us who labor and are heavy laden to come unto Him is absolutely realistic and absolutely the source of hope and healing.

NOTES

1. C. Terry Warner, and Terrance D. Olson, "Another View of Family Conflict and Family Wholeness," *Family Relations* 39 (October 1981): 493–503.

2. C. Terry Warner, *Bonds That Make Us Free: Healing Our Relationships, Coming To Ourselves* (Salt Lake City: Shadow Mountain, 2001).

3. To be ignorant of a law, including the law of the gospel, may mean we suffer the practical, temporal consequences of our ignorance. But we can not be accountable for that law to which we have not been exposed. This is important, for the solution to our ignorance of spiritual things is in being introduced to or confronted by them. If we have not been given the law, then as Jacob, from the Book of Mormon, reminds us:

"Wherefore, he has given a law; and where there is no law given there is no punishment; and where there is no punishment there is no condemnation; and where there is no condemnation the mercies of the Holy One of Israel have claim upon them, because of the atonement; for they are delivered by the power of him.

"But wo unto him that has the law given, yea, that has all the commandments of God, like unto us, and that transgresseth them" (2 Nephi 9:25, 27).

19

APOCALYPTIC IMAGINATION AND THE NEW TESTAMENT

Thomas A. Wayment

OVER THE COURSE OF HUMAN HISTORY the Lord has revealed to His prophets various apocalyptic dreams and visions. The terms *apocalyptic* and *apocalypse* are derived from a Greek word meaning to "reveal, disclose, or bring to light."[1] The term *apocalypse* also refers to the title of the portion of scripture known as the book of Revelation and has been used subsequently to describe writings that touch upon similar themes. In our day, the word *apocalyptic* describes a whole body of literature produced by early Christians and others. In the New Testament, for example, Matthew 24, Mark 13, Luke 17, and portions of 1 Thessalonians, 2 Thessalonians, and Jude contain apocalyptic revelations.

Unfortunately, we have had, and continue to have, a somewhat ambivalent attitude towards this type of revelation from the Lord. On the one hand, there are those who faithfully try to read and ponder it but often get confused by the strange symbolism or troubled by the disturbing picture painted in apocalyptic revelations. On the

---

Thomas A. Wayment is an assistant professor of ancient scripture at Brigham Young University.

other hand, there are those who become obsessed with its images and symbols and begin to focus their attention exclusively on this type of revelation, hoping to ascertain more perfectly the events of the last days. A middle ground must exist somewhere. However, it is often easier to avoid apocalyptic literature in order to steer clear of overindulgence. This paper will look at the social context in which many early Christian apocalypses were revealed and discuss, where possible, how the early Saints reacted to these new revelations.

The majority of apocalyptic literature in the New Testament is written in letter form, suggesting that it was meant to be read among the congregations and deliver a certain message to the Saints. If the book of Revelation were revealed today and delivered to the Church as new direction from the Lord, would we feel comforted, confused, or worried by it? Time has obscured many of the emotions felt by the early Saints upon hearing the book of Revelation or any such apocalyptic revelation for the first time, but we can look back and ascertain some of the principles upon which apocalyptic revelations are based. These principles may in turn help us to understand the function of apocalyptic revelation and ultimately gain from it a sense of hope and comfort.

DUALISM

One of the hallmark features of apocalyptic revelation is that it presupposes a dualistic worldview, a world where good is opposed by evil, darkness is confronted by light, and where God and His angels are opposed by Satan and his cohorts. In the New Testament, the war between the Saints of God and Satan is spoken of not only as a present reality but also as a future cataclysmic event.[2] Dualism is such an essential part of apocalyptic revelation that a text cannot be correctly described as apocalyptic without it.

A dualistic framework tends to influence any revelation. It is difficult to see past the language of struggle, war, death, and wickedness. Even though an apocalyptic revelation may have been delivered as a message of hope, we tend to look at the description of the conflict as the message of the text. For example, in Paul's second letter to the Thessalonians, are we supposed to focus on his description of the man of sin who sits in the temple or are we supposed to be comforted by the fact that the Second Coming is not immediately upon us? (2 Thessalonians 2:1–6). If we choose to look at the revelation as a description of struggles that will precede the Second Coming, we tend to ask questions regarding whom the man of sin is and why he is sitting in the temple pretending to be God. On the other hand, if we look at 2 Thessalonians as a message of comfort during times of trial, we tend to direct our focus on the message of hope and faith for those who are not deceived (2 Thessalonians 1:2, 11–12).

The description of two great opposing forces at work in the world is not the emphasis of apocalyptic revelation. The idea that good opposes evil and that darkness seeks to overthrow light can be stated without an apocalyptic framework (see 2 Nephi 2:11). President Harold B. Lee expressed a similar sentiment when he said, "There has ever been, and ever will be, . . . a conflict between the forces of righteousness and the forces of evil."[3] Apocalyptic literature with its dualistic perspective, however, provides a context for the description of how the forces of light will ultimately overcome the forces of darkness. Good will win, and darkness will be turned to light.[4] Dualism can help us to see that immediate victory may not be ours but that ultimate victory will surely be won. To the early Saints who faced tribulation and often severe persecution, a revelation promising an ultimate victory in which God personally intervenes would have had a significant appeal.[5]

A WORLD IN DECLINE

The concept that in the past the inhabitants of the world lived in a golden age is quite prevalent among many of the world's major civilizations.[6] Jews believe in a Garden of Eden, as do Christians, while the ancients Greeks believed in a golden age of civilization where heroes and demigods still wandered the earth. The natural corollary of this concept is that the world has continued to decline and that the current generation no longer lives in that golden age of the past but has degenerated into a state where the wicked prevail and the righteous suffer.[7] The faithful look forward to the return of this golden age, although they may use different terms to describe it. For Christianity and Judaism, one solution to the present difficulties is the coming of the Messiah or Savior, who will abruptly end the reign of the wicked.

Apocalyptic literature offers annihilation of the present world order as a solution to our present difficulties. It often describes the cataclysmic end of the world in vivid detail, using symbols and signs to amplify the image. The suddenness of the end of the world is a theme used to comfort those who are awaiting it and at the same time to strike fear into those who choose to oppress the meek. In the closing lines of the book of Revelation, the Lord reminds us of the swiftness of the His coming when He says, "Surely I come quickly" (Revelation 22:20). The benefit of history permits us the opportunity to see that "quickly" in this phrase has already extended nearly two millennia, but at the same time we know that for the wicked this will not have been enough time to prepare. Apocalyptic revelations are intended in many respects to act as a reminder of impending disaster.[8] Every dispensation has faced the uncertainty of the future as well as the reality that continued wickedness cannot be sustained indefinitely. The Lord will not permit us to continue to revel in our wickedness.

The Apostle Paul, as well as John the Beloved, sought to warn the early Saints that an age of darkness was soon to be felt on the earth. Paul taught that an age of apostasy or rebellion was soon to come that would precede the Second Coming of the Lord. Paul taught, "For that day shall not come, except there come a falling away first" (2 Thessalonians 2:3). To his beloved traveling companion, Paul was more explicit concerning the age of darkness to come. He taught:

"The time will come when they will not endure sound doctrine; but after their own lusts shall they heap to themselves teachers, having itching ears;

"And they shall turn away their ears from the truth, and shall be turned unto fables" (2 Timothy 4:3–4).

John taught in his first general epistle, "Even now are there many antichrists; whereby we know that it is the last time" (2:18).

The degradation and wickedness of the present generation is a sure sign that the end is nigh at hand.[9]

FINDING HOPE IN APOCALYPTIC DESTRUCTION

One of the underlying principles that governs our perception of apocalyptic literature is our own understanding of our future destiny and the destiny of the government under which we exist. If we view our current situation as another evidence of universally declining morality and goodness, it is easier to consider the fall of that government as a positive occurrence. On the other hand, if we view our nation as divinely inspired and on course with the commandments and principles of the gospel, we view a cataclysmic end of the government negatively. In reality, the choice is not so obvious since most worldly governments tend to fall somewhere between these two extremes. It has been stated that apocalyptic literature is born out of a frustration over the loss of one's homeland, government, or individual security.[10] In considering the plight of the early Christians, we find a people who lack a national identity as well as the possession of a specific homeland. For the first several hundred years they also lacked public places of worship where they felt welcome.

From the evidence left to us by the early Christians, we learn that for the first two hundred years life was a struggle. Christians were often put to death for simply being Christian, they were cast out of the Jewish synagogues (see John 9:22), and they did not have a national homeland where they could establish laws that were in accordance with their beliefs.[11] In many areas they were treated with hostility by government officials and in Jerusalem they were at times met with open hostility. The world was not a welcome place for them. In this context is it any surprise that the early Saints found comfort in such revelations as the book of Revelation, Matthew 24, 2 Thessalonians, and elsewhere?[12] The early Church fathers felt that even in their day the end of the world would be a welcome event.[13] We learn from our own history that apocalyptic fervor was heightened during the early days of this dispensation when the Saints were forced to leave their homes and often faced inhospitable circumstances that appeared to be acceptable to government leaders. The *Millennial Star* ran a regular series during the early days of the church entitled "The Signs of the Times." In our current day it is difficult to appreciate the feelings of a people whose circumstances were very different from our own.

PERSECUTION OF THE SAINTS

There can be no doubt but that the early Christians suffered severe persecution. The book of Revelation itself has been called "persecution literature."[14] It is helpful to the modern reader to keep in mind that the majority of apocalyptic writings were delivered during times of great duress and persecution.[15] For those who enjoy a peaceful situation it is difficult to understand the way in which severe persecution can substantially alter one's worldview. For example, in 1 Corinthians, Paul states that "God hath set forth us the apostles last, as it were appointed to death: for we are made a spectacle unto the world" (1 Corinthians 4:9). It is a foreign idea to us today that the Apostles are literally appointed to die for the cause, a statement that would shortly be fulfilled by Paul.

When John the Revelator saw the events of the fifth seal, or the events of his own day, he saw under the altar those who had been slain for their testimony (Revelation 6:9). He then asks, "How long, O Lord, . . . dost thou not judge and avenge our blood on them that dwell on the earth?" (Revelation 6:10). Instead of a positive response or even an indication that the wicked would be punished, John is told that persecution will continue until his fellow servants and brethren are killed likewise (Revelation 6:11). The entire description of the events of the fifth seal reveals a period of martyrdom for the faithful. No other event is spoken of during the fifth seal. History records that during the time of the writing of the book of Revelation, the first programmatic persecution of Christians was carried out under the Roman emperor Domitian. We even learn that being a Christian under Domitian was a crime.[16] One modern observer has noted that the term *apocalypse* begins to take on its modern-day meaning of doom and destruction under the reign of Domitian and that before his reign of terror the term was used by

Christians in its more neutral sense as simply a "revelation."[17] While we probably gain little in recounting the horrors of the first two Christian centuries other than a feeling of sympathy and compassion for those who were killed for the faith, it does help us to realize that our day is in many ways different than theirs. Our friends, families and leaders are not being tortured and killed.

What is shocking to us now was a reality for them. Apocalyptic literature was one means through which the Lord extended a message of hope to His people in extreme circumstances.

TRIBULATION TO DEFINE TRUE CHRISTIANS

It is troubling to think of the nature of trials as taught by the Prophet Joseph Smith when he said: "There is no safety only in the arm of Jehovah. None else can deliver and he will not deliver unless we do prove ourselves faithful to him in the severest trouble, for he that will have his robes washed in the blood of the Lamb must come up through great tribulation, even the greatest of all affliction."[18] It may be difficult to comprehend the fact that the Lord often allows His Saints to be persecuted in order to refine them. The Lord often has a greater good in mind than our finite minds can readily comprehend.[19] This doctrine is much easier to live in principle than in person.

In the New Testament there are several instances where the Apostles teach that tribulation is a means of determining those who are truly faithful. Paul points to this measure of Christian discipleship most clearly when he says, "Who shall separate us from the love of Christ? shall tribulation, or distress, or persecution, or famine, or nakedness, or peril, or sword?" (Romans 8:35). He further urges the Thessalonian Saints "that no man should be moved by these afflictions" (1 Thessalonians 3:3). In times of trial it is easy to see how some would collapse under the weight of torture, trial, and persecution, but for many of the early Saints affliction became a measure of true discipleship.[20] The Apostle John taught a similar concept when he wrote, "Blessed are the dead which die in the Lord" (Revelation 14:13). This statement carries with it the connotation that some have not died in the Lord, or in other words have fallen away. Likewise, Paul exhorted the Saints to continue in the faith, reminding them that "we must through much tribulation enter into the kingdom of God" (Acts 14:22).[21]

This measure of discipleship may seem somewhat difficult for us to appreciate. In times of relative peace this measure of discipleship may be based more on our ability to endure temptation, but we are nonetheless under obligation to remain faithful regardless of our circumstances. President Ezra Taft Benson said it so well, "God will have a humble people. Either we can choose to be humble or we can be compelled to be humble."[22] The Lord has not always revealed why or when He has used persecution as a means of discerning true discipleship, but we know that He wants us to be pure and that He will do whatever it takes to achieve that end.

REMINDER FOR CONTINUED OBEDIENCE

When we think of the calamities that have faced the Saints of God we often direct our attention to those who succeeded in overcoming trial and tribulation. For a moment, however, we should consider another possibility. Impending doom and destruction may heighten the spiritual readiness of those who were already waiting, but what is the effect on those who have delayed their preparations? Apocalyptic revelations carry a unique answer to this question. Those who are delaying their own repentance are in danger of being consumed.

We can sense this attitude in the epistles of Paul. Although probably the majority of Paul's converts continued to follow in the faith, there were some whose spiritual fortitude began to slacken. In Paul's second general epistle to the Saints of Thessalonica, it appears that some had quit their jobs, possibly in anticipation of the Second Coming. Paul reports, "We hear that there are some which walk among you disorderly, working not at all, but are busybodies" (2 Thessalonians 3:11).[23] Whatever the nature of their actions, it becomes a matter of concern for Paul, who sees their attitude as slothful and commends the members of the Church to discontinue association with them if they will not repent (2 Thessalonians 3:14). These members appear to be guilty of being slothful and apathetic in their duties as Christians. There is no specific sin attributed to them. This type of attitude can only be tolerated if there is plenty of time to repent and there is no danger that life will be cut short. An apocalyptic framework heightens this message by vividly pointing out the sudden destruction that will overtake the wicked. An apocalyptic revelation can help the slothful to see that there is no way of determining how long the present peace will prevail and that the wicked can be overtaken suddenly and with very little warning.

In several instances we find Paul exhorting the Saints to greater obedience because of the calamities that lie ahead. In 1 Corinthians Paul exhorts the Saints with the statement, "Brethren, the time is short, . . . for the fashion of this world passeth away" (1 Corinthians 7:29–31). In his first epistle to the Saints of Thessalonica, he warns, "Let us not sleep, as do others; but let us watch and be sober" (1 Corinthians 5:6).

Regardless of how many years exist between our current day and the day of wrath to come, the time to repent is now. We have recently felt some of this counsel in the words of President Gordon B. Hinckley when he said, "I need not remind you that we live in perilous times."[24] Similar to Paul's exhortation to the early Saints, President Hinckley used this occasion to remind us that obedience is still expected in the present. He taught, "Occasions of this kind pull us up sharply to a realization that life is fragile. . . . We have been counseled again and again concerning self-reliance, concerning debt, concerning thrift."[25] The uncertainty of the world's future provides an excellent context for a reminder to continue and even heighten obedience. After all, we want to be ready to meet Him when He comes to gather in His elect.

PESSIMISM WILL NOT PREVAIL

In looking at previous times of trial and tribulation, it is interesting to note that moderate optimism can easily be replaced by a minimal amount of pessimism. For some reason equal amounts of optimism and pessimism do not weigh the same in the scale of our hearts. What was once a moderate hope that life is good and that peace and plenty will continue can immediately be replaced by pessimism based on one singular act of destruction. Hope takes time to grow and must be nurtured, while fear can seize our hearts without any preparation. One school of thought has taught that the nature of apocalyptic prophecy is a pessimism in the ability of this world to continue to exist as it does.[26] This view, however, fails to adequately describe the end vision of apocalyptic thought and prophecy. In nearly all apocalyptic revelations there is the ultimate promise that the good will triumph, God and His Saints will be vindicated, justice and mercy will reign, and the earth will be ruled by a hand of righteousness.[27] In reality it depends upon which part of the vision we direct our attention.

Peter spoke against a growing pessimism in his own day when he said, "There shall come in the last days scoffers, walking after their own lusts, and saying, Where is the promise of his coming?" (2 Peter 3:3–4). Elder Neal A. Maxwell eloquently summarized the sentiment of these verses when he said, "Such cynicism mistakes the successive casts on the mortal stage for the absence of a Director or a script."[28] One modern commentator who has studied apocalyptic thinking through the ages has stated that "the rhetoric of Doomsday is a counsel of despair."[29] Indeed this is a legitimate understanding of apocalyptic literature, but isn't a message of hope equally represented? The present age and decline cannot continue to spiral out of control, there must be an end to all wickedness. For the faithful this is not new. Apocalyptic revelation teaches us that the end is near with an emphasis on hope for a positive outcome. To the righteous the message is not doom but happiness. President Marion G. Romney taught: "If in the providence of God, holocausts come, the earth will not disintegrate or be rendered uninhabitable. . . . It will be part of the prophet's road to the dawn of a glorious millennium of perfect peace."[30] The book of Revelation, the epitome of apocalyptic literature, ends with a vision of the earth in its celestial glory, where the Saints enjoy eternal splendor.

CHRIST WILL COME AGAIN

As part of the positive outlook of apocalyptic revelation, we learn that all of the doom and destruction are finalized in the event of the Second Coming. There is little, if any, evidence to suggest that the Saints will continue to experience physical suffering after Christ's Second Coming. Viewed in such a light, one can sense that the trials and tribulation that precede this great event are part of Satan's plan to mislead the weak and to tear down the faithful. The fact remains, however, that Christ will come in "power and great glory" (Matthew 24:30). At His Coming those who appear to have lost the battle in the eyes of their adversaries will be resurrected. The resurrection of the righteous dead is one of the crowning events of the apocalyptic end of the world. For a moment, we can imagine Christ coming in glory at the sound of the trump and all those who have died in the persecutions rising up to meet Him in one of the most glorious welcoming scenes this world has ever known. In that moment, the means and method of their death will seem insignificant. Those who die in faith or expect to die as martyrs can look forward to a glorious resurrected existence with Christ and His followers. In writing the epistle to the Hebrews, Paul expressed a similar sentiment when he taught, "Now no chastening for the present seemeth to be joyous, but grievous: nevertheless afterward it yieldeth the peaceable fruit of righteousness unto them which are exercised thereby" (Hebrews 12:11).

In looking at the symbolism of the book of Revelation, one is surprised at how often the figure of the Lamb of God appears among prophecies of the cataclysmic end of the world. This image of Christ as the Lamb of God is both weak and powerful. Sheep are one of the most docile of animals and were used in many of the sacrifices of the Mosaic covenant. They have come to symbolize the meek of the earth. Yet in a book where terror and destruction are prevalent it is somewhat surprising to find one of the main figures to be that of the Lamb. In considering this evidence, one scholar has noted that the Lamb image appears more often in the book of Revelation than in any other apocalyptic revelation.[31] If, however, we consider the larger purpose of apocalyptic literature, we see an interesting image being developed. That which was formerly meek and lowly now reigns supreme. The Lamb which was sacrificed for the benefit of mankind is now victorious. The image of the Lamb of God can help us see that our own struggles may result in something glorious.

ULTIMATE VICTORY

Approaching apocalyptic literature from the standpoint of audience and social setting cannot provide answers to all of the questions raised by this enigmatic body of literature. It does, however, help us to see that there may have been another intent besides simply revealing the events that would precede the Second Coming. Understanding such things as the worldview of apocalyptic revelation helps us to sense the duality of the world's existence. The moral decline of the present age can then be understood as a pattern of the world's progression or degression. Placing ourselves in this context helps us to feel and appreciate the sufferings of those who have gone before us and at the same time feel that we are brothers and sisters in their struggles and they in ours. We share a similar fate, although it may be separated by centuries of time. Their sufferings were not unlike ours, and their glory will be similar to ours.

We can also sense that many, if not all, apocalyptic revelations were delivered in times of great distress and persecution. Often the Saints were in a position where they were being persecuted for their faith. To these Saints, apocalyptic revelation was a message of hope and promise. They could hope for a glorious resurrection to come and exaltation for having proven themselves faithful despite all adversity. Persecution has been in times past a means of separating the wheat from the chaff. Paul recognized this tendency and warned the Saints to hold fast to the promises made to them. Although immediate victory may not be won, ultimate and complete victory will be.

NOTES

1. Frederick W. Danker, ed., *A Greek-English Lexicon of the New Testament and other Early Christian Literature*, 3d ed. (Chicago: University of Chicago Press, 2000), s.v. àpokalúptō.

2. Revelation 6:9–11 describes the events of the fifth seal, the time of the Apostle John, as one of tribulation and suffering. The hope of this age is that they will live a glorious existence after they have suffered martyrdom.

3. Harold B. Lee, "A Time of Decision," *Ensign*, July 1973, 31.

4. Richard D. Draper, *Opening the Seven Seals: The Visions of John the Revelator* (Salt Lake City: Deseret Book, 1991), 8, states that the book of Revelation

emphasizes the ultimate but not the immediate triumph of good over evil. Cf. Stephen E. Robinson, Warring against the Saints of God, *Ensign,* January 1988, 37.

5. This may have been the case with the Jewish insurrection of A.D. 67. It is plausible that those who opposed the Roman army were buoyed up by a hope that God would intervene as promised in the book of Daniel. J. Marcus, "The Jewish War and the *Sitz im Leben* of Mark," *Journal of Biblical Literature* 3 (1992): 447. See Martin Hengel, *The Zealots: Investigations into the Jewish Freedom Movement in the Period from Herod I until 70 A.D.,* trans. David Smith (Edinburgh: T & T Clark, 1989), 242–45.

6. Arthur O. Lovejoy and George Boas, *A Documentary History of Primitivism and Related Ideas in Antiquity* (Baltimore: Johns Hopkins Press, 1935), 1:2.

7. C. Wilfred Griggs, "Manichaeism, Mormonism, and Apocalypticism," in *Sperry Lecture Series: April 12, 1973* (Provo: Brigham Young University Press, 1973), 19.

8. Hugh W. Nibley, "The Last Days, Then and Now," in *The Disciple as Scholar: Essays on Scripture and the Ancient World,* ed. Stephen D. Ricks, Donald W. Parry, and Andrew H. Hedges (Provo, Utah: FARMS, 2000), 269–303.

9. Some of the early publications of the Saints in our dispensation bear names that indicate an awareness that the last days were upon them: *Millennial Star, Times and Seasons,* and *Zion's Watchman.* Cf. Glen M. Leonard, "Early Saints and the Millennium," *Ensign,* August 1979, 43. In 1840 the *Millennial Star* ran an article that stated, "We shall have reason to feel assured that the Second Advent is near, with the same assurance which we feel in regard to the near approach of summer when we see the trees put forth their leaves and blossom" (*Millennial Star* 1, no. 4 [August 1840]: 75).

10. Ithamar Gruenwald, *From Apocalypticism to Gnosticism: Studies in Apocalypticism, Merkavah Mysticism and Gnosticism* (Frankfurt: Verlag Peter Lang, 1988), 1–11.

11. Pliny, *Epistulae* 10.96, in *Pliny: Letters and Panegyricus,* Loeb Classical Library, trans. Betty Radice (Cambridge, Mass.: Harvard University Press, 1969), 285–91. The Roman historian Tacitus felt that Christians should be rooted out because they were a pernicious superstition (*Annals* 15.44), while Minucius Felix calls Christianity a foolish superstition (*Octavius* 9.3), in *Tertullian: Apology and De Spectaculis; Minucius Edix: Octavius,* Loeb Classical Library, trans. Gerald H. Rendall (London: William Heineman Ltd., 1931), 337.

12. The list of apocalyptic revelations should include also Mark 13, Luke 17 and many other more abbreviated references to the scenes and events of the Second Coming; e.g., 2 Peter 3; 1 John 2:18–29.

13. Richard Lloyd Anderson, "Clement, Ignatius, and Polycarp: Three Bishops between the Apostles and the Apostasy," *Ensign,* August 1976, 51.

14. Reed C. Durham, "Revelation: The Plainest Book Ever Written," *New Era,* May 1973, 22.

15. Cf. Philipp Vielhauer, "Apocalypses and Related Subjects," in *New Testament Apocrypha,* ed. Wilhelm Schneemelcher, trans. R. McL. Wilson (Louisville, Kent.: Westminster/John Knox Press, 1991), 2:558–59.

16. Draper, *Opening the Seven Seals,* 8.

17. Morton Smith, "On the History of Apokalyptō and Apokalypsis," in *Apocalypticism in the Mediterranean World and the Near East: Proceedings of the International Colloquium on Apocalypticism, Uppsala, August 1217, 1979,* ed. David Hellhom (Tübingen: Mohr, 1983), 17.

18. Dean C. Jessee, ed. and comp., *The Personal Writings of Joseph Smith* (Salt Lake City: Deseret Book, 1984), 285, spelling and punctuation corrected.

19. Cf. 2 Corinthians 1:5–7.

20. William Meeks, "Social Functions of Apocalyptic Language in Pauline Christianity," in Hellhom, *Apocalypticism,* 692. Based on the numerous references to enduring in times of affliction, Meeks has been led to state that Paul uses persecution as a test of Christian identity.

21. An unfortunate corollary to this is a report by the Roman governor Pliny, who noted with glee that he had been successful in turning away many of the Christians and uprooting their pernicious superstition (*Epistulae* 10.96).

22. Ezra Taft Benson, "Beware of Pride," *Ensign,* May 1989, 6.

23. The word "busybody" corresponds to the Greek term *periergazomai,* which indicates a person who goes around and around doing something but never getting anything done, or in essence someone who is not really doing anything.

24. Gordon B. Hinckley, "The Times in Which We Live," *Ensign,* November 2001, 72.

25. Ibid., 73.

26. Elisabeth Schüssler Fiorenza, "The Phenomenon of Early Christian Apocalyptic," in Hellhom, *Apocalypticism,* 303; P. Vielhauer, Apocalypses and Related Subjects; Paul D. Hanson, *The Dawn of Apocalyptic,* rev. ed. (Philadelphia: Fortress Press, 1979), 1–9, 2526.

27. Walter Schmithals, *Die Apokalyptik: Einfürung und Deutung* (Göttingen: Vandenhoeck & Ruprecht, 1973), 9–21.

28. Neal A. Maxwell, "The Tugs and Pulls of the World," *Ensign,* November 2000, 35.

29. Frank L. Borchardt, *Doomsday Speculation as a Strategy of Persuasion: A Study of Apocalypticism as Rhetoric* (Lewiston, New York: Edwin Mellen Press, 1990), 114.

30. Marion G. Romney, "The Price of Peace," *Ensign,* October 1983, 7.

31. John J. Collins, *The Apocalyptic Imagination: An Introduction to Jewish Apocalyptic Literature,* 2d ed. (Grand Rapids, Mich.: Eerdmans, 1998), 278–79.

20

TWILIGHT IN
THE EARLY CHURCH

W. Jeffrey Marsh

*B*Y THE TIME THE EPISTLES OF JOHN were written (about A.D. 100), the apostasy was well under way. The flame of faith initially lit by the Savior flickered and dimmed, and the long night of darkness foreknown and foretold by the Savior and His Apostles began to engulf the early Church (see Matthew 24:24; Acts 20:29; Galatians 1:6; Jude 1:4; Revelation 2:2). Apostles were slain, "ordinances were changed or abandoned. The line was broken, and the authority to confer the Holy Ghost as a gift was gone. The Dark Ages of apostasy settled over the world."[1]

Many in modern Christianity deny that a universal apostasy from the early Church ever occurred.[2] Yet "the church founded by Jesus and the apostles did not survive and was not expected to. . . . Jesus himself insisted that the Light was to be taken away. . . . [He] announced in no uncertain terms that his message would be rejected by all men, as the message of the prophets had been

W. Jeffrey Marsh is an associate professor of ancient scripture at Brigham Young University.

before, and that he would soon leave the world to die in its sins and seek after him in vain."[3]

The Greek word *apostasía*, from which we derived the English word *apostasy*, "is constructed from two Greek roots: the verb *hístēmi*, 'to stand,' and the preposition *apó*, 'away from.' The word means 'rebellion,' 'mutiny,' 'revolt,' or 'revolution,' and it is used in ancient contexts with reference to uprisings against established authority."[4] False teachers rebelled against Church authority, and their heretical ideologies were used to renounce the original doctrines established by Jesus Christ. Evidence for the apostasy is found in the New Testament record itself. The writings of the ancient Apostles, including those of John, predicted the mutinous falling away (see Acts 20:29; 2 Timothy 4:4; and 1 John 2:18–19) and declared that it was already upon them (see 1 Timothy 1:6; 1 John 2:18; 4:1). The scriptures also foretold of a future restoration, an event to occur in the latter days (see Matthew 17:11; 24:14; Acts 3:21; Revelation 14:6). Perhaps the best evidence an apostasy occurred is the fact that there was a Restoration (see D&C 1:14–17, 30). By 1820, Joseph Smith was told in his First Vision that God no longer acknowledged any church on earth as resembling the one He had established (see Joseph Smith—History 1:18–20).

The epistles of John were the last letters written by the sole-surviving leader of the early Church. They were penned to counter the apostate heresies which had already appeared in the Church by the end of the first century. What do we know about the author of these epistles? Which distinct heresies were addressed? What warnings do these epistles offer to prevent personal apostasy in our own day?

HISTORICAL SETTING AND AUTHORSHIP OF THE EPISTLES OF JOHN

"In none of these three epistles does the writer mention himself by name; but tradition assigns them to John" (Bible Dictionary, 715, "John, Epistles of")—that same John who labored with his brother James in their father's fishing business. He was a devoted follower of John the Baptist and was called by the Savior to become an Apostle. He is variously known as the author of the Gospel of John, John the Revelator, and John who, with Peter and James, was called to preside over the early Church. He also is often referred to as John the "beloved" because he was so loved by the Master.

Polycarp (bishop of Smyrna c. 69–155), knew John and regarded him as the author of 1 John. Athanasius accepts the epistles of John as canon in his festal letter of A.D. 367. All three letters were formally canonized at the Council of Carthage, A.D. 397. The first letter is to Church membership at large (a group referred to as "brethren," "children," and "beloved"). The second and third epistles are personal letters to the people mentioned (the "elect lady" in 2 John; and Gaius, Diotrephes, and Demetrius in 3 John).

This same Apostle is the traditional author of five books in our New Testament (Gospel of John, First, Second, and Third John; and Revelation). According to biblical scholars, these books were written in a different order than they appear in the New Testament. John apparently wrote the book of Revelation first (before A.D. 90–95), in which he described his call from the Lord to preside over the Church (see Revelation 1). Next, he wrote the Gospel of John (about A.D. 90), containing his testimony of Jesus Christ's life, mission, and ministry. Lastly, he penned the epistles First, Second and Third John (about A.D. 100) to correct the false doctrines which were already prevalent. Thus, the epistles of John are important letters because they provide a view of the early Church from its president—and the only surviving Apostle—at the time the apostasy had overwhelmed early Christianity.

JOHN'S MINISTRY

The New Testament record makes it clear that Peter was given the keys of the kingdom and called to lead the early Church after the death of Jesus Christ (see Matthew 16:19). Who, then, succeeded Peter? Modern Christianity is at a loss to explain. None of the charts showing succession in the early Church lists any of the Twelve as presiding after Peter's death—based on the assumption that all of them were killed. Tradition holds that Peter was arrested in Rome and crucified during the reign of Nero (the Roman leader who mercilessly persecuted Christians and blamed them for the burning of Rome in A.D. 64). It is said that at his own request Peter was crucified upside down because he considered himself unworthy to be crucified in the same manner as was the Savior (see John 21:18–19).[5] One by one the original Apostles called by Jesus were similarly slain. In *Foxe's Christian Martyrs of the World,* the deaths of all the original Apostles are chronicled except for John's.[6] Early records are mostly silent about what happened to him.

Interestingly, there are a few traditions claiming that John could not be killed. One claims that John was thrown into a cauldron of boiling oil, from which he miraculously escaped unharmed.[7] He was then exiled to Patmos (about A.D. 96). John stated that he was banished to Patmos for his "testimony of Jesus Christ" (Revelation 1:9). Following his imprisonment, he returned to Ephesus in A.D. 97.[8] It is assumed that this is where his epistles were written, though no place is mentioned in the letters.

What happened to the Apostle John after his move to Ephesus? In a revelation received in April 1829, the Prophet Joseph Smith learned the answer. John had such great love for his Lord and his fellowmen that he asked the Savior for power over death and permission to continue ministering on earth to bring more souls unto Christ (see John 21:20–23; D&C 7:1–8). The Savior granted his desires, saying, "Verily, verily, I say unto thee, because thou desirest this thou shalt tarry until I come in my glory and shalt prophesy before nations, kindreds, tongues and people"(D&C 7:3). He referred to John as "flaming fire and a ministering angel" who would continue to minister "for those who shall be heirs of salvation" (D&C 7:6). Thus, John is still on the earth performing a great and important mission to prepare "nations, kindreds, tongues and people" for the time when the Savior will return in His glory.[9]

John was apparently the only surviving Apostle in the Church after A.D. 100. None of the early Christian bishops nor early Church historians point to any other leader.

John the Beloved presided over the early Church from the death of Peter to the apostasy. He continued to minister on earth for the Lord until the time of the Restoration in the latter days.

Thus, John witnessed the birth, loss, and restoration of the gospel over a span of two millennia.

DANGERS BESETTING TRUE FAITH

Early Church members began adopting the methodologies of Greek philosophy, believing, as Clement of Alexandria later explained, that those who desired to be partakers of the power of God, could only do so by "philosophizing."[10] Greek philosophy began to infiltrate Christian theology so that "by the fourth century, Christian theologians had [completely] rearticulated Christian belief and understanding using the content and methods of philosophy."[11]

In his epistles, John specifically addressed four doctrinal challenges to the faith of the early Saints arising from "philosophizing": gnosticism, docetism, rebellion against authority, and gross misunderstanding about God's true nature and character.

Gnosticism. The term "gnosticism" comes from the Greek *gnosis,* meaning *knowledge.*[12] Gnostics claimed they had "special revelations from God about mysteries unknown by everyone else. They maintained that they had a special knowledge which was not available to all."[13] There was precedent for such claims (see 1 Corinthians 2:6–7), but with gnosticism, man's reasoning became more important than revelation, knowledge more important than Spirit and testimony. This is precisely the description the ancient prophet Nephi gave of apostate Christianity: "For it shall come to pass in that day that the churches which are built up, and not unto the Lord. . . . *shall teach with their learning, and deny the Holy Ghost. . . . And they deny the power of God*" (2 Nephi 28:3–5, emphasis added).

With gnosticism, there was no need for an atoning Savior but only for one who taught the secret knowledge. Good works were of little value. The proper function of religion was to teach a knowledge *(gnosis)* of secret mysteries. Salvation was achieved by the release of the spirit from the flesh and from the bondage of the material world into a heavenly realm. Gnostics claimed that the secret knowledge they had would allow an individual to ascend through multi-layered spheres of heaven until he or she could ascend into the presence of the divine substance, the unknowable God.

Gnostics claimed to have the very knowledge imparted by the Lord to the Apostles after His Resurrection.[14] Although gnostics varied in their practices and beliefs, a relatively common theme among them was "that human souls . . . do not belong in this material world (which is often described as evil and ignorant), and they can be saved only by receiving the revelation that they belong in a heavenly realm of light (the *plēroma* or 'fulness'). . . . Ascent to this realm is sometimes through baptism, sometimes through elaborate cultic rituals (often involving anointing), sometimes more through philosophical reflection. Some gnostic groups had their own hierarchy and virtually constituted a counterchurch."[15] The charges of the early Christian fathers (Irenaeus and Polycarp) against gnostics were "not that they invent new absurdities, but that they misrepresent true and familiar doctrines. . . . They use *genuine logia,* but give them a false twist. . . . Their teachings look perfectly orthodox, . . . their fault is not in appealing to noncanonical writings, but in counterfeiting such, . . . they imitate the sacrament, . . . they fake prophecy, . . . They counterfeit revelation with potions and drugs, . . . they parody marriage rites, . . . baptism, . . . and anointing. . . . They feign miraculous healings, . . . They do not (except for Marcus) change the scriptures but misinterpret them. . . . they are bad interpreters of the good word, mixing poison with good wine. . . . They mix chalk with milk."[16] One wonders how much of the true doctrine was left by the time these observations were made.

John's response to such doctrinal nonsense was pointed. The gospel of Jesus Christ was not veiled with darkness but had been proclaimed openly so that all might have an opportunity for eternal life:

"That which we have seen and heard declare we unto you, that ye also may have fellowship with us: and truly our fellowship is with the Father, and with his Son Jesus Christ.

"And these things write we unto you, that your joy may be full.

"This then is the message which we have heard of him, and declare unto you, that God is light, and in him is no darkness at all"

(1 John 1:3–5.) The Apostle Paul also made a point of countering gnostic heresies in his letter to Colossae, declaring that the "mysteries" of God were revealed to all through Christ and that Christians should not feel inferior to those who came preaching any other doctrine (see Colossians 1:26–27; 2:2–3).

John indicated that gnostics who taught with esoteric insight, ignoring the Spirit, were not of God: "They are of the world: therefore speak they of the world, and the world heareth them.

"We are of God: he that knoweth God heareth us; he that is not of God heareth not us. Hereby know we the spirit of truth, and the spirit of error" (1 John 4:5–6).

The gnostic tradition continued to eat away at the plain and precious doctrines established by Jesus Christ, until not only the doctrines disappeared, but the fundamental meaning of those doctrines was also lost: "Whosoever transgresseth, and abideth not in the doctrine of Christ, hath not God. He that abideth in the doctrine of Christ, he hath both the Father and the Son" (2 John 1:9).

Docetism. Another heresy contemporary with Gnosticism was a belief which denied Christ's humanity, denied His virgin birth, His suffering in Gethsemane, His Crucifixion and Resurrection. Docetism falsely assumed that all matter was evil and concluded therefore that Christ could not have been a material being. "They deny that the Son assumed anything material. For [according to them] matter is indeed incapable of salvation."[17] If matter was evil, God had to be nonphysical. "They regarded any Creator God as wicked."[18]

Thus "the first major test to faith . . . was not denial of Jesus Christ's deity, it was rejection of his humanity."[19] Docetists claimed that Christ did not come in the flesh upon the earth but only "seemed" (from the Greek *dokei*) to have appeared in the flesh. They taught that Christ did not suffer for mankind in Gethsemane and on the cross but only seemed to. He did not resurrect with a physical body, but only seemed to have done so. Such teachings, if accepted, would totally undermine the reality of the gospel as declared by Jesus Christ Himself:

"Behold I have given unto you my gospel, and this is the gospel which I have given unto you—that I came into the world to do the will of my Father, because my Father sent me.

"And my Father sent me that I might be lifted up upon the cross; . . . that I might draw all men unto me, that as I have been lifted up by men even so should men be lifted up by the Father, to stand before me, to be judged of their works" (3 Nephi 27:13–14; emphasis added).

John's testimony was similarly forthright: "In the beginning was the Word, and the Word was with God, and the Word was God. . . .

"And the Word was made flesh, and dwelt among us, (and we beheld his glory, the glory as of the only begotten of the Father,) full of grace and truth" (John 1:1, 14). Christ had come in the flesh as the divine Son of the Father, and John was an eyewitness who had known Him personally:

"Brethren, this is the testimony which we give of that which was from the beginning, which we have heard, which we have seen with our eyes, which we have looked upon, and our hands have handled, of the Word of life;

"(For the life was manifested, and we have seen it, and bear witness, and show unto you that eternal life, which was with the Father, and was manifested unto us;)

"That which we have seen and heard declare we unto you" (JST 1 John 1:1–3).

John warned that there were already many "antichrists" among them whose heretical teachings betrayed their lack of faith (see 1 John 2:18–19). Christians living in the second century attempted to repudiate docetism with a baptismal confession known as the Apostle's creed:

> We believe in God Almighty
> And in Christ Jesus, his only Son, our Lord
> Who was born of the Holy Spirit and the Virgin Mary
> Who was crucified under Pontius Pilate and was buried
> And the third day arose from the dead
> Who ascended into heaven

And sits on the right hand of the Father

Whence he comes to judge the living and the dead.[20]

John assured the Saints that it was possible for them to have a certain knowledge of the Lord's reality without having seen the Lord personally. They could trust in the testimony of those who had seen Him (see 1 John 2:14; see also D&C 46:13–14). He reminded them that the spiritual witness from the Holy Ghost (the "unction" or anointing of the Spirit) confirmed that Jesus is the Christ, the divine Son of God, the Redeemer of all mankind: "But ye have an unction from the Holy One, and ye know all things. . . .

"But the anointing which ye have received of him abideth in you, and ye need not that any man teach you: but as the same anointing teacheth you of all things, and is truth, and is no lie, and even as it hath taught you, ye shall abide in him" (1 John 2:20, 27). He further testified that these witnesses—intelligent assurances from the Spirit—were greater than any "witness of men" to the contrary (1 John 5:9). John's testimony about the atoning sacrifice of Jesus Christ is the very foundation upon which eternal life rests.

To deny Christ's humanity undermines the Atonement. If Christ had not really suffered for our sins, our sins would remain eternally unremitted, and all expectations for eternal life would be shattered (see 2 Nephi 9:8–9). Without Christ's sacrifice, there would be no "gospel"—no "good news." John's fervent testimony in his writings is that he was an eyewitness of the Savior's mortal ministry, had been in the Garden of Gethsemane with Him, and later saw the resurrected Lord. Almost half of his Gospel deals exclusively with the events of Christ's passion (see John 12–20).

Docetists also denied the reality of Christ's death and Resurrection, reasoning that if matter was evil, how could Christ be anything but a spirit? John declared plainly that anyone who denied the truth of Christ's actual life and suffering in the flesh was anti-Christ:

"Beloved, believe not every spirit, but try the spirits whether they are of God: because many false prophets are gone out into the world.

"Hereby know ye the Spirit of God: Every spirit that confesseth that Jesus Christ is come in the flesh is of God:

"And every spirit that confesseth not that Jesus Christ is come in the flesh is not of God: and this is that spirit of antichrist, whereof ye have heard that it should come; and even now it is already in the world. Ye are of God, little children, and have overcome them; because greater is he that is in you, than he that is in the world" (John 4:1–4).

"As C. S. Lewis put it, "There is no good trying to be more spiritual than God. God never meant man to be a purely spiritual creature. That is why He uses material things like bread and wine to put the new life into us. We may think this rather crude and unspiritual. God does not: He invented eating. He likes matter. He invented it.""[21]

To deny Christ's reality and divinity was to deny God the Father: "Whosoever denieth the Son, the same hath not the Father: [but] he that acknowledgeth the Son hath the Father also" (see 1 John 2:23). "Whosoever transgresseth, and abideth not in the doctrine of Christ, hath not God. He that abideth in the doctrine of Christ, he hath both the Father and the Son" (2 John 1:9).

John implored the Saints to cling to the truth they had already received, reminding them of the ultimate promise accompanying it:

"Let that therefore abide in you, which ye have heard from the beginning. If that which ye have heard from the beginning shall remain in you, ye shall continue in the Son, and also in the Father.

"And this is the promise that he hath promised us, even eternal life" (1 John 2:24–25).

Rebellion against Authority. A third heresy John condemned was that of rebellion. The apostasy of the early Church was the result of an internal dissension—a mutiny, a hostile takeover from shareholders—wolves who masqueraded as sheep. In his third letter, John described how some local leaders, blinded by pride and arrogance, even refused to acknowledge the authority of the Apostles:

"I wrote unto the church: but Diotrephes, who loveth to have the preeminence among them, receiveth us not.

"Wherefore, if I come, I will remember his deeds which he doeth, prating against us with malicious words: and not content therewith, neither doth he himself receive the brethren, and forbiddeth them that would, and casteth them out of the church.

"Beloved, follow not that which is evil, but that which is good. He that doeth good is of God: but he that doeth evil hath not seen God" (3 John 1:9–11).

John's letters were a refutation of this brazen belligerence. He warned that to give credence to such apostates would be to countenance their cause:

"If there come any unto you, and bring not this doctrine [true doctrine], receive him not into your house, neither bid him God speed:

"For he that biddeth him God speed is partaker of his evil deeds" (2 John 1:10–11).

The phrase "God speed" meant to welcome one into the home, to accept him as a guest. It was this kind of help that enabled itinerant heretics to aspire to Church leadership and to carry on their deceptive work of darkness. John's warning to the Saints was that to commit the sin of assisting and upholding those who preached false doctrine was to become a partaker of their evil deeds.

Misunderstandings about God's Nature. One of the first things to be jettisoned during any apostasy is a correct understanding of God's true nature and character because God can only be known by revelation. He either reveals Himself or remains forever unknown (see Jacob 4:8). When revelation ceases, so does the true knowledge of God—what He is like, who He is, and how we can become like Him.

The word John used more than any other to describe God was *love.* "God is love" is the central and most dominant theme in his epistles (see 1 John 4:8, 16). Divine love is the enabling power to overcome the world and lay hold on eternal life. "That love," Elder Bruce R. McConkie observed, "is the foundation upon which all personal righteousness rests. . . . All the purposes and plans of Deity are based on his infinite and eternal love; and . . . if men will personify that love in their lives, they will become like the Lord himself and have eternal life with him."[22]

God loves us, John testified, because:

• He has invited us to have fellowship with Him and His Son (1 John 1:3).

• He provided a way for us to be born again, enabling us to experience His divine love, to come to know Him, and to become like Him (see 1 John 2:29; 1 John 3:8–10; 1 John 4:7).

• He has created us as His sons and daughters, and will bestow upon those who accept Christ and His gospel—by taking upon themselves the name of Christ through baptism, honoring His name through faith and righteousness, and becoming sanctified through the Spirit—unfathomable blessings, and make them joint-heirs with Christ in a glorified and exalted state (see 1 John 3:1–2).

• He answers our prayers (see 1 John 3:22–23; 1 John 5:14–15).

• He gives us His Spirit (1 John 3:24; 1 John 4:13).

• He perfects His love in us (see Joseph Smith Translation 1 John 4:12).

• The greatest manifestation of God's love is the gift of His Eternal Son (see 1 John 3:16).

"In this was manifested the love of God toward us, because that God sent his only begotten Son into the world, that we might live through him.

"Herein is love, not that we loved God, but that he loved us, and sent his Son to be the propitiation for our sins" (1 John 4:9–10). *Propitiation* means to pay the price for, to bring comfort, to bring about reconciliation. Christ's voluntary atonement is the ultimate expression of true love and is the source of our adoration for Him: "We love him, because he first loved us" (1 John 4:19).

John also declared that Jesus Christ's love for us has also been manifest in specific ways:

• He is the advocate with the Father for all mankind (see Joseph Smith Translation, 1 John 2:1–2).

• He is our only hope for eternal life because there is no other Savior, no other philosophy or way or means to attain it:

"And this is the record, that God hath given to us eternal life, and this life is in his Son.

"He that hath the Son hath life; and he that hath not the Son of God hath not life.

"These things have I written unto you that believe on the name of the Son of God; that ye may know that ye have eternal life, and that ye may believe on the name of the Son of God (1 John 5:11–13).

• If we will confess our sins and repent of them, His atonement will cleanse us (see 1 John 1:7–9). Through faith, obedience, and love, we can be born of God and, because of Christ, we can achieve victory over the world.

• He willingly laid down his life for us (see 1 John 3:16). He had *to will* to die because His life could not be taken from Him (see John 10:17–18).

• His atoning sacrifice is the enabling power of our spiritual rebirth, giving us power over sin (see JST 1 John 3:5–9).

There were a few individuals in John's day who taught that church members could deny the doctrine of Jesus Christ and still have fellowship with the Father. John's letters to the Church correct this false thinking. He pointed out that one cannot deny a testimony of Jesus and be one with the Father (see 1 John 2:23). John wrote to teach the Saints "how to gain fellowship with God; how to know God and Christ; how to become the sons of God; how to abide in the light and love the brethren; how to dwell in God and have him dwell in us; how to be born again and gain eternal life."[23] As President David O. McKay described, "next to the affection we have for our home and loved ones, we prize the loyalty of friends, but even more precious is the true feeling of brotherhood in Christ."[24]

How can we show our love for Heavenly Father and Jesus Christ? We do so by keeping the commandments and avoiding sin (see 1 John 3:1–24), by walking in the light (1 John 1:6–7), by walking in truth and abiding in true doctrine (2 John 1:4; 2 John 1:9; 3 John 1:4), and by showing greater love to one another (1 John 2:9–11; 1 John 3:5, 11, 14–18, 22–23; 1 John 4:7–8, 11–12, 19–21).

John's Counsel on Avoiding Personal Apostasy

The epistles of John are filled with counsel about avoiding personal apostasy:

• He cautioned that it is impossible to claim to be in the light, and hate other church members: "He that saith he is in the light, and hateth his brother, is in darkness even until now. He that loveth his brother abideth in the light, and there is none occasion of stumbling in him" (1 John 2:9–10).

• He warned about being deceived by false spirits and gave counsel about the need to discern truth from error (see 1 John 4:1–3).

• He noted how pride can lead to self-deception: "If we say that we have no sin, we deceive ourselves, and the truth is not in us" (1 John 1:8). But "if our heart condemn us not, then have we confidence toward God" (1 John 3:21).

• He further testified that when we are filled with Christ's perfect love (or charity), that we may "have boldness [spiritual confidence] in the day of judgment. . . . There is no fear in love; but perfect love casteth out fear" (1 John 4:17–18). The Prophet Joseph Smith similarly taught that "until we have perfect love we are liable to fall and when we have. . . . perfect love . . . then it is impossible for false Christ's to deceive us."[25]

• John also had compassion on those who had not yet fallen away, but whose faith was weak. He noted that they need our prayers: "If any man see his brother sin a sin which is not unto death, he shall ask, and he shall give him life for them that sin not unto death" (1 John 5:16). The Prophet Joseph Smith also said: "I charged the Saints not to follow the example of the adversary in accusing the brethren, and said, 'If you do not accuse each other, God will not accuse you. . . . If you will throw a cloak of charity over my sins, I will over yours—for charity covereth a multitude of sins. What many people call sin is not sin."[26]

Witness for the Truth

John wrote to counteract the apostasy that was already under way at the end of the first Christian century. His epistles describe the rebellion against true priesthood authority and the rise of false teachings that drove the Church into obscurity and darkness. The fact that the Lord described His restored gospel as having come "out of obscurity and out of darkness" indicates how complete the apostate darkness was (see D&C 1:30). John's letters denounced the apostate heresies being taught, made declarations about God's love, and testified that God's plan for our salvation is based on that infinite love.

John bore testimony that he was an eyewitness of the resurrected Christ. He challenged us to stand as witnesses of Jesus Christ ourselves and reminded us that "whosoever shall confess that Jesus is the Son of God, God dwelleth in him, and he in God" (1 John 4:15). John's greatest joy was to know that those he loved lived by the truth: "I rejoiced greatly that I found of thy children walking in truth, as we have received a commandment from the Father" (2 John 1:4). "I have no greater joy than to hear that my children walk in truth" (3 John 1:4).

NOTES

1. Boyd K. Packer, in Conference Report, April 2000, 7.

2. Some notable exceptions of Christian writers who agree that significant changes occurred, and that modern Christianity no longer resembles the early Church, include David W. Bercot, *Will The Real Heretics Please Stand Up* (Tyler, Texas: Scroll Publishing, 1989); and Mark A. Noll, *Turning Points: Decisive Moments in the History of Christianity* (Leicester, England: Baker Books, 1997).

3. Hugh W. Nibley, "The Passing of the Primitive Church," in *When the Lights Went Out—Three Studies on the Ancient Apostasy* (Provo, Utah: FARMS, 2001), 2–3.

4. Kent P. Jackson, *From Apostasy to Restoration* (Salt Lake City: Deseret Book, 1996), 9.

5. See Joseph Fielding Smith, *Doctrines of Salvation* (Salt Lake City: Bookcraft, 1956), 3:151–52.

6. *Foxe's Christian Martyrs of the World* (Uhrichsville, Ohio: Barbour Publishing, 1989), 5–10.

7. Tertullian has an intriguing description of Rome in his book, *The Prescription Against Heretics* (written about A.D. 200), "where the Apostle John was first plunged, unhurt, into boiling oil, and thence remitted to his island exile"

on the isle of Patmos (see chapter 36). Another source for this tradition comes from the bishop of Lyons, France, Irenaeus (A.D. 135–200) who had listened to Polycarp describe having heard personally from the Apostle John. (See Eusebius, *Ecclesiastical History* 5:20; 4–7, and Irenaeus, *Against Heresies* 5:30.3; See also Richard L. Anderson, "What Do We Know of the Life of John the Apostle after the Day of Pentecost?" *Ensign*, January 1984, 50–51.

8. Eusebius, *Ecclesiastical History*, 3.20.8–3.23.6. Irenaeus states that John wrote his Gospel "during his residence at Ephesus in Asia" (*Against Heresies* III, 1, 1).

9. See Bruce R. McConkie, *Doctrinal New Testament Commentary* (Salt Lake City: Bookcraft, 1972), 3:371.

10. See Clement of Alexandria, *Stromateis* (Washington, D.C.: Catholic University of America Press, 1991), 55.

11. Noel B. Reynolds, "Why Early Christianity Adopted Greek Philosophy," *Insights* (Provo, Utah: FARMS, 2001), 21, no. 10 (2001): 2.

12. An extension of the word *gnosis* is "diagnosis" (meaning "to know thoroughly," from *dia*, "through or thorough;" and *gnosis*, "to know").

13. *Zondervan Handbook to the Bible* (Grand Rapids, Mich.: Zondervan Publishing, 1999), 725.

14. Nibley, "The Forty-Day Mission of Christ," in *When the Lights Went Out*, 55.

15. Raymond E. Brown, *An Introduction to the New Testament* (New York: Doubleday, 1997), 92.

16. See Nibley, "Forty-Day Mission," 75–76, footnote 61, where original sources to all the above statements are given.

17. David W. Bercot, ed., *A Dictionary of Early Christian Beliefs* (Peabody, Mass.: Hendrickson Publishers, 1998), 305.

18. *The Age of Catholic Christianity* (n.d., n.p.), 66.

19. *The Age of Catholic Christianity*, 68.

20. *The Age of Catholic Christianity*, 69.

21. C. S. Lewis, *Mere Christianity* (New York: Macmillan Publishing, 1952), 65.

22. Bruce R. McConkie, *Doctrinal New Testament Commentary* (Salt Lake City: Bookcraft, 1973), 3:371.

23. McConkie, *Doctrinal New Testament Commentary*, 3:371.

24. David O. McKay, in Conference Report, April 1956, 123.

25. *Teachings of the Prophet Joseph Smith* (Salt Lake City: Deseret Book, 1976), 9.

26. *Teachings of the Prophet Joseph Smith*, 193.

INDEX